Imagining a Medieval English Nation

MEDIEVAL CULTURES

SERIES EDITORS

RITA COPELAND
BARBARA A. HANAWALT
DAVID WALLACE

Sponsored by the Center for Medieval Studies at the University of Minnesota

Volumes in this series study the diversity of medieval cultural histories and practices, including such interrelated issues as gender, class, and social hierarchies; race and ethnicity; geographical relations; definitions of political space; discourses of authority and dissent; educational institutions; canonical and noncanonical literatures; and technologies of textual and visual literacies.

For more books in the series, see pages 349–52.

IMAGINING
A MEDIEVAL
ENGLISH NATION

KATHY LAVEZZO, EDITOR

Medieval Cultures, Volume 37
University of Minnesota Press
Minneapolis
London

Published by the University of Minnesota Press
111 Third Avenue South, Suite 290
Minneapolis, MN 55401-2520
http://www.upress.umn.edu

Library of Congress Cataloging-in-Publication Data

Imagining a medieval English nation / Kathy Lavezzo, editor.
   p.   cm. — (Medieval cultures ; v. 37)
   Includes bibliographical references and index.
   ISBN 0-8166-3734-2 (alk. paper) — ISBN 0-8166-3735-0 (pbk. : alk. paper)
   1. English literature—Middle English, 1100–1500—History and
criticism.   2. National characteristics, English, in literature.   3. Nationalism
and literature—England—History—To 1500.   4. Nationalism in literature.
5. England—In literature.   I. Lavezzo, Kathy.   II. Series.
PR275.N29 I43 2003
820.9'358—dc22   2003015322

12 11 10 09 08 07 06 05 04   10 9 8 7 6 5 4 3 2 1

CONTENTS

Introduction

Kathy Lavezzo

At least since Benedict Anderson breathed new life into the thought of Walter Benjamin, Ernst Renan, and Victor Turner, nationalism has constituted a prominent conceptual feature of contemporary literary and cultural studies. Following the lead of Perry Anderson, Anthony Giddens, and others, academics in English literary studies, by and large, have restricted their analyses to artifacts produced since the late eighteenth century, when the American and French revolutions launched the processes that gave rise to both a modern state founded on popular sovereignty and the appearance in the lexicon of the word "nationalism" (Anderson, *Imagined Communities,* 116–19).[1] But, as John Armstrong points out, this starting date presumes that, because a period of absolutism that rejected ethnic differentiation immediately preceded the revolutions, the rise of modern nationalism is unprecedented in England (*Nations,* 4). A deeper historical gaze, however, reveals pre-Enlightenment structures of communal thinking that strikingly correlate with the forms of modern nationhood. Theorists on nationalism such as Benedict Anderson, Ernest Gellner, and Liah Greenfeld have argued that while the Enlightenment may have ushered in the era of nationalism, national communities began to be imagined, if not realized, in western Europe with the advent of print capitalism and the Protestant Reformation. Likewise, literary critics such as Richard Helgerson, Jean Howard, and Claire McEachern have demonstrated how the emergence of national sentiment in England can be pushed back to the sixteenth century. Such developments are unquestionably significant; yet to acquire a full understanding of the earliest representations of English community in literary artifacts, we must extend our gaze still farther back in the history of the West, to the Middle Ages.

The argument against the presence of any form of nationalism in medieval Europe, incipient or otherwise, is well known, partly due to the influential claims made by Hans Kohn regarding the supposedly utter dominance of the universal Christian church in the West. According to Kohn, a "founding father" of contemporary scholarship on nationalism, identification with a *res publica generis humani* under one *ecclesia universalis* that transcended ethno-political ties superseded all other social forms in the medieval Occident (*Idea*, 78–96; Hayes, *Historical Evolution*). The myth of a medieval West so thoroughly saturated with universal Christian thought as to render virtually impossible national sentiment has been perpetuated in contemporary debates on nationalism in large part by Benedict Anderson. For Anderson, the occidental Middle Ages was a time dominated by "three fundamental conceptions": faith in holy truth-languages aimed at the "alchemic absorption" of peoples into a centripetal and hierarchically imagined world; allegiance to sacral monarchies ruling over subjects dwelling in territories lacking fixed boundaries; and belief in a "simultaneity-along-time" that dissolved the respective histories of particular peoples into one providential past (*Imagined Communities*, 14–24). Both Anderson's and Kohn's insistence on the lack of medieval precedents to the nation reflects the general tendency of post-Enlightenment Western intellectuals to invest all products of their culture with modernity, that is, newness. Essential to this fantasy is the construction of a premodern time when thinking the nation (and other "modern" forms) was impossible; hence the ironic insistence of otherwise historically rigorous writers such as Anderson upon viewing the Middle Ages as a time during which only universalist, not particularist, social structures existed. But as Bruno Latour has taught us, the forms of premodernity are not always so different from or "other" to contemporary life as we moderns believe them to be.[2]

The myth of a universal sacral West promulgated by Anderson, Kohn, and other like-minded critics, unfortunately, has tended to dominate academic thinking among social theorists and literary critics, despite the existence of a coterminous scholarly tradition that finds in medieval culture evidence of political structures—as well as structures of feeling—that anticipate the nation-state and the nationalist discourses of modernity.[3] An early argument for nationalism in medieval Europe appears in the work of Johan Huizinga, who claims that the concept of imperial dominion within Latin Christendom did not prevent the development of the national European configurations, a process that, for Huizinga, led to the establishment of a "framework within which national consciousness and a sense of fatherland evolve[d] in Europe . . . by around 1100"

(*Men and Ideas*, 100). In Huizinga's account, Christianity at times even contributed to national divisions, as it did in the case of the Crusades, which brought the members of Latin Christendom "together again and again in martial equipment, battle array, and a more or less sanctified rivalry" (108). Huizinga is hardly alone in his contention. In the scholarship of Marc Bloch and Hugh Seton-Watson on language, Vivian Galbraith on Latin chroniclers, Ernst Kantorowicz on political theology, Gaines Post on legal theory, Susan Reynolds on lay collectivities, and Joseph Strayer on laicization, we find but a sampling of scholarship over the last half of the twentieth century that suggests how analysis of the problem of nationalism should be extended back to the Middle Ages.[4]

To be sure, although this body of scholarship provides a precedent for critical work on medieval nationalism, it also has been complicated at times by the political agendas of its authors. In the particular example of England, some medievalists have productively turned an analytical eye toward the problem of medieval English national identity, while other scholars have focused on the Middle Ages in England with a gaze more patriotic than analytic. Indeed, if we turn to nineteenth-century scholarship on the medieval legends of Arthur and Robin Hood, we find that the Victorian dawn of the contemporary discipline of medieval literary study was clouded over by national and imperial impulses.[5] As Stephanie Barczewski recently has pointed out, literary criticism on the Robin Hood legend contributed to the construction of a "Merrie England" imagined to rescue late Victorian England from the dangers of industrialism. Thus it "is not the England of the mine and the workshop" that Robin Hood represents, according to William Winter in his 1892 *Shadows of the Stage*, but "the England of the feudal times . . . England in rush-strewn bowers and under green boughs" where one can listen to "the merry note of the huntsman commingled, far away, with the horns of Elfland faintly blowing" (272).[6] Winter offers here and elsewhere a nationalistic and pastoral image of England that resounds with the "blessed plot" and "demi-paradise" threatened by internal strife in Shakespeare's *Richard II* (II.i.43–50) even as it reifies Victorian fantasies of a late medieval golden age. If literary critics such as Winter saw in the Robin Hood legend an idyllic rural past capable of revitalizing an England enervated by modern life, other intellectuals rendered Arthur a figure for the triumphs of the empire. Such efforts, as Barczewski points out, comprised part of a nationalistic, if counterintuitive, bid for the English origins of the genre proffered by English academics with increasing stridency over the course of the nineteenth century. In his 1897 study on medieval romance, for example, George Saintsbury acknowledges the presence of classical, French, Celtic, and Oriental influences in medieval Arthurian literature, but claims that such foreign elements "are all co-ordinated, dominated, fashioned anew by some thing which is none of them, but which is the English 'genius'" (*Flourishing*, 137–38, 146–47; cf. Barczewski, *Myth*, 112). With his construction of a precocious English literary talent capable of subduing and remaking its sources and analogues, Saintsbury projects on the medieval writer the role of linguistic colonizer. The numerous foreign influences on English Arthurian romance are transformed fantastically by Saintsbury from anxiety-producing literary predecessors into the objects of a kind of English literary imperialism.

The examples of Saintsbury and Winter point to the English nationalism that we might most readily expect to find in scholarship on medieval England. Academics also have celebrated Middle English literature, however, with the intent of glorifying nations other than England. Some forty years after Saintsbury, in a book that remains "cherished today as one of the classical investigations in Chaucer scholarship," we find an unsettling complicity of academic work on the "father" of English poetry with prewar German national ideology (Utz, "Inventing," 16).[7] As Richard Utz recently has demonstrated, Will Héracourt's *Die Wertwelt Chaucers* (1939) adopts a *nationalpsychologische Methode* ("national-psychological method") that was mutually constitutive with the ideological objectives of the Third Reich. In *Die Wertwelt*, the German philologist maintains that Chaucer displays a preference for German over Romance words in his literary oeuvre. As found in such works as *The Canterbury Tales* and the *Legend of Good Women*, these "German expressions signify the hereditary, but always freshly lived and realistically-felt paternal property, the healthy, living power of the people," according to Héracourt (*Die Wertwelt*, 360 f.; Utz, "Inventing," 16). Despite "the French tendrils" of a Romance courtly lexicon, "the basic stock *(Grundstamm)* of ethical notions of German(ic) origin" are strong enough to challenge the exclusivity of the nobility with "signs of an awakening national spirit" (*Die Wertwelt*, 361, 354; Utz, "Inventing," 15–16). As Utz's decision to translate *stamm* as not "trunk" but "stock" suggests, the botanic and arboreal metaphors typical of philology are put, unsurprisingly, in the service of a racial nationalism in Héracourt's work (*Oxford Duden German Dictionary* s.v.

"stamm").[8] The additional definitions of *stamm* as tribe, clan, and above all blood complement Héracourt's claim elsewhere in *Die Wertwelt Chaucers* that Chaucer's *blut* or blood enables the representation of a *Volksideal* or national ideal in his literary corpus.

Héracourt certainly is not the last medievalist to inflect his work in terms of his own national ties. Moving from prewar Germany to post–World War II America, we can consider the historical work of Joseph Strayer, in which Norman Cantor has identified what he calls a Wilsonian agenda (*Inventing*, 277–86). Strayer contends in his 1940 essay on laicization that, by the end of the thirteenth century, "lay rulers, rather than the pope, could count on the primary allegiance of the people" in medieval Europe ("Laicization," 77). As Cantor points out, Strayer's emphasis on medieval loyalty to the state reflects less the political conditions of thirteenth-century England or elsewhere than the American exceptionalism of a twentieth-century medievalist. That exceptionalism would develop in the fifties and beyond into a cold war liberalism that emerges not only in Strayer's assertion in the preface to *On the Medieval Origins of the Modern State* (1970) that he "believe[s] that the state has succeeded in getting large numbers of men to work together effectively, and that the state can embody human ideals and human aspirations just as well as any other form of social organization," but also in that medievalist's employment by the CIA (*Medieval Origins*, 261–62; Cantor, *Inventing*, 261–62).[9]

The examples of Winter, Saintsbury, Héracourt, and Strayer may well give us pause, insofar as they demonstrate how modern work on medieval England at times has been implicated in nationalisms responsible for the English Empire, the German Holocaust, and the Cold War. Yet the biases of such scholarship also give a certain urgency to critical work on medieval nationalism. At stake in the problem of medieval nationalism is not only our comprehension of the past but also the dismantling of contemporary national fantasies—fantasies that no doubt continue to mobilize medieval scholarship. We can find a remarkable, early call for that sort of critical work in the writings of a pioneer of early English studies, Frederick Furnivall. To be sure, in certain respects the Victorian scholar-adventurer seems to epitomize the national inclinations of his time. Furnivall founded the Early English Text Society—still the most important publication series for work in Middle English—in 1864 to enlarge the historical range of the *Oxford English Dictionary*, itself an editorial project that came to contribute, as John Willinsky puts it, to a "particularly English claim on science and civilization" (*Empire,* 6).[10] At times Furnivall's institutional correspondence to supporters of the *OED* and members of EETS reveals his desire to seize upon his readers' English sentiment as a means of generating support for both editorial projects. In a London Philological Society pamphlet, for example, Furnivall maintains that he and the other *OED* editors "have set ourselves to form a National Portrait Gallery, not only of the worthies, but of all the members, of the race of English words which is to form the dominant speech of the world"; and in an EETS Committee Report Furnivall writes that "the love of the Fatherland" and "duty to England is the motive of the Society's workers" (Murray, *Caught,* 137; Benzie, *Furnivall,* 131–32). Yet for all his attempts to make the maintenance of EETS a matter of allegiance to England, Furnivall also displays a more critical awareness of the medieval English past. For example, in the foreword to his 1868 edited volume of medieval courtesy books, Furnivall infers of the aristocratic youths "to whom the *Babees Boke,* &c., were addressed" that "dirty, ill-mannered, awkward young gawks must most of these hopes-of-England have been, to modern notions" (*Early English Meals,* lxii). The inauspicious future that the unkempt and brutish character of the noble children seems to foretell points to the problem of beginnings that is closely bound with any nationalistic look at the medieval English past. If, to cite Anderson, "nations . . . always loom out of an immemorial past," any critical view of England's past troubles the desire to find in it signs of consequent English glories (*Imagined Communities,* 11). Furnivall is well aware of the disapprobation that his negative characterization of not only the children but also the kings, homes, and streets of medieval England as dirty might occasion:

> If it be objected that I have in the foregoing extracts shown the dark side of the picture, and not the bright one, my answer is that the bright now—of the riches and luxury in England— must be familiar to all our members, students (as I assume) of our early books, that the Treatises in this Volume sufficiently show this bright side, and that to me, as foolometer of the Society, this dark side seemed to need showing. (*Early English Meals,* lxvii)

Endowing himself with the license of the jester, Furnivall asserts the need for a balanced perspective on the past, a view that, as the editor well knows, not all of his Victorian readership would endorse. While the tenor of these lines iterated by the resident "foolometer" of EETS asks us to dismiss them as the mere rants of a notorious eccentric and devil's advocate, the methodological message they contain merits more serious consideration.

Furnivall makes a noteworthy, early case for medieval England as the object of not nationalistic appreciation but critical investigation. Even more trenchant analysis would emerge in work such as Barnaby Keeney's 1947 essay on medieval nationalism. In contrast to Héracourt's projection of a racialized national identity into the medieval past, for example, Keeney points out how similar historical myths were manufactured by late medieval English writers such as Pierre Langtoft, who met his readers' desire for "a common origin with their fellow countrymen" by "show[ing] that Briton, Anglo-Saxon and Norman had fused to form the Englishman," a feat that required the historian to "deliberately falsif[y] his source" at least once ("Military Service," 536). Both Keeney's work, as well as more recent analytical inquires into medieval English nationalism, demonstrate how scholarly quests for the presence in the medieval past of authentic Englishness—or, to borrow from Slavoj Žižek's vocabulary, an English "Real" or "nation-thing"—are doomed to failure. The idea of "England" as the protagonist of a gripping national tale of precocious birth in the Anglo-Saxon period, maternal nurturing and plucky survival during the Norman Conquest, and triumphant dominance in modernity is a teleology that no longer holds. What critical work such as Keeney's can do, however, is remind us how the national rhetoric present in the very origins of the discipline of medieval studies could have taken its cue from national mythologies extant in medieval English culture itself.

As the work of Keeney and like-minded critics demonstrates, while England lacks the national teleology that has been ascribed to it, rhetorics of Englishness have a long history. Indeed, close examination of English medieval literature and culture not only offers us an important prehistory to modern formulations of nationalism, but also presents us with at least one striking premodern analogue to contemporary theoretical work on the topic. At one point in his account of the history of the Britons in his *Polychronicon* (ca. 1327–ca. 1360), the Cheshire monk Ranulph Higden engages in a remarkable critical detour that queries the Arthurian legend as it appears in Geoffrey of Monmouth's *Historia Regum Brittaniae* (1136). While Geoffrey describes Arthur overcoming both the king of France and the emperor of Rome, Higden remarks, no Roman or Frankish histories record such Arthurian exploits. While Geoffrey wonders at the absence of Arthur in the work of Gildas and Bede, Higden tells us that he marvels at Geoffrey's extensive praises of a man ignored by credible and established chroniclers.[11] Endeavoring to account for Geoffrey's portrayal of Arthur, Higden suggests that we might understand the presence of an unbelievably mighty Arthur in the *Historia* if we consider that such heroes may be constructed not for their own sake but for the sake of a nation:

> But perhaps it is the manner of every nation to extol in excessive praise some one from their members, as the Greeks do their Alexander, the Romans their Octavian, the English their Richard, the French their Charles; and thus it follows that the Britons overly extoll their Arthur. That happens often, as Josephus says, for beauty of the story, for the pleasure of the readers, or to praise their own blood.[12]

Nations, Higden tells us (with the help of Josephus), are given to constructing heroes whose exceptionally grand qualities testify to the grandeur of their people. In a move that strikingly looks toward modern work on the nation as artifact, Higden admits here that part of the work of national history is that of giving pleasure, of offering a fantasy that creates a sovereign nation. Higden's remarks provoke a strident rebuttal of the monk by his Middle English translator John Trevisa, a Cornishman who is clearly an Arthurian enthusiast (Waldron, "Celtic Complex"). But Higden's thinking on the tendency of nations to render their heroes larger than life also proves so powerful as to make even Trevisa concede that "it may wel be þat Arthur is ofte overpreysed and so beeþ meny oþere" and even refer to Augustine's remarks on the overvaluation of Greek heroes (Higden, *Polychronicon*, 5.339). Higden thus offers an explication of Geoffrey's nationalism so forceful as to make even the Celtic patriot Trevisa give pause. We might safely presume, however, that Higden's powerful critique did not gain the attention of late-nineteenth-century Arthurian scholars such as Jessie Weston, who maintains in *The Legend of Sir Gawaine* (1897) that "we may... believe that [Arthur] really lived" (3) or S. Humphreys Gurteen, who declared in *The Arthurian Epic* (1895) that "to disbelieve in the historic existence of such a personage as Arthur simply shows an unhealthy skepticism" (97; Barczewski, *Myth*, 144). What the late Victorian nationalist Gurteen would term "unhealthy skepticism" we may well call impressive critical acumen on the part of the universal chronicler Higden.

Of course, despite the remarkable example of Higden, certain obstacles appear to undermine our critical investigation of medieval English nationalism. Above all, the risk of anachronism seems to oppose such a project. If we restricted our inquiry into the history of English nationalism to the period after words such as "Englishness" and "nationalism" entered the lexicon, we would look no further back than 1804. "Nation," on the other hand, is a much older word, with etymological roots in the Latin *natio,* whose identification with the goddess of birth and definition as breed, stock, and race both testify to the deep biological and racial structure that often underlies national feeling (Lewis and Short, *New Latin Dictionary,* s.v. "natio, nationis"). Then again, "nation" also notoriously resists definition, in part due to its constitution through the imagination. In Anderson's formulation, nations are imagined because of the literal impossibility of all the members of a community experiencing face-to-face contact with each other (*Imagined Communities,* 6). To use a more psychoanalytic register, national fantasy can refer to a style or technique of articulating impossible individual psychic desires, whether for wholeness and loving camaraderie or for a grand past punctuated by idealized heroes such as Arthur. Kathleen Davis addresses such yearnings in her essay for this volume, which delineates the ineluctable contingency of a medieval English nation ever desirous of eternity. The status of nation as artifact also comprises the sort of social action ascribed to art by Kenneth Burke and Fredric Jameson, insofar as constructions of the nation respond imaginatively to sociohistorical crises (civil uprisings, economic troubles, etc.). For example, as Claire Sponsler points out in her contribution to this collection, in the Statutes of Kilkenny and elsewhere we see "the colonists' increasingly loud proclamations of their Englishness" precisely when those settlers were increasingly going native. The bundle of attributes that the members of a nation are imagined to share are far from stable, but instead can range

from the diachronic (territory) to the synchronic (history), from the biological (race) to the cultural (religion, language, etc.) and to the political
(the state). Coterminous with the various fantasies of sameness, union,
and wholeness that nationalism entails are fantasies of difference, the
construction of others whom the nation is "not" and whom the nation
surmounts, such as the stereotypically brutish Irish denounced by medieval English polemicists bent on asserting their own civility. Though,
as several essays in the volume demonstrate, making medieval "England"
also depended on the appropriation of strangers both within (women,
the poor, merchants) and without (Ireland, France, Italy) its boundaries
even as it excluded those same others.

    The medieval valences of "nacioune" as "race of people," "political
country," "nationality" in fact do overlap significantly with the constellation
of characteristics ascribed to modern nations. But the very indeterminacy
of the modern "nation," as well as that term's fundamental relationship
with fantasy, suggests the limitations of arguments about nationalism
(whether in the Middle Ages or in modernity) based on lexicography.
The notoriously slippery meaning of "nation" demonstrates how words
hardly secure meaning and identity. As recent work on medieval representations of other ostensibly modern notions make clear, we need not
prove the codification of a concept in a language in order to analyze that
notion, since any full codification of such charged terms as "race," "homo-
sexuality," and "nation" is itself an impossible desire.[13] In *Nations and
Nationalism since 1780*, a text invested in the modernity of nationalism,
Eric Hobsbawm tellingly acknowledges that "the word 'nation' is today
used so widely and imprecisely that the use of the vocabulary of nationalism today may mean very little indeed" (9). Hobsbawm's certainty about
the nation's newness and his uncertainty about the nation's definition
exemplifies Larry Scanlon's incisive observation in his contribution that
"the modernist's commitment to the uniqueness of the present...runs
aground on the same logical problems" inherent in the "medievalist's
fear of anachronism." Hobsbawm does attempt to evade the contradictions he produces, claiming that the novelty of the nation accounts for
its fuzziness, that what is "historically novel, emerging, and changing"
never fits "into a framework of permanence and universality" (6). Yet
that fuzziness can just as easily serve as grounds for inquiry into premodern nationalism. If we cannot determine precisely what a nation is

today, how can we be sure of its modernity? How can we verify that thinking the nation was impossible in medieval England?

Certain phenomena suggest that it indeed was possible to imagine an English community in the Middle Ages. On the question of the shared past claimed by the nation, we can turn to the national chronicles written in late medieval England, above all the immensely popular *Brut*.[14] On the issue of territory, we can turn to the appearance around 1360 of the Gough Map, whose detailed and accurate portrayal of Britain is unprecedented in Europe.[15] On the subject of language, we can point to the introduction of the vernacular into the spaces of the classroom, the court, and Parliament in the fourteenth century, as well as the transformation, to use David Crystal's words, of the "trickle" of texts in Middle English into "a flood" during this period (*Cambridge Encyclopedia*, 34). On the problem of social organization, we can shore up the emergence of neither knights, priests, nor plowmen but the horizontally bound "new men" described by Anne Middleton (lawyers, merchants, poets, bureaucrats). And, along more explicitly political lines, we can consider the fact that, by even the mid-thirteenth century, there "stretched from Westminster throughout the land" a "web of bureaucracy" that administered the law, levied taxes, regulated currency, licensed markets, and raised troops (Turville-Petre, *England*, 8; Harding, *Law Courts*; Harriss, *Public Finance*; Britnell, *Commercialisation*; Keeney, "Military Service"). Particularly notable, perhaps, is the culmination of the juridical separation of England from Rome (of civil law from canon law) with the laicization of the King's Bench in 1341.[16] Even as such phenomena point to the establishment of a medieval state whose secular authority came from the Crown, other phenomena suggest certain aspects of the dissemination of power more characteristic of the nation-state (Breuilly, *Nationalism*). Minor rural nobility gained a voice in political affairs when Edward I included them in the holding of Parliament from 1297 on (Roskell, *Parliament*). These members of the squirearchy hardly lived up to their designation as the "Commons" in any real sense of the word. But it was also during the fourteenth century that the powers of the peasant majority were first asserted with any force (as the status of the *nativi* rose after 1350–51 and came to a head in 1381).

This brief and incomplete list may seem to lump together cultural and historical phenomena and hence confuse fiction and fact. But, to cite Sarah Radcliffe, "no easy hierarchies are set up between discourses and practices of nationhood" ("Gendered Nations," 5–6). The intimate relation between the "objective" and the "subjective" or "ideal" and "actual" aspects of the problem of nationhood refuses the divorcing of such binaries as well as their ranking. To stress how medieval England was imagined in chronicles, for example, is to assert the historical agency of fantasy. And conversely, to emphasize such "realities" as medieval England's lay bench is to assert the state's own imaginary; L. O. Aranye Fradenburg puts this in Lacanian terms in her contribution to this volume when she notes how "social and economic apparatuses are the very means by which desires circulate." Fantasy drives the law even as the law fashions identities by regulating the rights and duties of the people who inhabit the perceived space of the nation. Instead of parsing out the cultural from its perceived others, it is crucial to consider how a variety of phenomena worked in conjunction to make it possible to imagine an English nation in the late Middle Ages. Bringing the problem of nationalism into English medieval studies thus would mean exploring the conception of an English community within manifold cultural and political arenas such as the law (the development of the common law), the church (Wyclif, the *ecclesia anglicana*, monastic nationalism), the scriptorium (national historiography, the rise of the vernacular), the military (English feeling and the Hundred Years War), and the court (the cult of Arthur, English fin amor).

Some progress toward this goal has been made through the emergence over the past decade of a growing body of academic work on nationalism and medieval English literature (Peter Brown, Jeffrey J. Cohen, Judith Ferster, John Gillingham, Patricia Ingham, Leslie Johnson, Lee Patterson, Felicity Riddy, Lynn Staley, Edith Tatnall, David Wallace). This trend has culminated in the 1996 publication of the first book-length study of the topic, Thorlac Turville-Petre's *England the Nation*. As Lee Patterson has argued, Turville-Petre's book constitutes a crucial step forward in the analysis of nationalism in England, insofar as the book uses literary texts produced during the fifty years before the Hundred Years War to reveal how medieval England met "the contemporary criteria of nationhood—territory, people and language" (Patterson, Review, 326). Much work, however, remains to be done both on the English nationalist texts that appear outside of Turville-Petre's fifty-year focus, as well as on works produced within this time frame that are not discussed by Turville-Petre. Extending and complicating recent arguments by Turville-Petre, Susan Reynolds, and other medievalists, *Imagining a Medieval English Nation* gathers the work of ten literary critics who apply a variety of interdisciplinary and theoretical methodologies to the problem of a medieval English nation.

Taken together, these original essays offer a theoretically informed and wide-ranging investigation of the multiple representations of "England" produced during the Middle Ages. Thus, while the volume suggests how a discourse of English identity may be located in the medieval period, it also affirms that what constituted "England" during the Middle Ages was hardly fixed. The Middle Ages did not see the birth of a unified English community, but instead witnessed the construction of multiple, contingent, and conflicting "Englands," each geared toward the respective needs of different social groups (monarchic, Lollard, monastic, etc.) engaged in national discourses. By maintaining the variety of nationalisms present in medieval England, *Imagining a Medieval English Nation* offers no single answer to the question of the relationship between medieval and modern nationalisms. Far from adopting either a teleological or constructionist approach to history, it is precisely the goal of this volume to open up the old binaries that govern thinking on the relationship between premodernity and modernity.[17] Instead of assuming an "either/ or" stance toward medieval culture, we urge a more flexible methodology that embraces the wide variety of possible relationships between the present and the past, relationships that cannot be described adequately through either Whiggism or constructionism. Thus while some essays point to aspects of medieval English nationalism that look toward the modern nation, others address concepts of the nation that were not adopted in later periods. By demonstrating the multiplicity of "England" we aim to provide not a limited but rather a liberating account of the past. As critics writing about nationalism within a discipline whose origins are themselves nationalist, we can perhaps never fully escape our own implication in nationalist discourses of England. But through our attention to the many different stories of England told in the Middle Ages, we can hope to provide a stance of resistance to those oppressive myths of a monolithic and predestined English nation that have been promulgated by nationalist projects.

CONTENTS OVERVIEW

The following original essays engage with the problem of nationalism in medieval England through a variety of approaches to an interdisciplinary array of texts (ranging from Latin and vernacular historiography to Lollard tracts, Ricardian poetry, and chivalric treatises). These essays not only challenge traditional preconceptions regarding the origins of the nation, but also complicate theories about the workings of nationalism. For example, if, as Anderson, Gellner, and other critics point out, the nation is imagined, the analysis of nationalism can benefit much from that theoretical discourse that has taught us the most about the way fantasy works, psychoanalysis and, in particular, its Lacanian manifestations. The volume opens with an essay by L. O. Aranye Fradenburg that engages and complicates psychoanalytic theory to address the fantasies of sacrifice that bind national and chivalric culture in late medieval England. In "Pro Patria Mori," Fradenburg argues that the premodern notion of the production of glory through dying for the fatherland can help us address some of the controversies about how community was imagined in late medieval England. Building upon both the work of Ernst Kantorowicz and Gaines Post in their early essays on this subject and recent scholarship in chivalric culture, Fradenburg specifically criticizes the supposed opposition between war crimes and chivalric sacrifice. The constitutive role of desire in nation making, Fradenburg points out, reveals that those pleasures (such as the violence and waste endemic to *chevauchée*) do not clash with the good of the nation; rather, "the desires that must be renounced are kissing cousins to those that desire their renunciation." Through her analysis of chivalric texts such as the *Pageant of the Earl of Warwick* and Caxton's version of Ramon Lull's *Book of the Order of Chivalry*, Fradenburg demonstrates how the sublime object of national ideology relates less to virtue than a *jouissance* that is as destructive as it is creative and as vicious as it is munificent.

A similar paradox about national fantasy emerges in Andrew Galloway's contribution to the volume, which focuses upon the chronicles of Ranulph Higden and Thomas Walsingham. While the emphasis both chroniclers place upon threats to the good of the realm suggests the undermining of English identity, these writers nevertheless contribute to the idea of England insofar as it constitutes a presumed object of inquiry.

Galloway offers here a new wrinkle on Turville-Petre's insight regarding how "concepts of nationhood become dominant when the nation is perceived to be under threat from outside attack or influence" (*England the Nation*, 4). Turville-Petre emphasizes the construction by English chroniclers of "national unity" as "the *good* that can be set against the evil[s]" (4) that threaten it, but in "Latin England," Galloway demonstrates how England not as solution but as *problem* nevertheless becomes a kind of "badge of national identity." Higden's Ockhamist obsession with the problematic *varietas* or diversity of England "etches the boundaries and the importance of the secular nation more deeply" as the assumed arena for his intense pursuit. And Walsingham's Augustinian satire of the caste dynamics of the 1381 Rebellion, "and the underlying conflicts it derives from, emphasize the secular English community as the focus of all his historical fascination and his narrative energy and craft."

As the title of Galloway's essay suggests, both Higden and Walsingham wrote their chronicles in Latin. Through his analysis of how Latin historiography fashions England, Galloway challenges the long-standing notion that only vernacular texts can imagine nations. For Benedict Anderson and other theorists of the nation, Latin and other "imperial" languages enable the imagining of global communities such as the universal Christian brotherhood, while "native" languages enable the imagining of the national communities from which they spring and to which they refer. Galloway, however, makes the radical claim that late medieval English writers in Latin such as Higden and Walsingham, even more than their vernacular counterparts, fashioned themselves as writers for England. By dint of their vast dissemination, as well as their explicitly national vision and authorial self-consciousness, Higden's and Walsingham's Latin chronicles suggest how it is not in the Middle English but in the Latin literary corpus that we find the best examples of national textual community late medieval England had to offer.

While Galloway turns the typical presupposition about the social aspects of Latin texts on its head, Jill C. Havens in her essay pushes the rise of English as an instrument for national acculturation back to the medieval period. For most theorists of the nation, the universalizing effects of Latin's hegemony would not erode until the seventeenth century. However, in "'As Englishe is comoun langage to oure puple': The Lollards and Their Imagined 'English' Community," Havens posits that the massive vernacular productions of the Lollard movement—that is, the circulation of some 250 Wycliffite Bibles in England—constitute a crucial moment in the rise of English as a medium for imagining an English community. According to Havens, the unusually large volume, exceptional organization, and remarkable complexity of the Lollard book trade render it a phenomenon comparable with the vernacular print-capitalism so crucial to Anderson's argument about the dawn of nationalism in early modernity. Through careful attention to Lollard translation debate documents, moreover, Havens shows the nationalist strategies of authorizing the vernacular at work in Lollard culture, which strove both to endow English with the sacral authority that was assigned officially to Latin and to "mak[e] the mother tongue imperative to national security." By analyzing the role of Lollardy in legitimizing Middle English, Havens also challenges presumptions about the homogenizing effects of religion in the Middle Ages. As Havens demonstrates, Christianity at times actually fostered the growth of nationalism in medieval England, whereby "the Bible became to [the Lollards] the *liber vitae Anglicanae* in which the English were the *populus Dei*, the chosen people of Israel."

The Lollards may constitute the religious group most identified with vernacular production in medieval England, yet in the literary arena, it is above all Chaucer whom we think of in connection with the emerging legitimization of English. By dint of his status as the "father" of English poetry, Chaucer, more than any other medieval English writer, also has acquired the role of the originator of English nationalist sentiment. All too often, however, the "Englishness" of Chaucer constitutes something assumed and never analyzed in any detail. And those elaborations of Chaucer's nationalism that do exist problematically appear in texts whose own national agendas preclude any critical assessment of the poet's work. Peggy A. Knapp and Kathleen Davis do much to remedy this problematic state of affairs in medieval studies in their respective interrogations of Chaucer's poetry. In "Chaucer Imagines England (in English)," Knapp offers a much needed historicization of the term that lies at the heart of Benedict Anderson's influential book. In its representation of "ymagi-nacioun" and related words such as "fantasye," "resoun imaginatyf," and "engyn," Chaucer's literary oeuvre departs from medieval philosophy's devaluation of *imaginatio* (or *phantasia*) as an illusory mental faculty in need of control by the intellect. Rather, the poet depicts "ymagina-cioun" as a dynamic "even an aggressive, intellectual process" that forms images that incite both emotion and action. Imagination has powerful consequences for Chaucer, consequences that suggest, for Knapp, modern work on imagination by Hume, Wittgenstein, and others.

Knapp's reposte to Anderson involves more than imagination, and in part returns us to Galloway's critique about the role of language in national fantasy, though with starkly different results. Galloway's essay demonstrates how, while Latin possessed the prestige Anderson claims it did in the Middle Ages, that language nevertheless could be marshaled for English purposes. Knapp, on the other hand, troubles our idea of premodern Latin's reputation as an "emanation of reality" by pointing out how, even in the early Middle Ages, the Latin Bible "could not be defended as the uniquely delivered Word" since it "was the original language of neither the Old nor the New Testament." Similarly, in the case of *The Canterbury Tales,* religious figures as diverse as the Pardoner and the Parson all point to a "cultural world" that was familiar with Latin but not reverent toward it in the manner Anderson suggests. Knapp ends her piece by querying a third component of Anderson's thesis, the modernity of the homogeneous, empty time of the nation. Though, for example, *The Miller's Tale*'s references to a second flood invoke a distinctly medieval typological conception of time, that fabliau *"only works because* Alison, Nicholas, John, and Absolon act in the same time frame unaware of each other's plots." As Knapp well demonstrates, through its dependence on the idea of "meanwhile," *The Canterbury Tales* suggests the "confidence" in the "steady, anonymous, simultaneous activity" of the members of a community Anderson locates in the modern novel (*Imagined Communities,* 26).

In "Hymeneal Alogic: Debating Political Community in *The Parliament of Fowls*," Kathleen Davis focuses on one of Chaucer's early poems to analyze the vexed relationship between the sex/gender system and the problem of medieval English identity. In a move similar to Galloway's in "Latin England," Davis emphasizes how *Parliament* conjoins linguistic, social, geographic, and feminine space to make possible the communal territory of political debate that is reflected in the varied scholarship on the politics of the poem. *Parliament,* that is, offers no fantasy of a unified nation, but it does produce "England" as the given site of social contestation. Davis focuses on the way that English space is produced through the management of the vexed temporality of nations. As critics such as Renan and Homi Bhabha have taught us, the claim of timeless-

tionship between a nation and its others, whereby the center excludes the very things it needs and deviant practices paradoxically can transform marginal groups into the guarantors of national welfare.

Both Smith's analysis of the new category of merchants in *Piers* and Davis's interrogation of woman in *Parliament* suggest how making England entailed the management of others living in the space of the nation. Of course, the negotiation of others located beyond a nation's boundaries (i.e., foreign nations and peoples) is also crucial to the construction of the nation; hence the Hundred Years War and its production of the French as enemies to England figures prominently in what scholarly accounts we have of medieval Englishness. Still more interesting, perhaps, than the strategies of opposition and exclusion that we immediately identify with the nation's response to the foreign is the constitutive role such others play in the making of England itself. Smith suggests as much when he remarks upon how the Hundred Years War, deemed to be a prime contributor to English identity, was funded by a "vast flow of foreign monetary capital." Smith indicates that we might best think of the war in terms of counter transferences, both psychic and material, between England and its "extimate neighbor," such as the French capture of Edward's ship the *Christopher* and its eventual English rescue during the battle of Sluys in 1340. Peggy Knapp makes a similar point when she notes how, while Chaucer is the "Father of English Poetry," his "productions were in fact translations from Latin, Italian, and French 'originals.'"

The topic of translation is taken up more extensively in Lynn Staley's essay for the volume, "Translating 'Communitas,'" whose focus recalls not only the *translatio studii* embodied in Chaucer's literary projects but also the related and more overtly political *translatio imperii*. Turning us from the relatively successful reign of Edward analyzed by Smith to the king's notoriously ineffectual successor, Staley analyzes Richard II's efforts during the 1390s to mimic the strategies of rule that had been practiced in the French court as early as 1250. "Translating 'Communitas'" traces the development of a French myth of sacramental kingship that culminated in Charles V's winning self-fashioning through "myths of descent" and "cultic symbols" that were "rooted in vernacular textuality." Charles scrupulously deployed vernacular texts such as *Le Songe du Vergier* (1378) to "deal with both internal and external threats to his position" and create "for himself an image that came to be identified with that of France itself." During the 90s, Richard II attempted to appropriate that discourse to prop up his own authority in the face of events such as the 1381 Rebellion and the Merciless Parliament of 1387/8. But certain factors ensured that such a project would only emerge as anachronistic and emptied of the legitimacy enjoyed by Richard's French counterparts. Wyclif's "stark dismissal of a whole universe of meaningful signs, of images" such as the communal host "that embodied...a divine essence," "began a process by which authority itself could be ignored or rejected," above all, the very sacramental authority successfully utilized in France. Richard fruitlessly attempted to "define himself as sacred space" in artifacts such as the Wilton Dyptich precisely when "the very subject of signs, of sacramental reality, was a subject of contestation" in England. Staley ends her essay with a look at how Chaucer confirms in *The Nun's Priest's Tale* the inappropriateness of *translatio* as a Ricardian strategy. The near disaster resulting from "Chauntecleer's fascination with his own image of magnificence" points to a world, Staley contends, "whose contingencies cannot allow a simple borrowing of signs from another culture and time."

Through her analysis of how Richard II traveled abroad for his ideas about royal supremacy, Staley not only provides an invaluable assessment of what went wrong for the king; she also demonstrates how national projects are not autonomous but relational, whereby the example of other sociopolitical communities inspires national projects in England. Yet, as we also know, Richard not only went to France to consolidate English identity, he also went to Ireland. In "The Captivity of Henry Chrystede: Froissart's *Chroniques,* Ireland, and Fourteenth-Century Nationalism," Claire Sponsler analyzes a section in Jean Froissart's *Chroniques* in which Anglo-Irish colonist Henry Chrystede recounts his role in the Ricardian effort to colonize Ireland. As a man who "went native" while imprisoned by native Irish forces during the Anglo-Irish conflicts, Chrystede is entrusted by the king with the task of explaining (in Gaelic) how to live as a proper Englishman to four Irish kings whom Richard has conquered. Chrystede's job testifies to the role of performativity in the construction of national identity: one can become an Englishman, Chrystede's work implies, simply by learning how to act like an Englishman. Richard's employment of the not-quite-Irish and not-quite-English

Chrystede also demonstrates the uses of hybridity in national projects, whereby the work of incorporating "others" into England may be best undertaken by a man himself possessed of a "mongrel identity."

Yet among the wealth of implications Sponsler teases out from Frois-sart's tale of Chrystede, foremost among them are the unsettling de-stabilizations of identity that result when cultures and nations collide. Thus Chrystede reveals not only the benefits but also the dangers that those possessors of "mongrel identities" pose the nation. As a captivity narrative that offers not the stereotypical image of a savage Ireland but instead describes the island as a site of important opportunities for so-cial and economic advancement, Chrystede's story "starkly confronts the invader culture with the unpleasant truth that perhaps not everyone agrees that it is superior...." Conversely, Chrystede's inability to "as-semble his various identities into one synthetic whole" and his obliga-tion to move "among them according to his changing circumstances" point to his own fraught positioning. Sponsler thus provides a provocative and poignant account of the consequences of nationalism for its hybrid subjects, from the Anglo-Irish Chrystede, the French and English aristo-cratic readers of Froissart, to the historian himself, a man, Sponsler points out, who was both displaced from the England he once called home and possessed of "a professional interest in what happens" when cultures and nations collide.

The volume closes with a reassessment of his own claims on En-glish nationalism by Thorlac Turville-Petre, who, among other things, emphasizes the importance of historicizing Englishness. Additionally, through a reading of the prologue to *Sir Gawain and the Green Knight,* Turville-Petre demonstrates what the volume elsewhere makes evident, that nationalism is intertwined with a certain internationalism in the late fourteenth century.

NOTES

1. On the usage of the term "nationalism" in the nineteenth century, see Kemailäi-nen, *Nationalism.*

2. Scholarly work offering a revisionist history that counters the problematic char-acterization of the Middle Ages as "other" to the "modern" historical period it precedes in-cludes Fradenburg and Freccero, "Caxton"; Aers, "Rewriting" and "Reflections"; Patterson, *Negotiating.* For a similar critique of Anderson, see Johnson, "Imagining Communities," 5.

3. By "structures of feeling" I refer to Raymond Williams's notion of that inchoate and inexpressible aspect of lived experience that grounds individuals' ideological investments. Affective rather than intellectual, structures of feeling inhabit the preconscious and hence their relationship to the official consciousness of a culture is often obscure.

4. With the exceptions of Reynolds, *Kingdoms*, and Seton-Watson, "Language," selections of these scholars' work (and that of others, including Huizinga) appear in *Nationalism*, ed. Tipton.

5. The politics of medieval scholarship has received much attention over the past fifteen years. For examples of such work and references to like-minded inquiries into the history of the discipline, see the introduction and essays contained in *Medievalism*, ed. Bloch and Nichols. John Ganim's essay "The Myth of Medieval Romance" is of particular interest, since it provides an important account of scholarship on romance from the eighteenth century onward as "a continually contested terrain, problematizing the political implications its proponents wish to draw" (148). On the manner in which nationalism has informed scholarly work on Old English as early as the Renaissance, see Frantzen, *Desire*, and *Anglo-Saxonism*, ed. Frantzen and Niles. On the politics of the popular medievalisms of the nineteenth century, see Chandler, *Dream*, and Girouard, *Return*.

6. Cited and analyzed in Barczewski, *Myth*, 106–7. A classic analysis of the history of constructing an idealized pastoral past as a means of criticizing and resolving contemporary problems in England is Williams, *Country and the City*. See also Ganim, "Myth," and the scholarship cited in Barczewski, *Myth*, 107 n. 52.

7. An important and wide-ranging account of the ideology of Chaucer criticism appears in Patterson, *Negotiating*, 3–39.

8. On the Romantic use of the tree in nineteenth-century Germanic philology, see Frantzen, *Desire*, 64–65.

9. Cf. Strayer's somewhat innocuous characterization in "Laicization" of the power of the modern state as "attempt[s] to control social services, such as education, to regulate family relationships, and to confiscate all, or part of the church's property" (77) and his interest in "Historical Experience" in Poland and Czechoslovakia as states whose "strong personalities assert themselves even under Communist control" (25). Strayer demonstrates the relationship between cold war ideology and historical scholarship on the Middle Ages; much work remains to be written on the question of cold war politics of medieval literary studies, although Lee Patterson (*Negotiating*, 41–76) does engage with the humanist impulses of Chaucer criticism. On the relationship between literary critical work and cold war politics, see Lauter, "Sheep," Epstein, "Counter-Intelligence," and Ninkovich, "New Criticism." For a book-length study of the Cold War and the humanities generally, see Saunders, *Cultural Cold War*.

10. On the intersection of national, imperial, and gendered interests in EETS—and, in particular, the inclusion of the Bombay Asiatic Society among the members of EETS—see Biddick, *Shock*, 92–96.

11. On Higden's criticism of the Arthurian legend, see also Brown, "Higden's Britain."

12. "sed fortassis mos est cuique nationi aliquem de suis laudibus attollere excessivis ut quemadmodum Graeci suum Alexandrum, Romani suum Octavianum, Angli suum Ricardum, Franci suum Karolum sic Britones suum Arthurum praeconantur. Quod

saepe contingit, sicut dicit Josephus, aut propter historiae decorem, aut propter legentium delectiationem, aut ad proprii sanguinis exaltationem": Higden, *Polychronicon*, 5:336. My translation, in consultation with Trevisa.

13. John Armstrong makes a related point when he claims in *Nations before Nationalism* that just as we shouldn't assume that phenomena bearing the same names are necessarily similar, we shouldn't presuppose that "because movements in cultures remote in time or space from modern Europe employ very different terms, the phenomenon of ethnic identification must be absent" (10).

14. Composed first in Anglo-Norman during Edward I's reign and later translated into both Latin and English, the *Brut* aimed at most if not all classes of English society. Appearing in over two hundred manuscripts, the vast majority of which are in English, the *Brut* "was owned all over the country by nobility, gentry, merchants, clerics and academics" (Riddy, "Reading," 326–27). We should also note that the first national chronicle in the vernacular in Europe is the *Anglo-Saxon Chronicle*.

15. Cf. the four maps of England Matthew Paris included in his thirteenth-century Latin chronicles. While less accurate and detailed than the Gough Map, they nevertheless constitute an unparalleled enterprise in Europe. On the Gough Map, see Harvey, "Cartography," 495–96, and Parsons, *Map*. On Matthew Paris's maps, see Thorlac Turville-Petre's discussion of them at the start of *England the Nation*, 1–5, and the scholarship he cites.

16. The benches of the common law courts were laicized during Edward I's reign. On the court system, see Harding, *Law Courts*, Ormrod *Reign*, and Justice, *Writing*, 42.

17. John Ganim advocates a similar approach to questions of periodization and methodology in "The Literary Uses of the New History."

REFERENCES

Aers, David. "Rewriting the Middle Ages: Some Suggestions." *Journal of Medieval and Renaissance Studies* 18 (1988): 221–40.

———. "Reflections on Current Histories of the Subject." *Literature and History*, n.s., 2 (1991): 20–34.

Anderson, Benedict. *Imagined Communities: Reflections on the Origin and Spread of Nationalism*. Rev. ed. London and New York: Verso, 1991.

Anderson, Perry. *Lineages of the Absolutist State*. London: N.L.B., 1974.

Armstrong, John. *Nations before Nationalism*. Chapel Hill: University of North Carolina Press, 1982.

Barczewski, Stephanie L. *Myth and National Identity in Nineteenth-Century Britain: The Legends of King Arthur and Robin Hood*. Oxford: Oxford University Press, 2000.

Benjamin, Walter. *Illuminations*. London: Fontana, 1973.

Benzie, William. *Dr. F. J. Furnivall: Victorian Scholar Adventurer*. Norman, OK: Pilgrim, 1983.

Bhabha, Homi. "DissemiNation: Time, Narrative, and the Margins of the Modern Nation." In his *The Location of Culture*, 139–70. London and New York: Routledge, 1994.

Biddick, Kathleen. *The Shock of Medievalism*. Durham and London: Duke University Press, 1998.

Bloch, Howard R., and Stephen G. Nichols, eds. *Medievalism and the Modernist Temper*. Baltimore and London: Johns Hopkins University Press, 1996.

Bloch, Marc. *Feudal Society*. 2 vols. Trans. L. A. Manyon. Chicago: University of Chicago Press, 1964.

Breuilly, John. *Nationalism and the State*. Manchester: Manchester University Press, 1982.

Britnell, R. H. *The Commercialisation of English Society, 1000–1500*. Cambridge: Cambridge University Press, 1993.

Brown, Peter. "Higden's Britain." In *Medieval Europeans: Studies in Ethnic Identity and National Perspectives in Medieval Europe*, ed. Alfred P. Smyth, 103–18. New York: St. Martin's, 1998.

Burke, Kenneth. *The Philosophy of Literary Form: Studies in Symbolic Action*. 2d ed. Baton Rouge: Louisiana State University Press, 1967.

Cantor, Norman. *Inventing the Middle Ages: The Lives, Works, and Ideas of the Great Medievalists of the Twentieth Century*. New York: William Morrow, 1991.

Chandler, Alice. *A Dream of Order: The Medieval Ideal in Nineteenth-Century English Literature*. Lincoln: University of Nebraska Press.

Cohen, Jeffrey Jerome, ed., *The Postcolonial Middle Ages*. New York: St. Martin's, 2000.

Crystal, David. *The Cambridge Encyclopedia of the English Language*. Cambridge: Cambridge University Press, 1995.

Epstein, William. "Counter-Intelligence: Cold-War Criticism and Eighteenth-Century Studies." *English Literary History* 57 (1990): 63–100.

Ferster, Judith. "England as a Political Nation." In her *Fictions of Advice: The Literature and Politics of Counsel in Late Medieval England*, 16–42. Philadelphia: University of Pennsylvania Press, 1996.

Forde, Simon, Lesley Johnson, and Alan V. Murray, eds. *Concepts of National Identity in the Middle Ages*. Leeds: University of Leeds Press, 1995.

Fradenburg, Louise, and Carla Freccero. "Caxton, Foucault, and the Pleasures of History." In *Premodern Sexualities*, ed. Louise Fradenburg and Carla Freccero, xiii–xxiv. New York: Routledge, 1996.

Frantzen, Allen. *Desire for Origins: New Language, Old English, and Teaching the Tradition*. New Brunswick: Rutgers University Press, 1990.

Frantzen, Allen J., and John D. Niles, eds. *Anglo-Saxonism and the Construction of Social Identity*. Gainesville: University Press of Florida, 1997.

Furnivall, Frederick J., ed. *Early English Meals and Manners*. EETS o.s. 32. 1868. Reprint, London: Kegan Paul, Trench Trübner and Co., 1894.

Galbraith, Vivian. "Nationality and Language in Medieval England." *Transactions of the Royal Historical Society* 23 (1941): 113–28.

Ganim, John. "The Literary Uses of the New History." In *The Idea of Medieval Literature: New Essays on Chaucer and Medieval Culture in Honor of Donald R. Howard*, ed. James M. Dean and Christian K. Zacher, 209–26. Newark: University of Delaware Press, 1992.

———. "The Myth of Medieval Romance." In *Medievalism*, ed. Bloch and Nichols, 148–66.

Gellner, Ernest. *Thought and Change*. London: Weidenfeld and Nicholson, 1964.

————. *Nations and Nationalism*. Oxford: Blackwell, 1983.

Geoffrey of Monmouth. *The History of the Kings of Britain*. Trans. Lewis Thorpe. London: Penguin, 1966.

Giddens, Anthony. *The Nation-State and Violence*. Cambridge: Polity, 1985.

Gillingham, John. "Henry of Huntington and the Twelfth-Century Revival of the English Nation." In *Concepts of National Identity*, ed. Forde, Johnson, and Murray, 75–102.

Girouard, Mark. *The Return to Camelot*. New Haven: Yale University Press, 1981.

Greenfeld, Liah. *Nationalism: Five Roads to Modernity*. Cambridge: Harvard University Press, 1992.

Gurteen, S. Humphreys. *The Arthurian Epic: A Comparative Study of the Cambrian, Breton, and Anglo-Norman Versions of the Story and Tennyson's Idylls of the King*. New York and London: G. P. Putnam's Sons, 1895.

Harding, Alan. *The Law Courts of Medieval England*. London: Allen & Unwin; New York: Barnes and Noble, 1973.

Harriss, G. L. *King, Parliament and Public Finance in Medieval England to 1369*. Oxford: Clarendon, 1975.

Harvey, P. D. A. "Local and Regional Cartography in Medieval Europe." In *The History of Cartography*. Vol. 1. ed. J. B. Harley and David Woodward, 464–501. Chicago and London: University of Chicago Press, 1987.

Hayes, Carleton J. H. *The Historical Evolution of Modern Nationalism*. New York: Smith, 1931.

Helgerson, Richard. *Forms of Nationhood: The Elizabethan Writing of England*. Chicago: University of Chicago Press, 1992.

Héracourt, Will. *Die Wertwelt Chaucers: Die Wertwelt einer Zeitwende*. Heidelberg: C. Winter, 1939.

Higden, Ranulph. *Polychronicon, together with the English Translations of John Trevisa and of an Unknown Writer of the Fifteenth Century*. Ed. Churchill Babington and Joseph Lumby. 9 vols. Rolls Series 41. London: Her Majesty's Stationery Office, 1865–86.

Hobsbawm, E. J. *Nations and Nationalism since 1780: Programme, Myth, Reality*. Cambridge: Cambridge University Press, 1990.

Howard, Jean E. *Engendering a Nation: A Feminist Account of Shakespeare's English Histories*. New York: Routledge, 1997.

Huizinga, Johan. *Men and Ideas: History, the Middle Ages, the Renaissance*. Trans. James S. Holmes and Hans van Marle. New York: Meridian, 1959.

Ingham, Patricia. *Sovereign Fantasies*. Philadelphia: University of Pennsylvania Press, 2001.

Jameson, Fredric. *The Political Unconscious: Narrative as a Socially Symbolic Act*. Ithaca and New York: Cornell University Press, 1981.

Johnson, Leslie. "Imagining Communities: Medieval and Modern." In *Concepts of National Identity*, ed. Forde, Johnson, and Murray, 1–20.

————. "Etymologies, Genealogies, and Nationalities Again." In *Concepts of National Identity*, ed. Forde, Johnson, and Murray, 125–36.

Justice, Steven. *Writing and Rebellion: England in 1381*. Berkeley and Los Angeles: University of California Press, 1994.

Kantorowicz, Ernst. *The King's Two Bodies: A Study in Mediaeval Political Theology*. Princeton: Princeton University Press, 1957.

Keeney, Barnaby. "Military Service and the Development of Nationalism in England, 1272–1327." *Speculum* 22 (1947): 534–49.

Kemailäinen, Aira. *Nationalism: Problems Concerning the Word, the Concept and Classification.* Jyväskylä: Kustantajat, 1964.

Kohn, Hans. *The Idea of Nationalism: A Study of Its Origins and Background.* New York: Macmillan, 1944.

———. *Nationalism.* Princeton: Princeton University Press, 1955.

Latour, Bruno. *We Have Never Been Modern.* Trans. Catherine Porter. Cambridge: Harvard University Press, 1993.

Lauter, Paul. "Little White Sheep, or How I Learned to Dress Blue." *Yale Journal of Criticism* 8 (1995): 103–30.

Lewis, Charlton T., and Charles Short, eds. *A New Latin Dictionary.* Rev. ed. New York: American Book Company, 1907.

McEachern, Claire Elizabeth. *The Poetics of English Nationhood, 1590–1612.* Cambridge: Cambridge University Press, 1996.

Middleton, Anne. "Chaucer's 'New Men' and the Good of Literature in the *Canterbury Tales.*" In *Literature and Society,* ed. Edward W. Said, 15–56. Baltimore: Johns Hopkins University Press, 1980.

Murray, Elisabeth. *Caught in the Web of Words: James Murray and the Oxford English Dictionary.* New Haven: Yale University Press, 1977.

Nairn, Tom. *The Break-Up of Britain.* London: Verso, 1983.

Ninkovich, Frank. "The New Criticism and Cold War America." *Southern Quarterly* 20 (1981): 1–24.

Ormrod, W. M. *The Reign of Edward III: Crown and Political Society in England, 1327–1377.* New Haven and London: Yale University Press, 1990.

Parsons, E. J. S. *The Map of Great Britain circa A.D. 1360, known as the Gough Map: An Introduction to the Facsimile.* Oxford: Oxford University Press, [1970].

Patterson, Lee. *Negotiating the Past: The Historical Understanding of Medieval Literature.* Madison: University of Wisconsin Press, 1987.

———. "Making Identities in Fifteenth-Century England: Henry V and John Lydgate." In *New Historical Literary Study: Essays on Reproducing Texts, Representing History,* ed. Jeffrey N. Cox and Larry J. Reynolds, 69–107. Princeton: Princeton University Press, 1993.

———. Review of Thorlac Turville-Petre's *England the Nation. Studies in the Age of Chaucer* 19 (1997): 324–28.

Post, Gaines. "Two Notes on Nationalism in the Middle Ages." *Traditio* 9 (1953): 281–320.

———. "'Blessed Lady Spain': Vincentius Hispanus and Spanish National Imperialism in the Thirteenth Century." *Speculum* 29 (1954): 198–209.

Radcliffe, Sarah. "Gendered Nations: Nostalgia, Development, and Territory in Ecuador." *Gender, Place, and Culture* 3 (1996): 5–21.

Renan, Ernst. "Qu'est-ce qu'une nation?" In *Oeuvres Complètes,* 1:887–906. Paris: Calmann-Lévy, 1947–61.

Reynolds, Susan. *Kingdoms and Communities in Western Europe, 900–1300.* 2d ed. Oxford: Clarendon, 1997.

Riddy, Felicity. "Reading for England: Arthurian Literature and National Consciousness." *Bibliographical Bulletin of the International Arthurian Society* 43 (1991): 314–32.

Roskell, John Smith. *Parliament and Politics in Late Medieval England*. London: Hambledon Press, 1981.

Saintsbury, George. *The Flourishing of Romance and the Rise of Allegory*. Edinburgh and London: C. Scribner's Sons, 1897.

Saunders, Frances Stonor. *The Cultural Cold War: The CIA and the World of Arts and Letters*. New York: New Press, 1999.

Scholze-Stubenrecht, W., and J. B. Sykes, eds. *The Oxford-Duden German Dictionary: German-English/English-German*. Oxford and New York: Clarendon Press, 1997.

Seton-Watson, Hugh. "Language and National Consciousness." *Proceedings of the British Academy* 67 (1981): 1–18.

Staley, Lynn. *Margery Kempe's Dissenting Fictions*. University Park: Pennsylvania State University Press, 1994.

Strayer, Joseph. "The Laicization of French and English Society in the Thirteenth Century." *Speculum* 15 (1940): 76–86.

———. "The Historical Experience of Nation-Building in Europe." In *Nation-Building*, ed. Karl W. Deutsch and William J. Foltz, 17–26. New York: Atherton Press, 1963.

———. *On the Medieval Origins of the Modern State*. Princeton: Princeton University Press, 1970.

Tatnall, Edith. "John Wyclif and *Ecclesia Anglicana*." *Journal of Ecclesiastical History* 20 (1969): 19–43.

Tipton, C. Leon, ed. *Nationalism in the Middle Ages*. New York: Holt, Rinehart and Winston, 1972.

Turner, Victor. *Dramas, Fields, and Metaphors: Symbolic Action in Human Society*. Ithaca: Cornell University Press, 1974.

Turville-Petre, Thorlac. *England the Nation: Language, Literature, and National Identity, 1290–1340*. Oxford: Clarendon, 1996.

Utz, Richard J. "Inventing German(ic) Chaucer: Ideology and Philology in German Anglistics before 1945." *Studies in Medievalism* 8 (1996): 5–26.

Waldron, Ronald. "Trevisa's 'Celtic Complex' Revisited." *Notes and Queries* 36 (1989): 303–07.

Wallace, David. *Chaucerian Polity: Absolutist Lineages and Associational Forms in England and Italy*. Stanford: Stanford University Press, 1997.

Weston, Jessie L. *The Legend of Sir Gawaine: Studies upon Its Original Scope and Significance*. London: Nutt, 1897.

Williams, Raymond. *The Long Revolution*. New York: Columbia University Press, 1961.

———. *The Country and the City*. London: Paladin, 1973.

———. *Marxism and Literature*. New York: Oxford University Press, 1977.

Willinsky, John. *The Empire of Words: The Reign of the OED*. Princeton: Princeton University Press, 1994.

Winter, William. *Shadows of the Stage*. New York: Macmillan, 1892.

Žižek, Slavoj. *The Sublime Object of Ideology*. New York: Verso, 1989.

PART I

THEORIZING THE
MEDIEVAL ENGLISH NATION

Pro Patria Mori

L. O. Aranye Fradenburg

*To a knyght apperteyneth that he be lover
of the comyn wele. For by the comynalte of
the people was the chyvalrye founden &
establysshed. And the comyn wele is gretter
& more necessary than propre good and
specyall.*

       —The Book of the ordre of chyualry

*The conclusion that the phenomena of
patriotism and nationalism are recent
because the words and concepts are recent
is . . . misleading. . . . On the same basis one
might conclude that there were no cosmic
rays in the Middle Ages.*

       —Johan Huizinga

Imagining community is a work of desire, as Benedict Anderson pointed out when referring to the love people feel for the nations they dream into being.[1] Communities—their social structures, architecture, marketing practices, secret places—are not only imagined but also made by desire (Deleuze and Guattari, *Anti-Oedipus,* 6). They are our "territorializations," our complex and shifting ecologies of *habitus* and habitation.[2] We participate in the histories of their enjoyment; we are there (where else?) when they assemble and fall apart, take (over) place and dwindle, in the course of their attempts to get as close to *jouissance* (impossible or unbearable amounts of enjoyment) as possible.[3] Individual and group desires are never independent of one another. Group subjectivities relay desire from one member to another. They consist of shifting codifications of enjoyment, codifications worked out by the law as well as by the transgressions that depend upon it. They transmit enjoyment, and thereby construct territory of every kind, mapping urban centers ("gay" neighborhoods, financial centers, museum districts), the "land" (national parks, theme parks, car parks), and so forth. And group subjects participate in the logic of transmission: the production of change (e.g., receiving information from the past, the future, the core, the periphery, the inside, the outside) through techniques of replication and dissemination.

Territory cannot maintain itself without constant differentiation (Deleuze and Guattari, *Capitalism*, 313). This means active interdependence between many different levels of biological/social organization. Ecologies survive by means of re/production; the continued life of all elements in an ecology depends on how each negotiates the border between the inside of the territory and the outside, the familiar and the unfamiliar, the "same" and the "other." What counts is *how* these negotiations are styled. The groups and modes of enjoyment that make up human ecologies are realizations of technologies of transmission, which gives them enormous power, including the power to give sacrifice its meaning.[4] Though an individual subject can sacrifice to the demands of its own exacting moral strictures, only in the context of the group can the social and economic value of sacrifice be fully determined: one may die on behalf of the other, even or especially on behalf of the other inside oneself, but group processes—and therefore language—will determine the value of the life thus relinquished, and distribute favor(s) accordingly. Henry of Ghent "praised the magnanimity of a soldier's sacrifice if dictated by love," quoting the Song of Solomon 8:6, "for love is as strong as death," to "demonstrate that a soldier's sacrifice for his friends was a work of charity and of faith"; "he accepted Cicero's religion: *Patria mihi vita mea carior est*, 'The fatherland is dearer to me than my life.'"[5] Western ethical and political thought closely associates sacrifice with patriotism and patriotism with nations or empires. Insofar as medieval polities are regarded as postimperial or prenational, they may also be regarded as post- or prepatriotic. For example, many histories of France and

England have begun with the Picts or the Celts or the Gauls as though they were part of a progression toward nationhood; medieval polities are treated as hybrid forms somewhere in the middle of this development, and therefore *inevitably* lack certain features of nationhood that emerge in later times, however busy they may be adding ones that weren't there earlier. This kind of nationalist narrative, aspects of which are uncomfortably recapitulated in New Historicist writing, has obscured the importance to the study of nationalism of polities whose histories seem less amenable to developmental narrative. The "fragmentation" of medieval Germany and Italy, or the variousness of Spain, did not prevent them from becoming important modern nations, and equally did not prevent medieval Germans and Italians and Spaniards from glorifying their "fatherland" (Post, "Two Notes," passim). Patriotic discourse was prominent in communities on the "margins" of Europe, and/or in communities whose sovereignty was consistently menaced—the northern communities most threatened by German imperialism, such as Denmark, and England's "Gaelic fringe."[6] Not only did the putative underdevelopment of national apparatuses in Scotland, Wales, and Ireland not inhibit patriotic discourse, but there is every reason to think that English patriotic discourse developed as a consequence of its exchanges with its independent-minded neighbors.[7]

Two common assumptions about the Middle Ages further obscure the possibility that medieval political subjects loved their countries, or that this love was materially meaningful: the Middle Ages is the time of the group mind, and if love of one's country is a *particular* love, it will not survive competition with the Church and the (hope of renovated) Empire; the Middle Ages is also the time of semi-private loyalties, which crisscross political boundaries too often to permit of passionate identifications with one particular territory.[8] But multiple loyalties are not necessarily weakened loyalties.[9] In *The Just War in the Middle Ages*, Russell argues that "[d]efense of the Holy Land and the church gave rise to defense of the *patria*," and "nourished the just wars of states . . . claiming sovereignty" (297); Alan Forey notes that in the thirteenth century the military orders were increasingly "expected to give service against . . . Christian states" (*Military Orders*, 297). The Spanish Templars, defending themselves to James II at the time of their arrest, (futilely) reminded him of their loyalty to King Pedro: "the brethren fortified and garrisoned their castles with their forces with the intention of dying with the lord king or preserving the kingdom for him, and they defended him and his land" (Forey, *Military Orders*, 221; citing Finke, *Papstuttum*, c. 72 doc. 48).

Loyalty to lord, then, does not exclude loyalty to *paÿs*, *natio*, or *patria*, or *ecclesia*. Alain de Lille's handbook on the art of preaching explains that soldiers were especially ordained "that they should defend their native land *(ut patriam suam defendant)*, and that they should repel the attacks of the violent upon the Church."[10] Treatises on chivalry commonly emphasize the multiple responsibilities of the knightly order, which, according to *The Boke of Knyghthode*, is "principaly to be occupied in kepying and defendyng the Cristyn feythe, [th]e rigth of the Chirch, the lond, the contre and the comin welefare of it" (*Epistle*, ed. Bühler, 121).[11] Geoffroi de Charny explains that great personages are necessary to society because they "expose themselves to the physical dangers of battle in defense of their people and their land" *(leur peuple et de leurs terres)* (Kaeuper and Kennedy, "*Book*," 140–43).[12]

Multiple allegiances cannot cause confusion and anxiety unless they are strong allegiances in the first place; provoking conflicts between them can bring those strengths to the foreground, reinforcing the very ties whose exclusivity seems threatened. Certain allegiances may be sublimed at certain moments and others abjected, but these differences of value have meaning only in relation to one another. Just as there is never only one community, there is no glorious individual without the group. If particular interests—personal, familial, regional, "class"—complicate the formation of national polities, they are also essential to the process. The "extraordinary" and the "ordinary" are mutually constitutive. Citing Otto Hintze's view that states rely on class structures, Joachim Bumke, in *The Concept of Knighthood in the Middle Ages*, writes that

> ... "the nature of the concept of class" is to be seen in the fact "that in a political lordship grouping ... the *meliores et majores terrae* (the superior and greater men of the land) 'represent' the whole, the 'Land' or the 'empire' before the ruler" in a corporate organization. ... (116, citing Hintze, "Typologie," 229 ff.)

Adrian Hastings has more recently argued that nationhood depends on the formation of both "horizontal" and "vertical" bonds (*Construction*, 4). *The Book of the ordre of chyualry* seems to be saying something like this when it remarks that if kings or princes were not "noblesse" of chivalry "incorporate," they would not be "suffysaunt" nor worthy to be lords of "countrees" (Caxton, *Book,* 47).

Sacrifice does its best political work by subliming (into existence) an elite *within* the community. It defines extraordinary persons by, through, and for the group. In military culture—for Freud, the most venerable example of group psychology—ranking does not militate against group identification (*Group Psychology,* 32–35). To this day military organizations remain both very hierarchical *and* specially sublime instances of the patriotism felt by ordinary citizens. *Everybody's* sacrificial enjoyment depends on creating differential values for particular (kinds of) lives.

In the later Middle Ages, the right of the *meliores et majores terrae* to represent the "land" is increasingly linked to their putative willingness to sacrifice their important, exemplary lives, and therefore depends (in circular motion) on the high value of the lives they sacrifice. This circularity is a prime example of the group's power of relay, of the group's ability to forge value by handing things off from one member or faction to another; as we shall see, it is also reinforced by chivalry's spectacular use of the (mirror) image to perform the function of relay (see "Ethics for Strong Bodies," below). The consequences of this group performativity were profound: chivalric treatises of the later Middle Ages enjoined knights to be "lovers of the common weal," glorified knightly sacrifice on behalf of lord and people, and thereby (re)developed patriotic discourse on behalf of European nationalism. *Amor patriae in radice charitatis fundatur*—"Love for the fatherland is founded in the root of a charity which puts, not the private things before those common, but the common things before the private" (Kantorowicz, *King's,* 242, citing Tolomeo of Lucca, *De regimine principum,* c. 4, 41). Chivalry's extensive use of ecclesiastical resources made it an important model for the cross-channelling of secular and religious "sentiment," just as its admiration for classical literature fostered the creation of the national "histories" subsequently repudiated by humanist historians hoping to cancel their debts to the passionate mythmaking of the barbaric ages that preceded the invention of "true historical criticism."[13] Chivalry drew on clerics and mysticism and identificatory devotional piety to make it sublime; increasingly dependent on the fighting forces of Christendom, the Church in turn produced sacralized warfare and lent its ritual power to the "ordaining" of knights as though their "office" were analogous to the priesthood.[14]

The monarchy made similar contributions. Hoping to foster the chivalric sentiments of the nobility whose support it needed for warfare, it found out many ways of subliming the sacrifices made by "the order of knighthood" on behalf of rulers. But this was not simply an attempt to "restrain" the power of the nobility; it was an attempt to solemnize the value of the monarch and his people by solemnizing the exemplary personages who mediate between them. Sublimity can be mutually reinforcing, with mirrors. According to Richard Barber, "when the secular orders appeared, they were both nationalist and personal to the monarch" (*Knight*, 305). The Order of the Star and the Order of the Garter were both founded by kings (Jean II of France and Edward III of England respectively) who intended them as spectacular examples of the monarch's patronage of chivalry on behalf of *paÿs* and people.[15] But they also consecrated the concerns of knights like Geoffroi de Charny, part of Jean II's intimate circle of reformist policy wonks, who was devoted to the idea of loyalty to liege lord, to the idea of the common weal, and to the *paÿs*, the "natural country" as *The Book of the ordre of chyualry* puts it (Caxton, *Book*, 15).

Chivalric sacrifice can circulate sublimity because knights sacrifice on behalf of monarch and peoples, who are made worthy of sacrifice because knights sacrifice for them. In other words, sacrifice is performative, and this performativity enables the circulation of sublimity. Towns were part of this loop-de-loop; Juliet Vale argues that tournaments and *fêtes* in the Low Countries and in England that pitted important townies against the nobility were evidence for widespread "cultural interaction between noble and bourgeois."[16] A realm's possession of a populous and prosperous city was evidence of its importance and hence could play a role in determinations of sovereignty (Fradenburg, *City*, 22, n. 12.) The "Prologue" to Caxton's edition of "Caton" (dedicated to the city of London) laments the diminution of London's prosperity, "the cause [of which] is that ther is almost none / that entendeth to the comyn wele but only euery man for his singuler prouffyte / O whan I remember the noble Romayns / that for the comyn wele of the Cyte of Rome / they spente not only theyr moeuable goodes / but they put theyr bodyes & lyues in Ieopardye & to the deth" (Crotch, *Prologues*, 77).

By the time of Caxton's writing, this passage would relay both classical themes of sacrifice on behalf of the "comyn wele" and the ethics of integrity developed by political thinkers like Aquinas and John of Salisbury. Caxton's interest in the power of moral discourse to incite sacrifice, economic and otherwise, is given a wider context in the *Proem* to his translation of the *Polychronicon,* where histories are praised because they have "moued ryght noble knyghtes to deserue eternal laude whiche foloweth them for their vyctoryous merites / And cause them more valyantly to entre in Ieopardyes of batayles for the defence and tuicion of theyr countrey / and publyke wele" (Crotch, *Prologues,* 65). Caxton's role in appropriating chivalric techniques of glorification on behalf of mercantile culture is well known; in his *Cato,* he stresses that sacrificing one's goods for the common weal is much the same as sacrificing one's body in its defense. The wealth of London is the city's imaginary body. Thus Caxton's concern for the "wele" of the city of London, and the fragility of inheritance and virtue within it (noted also by the Host in *The Monk's Prologue* to *The Canterbury Tales*), is not evidence of a narrow allegiance, nor is the market he is cultivating alien to chivalric economies, whose claim to transcend mere exchange has been too often accepted as a description of medieval reality by historians who at the same time depreciate its common sense. If the economy of sacrifice means to get back with interest whatever it gives away (Derrida, *Gift*), it is far from foolish. This is a point we should consider when we try to understand the meaning of "modernity." Far from inhibiting the development of the nation-state, chivalric culture was largely responsible for the subliming of secular militancy on which centuries of European nationalist sentiment, linking group enjoyment to the protection of gold mines or petroleum resources, would come to rely.

This essay explores late medieval chivalric culture's foregrounding of sacrificial *jouissance,* and its contributions to nation formation, as a particular moment in the "history of the signifier"—when signifiers of secular community ("*patria,*" "country," "common weal") are sublimed by their performance of an "apotheosis of sadism" (Lacan, *Seminar,* 262), by a sado-masochistic rewiring of the group body (Rickels, *Case,* 18), and hence a massive intensification of the corporeal, psychic, and social enjoyment of identification with a "common" imaginary body *by losing, and also regaining in sublimer form, singularity*—thus enabling loss to be enjoyed by the patriot, to become the patriot's *jouissance,* because he is "held together" (while losing himself on the killing fields) not even simply by his participation in a super group but by the exemplary singularity his sacrifice confers upon him. By means of the get-it-back-with-interest economy of sacrifice, what chivalry donates to *patria* is the real entitlement of the patriot to atrocity and other forms of *jouissance* on the grounds of his sacrifice; the dissolution caused by *jouissance* is perfectly supported by the image of the dissolution of singularity through sacrifice, a singularity that returns to the subject with interest *because* it has risked this double-dissolution caused by an unusual conjunction between *jouissance* and the Good. The plasticity of this mode of enjoyment as well as its power of concentration, its ability to deliver on all points, has made it a powerful legacy indeed.

The Germans Should Not March with the French

At one time the idea of medieval nationalism found favor with a number of historians who felt the resonance of remarks like that of Gervase of Prémontré with the nationalist alliances that produced the world wars of the twentieth century. The lived history of scholars like Kantorowicz and Huizinga prompted them to ask certain questions about the past that lost favor in the Reaganomical heyday of the New Historicism but were restored as interesting when Russia and the Balkan states began, in the later 1980s and 1990s, to repeat the past with so little apparent difference. The revelations of earlier twentieth-century history—e.g., that passionate nationalism neither requires nor is obviated by complicated administrative and media technologies—enabled Huizinga to posit that

> The Crusades, far from uniting in the faith what was divided by language, descent, and allegiance, reinforced the national enmities of the peoples of Latin Christendom by bringing those peoples together again and again in martial equipment, battle array, and a more or less sanctified rivalry. ("Pariotism," iii, 108–09)

The events that have followed the breakup of the Soviet Union do not encourage the technological progressivism that underlies so many discussions of nationhood, and especially disfavor the notion that irrational or religious or ethnic ("racial") nationalism must ipso facto predate trade commissions and butter mountains (not that there is anything self-evidently sane about butter mountains). Likewise the significance of the contributions made by the medieval Church to the history of European nationhood may now come into sharper focus, in particular the creation of discursive and legal forms for the purpose of sanctifying, and thereby de/reterritorializing, militancy. Hastings, in *The Construction of Nationhood*, points out that "[o]ne wide-ranging context for the religious shaping of nationalism is that of a contested frontier" (190). Earl Jeffrey Richards, in his discussion of nationalism in the work of Christine de Pizan, usefully describes the Crusades as a means of "displacing national differences to the realm of salvation history" ("Cultural Nationalism," 75). When the *Chanson de Roland* vernacularized the "Saracen" invasion of Europe, Karl Uitti writes, "'France' does not replace 'Empire' in Roland. It embodies and renews it.... Christian unity [is] represented by 'dulce France'" ("Alexis," 138).[17]

The Crusades played a significant role in subliming knightly sacrifice, through the sacralizing of militant pilgrimage to the Holy Land, especially in the form of the papal indulgences that came to be associated, however ambiguously, with just or holy war. Those knights who have gone "ouer the see in pylgremage" and there fight the enemies of the cross are "martirs yf they deye / For they fyghte for tenhaunce the holy feyth catholyk" (Caxton, *Book*, 37). Pope Leo IV's 853 appeal for the protection of Rome from the "Saracens" says that such warriors also die on behalf of the fatherland: "'he who dies in this battle...died for...the salvation of the *patria*, and the defence of Christianity'" (Keen, *Chivalry*, 46). As the historian G. G. Coulton has argued, the Crusades were opportunities for different European nations to meet, compete, and relish their differences ("Nationalism," 17, 20).[18] Guibert of Nogent hilariously calls his account of the First Crusade *Gesta Dei per Francos*, "The Acts of God as Performed by the French" (Richards, "Cultural Nationalism," 79). Coulton cites contemporary accounts of "the jealousies of the detachment of the several nations" at the capture of Lisbon ("Nationalism," 19, citing *Memorials of Richard I*, cxlii–clxxx). Gervase of Prémontré, bishop of Séez, appealed to the long history of these jealousies when writing to Innocent III about the pilgrim armies:

> I tell you confidently—and I believe there are many who agree
> with me here—that it is very important for this business [of
> the Crusade] that the Germans should not march with the French;

for we can not find in history that they ever were at accord in
any momentous common enterprise. (Coulton, "Nationalism,"
19, citing Hugo, *Antiquitatis*, 4)

Later chivalric ordinances were sufficiently concerned about these antag-
onisms to rule out hate speech, at least when it led to physical violence.
Item 34 of the "Ordinances of War Made by King Henry V at Mawnt"
provide that "nomaner man gyve no reproche to none other, because of
the cuntrey that he is of, that is to say be he Frenshe, Englissh, Walsh, or
Irissh... thorough the whiche vilony saying may falle sodeyn man-
slaughter... alle suche barratourz shal stond at the kynges will, what
deth thay shall have for their noys makyng" (Twiss, *Black Book*, 469).

Tournaments also provided common ground for the purpose of national competition; "French" knights fight against "English" knights who
fight against "German" knights. According to his biographer, William
Marshall feels that the knights of France are "definitely superior to their
close relatives who formed the chivalry of England."[19] Boucicaut holds
an "enterprise" on the frontier between Boulogne and English Calais
and provides that "enemies of France could choose whether they were to
contend with real lances or with blunted tilting weapons"; if an English
knight appeared "who wished to tilt with Boucicaut he would strike the
shield of the Marshal which was reserved for foes of the realm of France"
(Painter, *French Chivalry*, 52). All very friendly in its way.

Chivalric writing is also full of learned observations about the behavior and obligations of knights not only *en son paÿs* but also *en autres:*
Knyghthode and Bataile (ed. Dyboski and Arend, pt. II, st. 6, lines 660–
62) explains that "Confederat men aydaunt is to se, / That is to se, by
trewce or toleraunce, / As Frensh ar suffred here, and we in Fraunce."[20]
In *The Tree of Battles,* Honoré Bonet often lays down the law when territorial borders are causing problems: if a German goes to Paris "to become
acquainted with the gentle manners of France," finds "a knight or squire
bearing the arms of his house, and confronts him, as roughly as the
Germans are accustomed to do," is the German free to offer the Frenchman "wager of battle"? Or, can "an English student dwelling at Paris for
purposes of study" be imprisoned? (c. 127, p. 204; c. 86, p. 180).

Love of country also finds its way into "the later knighting ceremonies," which, Barber notes, "contain a prayer that the new knight
may use his weapons faithfully in the service of the kingdom of France,

or England, or Castile, as the case may be; so the international ideal is not emphasized, and the brotherhood is first and foremost composed of the knights of one nation under their ruler" (*Knight*, 295). Caxton's famous coda to *The Book of the ordre of chyualry*, which echoes a long tradition of complaint about knightly sloth and effeminacy, makes the "exercise of arms" a patriotic matter: he reminds "ye knyghtes of Englonde" not only of the legendary courage of British knights as described in Arthurian literature but also "of the noble actes syth the conquest / as in Kyng Rycharde dayes cuer du lyon / Edwarde the fyrtste / and the thyrde / and his noble sones / Syre Robert Knolles / Syr Johan hawkwode / Syr Johan chaundos / & syre gaultier manuy rede froissart," and the victorious and noble "harry the fyfthe / ande the capytayns vnder hym" (50). *Knyghthode and Bataile* imagines the ceremonies it describes as transmitting national glory: "Justise is heer peasibilly to stonde / And al the world shal telle of Engelonde, / And of the kyngis high magnificence" (pt. V, st. 100, lines 2920–22).

The Crusades not only provided *eine anderere Schauplatz* for the mobilization of European nationalisms, but also helped to delineate the home territories. Gerald of Wales's *Journey Through Wales* brilliantly exemplifies how a carefully etched territorialization of community, far from eliding "elsewhere," depends on it, and vice versa. Gerald is part of an entourage that goes on pilgrimage through Wales to preach a new Crusade in the Holy Land, and along the way Wales takes shape through Gerald's descriptions of local topographies and histories and present-day customs. So we have come round again to three important points: that the well-being of the territory depends on openness to multiple ecologies within and without it, that one territorial assemblage ("dulce France") can be used to exemplify another ("Empire"), or provide a home or origin or promised land for another; and (most obviously, but still worth repeating) that shared borders mean intimacy and *therefore* conflict.

The Sublime

Enjoyment depends on both obeying and transgressing the law, that is, the kinship and linguistic structures (including erotic prohibitions and permissions) we begin to internalize from the moment of our birth. The law that structures our subjectivity is neither a "good" law nor a "bad." It

ject, the more likely is this service to get us near *jouissance*. Such acts
of devotion depend on unintelligibility and non-knowledge, like any act
of faith.[22] There is no risk in fighting for an agency whose power to reward is *really* self-evident and beyond question. The obscenity of submission to the arbitrariness of the law is, in this sense, itself a source of
sublime effects.

Sublime objects (one's brother-in-arms, one's city, one's lady) are
often pitted against each other in aristocratic literature, but these oppo-
sitions are far from fundamental and multiply into potentially endless
contradictions. The love of one's brother-in-arms can be pitted against
love for the larger military group; the love of one's brother-in-arms can
be pitted against the love of one's lady; one's brother-in-arms can *be*
one's lady. The structures and processes that produce erotic love or ag-
gressivity in the subject are not alien to those that produce community-
love. We set at odds our love for God, country, and sweetheart when
we want to substantiate the sublimity of our objects by fighting over
them instead of for them—which is to say, when we want to vary the
particular kinds of sacrificial enjoyment at stake in winning the lady of/
or the land.[23] And war directly inspires desire for personal as well as
community love-objects. To this day, soldiers get engaged before or during or after they go to war, prompted by the service of one desirable object or means of excitation to the service of another. Since war makes
soldiers realize how precious their love is, how much it is worth protecting, war enhances the precariousness and hence sublimity of the love-
object at home. (During the rejoicing that welcomed home the crew-
members of the American spyplane shot down over China in 2001, one
of the returning heroes announced his engagement on television, to
great applause.)

Certainly moralists throughout the Middle Ages reprobated love of
ladies for the dangers it posed to military preparedness. The theme of
knightly "effeminacy" appears frequently in later medieval homilies and
secular literature like Gower's "Complaint Against Chivalry" (Fradenburg, *City*, 212–13, and, e.g., Gower, *Vox Clamantis*, V, 4). But the arts of
rule in the Middle Ages offer plenty of examples of love as stimulant to
the pursuit of arms and glory. *The Book of the ordre of chyualry* says (without taking it back) that "no man may more honoure and loue Chyualrye /
ne more for hym maye not he do / Than that *deyeth for loue* & for

to honoure the ordre of Chyualrye" (Caxton, *Book,* 17). So martial and solemn a document as *The Roll of Arms of the Princes . . . Who Attended . . . the Siege of Caerlaverock* (1300) remarks of Robert Lord Clifford (after its puff-piece on his and his armigerous ancestors' fantastic feats of arms [against Scotland and unicorns respectively]), that "If I were a young maiden, / I would give him my heart and person, / So good is his fame" ("Si je estoie une pucelette, / Je li donroie quer e cors, / Tant est de li bons li recors") (ed. Wright, 11–12). The entry for William de Ferrers mentions that he "long endured great sufferings" *(por ki long tens souffri granz maus)* for the countess of Gloucester (21). Explaining how some good knights may be inspired to bestir themselves to fight on behalf of *payïs* or faith as well as for their personal holdings, so thoughtful a servant of the common weal as Geoffroi de Charny remarks that some knights are so fortunate as to have ladies to "command them to set out and put all their efforts into winning renown . . . these ladies urge them on to reach beyond any of their earlier aspirations" (Kaeuper and Kennedy, "*Book,*" 95). Sublimity can be substantiated either by beating rivals or joining them (*The Art of Courtly Love* does both), by drawing on the excitement of conflict or the deep pleasures of narcissistic reflection. The indifference of sublimity to consistency, sometimes registered as its "fickleness" (Fortune, Fame), is the paradoxical ground of its power to fascinate.

THE HORROR, THE HORROR

In his essay "Thoughts on War and Death," Freud suggests that the depression of civilians during World War I resulted from a desublimation of the state. In wartime, the state's criminality can scarcely be disguised. The state does the very things it forbids its own citizens to do, and accuses its enemy state of doing—raping, pillaging, murdering, etc. Hence the murkiness of discussions of "atrocity."[24] One of the most common responses to recent revelations of Senator Kerry's activities in Vietnam is that "war is a gray area, everything is happening so fast you can't tell what's going on," similar to the "gray area" explanations given for police shootings of civilian suspects. Contemporary accounts of the Hundred Years War repeatedly lament the inability of soldiers to follow the rules of war. Apparently, no amount of training can reliably prepare us for self-possession on the battlefied, a place where what goes on is finally unknowable because no reliable subject is there to know it.

Whenever the group faces death, the subject can scarcely avoid producing the symptom of bewilderment over the nature of the agency to which she is sacrificing her *jouissance*. War always creates uncertainty. If, in keeping with the *Iliad*'s reservations about Helen, we doubt the sublimity of the object of war, this must mean that the sublimity of the object of war is an *effect* of this doubt. Again, the very precariousness of sublime effects contributes to their sublimity. On the level of the group, at least, we love to make war because we can be of two minds about it. Patriotism, of course, defends against this kind of sublimation; it does not identify the state's actions as criminal (atrocious, hence unworthy of sacrifice) but as necessary to the group (worthy of, indeed *requiring*, sacrifice). But the borderline between what is and is not sacrifice-worthy is always negotiable. Indeed, the mobility of this borderline is what permits us, during war, to achieve the absurd enjoyment characteristic of faith. The revelation of arbitrariness during wartime is destabilizing, but, with respect to desire, in a very precise way: it's not just that the undoing of categories (just/unjust) can plunge us into melancholy, but that submission to the arbitrary law, to its un-reasonability, gets us as close to *jouissance* as anything can, a proximity quite capable of producing melancholy and many other symptoms of decomposition and fragmentation. To submit to a necessity whose necessity cannot be certified is to submit to the arbitrariness of the law.

The coincidence of ideality with atrocity, much lamented in discourses on chivalry, is thus no coincidence; it gives rise to the enjoyment of the state as well as of war.[25] The group subject, sometimes ingroupified as an "exemplary" subject, is "entitled" to a *jouissance* denied ordinary subjects, and this entitlement takes place through the medium of the law. Those whose sacrifices are "sweetest" to the community are those most entitled to enjoyment.[26] Ramon Lull's influential myth of the origins of chivalry is designed to justify the entitlement of knights, not merely to respect, but to wealth, leisure, and servants. De Charny similarly presents those who bear the burden of arms on the battlefield as entitled to lives filled with pleasure at home (Kaeuper and Kennedy, "*Book*," 117). Men of privilege are exemplary but also extraordinary, upholding norms and the people's profit "before" their "particular will" but nonetheless singularly entitled to pleasure (140–41).

The sovereign right to wage a just or holy war is linked to the question of authority and hence to the right to make law on behalf of the common good; doing violence or constraining freedoms on behalf of particular interests is transgressive *jouissance*. When medieval chivalric treatises distinguish between atrocity and legitimate violence, giving knights special responsibility for the protection of the weak from injury, the weak are understood to be those deprived of powerful voices to speak for them at law, primarily widows and orphans.[27] Legists and canonists are among the most important sources for the sentiment of *pugna pro patria,* a maxim, as Gaines Post points out, drawn from "the moral *Distichs* attributed to Cato and read by school boys throughout the Middle Ages" (and published by Caxton) ("Two Notes," 281). Russell writes that the idea of the "just war reveals its fullest significance" when the "ideology of the secular state" is being developed during and after the Investiture Contest; canonists and theologians alike "viewed the defense of the *patria* as the primary just cause, emphasised public authority and condemned the . . . cruelty of war" (*Just War,* 296–97, 299). Chivalric writing, as Bonet's work exemplifies, in turn draws on legal codes and styles of commentary, reinforcing the links made by medieval society between the privilege of bearing arms and privilege at law, including privilege to make or administer law. The international law being developed in such treatises is a *logical* outcome of medieval warrior society and its stylizations of power: war—more precisely, the enjoyment at stake in it—by any means possible.

In the later Middle Ages, complaints against wartime atrocity rarely disturbed the practice of war not because the idealism of the one was so disengaged from the horrors of the other, but because they issued from the same passional logic: submission to codifications and rules is a form of enjoyment, and the enjoyment of atrocity depends upon the law. Honoré Bonet begins *The Tree of Battles* by lamenting that it is also a "Tree of Mourning," but he does not seem to have composed his ambitious application of canon law to military obligation in order to ameliorate this suffering. His lament honors the *sentement* so piteously and fearsomely characteristic of nobility and its sublime sacrifice of security. Moreover, Bonet makes a number of observations about the suffering of the poor during the Hundred Years War, but outlawing the military activities that lead to this suffering seems also not to be his primary intention. So, are these *outbreaks* of feeling? Moments that occur only when the code of chivalry breaks down and, as in *The Knight's Tale*, shows us the burning sheep-pens and clothered blood? Or are these moments interior to the workings of chivalric law? What is crucial to remember is that codification is itself a means of opening the door to *jouissance*. And since codification implies or even constitutes the group (codification is always addressed to a community), it is a means to mobilize. The idea—revisited by Freud in *Civilization and Its Discontents* as well as in "Thoughts on War and Death"—that the history of civilization might consist of a gradual subjection of desire to the law of sacrifice is usefully complicated by Lacan's insistence that "the genesis of the moral dimension . . . is located nowhere else than in desire itself" (*Seminar*, 3). The "moral dimension" of our experience is a *form* of desire. The desires that must be renounced are kissing cousins to those that desire their renunciation.

The heightening of nationalist feeling during the Crusades may therefore help to explain why the Crusades were, from their inception, atrocious—compelled to go above and beyond the call of duty, *jouissance* dead ahead. Brutality was homegrown and at home in Europe (Charlemagne's treatment of the Saxons, the Albigensian Crusade; Coulton, "Nationalism," 16). When, in the *chevauchées* of the Hundred Years War, soldiers mutilated the dead or burned the crops left to the living, they were acting out the relation of the sublime to excess, outrage, and arbitrariness. Christine de Pizan's *Othea*, like Chaucer's description in *The Knight's Tale* of Theseus's siege of Thebes, draws on *chevauchée* and counterordinance to describe the atrocities of Busiris, who killed men "in his templis with knyvis, and made sacrifices to his goddis," and thus broke the commandment against theft: "Seint Austyn seith that in this is defendid al vnleifful vsurpacioun of othir mennys thingis, as sacrilege, al raveine, al thing takin by force and be lordschipe of the pepil withoute reson" (Bühler, *Epistle*, 53). The "particular profit" forbidden but also given to knights reaches a certain apex in the extreme rapaciousness of Busiris, who, instead of making sacrifices for the people, sacrifices people in the hope of improving his fortunes; sacrificing humans is the dark "opposite" of sacrifice for humankind.

The figure of Busiris gives us the Hundred Years War as horror story, turning atrocity into monstrosity (Busiris acts "contrary to mankindeli nature"). Because it is made and not begotten, sublimity can be cruel, exacting, capricious as well as radiant and magnanimous—or both at once (Fame and Fortune). Monstrosity and beauty intersect; fascination and petrifaction, rapture and trauma, the overfamiliar and the strange are perilously intimate; so can righteousness and extreme humility be perilously intimate with motiveless malignity. The contradictions critics have seen in Chaucer's *Knight's Tale* may or may not be in the eye of the beholder, but either way they screen (that is, show *and* hide) the unnerving power of *jouissance*.

THE LAW DOES NOT
REPLACE LAWLESSNESS

Sacrificial *jouissance* is the raison d'être of the chivalric culture of the later Middle Ages because, at least in certain circumstances, it really can be sweet to die, and as we are told, it is particularly sweet to die on behalf of one's country. The signifier of "community"—whether fatherland, nation, country, people, public good—magically turns singularity into a characteristic of the group, not just of the exemplary individual. It has enormous power to put the drives through their paces because it redefines their relation to the law every time it shifts (it turns "war" into "terrorism," "protesters" into "anarchists," and so on). The medieval distinction between common and singular interests has, interestingly, been upheld by historical narratives about nations. For example, feud gives way to "public" justice, a self-evident improvement.[28] On the other hand a foolishly chivalric (sacrificial) approach to war and politics gives way to the artful calculation of interests (Burckhardt). The "modern" always has better technology, which seems also to mean that it has the nation. But of course these are not easy associations to sustain. The nation is ancient as well as modern (Suleri, *Rhetoric*, 3–4). Taxation is one of the world's oldest administrative technologies. Marx had to theorize the "Asiatic" mode of production in order to account for the sophistication of long-dead bureaucracies.[29] Nor does the coexistence, at any given time, of different forms of polity necessarily imply different stages of "development," technological or otherwise. David Wallace has reminded us recently of the great variety of polities in the late medieval world (*Chaucerian Polity*, 9–11). It appears we may have dreamed that Boccaccio's

Florence belonged to a different time from Chaucer's England, so that medieval monarchy might seem remote from the political form of the republic, ignorant of different arrangements of power and privilege, a world unto itself, unwilling or unable to get on line with the timeline.

But there is no time "before" calculation or technology, and no time "after" *jouissance*. We cannot assume that information technologies and number-crunching have more to tell us about the group bodies they inscribe than do the transmissions of popular song or mantling and feathering. The conferring on or withdrawal of sublimity from or by a signifier may be just as, or even far more, decisive for the workings of group desire than the development of a particular technological symptom; or, they may really amount to the same thing. Print might require patriotism rather than the other way round, not because "ideas" drive history (they don't) but because both print and patriotism are grounded in the materiality of the body, its organization by the law, and the resulting drives toward replication, reproduction, and production that produce economic and social activity in the first place. What matters is how and when a signifier is empowered to act as switchpoint between "particular" and "common" desires. Because fatherland always depends on an other, "natal," place, toward which one is obliged to orient oneself (Deleuze and Guattari, *Capitalism*, 312), the community is always decentered, and the signifier *patria* is *variously* linked to places, peoples, languages, techniques of living. Moreover, *patria* gives variousness a reason to live. The discourse of *patria* or nation can precede, follow, or displace the "actual" technologies (e.g., print) designed to artifice equivalence among subjects. Love of *patria* is not necessarily a more primitive or epiphenomenal sign of the nation than is a secretariat or justice by proxy. Social and economic apparatuses are the very means by which desires circulate.

Late medieval heraldry was love of the signifier as such. It scarcely even pretended to be utilitarian in its fantastic multiplication of signifiers of identity (crests, feathering, mantling, supporters); it was a love of the symbolic order, the law of signs, upheld by and upholding the spectral body through a proliferation of prosthetic "stand-ins." Heralds produced the codes that linked corporeal to spectral being by means of prostheses that are also signifiers—the arms that defend and also locate in the symbolic order whatever is inside or bears them. What emerges is of course that the signifier functions *as* prosthesis, marking the going-beyond of corporeality paradoxically essential to its survival. Thus heralds read and "descryve" the battlefield or the lists, make chronicles that extend memory, and act as custodians and judges of the arms that confer singularity as well as spectrality on their bearers. They bear the sign of the other (Lion King-at-Arms, Chandos Herald, Dragon Rouge Pursuivant), as icons of the enjoyment of naming and being named, "living examples" of the role of signification and administration in the enjoyment of conflict. Their manners with respect to signs must be impeccable. The fifth item of the "Othe of the Kynges of Armes in their Creacion" requires that

> Ye shal observe and kepe to your comyng and power all suche othes as ye made when you were create heraud, to thonour and worshippe of noblesse and integrity of lyvyng, namely, in eschewing of disclaundros places and dysclaundred persones and reproved. (Twiss, *Black Book*, 297)

They must keep their word; they must avoid people and places spoken ill of; their office is to report truth, to carry messages "as honorably and trewly as your will and reason can serve you, and gretely to thadvauntage of oure sovereyne lord and his realme."

How does a herald carry messages "trewly" and also "gretely to thadvauntage of oure sovereyne lord and his realme"? "Trewly" may mean something like "accurately"—"integrity of lyvyng" guarantees the reliability of one's transmissions, which is consistent with the narcissistic circuitry of chivalry (see below)—but there is no notion here of a loyalty to truth that transcends "thadvauntage" of the herald's particular sovereign and realm. Again, heralds are to embody the motto *honi soit qui mal y pense*, to be "[A]lwey more redy to excuse than to blasme any noble persone, on les than ye be charged to sey the trouth by the kyng, his conestable, and mareschal, or in any place judicial" (295, 297). But in this context *honi soit qui mal y pense* proposes the cultivation of a diplomatic interior, of an ethical integrity that can turn into secrecy. The chivalric life is devoted to the accumulation of signs of credibility, that is, of signs consistent with the hidden interior, all the way round to the trustworthiness that deserves credence because it *doesn't* speak, but which nonetheless creates the secret space in which "advantage" may be pursued.[30] Heralds are transmitters, "descryving" ceremonies so that their glory can spread, mapping the hottest spots of the territory by recording solemn "progresses." They are transformed by fantastic signifiers into credible repositories of information, and their sacrifice of particular identity makes love of country portable, gives country eyes, ears, and a firewalled interior so that it can walk abroad—"As Frensh ar suffred here, and we in Fraunce." It is possible that the chivalric cultivation of strong minds was not the obstacle but the sine qua non of the marking and valuing of calculation so often associated with early modernity.

Ethics for Strong Bodies

Chivalry was not simply a mask for brutality, nor was it an attempt to restrain brutality or an enervated and obsolescent ideological fantasy, but a "spectacular" mode of enjoyment, a technique of living that had lasting effects on "manners" (in Christine de Pizan's *Othea*, it's not just that chivalry is a way of living, it's that "mankyndli lyf" can be called "verrai chyualrie" [*Epistle*, ed. Bühler, 8]). Etiquette, protocol—these performances, through the perfection of their attention to the other, establish the trustworthiness of interiors, without which no interior can become a safe repository of one's own or the other's counsel. This ethical or ethicized interior keeps its word(s) so strongly that it ends by keeping its own counsel.

The creation of a psychic interior for the nonreligious was one of the most important ambitions of chivalric artistry (Fradenburg, *City*, 206–07, 209). Chivalric interiority is produced and shaped by mirroring and thus perfecting the warrior's prowess. The body of the warrior is trained by perfecting its potential *as* body (strength, endurance, agility, health), not by depriving it of strength, and the virtues of the warrior's perfected body must be matched by "justice / wysedom / charite loyalte / verite / humylite strength hope swiftnes & al other vertues semblable apperteyne to a kn3t as touchyng his soule" (Caxton, *Book*, 14). A knight "ought to gyue gretter passion to his corage than hongre ne thurste / hete ne colde maye gyue to his body" (Kaeuper and Kennedy, "*Book*," 26). In *The Book of the ordre of chyualry*, the knight's "cote" is given to him to signify "the grete trauaylles that a knyght must suffre for to honoure chyualrye"; just as the cote is the first thing to receive strokes, "Right so is a kny3t chosen to susteyne gretter trauailes than another man" (Caxton, *Book*, 36). Bonet writes that "strength of soul is the principal foundation [of battle], but strength of body is not to be neglected, for, if accompanied by strength of soul, it too, is a foundation of battle" (*Tree*, pt. 3, c. 3, p. 120; the virtue of strength is *fortitudo*, pt. 3, c. 4, p. 120). This focus on the virtue of the knight's body links chivalric sacrifice especially closely to the apotheosis of sadism that was the crucifixion of the marvelous undead body of Christ, "the divinization of . . . the limit in which a being remains in a state of suffering," that is, of the object's power of endurance (Lacan, *Seminar*, 262).

Chivalric ascesis structures enjoyment by establishing a narcissistic circuit between bodily exterior and psychic interior, thus enabling a distinctively close articulation of pride and sacrifice. We see this in reverse, so to speak, in *The Book of the ordre of chyualry*, where the "good heremyte" who teaches the "Rule & Ordre of Chyualrie" is a wise and valorous old knight who "fledde the world / by cause that the feblenesse of his body in the which he was by old age fallen / And that he dishonoureth not that / whiche that in honourable thynges and auenturous hadde ben longe tyme honoured" (Caxton, *Book*, 4). Penitence is his aim, but he withdraws his body from the world when its "feblenesse" threatens to shame all of chivalry and its honorable history. Of the fasting and vigils of the religious, de Charny remarks: "this is all nothing in comparison with the suffering to be endured in the order of knighthood" (*souffrir*; Kaeuper and Kennedy, "*Book*," 175). De Charny uses *souffrir* with some regularity to indicate the particular confluence of suffering and strength and therefore endurance he associates with the knightly order. The life of the knight is *si perilleuse service*, special because it is distinctively fraught with danger, meaning not only that the knight is often surrounded by perils but also that he cannot anticipate a time when danger will not be at his back (182). Knighthood is "of all the conditions of this world . . . the one above all others in which one would be required to live with the constant thought of facing death at any hour on any day," not only on the battlefield but also at court because people will want to destroy you (*cuidier mourir toutes heures et touz les jours*; 185).

"To live with the constant thought" means that the knight's life and mind are *unreservedly given over* to anxiety, to reading the signs of potential danger; it is not possible for a true knight to have his mind on something trivial. The constancy of the thought enables the anticipation of death at *every* hour on *every* day. The knight's interiority mirrors and thereby becomes an enduring receptacle for the confrontation with death characteristic of the battlefield; the unreserved anticipation of death is "deterritorialized," a "line of flight" sets it free from green fields and

gives it or turns it into the absolute intensity that is interiority's version
of immensity. Sublimity is produced by projecting the battlefield's antici-
pations of and confrontations with death into an interiority that can
stretch them out beyond the limits of field or moment; the singularity
and single-mindedness of this interior is then re-territorialized by the
rest of the knight's life, that is, the time he spends at court, which affords
no respite despite its reputation for same (distractions, etc.), and by other
evidences of single-mindedness. Of Jehan de Bretaigne (John of Brittany,
afterwards earl of Richmond), the Caerlaverock *Roll of Arms* remarks
that he deserved preference "For having served his uncle, / Laboriously
from his infancy, / And abandoned entirely / His father and other relations, / To dwell in his household, / When the King had occasion for
men" ("Si le avoit-il ben deservi / Cum cil ki son oncle ot servi / De se
enfance peniblement, / E deguerpi outréement / Son pere e son autre
lignage; ed. Wright, 9–10 and n. 3).

Knightly sacrifice is living when living also means dying. All souls
do it, but the knight wants to be "sovereignly mortal" (Blanchot, *Space*,
96); his relation to the facts of life and death is sublime because displaced, reflected into *eine anderere Schauplatz* that then clarifies the
meaning of the entirety of the knight's life even when lived in places
where ambitious, privileged people carry on as though they were going
to live forever. Perhaps this is why the memento mori tradition flourished so well inside the very precincts of power it appeared to critique.
The entitlement of the nobility to pleasure and to the labor of others, asserted by de Charny as well as by Lull, is justified by the impossibility of
any knight ever really being able to enjoy such distractions. Lull, in Caxton's words, explains that "it behoueth also that the comyn peple laboure
the londes for to brynge fruytes and goodes / Wherof the knyght and his
beestes haue theyr lyuyng. / And that the knyght reste hym . . . & des-
porte hym . . . & that he ease hym / & delyte hym in thynges / Of which
his men haue payne & trauayl" (Caxton, *Book*, 10). At the same time Lull
would have agreed with de Charny's formulation that "These personages
and these lords were not raised up to have great periods of rest nor great
pleasures nor great delights, but to endure more & strive harder than
any of the others" (*pour avoir plus grans panes et travaulx;* Kaeuper and
Kennedy, "*Book*," 140, 141).

The development of interiority—*esprit,* "character," "values"—for
the territory and the group is another consequence of the close articula-

tion of pride and sacrifice enabled by the narcissistic circuitry of chivalry. If the body is a double for the body of the land and the group, its experience of interiority may also be. These replications depend on our willingness to believe in an imaginary body, a spectral body, one that "really" exists, existed, or will exist but cannot be fully phenomenalized in the present and in our presence (Derrida, *Spectres,* 6). The material body of the warrior is reflected into an inner structure of virtue through the mediation of an imaginary body, and that imaginary body can then be used to construct an interiority and exteriority for the group. The group body and mind "exist" only because we construct elaborate prostheses to interlink the group's members, and the most powerful of these prostheses is the signifier. Perhaps, then, the narcissistic circuitry of chivalry can help to explain why some of the most important developments in the history of the signifier in the later Middle Ages involved the cultivation of noble interiority *and* the integrity of the group: romance; the proliferation, in political literature, of organological metaphors; and the genre of the mirror for princes. Is the aristocratic body, including its prosthetic extensions (weapon, armor, ornament, costume, heraldry, poetry), a sign of complex inner beauty and strength? Of the integrity of the group? The sublimity of chivalry is enhanced by its pairing of beauty—youth, strength, physical integrity—with the good, with such fascinatingly equivocal results that it has been hard for scholars of chivalry to think about anything else.[31]

The specific contribution of the mirror for princes to the subliming of chivalric enjoyment is an ethics of integrity. In the *De regimine principum,* Aquinas explains that because "a man cannot adequately provide for his life by himself," helping being necessary to life, "it is natural for man to live in association with his fellows" (14). Aquinas focuses on the groupifying power of the signifier, specifically its power of transmission. We join in multitudes for the sake of our living, the chief sign of which is the sign itself: "This [meaning, the fact that we associate with each other for the sake of survival] is most clearly demonstrated by the fact that man uses words to communicate his thoughts fully to others" (15). The sign is both sign and maker of common good. "Our" dependence on integrity is also famously imagined by John of Salisbury in terms of what the body needs to survive, where the dependence of a body on the common good of its parts, like the dependence of a community on same, can only be guaranteed by a governor (Salisbury, *Policraticus*).

The figure that "stands for" more than private interests—Aquinas's sign, Salisbury's governor—enables sacrifice of distinctiveness on behalf of the community to produce distinction at the very moment when singularity is being ruled out. In Chaucer's *Tale of Melibee*, Prudence counsels the proud and irate lord that "it is good as now that ye suffre" (VII. 1479). The distinctive capacity of the individual body to feel pain, that is, to be vulnerable to disintegration, is the basis on which the willingness of an individual to endure pain confers distinction. But this capacity can be relayed fictively from one member of the group to others by means of the prostheses of example and gift. Patiently bowing to the example itself is (like) bowing to the law that demands Christ's suffering, and is also ipso facto to accept the gift of that suffering: "enclyne and bowe youre herte to take the pacience of our Lord Jhesu Crist," who, "as seith Seint Peter in his Epistles," "hath suffred for us."[32]

Prudence's emphasis on "unytee and pees" as "oon of the gretteste and moost sovereyn thyng that is in this world" (VII. 1500–01) is consistent with the linking of privilege to martyrdom characteristic also of de Charny's work.[33] In Scrope's translation of *Othea*, "Jhesu Criste" is "the god of bataill" and a "good kny3t"; like him, good knights "shoulde haue pite of nedi peopill" (*Epistle*, ed. Bühler, 58, 88, 105). Sacrifice establishes the capacity of the (love-)object to endure, sustain its integrity, and last forever, regardless of whatever abandonment, vilification, and torture its lover might visit upon it; the perfect object is always also the perfect transitional object.[34] Sacrifice of and entitlement to enjoyment are decisively intertwined when the suffering of knights is linked to the crucifixion (Lacan, *Seminar*, 262). Geoffroi de Charny says that men of prowess, "because of their great desire to reach [the] high honor [of battle] . . . do not care what sufferings they have to endure, but turn everything into great enjoyment" *(deduit)*.[35]

The concept of the common weal made it possible for the exemplary personages of the Middle Ages to "stand for" the people on whose behalf they sacrificed their lives to the constant awareness of death. In *The Boke of Knyghthode*, "Jon, Duke of Barry" is praised for his concern "for all the comon welleffare of [the] noble Royaulme" (*Epistle*, ed. Bühler, 123). De Charny explains that lords and rulers were chosen as governors "so that they might place the people's profit before their own" ("pour faire le proffit du peuple avant que le leur singulier"; Kaeuper and Kennedy, "*Book*," 140, 142). The translation of Vegetius's "De Re Militari" known as *Knyghthode and Bataille,* which probably played a part in the "love-day" between York and Lancaster in 1458, presents chivalry as the foundation (rather than ruination) of public concerns: "Res publica right comendabil is, / If chiualers and armys there abounde, / For, they present, may nothing fare amys, / And ther thei are absent, al goth to grounde" (pt. I, st. 46, lines 404–07).[36] "Riders in playn, footmen goth euery where, / By theyme the commyn wele is to conquere" (pt. II, st. 5, lines 654–55).[37] The relation is one of identification as well as necessity; so tight is the bond that "if a faut is founden in my dede, / Not oonly me, but al the commyn wele / So hurteth it, that gretely is to drede / Dampnatioun" (pt. III, st. 95, lines 1636–39). *The Book of the Knight of La Tour Landry* teaches by "ensaumple" of a "knight [who] had pite upon [a] mayde" that "eueri man and woman aught to haue pitee and sorw of the disese of thair frendes neigheboures, and upon the poure creatoures of God...and to weep pitously, as wepte the good ladyes after oure lorde Ihesu Crist, whanne he bare the crosse to be crucified, and suffre dethe for oure synnes" (Le May, "Allegory," 29, citing Geoffrey de la Tour Landry, *Book*). In *The Book of the ordre of chyualry,* the sword "is made in semblaunce of the crosse for to sygnefye hou our lorde gode vaynquysshed in the crosse the dethe of humayn lygnage / ... Al in lyke wyse knyght oweth to vaynquysshe and destroye the enemyes of the crosse / by the swerde" (Caxton, *Book,* 32). Chandos Herald's *The Life of the Black Prince,* describing the travails of the pass of Ronceveaux, illustrates how daring—or commonplace—these analogies could become: "But since the just God suffered death for us on the cross there was no such painful passage, for one saw men and horses, that suffered many ills, stumble on the mountain" (ed. Lodge and Pope, 54).[38]

Not only does *Othea* enjoin "[th]e good kny3t [th]at he shoulde haue pite of nedi peopill [th]at requireth [it]" (*Epistle,* ed. Bühler, 105), but in a quite different social and cultural location, Langland's *Piers Plowman* develops, in the figure of Piers, a significant alternative to the chivalric model of charitable, sublime suffering on behalf of the common good. Even here, however, the usefulness of chivalry's deployment of the spectral and spectacular body for the sublimation of secular sacrifice is evident: Langland identifies Piers the Plowman with the figure of "Christ-as-Knight" ("Is [th]is ihesus [th]e iuster [jouster]? ... Or is it Pieres [th]e plowman?").[39] A crowning example of the active interchange between the laicizing of sacrifice and the sacralizing of lay culture characteristic of the later Middle Ages, this figure at first portrays Christ as warrior against the enemies of humankind and then is appropriated by chivalric culture to enhance the value of its sacrifices.[40] It is itself a spectacular example of how the ethics of integrity works to instill in the subject, and to perform, the spectral image of the group body and of the special or singular body that stands for the group. Comparisons of knights to Christ, not just of Christ to knights, secularize and glamorize the later Middle Ages' "apotheosis of the neighbor," and further the migration of chivalric sacrificial idealism to other social locations.[41]

COUNTRY MATTERS

Historians of the European state have argued quite a bit over terminology. According to Huizinga, the conclusion that the phenomena of patriotism and nationalism are recent "because the words and concepts are recent is...misleading.... It is true that the word and the concept 'state' were...largely hidden behind that of the Church in the Middle Ages, [but] medieval society made good use of the concepts *regnum* and *civitas* to express things political" ("Patrotism," 99). According to Reynolds, the terms *natio* and *gens*, used often in the Middle Ages (and sometimes synonymously), were "thought of as a community of custom, descent, and government—a people" (*Kingdoms*, 256). Bartlett minimizes the role of nationalism in the formation of "conquest states" and "colonial societies" in the Middle Ages, but uses the term *natio* (translated as "blood" or "stock") frequently and unproblematically in his discussion of race relations, despite his insistence that "medieval ethnicity was a social construct rather than a biological datum" (*Making*, 101, 197). We have found it difficult to agree about which terms are relevant, what they mean, and how we know what they mean. Is it true that, as the *OED* suggests, in early uses of the term "nation" the "racial idea" predominates and later the "political" one? And what difference would that make if it were true?

One of the most important reasons for the impression of disarray these terminological debates can create is the homogeneity of the semantic fields on which they work. By this I don't mean that terms like "nation" or "people" have narrow semantic ranges; they don't. But their semantic ranges overlap to a considerable degree. *Patria* is given in Lewis and Short as "One's father land, native land or country, native place," which closely duplicates *natio*'s generalization of birthplace to land of one's birth to country (s.v. *patria, natio*). *Terra* is land, country, region, sometimes in collocation with *patria*. *Terra, patria,* and *natio* are often synonymous or apposite, and frequently appear in collocations with each other. Each emphasizes a particular aspect of the notion of territory (land as such, my father's land, my birthplace), but these are usually nuances, not striking differences.

But the very intimacy of these terms indicates the richness of the concept of territory: the earth, or its crust or surface, a particular section thereof, with everything that grows or dwells upon it and their interrelations, the experience of demarcation and identification, a living that inevitably acts upon the territory (hence the significance of nativity— something comes out of nowhere and there is no telling what the consequences will be) out of which unfolds the possibility of acting to reorganize organization. Historiographical discussions of *natio* should try not to put asunder what has so long been linked together: the semantics of the specificity *and* generalizability of people and places; the earth *and* life's reconfigurations of it.

The situation is not much different when we look at the equivalents of these terms in European vernaculars. "Country" makes its appearance in English in the late thirteenth and fourteenth centuries, with the following meanings: "a tract or expanse of land of undefined extent; a region, district" (*OED,* s. v. "country," I1); but *also* "a district having distinct physical or other characteristics," a definition that bridges "land of undefined extent" and "a tract or district having more or less definite limits in relation to human occupation, e.g. owned by the same lord or proprietor, or inhabited by people of the same race, dialect, occupation, etc." (*OED,* s.v. "country," 2). At least by 1300 the usage of "country" extended to "the land of a person's birth, citizenship, residence, etc.; used alike in the wider sense of native land, and in the narrower one of the particular district to which a person belongs" and by 1330 to "the territory or land of a nation; usually an independent state" (3). "Nation" is recorded as appearing in English around the same time as "country" (ca. 1300), with the following meanings: (I1) "an extensive aggregate of persons, so closely associated with each other by common descent, language, or history, as to form a distinct race or people, usually organized by a separate political state and occupying a definite territory"; I15 "a family, kindred"; also, later in the fourteenth century, (3) "a *particular* class, kind, or race of persons. Also man's nation, *human kind*" (my emphasis). Finally, unsurprisingly, the oldest of all: from at least 875 onward, "land" is (3) "a part of the earth's surface marked off by natural or political boundaries," "a country, territory," (4) "ground or territory as owned by a person or viewed as public or private territory."

Undoubtedly—probably inevitably—some of these meanings were more significant than others at times, and at different times, but clearly once *natio, patria, terra* or *land, country, nation* or *paÿs, terre* are in use, their meanings range easily from particular to general bonds, from earth to chunk of earth to property to political unit, from progenitors to kindreds to peoples. In other words, most of the categories fundamental to the plotting of European political history commingle freely in these semantic fields; they are not strung out along a timeline. It is inadvisable to make sweeping statements about "period" on the basis of a range of meanings that *recognizes* the links between families and states, familiar countrysides and socially constructed borders, rather than driving wedges between them. This is perhaps an unnecessarily complicated way of agreeing with Turville-Petre's formulation that "it is the similarities between medieval and modern expressions of national identity that are fundamental, and the differences that are peripheral" (*England*, v). We might only add that the similarities between faith in the soil and the love of superintending it are fundamental, and the differences peripheral.

NOTES

1. Ingham, *Sovereign Fantasies*, discusses Anderson at length in her second chapter, and see also her sixth chapter on militarism and sacrifice in Arthurian literature.

2. Deleuze and Guattari *(Anti-Oedipus)* argue that desiring-production is in various ways tied to material territory (for example, the privileging of agriculture over nomadism by farming societies and their heirs) but can be "deterritorialized," i.e., repeated with a difference in another context (e.g., "Labor Day"), and then "reterritorialized" (everyone goes "home" to work, experiencing the freshness of "return"). Pierre Bourdieu's concept of *habitus* as developed in *Outline of a Theory of Practice* is also important to this essay as a way of thinking about how enjoyment is culturally patterned.

3. Laurence A. Rickels, in *The Case of California*, uses the term "groupification" to designate the process whereby multiple assemblages are transformed into *a* group by means of identification. "Enjoyment" has become a common translation for *jouissance*, i.e., for libidinal excitation so powerful that it can be unpleasurable, but it is also used more broadly to designate other forms taken by the drives, like pleasure and desire; see Žižek, "Republics."

4. On the subject of sacrifice and chivalry, see L. O. Aranye Fradenburg, *Sacrifice Your Love*, esp. the Introduction for a theoretical discussion of sacrifice.

5. Kantorowicz, *King's*, 244, citing Henry of Ghent, *Quodlibeta*, fols. 594 ff. The section on "*Pro Patria Mori*" in *The King's Two Bodies* (232–72) has been invaluable to this essay, especially for its emphasis on the role played by *patria* in the medieval development of corporate fictions.

6. In "The Otterburn War from the Scottish Point of View," Alexander Grant critiques scholarly accounts of the Otterburn War that "'regard [Border conflicts in the 1380s] as no longer the simultaneous efforts of a nation in defence of their independence, but the selfish and disjointed expeditions of a lawless aristocracy'" (30; citing Tytler, *History*), concluding instead that Otterburn "symbolizes the final, triumphant, conclusion of Scotland's Wars of Independence" (54).

7. On this point see the essays in this volume by Sponsler, Staley, and Smith.

8. Reynolds notes that previous historical paradoxes regarding medieval communities—such as an apparent contradiction between individual concerns and the concerns of a larger community—might result from "combining together traditions of historiography produced by the varying interests of different historians and the political preoccupation of their times" (*Kingdoms*, xv).

9. Thorlac Turville-Petre argues for "overlapping identities," including religious ones, in the Middle Ages, and critiques the view "that a sense of national unity was held in check by membership of the universal Christian Church.... Such views reflect the fundamental misconception that one identity must exclude or diminish another" (*England*, 7, 40 ff). See also Lavezzo, "Another Country," Tatnall, "John Wyclif," Banton, "Monastic Reform," and (in this volume) Havens.

10. Translation from Alain de Lille, *Art of Preaching*, trans. by Evans, 150. "Ad hoc specialiter instituti sunt milites, ut patriam suam defendant, et ut repellant ab Ecclesia violenturum injurias, sed jam milites facti sunt praedarii duces aliorum, facti sunt abigeri": Alanus ab Insulis, *Summa de Arte Praedicatoria*, section 107, p. 186.

11. *The Boke of Knyghthode* is the preface to *Othea* in Bühlers MS L.

12. See also Keen on the "sharper emphasis" in the later Middle Ages "on the definition of true service as the service of a lawful ruler, defined as one who embodies in his authority the common weal of a people or city" (*Chivalry*, 234).

13. Benedict Anderson's idea that "the medieval Christian mind" was unable to conceive of either history or nation has many antecedents in Renaissance humanist texts (*Imagined Communities*, 23). On humanist historicism, see Fradenburg, "Amorous Scholasticism"; on the discrediting of chronicle history, see Fradenburg, "Troubled Times," and Turville-Petre's discussion of the regular use of biblical history "by chroniclers . . . as a backdrop to national history, to establish a comparative chronology and sometimes to demonstrate an unbroken genealogical succession" (*England*, 40–42).

14. See Kantorowicz, *King's*, 238–39 on "belief in the crusader's assumption to paradise" and similar glamorizations of secular war.

15. In *Edward III and Chivalry*, Juliet Vale remarks that "the significance of the [Order of the Garter's] institution as a unifying force in the kingdom seems to be generally recognized" (52). On the Order of the Star, see Kaeuper and Kennedy, "*Book*," 21, 34, 52–54.

16. The wives of prominent London citizens were invited to the festivities at Windsor in 1344, and Vale speculates that their husbands might have joined the "'all-comers'" who competed against the royal teams in various London locations (*Edward III*, 62–63).

17. See also Richards on the "review of nationalities in Charlemagne's army in the *Chanson de Roland*" ("Cultural Nationalism," 76).

18. Coulton argues that national energies were present in the institution of the Church itself, and that the Crusades, the universities, and monasticism all relied on an idea of nationalism in order to function. See also Huizinga, "Patriotism," 99 ff.

19. Painter, *French Chivalry*, 37, citing *Histoire de Guillaume le Maréchal*, II, lines 16388–91; see also I, line 4481. Gerald of Wales agreed (*De principis instructione liber*, in *Opera*, ed. Brewer, 8:318.)

20. Dyboski and Arend note that these lines "probably refer to . . . the employment of mercenary troops, and seem to hint at military conventions regarding them" (*Knyghthode*, p. 123, nn. 660–62).

21. On techniques of living—vocational, ethical, religious, affective, political—see Freud, *Civilization*, 26–34; also Foucault, *Care*, on the "development of the art of living under the theme of the care of oneself" (42–43, 45–47).

22. Derrida writes that "the knight of faith must not hesitate. He accepts his responsibility by heading off towards the absolute request of the other, beyond knowledge" (*Gift*, 77).

23. Elaine Scarry discusses the use of pain to substantiate intangible ideas (*Body*, 13 ff.).

24. Russell remarks that medieval canonists and theologians found it difficult to address "bloodshed," treating the Crusades "in functionally euphemistic and oblique terms such as *iter* and *peregrinatio*; rarely were they explicitly considered as the wars that they were" (*Just War*, 294–95). See also Keen, *Chivalry*, 44 f.

25. Deleuze and Guattari separate the "war machine" from the state while acknowledging that the latter depends frequently on the former, but through the mode of appropriation (*Capitalism*, 351–74). In my view, what enables the appropriation is the sacrificial enjoyment common both to the war machine and to statist forms.

26. Kantorowicz notes that medieval canonists "followed the model of the Digests when talking about the 'sweet' or 'sweetest fatherland'" (*King's*, 236).

27. See Allmand, *Society*, 26–27, on the oath "to maintain the honour of womanhood, . . . and to do this with our bodies, if need be" of a military order founded by the duke of Bourbon.

28. For a critique of this narrative, see Fradenburg, "Troubled Times."

29. Deleuze and Guattari's discussion of "The Barbarian Despotic Machine" in *Anti-Oedipus* makes for very interesting reading on early statist technologies (192–200).

30. On credence, secrecy, sacrifice, and militancy see Derrida, *Gift*, 11, 15, 101, 115.

31. On the relationship between beauty and the Good, see Lacan, *Seminar*, 217.

32. Chaucer, *Melibee*, VII. 1500–01. Keen cites, from the *Chanson de Guillaume*, Vivien's reproach to himself for having prayed to the Virgin to save him from death: "'Truly, that was a foolish thought, to seek to save myself from death, when the Lord God himself did not, when He suffered death upon the cross to save us from our deadly foe'"; Keen comments: "Christ's example on the cross is an inspiration to [the Christian soldier's] courage" (*Chivalry*, 51, citing lines 818–22, ed. Wathelet-Willem, 2:813).

33. See Kaeuper and Kennedy, "*Book*," 37, for discussion of de Charny's "striking" "appropriation of the concept of suffering righteously, or even martyrdom" for knighthood.

34. D. W. Winnicott's *Playing and Reality* regards the teddy bear and its ilk as opportunities for children to test the endurance of loved objects.

35. Kaeuper and Kennedy, "*Book*," 117; "quar pour le grant desir queuz ont de venir . . . a celui haut honneur, riens ne leur grieve qu'ilz aient a souffrir, mais leur tourne tout a tres grant deduit" (114).

36. Dyboski and Arend note of the untranslated "res publica" in these lines that "our author could not find an English word to render this exactly; *commonwealth*, according to the *OED*, does not appear before 1531, and *common weal* (found in the sense of 'state' in Robert Brunne, 1330), is used by our author in the sense of *salus publica*, cf. l. 262; but in ll. 655 and 1637, *common weale* corresponds to *res publica*" (Knyghthode, 36). Lewis and Short give *salûs* as "a being safe and sound; a sound or whole condition, health, welfare, prosperity, preservation, safety, deliverance"; "used in religious formulae for asking protection"; found in the Vulgate as "*verbum salutis*, salvation, deliverance from sin and its penalites." Lewis and Short, s.v. *salus;* the connection with the idea of defense is clear in the Sanskrit root meaning "to guard, *whence servus, servare; salvus, sollus;* cf. Gr. *Holos,* entire."

37. *Knyghthode,* n. 655, p. 123: "Veg[etius] has merely *magis reipublicae necessarios pedites;* the phrase [in translation] evidently means 'by them the State must win its victories.'"

38. "Mais puis qe dieux le droiter / Suffri mort pur nous en la crois / Ne fuist passage si estrois / Car home veoit gentz & chiuaux / Qui moult y suffroient des maux / Trebbucher p[ar]myla montaigne" (*Life,* ed. Lodge and Pope, p. 70, lines 2296 f.)

39. On this tradition, see Le May, "Allegory." In *Piers Plowman,* the narrator dreams of Piers carrying a cross: "That Pieres [th]e plowman was paynted al blody, / And come in with a crosse before comune peple, / And rigte lyke in all lymes to oure lorde ihesu"; Conscience cries out "'Is [th]is ihesus [th]e iuster? . . . Or is it Pieres [th]e plowman . . . ?' / Quod conscience & kneled [th]o, '[th]ise aren Pieres armes, / . . . ac he [th]at cometh so blody/ Is cryst with his crosse conqueroure of crystens'" (B.19.6–9, B.19.10–14).

40. Painter writes that after the eleventh century, the "suggestion that because a man was a noble he owed special obligations to the church and society. . . . seems to me to mark the beginning of religious chivalry" (*French Chivalry,* 66–67).

41. Lacan, *Seminar,* 152; also see Henry of Ghent, *Quodlibeta,* on the charity of knights, *supra* and n. 6.; and Tolomeo of Lucca on the sentiment *Amor patriae in radice charitatis fundatur* (Kantorowicz, *King's,* 242, citing Tolomeo of Lucca, *De regimine principum,* c. 4, 41).

REFERENCES

Alanus ab Insulis. *Summa de Arte Praedicatoria.* In *Patrologia Latina,* ed. J.-P. Migne, vol. 210. Turnhout: Brepols, 1976.

Alain de Lille. *The Art of Preaching.* Trans. Gillian R. Evans. Vol. 40. Kalamazoo: Cistercian Publications, 1981.

Allmand, C. T., ed. *Society at War: The Experience of England and France during the Hundred Years War* (Edinburgh: Oliver and Boyd, 1973).

Anderson, Benedict. *Imagined Communities: Reflections on the Origin and Spread of Nationalism.* Rev. ed. London and New York: Verso, 1991.

Aquinas, St. Thomas. *De regimine principum.* In *St. Thomas Aquinas on Ethics and Politics,* trans. and ed. Paul E. Sigmund, 14–29. New York: Norton, 1988.

Banton, Nicholas. "Monastic Reform and the Unification of Tenth-Century England." In *Religious and National Identity,* ed. Stuart Mews, Studies in Church History 18, 71–86. Oxford: Blackwell, 1982.

Barber, Richard. *The Knight and Chivalry.* New York: Scribner, 1970.

Bartlett, Robert. *The Making of Europe: Conquest, Colonization and Cultural Change, 950–1350.* Princeton: Princeton University Press, 1993.

Blanchot, Maurice. *The Space of Literature.* Trans. Ann Smock. Lincoln: University of Nebraska Press, 1982.

Bonet, Honoré. *The Tree of Battles.* Ed. G. W. Coopland. Cambridge: Harvard University Press, 1949.

Bourdieu, Pierre. *Outline of a Theory of Practice.* Trans. Richard Nice. Cambridge and New York: Cambridge University Press, 1977.

Bumke, Joachim. *The Concept of Knighthood in the Middle Ages.* Trans. W. T. H. and Erika Jackson. New York: AMS Press, 1982.

Caxton, William, ed. *The Book of the ordre of chyualry or knyghthode.* Westminster: Caxton, [1484?].

Chanson de Guillaume. Ed Jeanne Wathelet-Willem. Vol. 2. Paris: Société d'édition Les Belles Lettres, 1975.

Chaucer, Geoffrey. *The Riverside Chaucer,* ed. Larry D. Benson et al., 3rd ed. Boston: Houghton Mifflin, 1987.

Coulton, G. G. "Nationalism in the Middle Ages." *The Cambridge Historical Journal* 4 (1935): 15–40.

Crotch, J. B. *The Prologues and Epilogues of William Caxton.* EETS o.s. 176. London: Oxford University Press, 1928; Kraus Reprint Co., 1978.

Deleuze, Gilles, and Félix Guattari. *Anti-Oedipus: Capitalism and Schizophrenia,* Trans. Robert Hurley, Mark Seem, and Helen R. Lane. Minneapolis: Univeristy of Minnesota Press, 1983.

———. *Capitalism and Schizophrenia: A Thousand Plateaus.* Trans. Brian Massumi. Minneapolis: University of Minnesota Press, 1987.

Derrida, Jacques. *The Gift of Death.* Chicago: University of Chicago Press, 1991.

———. *Spectres of Marx: The State of the Debt, the Work of Mourning, and the New International.* Trans. Peggy Kamuf. New York: Routledge, 1994.

The Epistle of Othea. Ed. Curt Bühler. Trans. Stephen Scrope, EETS. o.s. 264. London: Oxford University Press, 1970.

Finke, Heinrich. *Papstuttum und Untergang des Templerordens,* vol. 2. Münster: Aschendorff, 1907.

Forey, Alan. *The Military Orders: From the Twelfth to the Early Fourteenth Centuries.* Toronto: University of Toronto Press, 1992.

Foucault, Michel. *The Care of the Self: The History of Sexuality.* Vol. 3. Trans. Robert Hurley. New York: Vintage, 1986.

Fradenburg, L. O. Aranye "Amorous Scholasticism." In *Speaking Images: Essays in Honor of V. A. Kolve,* ed. Charlotte C. Morse and Robert F. Yeager, 27–53. Asheville, NC: Pegasus Press, 2001.

———. *Sacrifice Your Love: Psychoanalysis, Historicism, Chaucer.* Minneapolis: University of Minnesota Press, forthcoming.

Fradenburg, Louise Olga. *City, Marriage, Tournament: Arts of Rule in Late Medieval Scotland.* Madison: University of Wisconsin Press, 1991.

———. "Troubled Times: Margaret Tudor and the Historians." In *The Rose and the Thistle: Essays on the Culture of Late Medieval and Renaissance Scotland,* ed. Sally Mapstone and Juliette Wood, 38–58. East Linton: Tuckwell, 1998.

Freud, Sigmund. *Group Psychology and the Analysis of the Ego.* Ed. and trans. James Strachey. New York: W. W. Norton, 1959.

———. *Civilization and Its Discontents.* Trans. James Strachey. New York: Norton, 1961.

Geoffrey de la Tour Landry. *The Book of the Knight of La Tour-Landry,* ed. Thomas Wright, EETS o.s. 33. London: EETS, 1868.

Gerald of Wales. *Giraldi Cambrensis Opera.* Ed. J. S. Brewer. London: Longman, 1861–91.

———. *The Journey through Wales.* In *The Journey through Wales and The Description of Wales,* trans. Lewis Thorpe. Harmondsworth: Penguin, 1978.

Gower, John. *Vox Clamantis.* In *The Major Latin Works of John Gower,* trans. Eric Stockton, 47–288. Seattle: University of Washington Press, 1962.

Grant, Alexander. "The Otterburn War from the Scottish Point of View." In *War and Border Societies,* ed. Anthony Goodman and Anthony Tuck, 30–64. London: Routledge, 1992.

Hastings, Adrian. *The Construction of Nationhood: Ethnicity, Religion and Nationalism.* Cambridge: Cambridge University Press, 1997.

Henry of Ghent. *Quodlibeta Magistri Henrici Goethals a Gandavo.* Paris, 1518.

Hintze, Otto. "Typologie der ständischen Ver fassungen des Abendlandes." *Historische Zeitschrift* 141 (1930): 229–48.

Hugo, C. L. *Sacrae Antiquitatis Monumenta Historica.* Etival: Heller, 1725.

Huizinga, Johan. "Patriotism and Nationalism in European History." In *Men and Ideas: History, the Middle Ages, the Renaissance,* trans. James S. Holmes and Hans van Marle, 97–158. London: Eyre and Spottiswode, 1959.

Ingham, Patricia. *Sovereign Fantasies.* Philadelphia: University of Pennsylvania Press, 2001.

Kaeuper, Richard W., and Elspeth Kennedy. *The "Book of Chivalry" of Geoffroi de Charny: Text, Context and Translation.* Philadelphia: University of Pennsylvania Press, 1996.

Kantorowicz, Ernst. *The King's Two Bodies: A Study in Mediaeval Political Theology.* Princeton: Princeton University Press, 1957.

Keen, Maurice. *Chivalry.* New Haven: Yale University Press, 1984.

Knyghthode and Bataile. Ed. R. Dyboski and Z. M. Arend. EETS o.s. 201. Oxford: EETS, 1935–36; New York: Kraus, 1971.

Lacan, Jacques. *The Seminar of Jacques Lacan: Book VII: The Ethics of Psychoanalysis, 1959–1960,* ed. Jacques-Alain Miller, trans. Dennis Porter. New York: Norton, 1992.

Lavezzo, Kathy. "Another Country: Aelfric and the Production of English Identity." In *New Medieval Literatures* 3, ed. Wendy Scase, Rita Copeland, David Lawton, 67–93. Oxford: Oxford University Press, 2000.

Le May, Sister Marie de Lourdes. "The Allegory of the Christ-Knight in English Literature." Ph.D. diss., Catholic University of America, 1932.

Lewis, Charlton T., and Charles Short, eds. *A New Latin Dictionary*. Rev. ed. New York: American Book Company, 1907.

Life of the Black Prince by the Herald of Sir John Chandos. Ed. Eleanor C. Lodge and Mildred K. Pope. Oxford: Clarendon Press, 1910.

Migne, J.-P. *Patrologia Latinae*. Turnhout: Brepols, 1976.

Painter, Sidney. *French Chivalry: Chivalric Ideas and Practices in Mediaeval France*. Baltimore: Johns Hopkins University Press, 1940.

Post, Gaines. "Two Notes on Nationalism in the Middle Ages." *Traditio* 9 (1953): 281–320.

Reynolds, Susan. *Kingdoms and Communities in Western Europe, 900–1300*, 2nd ed. Oxford: Clarendon Press, 1997.

Richards, Earl Jeffrey. "French Cultural Nationalism and Christian Universalism in the works of Christine de Pizan." In *Politics, Gender, and Genre: The Political Thought of Christine de Pizan*, ed. Margaret Brabant, 75–94. Boulder, CO: Westview Press, 1992.

Rickels, Laurence A. *The Case of California*. Baltimore: Johns Hopkins University Press, 1991.

Russell, Frederick. *The Just War in the Middle Ages*. Cambridge: Cambridge University Press, 1975.

Salisbury, John [of]. *Policraticus*. Vol. 5. Ed. and trans. C. J. Nederman. Cambridge: Cambridge University Press, 1990.

Scarry, Elaine. *The Body in Pain: The Making and Unmaking of the World*. Oxford: Oxford University Press, 1985.

Suleri, Sara. *The Rhetoric of English India*. Chicago: University of Chicago Press, 1992.

Tatnall, Edith C. "John Wyclif and the *Ecclesia Anglicana*." *Journal of Ecclesiastical History* 20 (1969): 19–43.

Tolomeo [of] Lucca. *De regimine principum*. Ed. Joseph Mathis. Vol. 3. Rome and Turin: Marietti, 1948.

Turville-Petre, Thorlac. *England the Nation: Language, Literature, and National Identity, 1290–1340*. Oxford: Clarendon Press, 1996.

Twiss, Sir Travers, ed. *The Black Book of the Admiralty*. Vol. 1. London: Kraus Reprint, 1965.

Tytler, P. F. *History of Scotland*. Edinburgh: William Tait, 1829.

Uitti, Karl D. "Alexis, Roland, and French 'Poésie Nationale.'" *Comparative Literature Studies* 32 (1995): 131–50.

Vale, Juliet. *Edward III and Chivalry: Chivalric Society and Its Context, 1270–1350*. Woodbridge: Boydell, 1982.

Wallace, David. *Chaucerian Polity: Absolutist Lineages and Associational Forms in England and Italy*. Stanford: Stanford University Press, 1997.

Winnicott, D. W. *Playing and Reality*. London: Routledge, 1991.

Wright, Thomas, ed. *The Roll of Arms of the Princes, Barons and Knights Who Attended King Edward I to the Siege of Caerlaverock, in 1300* . . . London: Hotten, 1864.

Žižek, Slavoj. *The Sublime Object of Ideology*. New York: Verso, 1989.

———. "Eastern Europe's Republics of Gilead." *New Left Review* 183 (1990): 50–62.

PART II

THE LANGUAGES OF ENGLAND

LATIN ENGLAND

ANDREW GALLOWAY

Scevola: . . . *My lord, I heard them all have a*
conceite of an Englishman, a strange people,
in the westerne Islands, one that for his
variety in habit, humour and gesture, put
downe all other nations whatsoever . . .
> —Thomas Heywood,
> *The Rape of Lucrece,* lines 1740–43

Thorlac Turville-Petre's *England the Nation,* linking English literary communities and anthologies with the emerging national status of the English language, calls out for a succession of appendices—or rather, in the spirit of his nondogmatic and open-ended work, with its provocatively pre-Ricardian stopping point, many further chapters, in what deserves to be a vast, collaborative project assessing the ideologies and contexts of national community in late medieval English-speaking areas.[1] A simple encompassing claim about nationalism in the period will not be satisfactory, but the time is long past when we can make a flat declaration that a pan-European Christian ideology and the preeminence of Latin rendered medieval culture incapable of nationalism (cf. Anderson, *Imagined Communities,* 15, 37–46).

Yet as Derek Pearsall's recent counterargument in "The Idea of Englishness" emphasizes, it remains debatable whether late medieval vernacular English literature even in its most self-confident instances and most overt royal promotion was truly symptomatic of, or merely wishfully prescriptive for, a broad context of nationalist outlook. Pearsall argues that the occasional associations of vernacular literature with nationalism strictly reflect the intermittent desires of the Crown, with no deeper or growing "national feeling" (15). And indeed, for the phrase to have meaning it must involve a sense of a territorially and culturally unified community exceeding the elite groups of the clergy or aristocracy, on the one hand, and also exceeding simple ethnic identity, on the other (see Smith, "National Identities"). Those who do make claims for the emergence in this period of such a notion, which of course implies some accompanying notion of "culture" susceptible to this application, often attribute it either to direct claims by vernacular, secular culture, or to a more general sentiment impelled or inspired by the century's gradual or more dramatic social changes (the consequences of the Black Death and the Hundred Years War are often posited [e.g., Danbury, "Propaganda"]).

Such debate about vernacular literature, culture, and patronage notwithstanding, these were not the only or indeed the primary sources for views of "the nation"—not, that is, until the Reformation rendered other sources defunct. Throughout the Middle Ages, monastic Latin writings were far from lacking in historical and thus at least potentially "nationalist" authority. An important appendix, then, to studies of ideas of Englishness would seem to be consideration of the Latin, monastic writers who had long enjoyed enormous authority for defining "England" and continued to do so into the fifteenth century, even though they did not enjoy a thriving or at least grateful posterity. To be sure, their authority in this period was not unchallenged: from our perspective, their position in this late period was one of historical futility. But the contributions of monastic Latin historians in the later fourteenth and early fifteenth centuries to notions of national community were able for a time to compete with, even flourish in, an increasingly secular and unified administrative state, and in the corresponding presence of increasingly authoritative claims for the English language and a diverse but very ambitious English literature. How did "England the nation" appear to them, and what did they contribute to its expression by others?

These questions, and the narrative features of late medieval chroniclers in general, have begun to receive attention, especially by literary scholars. Ranulph Higden's influential world chronicle of the 1330s and 40s, for example, has recently been considered in terms of how marginally he presents England in his text and in the maps associated with his chronicle, yet how emphatically he makes England the abundant provider to the world and center of the world's desires (Lavezzo, "Angels," chapter 2). Higden's chronicle has also been noted for a national vision that generally dismisses the legendary narratives of Brutus, founder of royal and aristocratic claims, in favor of "a more factual, rationcinative, less imaginative but no less fascinating account" of Britain (Brown, "Higden's Britain," 106). Other chroniclers of the Hundred Years War from mid-century have been considered in terms of how their "oral" style is implicitly imperialist, claiming territory for England with the superficial and naive ease of claiming the "speaking voice" of a text.[2] Careful consideration of late medieval Latin chronicles in these narrative and ideological terms offers a potentially major expansion of our vision of literary and cultural history in this period and a direct challenge to our sense of the vernacular roots and branches of early nationalist ideology. Further study is necessary not just because of the narrative vitality and social significance of works that, from the point of view of their medieval readers—including the kings who sometimes invoked the chronicles as testimonials of national territorial claims, or summoned their authors to royal councils[3]—were (in contrast to a general modern view of them) prominent, widely read, and authoritative sources for definitions of national culture. Such study is also rewarding for reasons with potentially broader significance in literary and cultural theory: how new visions of community arise within narrative traditions and institutions that themselves can no longer contain or even plausibly claim to represent, much less be readily authorized by, these visions. For it is the monastic writers, near the end of a long run of secure but increasingly embattled institutional and historiographical authority, who most advanced the terms of vernacular and secular national ideology, even if they were themselves as unlikely as modern scholars have generally been to desire or to acknowledge the debt of vernacular and secular culture to them.

I focus here on the two most influential and narratively powerful English Latin chroniclers of the later Middle Ages, perhaps not coincidentally writing from just before, through, and after the "Ricardian" period of dramatically inventive and socially engaged vernacular writings. I first take up Higden's *Polychronicon:* by design a nationally and "universally" comprehensive Latin history; by circumstance a work appearing just before the "take-off" of vernacular literature, whose popularity is extraordinary by any standard. The unpredictably varied and energetic reception of this highly self-conscious author and his national historical vision suggests, by its very diversity, that the *Polychronicon* achieved the most effective construction of a national textual identity and national model of authorship that England had yet seen, and more-over reveals that this appeared at a time when these features could be vigorously exploited by non- or even antimonastic English writers. The *Polychronicon* was translated by John Trevisa in 1385, Wyclif's sometime companion at Queen's College, Oxford, in a translation that includes many antimonastic remarks, and it was used heavily by Wyclif himself, even being a main source of the "Lollard chronicle of the Papacy" and other manifestly or putatively Lollard writings in English.[4] As I hope to make clear, there are reasons within Higden's work why it lent itself to these diverse uses so opposed to his own institutional agenda: its narra-tive construction and self-conscious cultural posture facilitate this dias-poric reception history. But although I will put some emphasis here on how much Trevisa's and some other writers' postures of vernacular authority owed to Higden's perspective, I shall focus less on Higden's influence on vernacular writers (which has been traced elsewhere, although I add a few further suggestions) than on Higden's modes of defining his own authority in relation to the vision of English culture he sets forth, and on a sampling of how these modes influenced other Latin monastic historians in the fourteenth century.

I then turn to the national vision of the chronicles by Thomas Wals-ingham, monk of St. Albans, which were begun in the last quarter of the century and continued into the first quarter of the next. Best known to literary scholars for his denunciations of the 1381 rebels, whose "rus-tic tragedy" he unfolded in a biting account of the 1381 Rebellion, he was also responsible for remarkable narratives of the Good Parliament and for perhaps the most heroic account extant of the Battle of Agincourt.[5] By considering first Higden's work of the 1340s, then Walsingham's writ-ings of the 1370s–1420s, I hope to suggest a trajectory of narrative in which the authority of a vision of national ideology and the authority of the late medieval monastic writer were increasingly under mutual pres-sure, but yielded the period's most forceful and significant articulations of vernacular and secular national culture. They surely did not start the idea of vernacular and secular nationalism, but by a path fraught with conflict both within and without their narratives, they made a formative contribution to it.

Too formative. By the next century, monastic chroniclers found they had insufficient grounds for assuming a national authority that would allow them to venture articulations of the nation. Later fifteenth-century Latin monastic chronicles are usually narrowly focused, local, or simply in-house histories, yielding the ambition for national history to the increasing numbers of vernacular chroniclers in English and French, although even these did not equal the earlier articulations of the secular nation presented by Higden and Walsingham (see Jacob, "Verborum," and Galloway, "Writing History," 272–76). Perhaps many appendices on this particular aspect of late medieval English nationalisms are not needed after all. The most significant and influential late medieval narrative constructions of England the nation by monastic, Latin writers, indeed by any writers before the Reformation, began with Higden and ended with Walsingham.

INTIMATE HISTORY AND VARIETAS: RANULPH HIGDEN'S *POLYCHRONICON*

Such constructions were never simple and direct, and indeed their intensity and fascination derive from their self-contradictions. In spite of its appearance to outsiders as a monolith of authority, the community of Latin historical writing was a divided domain in fourteenth- and early-fifteenth-century England—divided from an increasingly confident and literate vernacular culture; divided from a past of Latin writings whose very quantity and thus discrepancies made them seem increasingly less reliable; divided, indeed, by quarrels with other contemporary Latin chronicles. In contrast, a writer in the vernacular with the right patronage and sense of historical momentum could make a direct bid for representative national identity in spite of the lack of any monolithic presence: in spite of the relatively limited reach of any one dialect, the usually few manuscript copies, and relatively few readers of most vernacular writings—in spite, that is, of the need to invent out of whole cloth the full abstraction of "England the nation" as a linguistic, intellectual entity.

Thus Higden's first translator, the chaplain for Thomas, Lord Berkeley, and sometime Oxford scholar, John Trevisa, more than 'corrected' the monastic Latin world history by the Chester monk Ranulph Higden that Lord Berkeley had asked Trevisa to translate: Trevisa performed an

all-out sublimation of Higden's probing and pessimistic view of the difficulties of English linguistic and intellectual unity.[6] According to Higden,
after the Danish and then the Norman conquest, the language of the English became thoroughly *corrupta,* lapsing into a diversity of weird groan-
ings—*boatus et garritus,* Higden states; "strange wlaffyng, chyteryng,
harryng and garryng grisbittyng," Trevisa more compendiously and vigorously translates. This *corruptio* of some originally 'pure' and unified
national English *(nativa et propria Anglorum lingua)* is worsened, Higden goes on to declare, because English children—unlike the custom of
other nations *(contra morem caeterarum nationum)*—are forced to learn
French in school *(construere Gallice compelluntur).* Children of the nobility, Higden adds, are taught French from the cradle, and "country folk"
try to "frenchify" themselves *(rurales homines . . . francigenare satagunt)*
hoping to be assimiliated into fashionable society so that they might seem
more respectable *(assimilari volentes, ut per hoc spectabiliores videantur).*
As Trevisa pungently translates, "and oplondisch men wol likne hamsylf
to gentil men, and fondeþ wiþ gret bysynes for to speke Frenysh for to be
more ytold of" (2:158–61; fol. 50v).[7]

Higden's evaluation of the repression and disintegration of the English vernacular tongue is much richer than most contemporaneous
remarks against the use of French in England, although some Latin writers are similarly critical; in an early-fourteenth-century commentary on
Wisdom, for example, the scholar Robert Holkot remarked on William
the Conqueror's efforts to destroy the *lingua Saxonica* by requiring French
to be spoken in the *curia regis* and taught to school children, an anecdote
Holkot allegorizes as the devil's efforts to force human beings from an
early age to learn the "idiom of the infernal provinces," namely, lies.[8] Higden, however, uniquely emphasizes a materialist sense of national culture, especially the social and political structures creating and created by
language, and the material bases and effects of different kinds of knowledge. His chief concern from this perspective is England's cultural unity,
but as a problem to which he sees no solution.

For obvious modern reasons, Higden's own meditation on the social
dimensions of English language and knowledge and the larger historical
style and mode that makes this view possible have been overshadowed
by Trevisa's addition to the passage. Trevisa's remarks are indeed worth
quoting in any discussion of late medieval English ideas of community

for the sense of a "new world" that his statements convey, in their vision of the growing institutional authority of English in the decades after the "first plague" of 1349, and for the clever insistence on the significance of Trevisa's own time, place, native origins, and present literary activity in this shift:

> *Trevisa.* þis manere was moche yused tofore þe furste moreyn and ys seythe somdel ychaunged, ffor John Cornwal a mayster of gramere chayngede þe lore in gramer scole and construction of Freynsch into Englysh, and Richard Pencrych lirnede þat manere techyng of hym and oþer men of Pencryth. So þat now, þe yer of oure lord a þousond þre hundred foure score and fyve, of þe seconde kyng Richard after þe conqueste nyne, in al þe gramer scoles of Engelond childern leveþ Frensch and construeþ an Englysch, and habbeþ þerby avauntage in on syde and disavauntage yn anoþer: here avauntage ys þat a lirneþ here gramer yn lass tyme þan childern wer ywoned to do; disavauntage ys þat now childern of gramer scole conneþ no more Frensch þan can hire lift heele, and þat ys harm for ham and a scholde passe þe se and travayle in strange londes and in meny caas also; also gentil men habbeþ now moche yleft for to teche here childern Frensch. (2:161; fols. 50v–51)

An epochal tone is clear in the multiple dating clause for 1385, and the importance of this 'event' for Trevisa's own literary vocation is clear. Trevisa adroitly turns the "now" of his act of writing into a pivotal and capacious moment of intellectual, literary, cultural, and indeed universal history: in the context of his dating clause, his "now" implies not "after the first plague" but "from this nationally located moment of my writing on." With his sweepingly national claim for primary education ("al þe gramer scoles of Engelond"), and his equally sweeping claim of a language that now makes learning grammar easy for all English children, noble and ignoble, while making work in "strange londes" correspondingly more difficult, Trevisa makes the separation between himself and Higden seem centuries, rather than some forty years, and continents, rather than a few hundred miles. It only remains for Trevisa to reckon up the gains and losses, adding a touch of objectivity, even epic elegy, to his pronouncement about the birth of a fully, irrevocably unifying and isolating, national language, springing forth full-born from the grammar masters of his own native Cornwall.

With that final balance sheet of gains and losses, Trevisa appears attractively objective and self-conscious about his position straddling present and past. A direct model for such self-consciousness, however, lies at hand. Higden presents himself throughout as self-consciously belated in relation to his authorities and narrowly locatable in Chester, cultivating a posture of contemporaneity and local specificity that is defined in an implicitly national setting. The *Polychronicon* opens with a sprawling sentence that is confusing less because of bad grammar than because of its torturous way of emphasizing a belated relation to the Latin materials it gathers. Its thundering initial clause opens the work with what is in most copies a visually prominent *Post* ("After"), constituting his own capacious but belated "now":

> After the most famous writers of the arts [have lived, have written], for whom it was a pleasure to labor as long as they lived at the knowledge of things and the modesty of morals, they, just as they mixed utility with sweetness, justly ought to be praised in grand, solemn sounds, who have passed on to posterity by the benefit of writing the great deeds of the ancients.[9]

In this preface—the first of three he had produced by the time he stopped work on the *Polychronicon,* sometime after 1352—Higden elaborates this subservient relation to the past by declaring that he is a gleaner after the harvest, a dwarf on the shoulders of giants, a ridiculous figure piping on an oaten reed after great trumpetings. These postures of a latecomer allow Higden to assert the right not just to compile but also personally to respond to and critique historical authorities. Higden includes the names of his authorities within the text rather than in the margin, a practice first developed in history writing by Vincent of Beauvais in the thirteenth-century *Speculum Maius,* and, like Vincent's use of the word *actor* to designate his own comments, Higden also inserts the sign *R* (for "Ranulphus") to designate his comments.[10] So too, Trevisa inserts *his* name when he disagrees or wishes to explain further. (Trevisa retained this device for his translation of Bartholomeus Anglicus's *De proprietatibus rerum.*)[11] And in the longest, final version of the *Polychron-*

icon, completed during the last two decades of his life and at the highest point of national recognition in his lifetime, Higden altered the first letters of the first sixty chapters to spell out more directly the "now" of his writing, the place of his monastery and his own name: *PRESENTEM CRONICAM COMPILAVIT FRATER RANULPHUS CESTRENSIS MONACHUS* ("Brother Ranulph, monk of Chester, compiled the present chronicle").

This device, while not uncommon in Latin poems and sermon manuals, is unprecedented in history writing; thanks to Higden's use it quickly became a widespread fashion in both Latin and vernacular narratives.[12] V. H. Galbraith offered the balanced verdict that the acrostic was inserted "to combine the professional humility and anonymity of the monk with the very human instinct for fame" (Galbraith, "Autograph Manuscript" 5). But an appeal to "human instinct" dismisses too quickly the acrostic's specific contexts, associations, and consequences. Thanks to Galbraith's identification of an autograph manuscript of the *Polychronicon,* Higden's processes of self-definition, probably the result of his awareness of a very wide community of readers far from Chester, can be studied more closely than those of almost any other major fourteenth-century writer. This heavily carreted, emended, scraped, and rewritten manuscript reveals that Higden added the acrostic as well as many of his personal comments to the *Polychronicon* in the 1340s. In these late revisions, a reference to the acrostic is inserted in a seemingly incidental, marginal position, during a description of the history of English towns and cities, including Chester where "the present chronicle was labored at, as through the initials of the first book stands more fully clear"[13]—a remark thickly rubricated and repeated in the margin of the autograph manuscript, but by a later hand; the original is simply at the textual hierarchy of the rest of the text (fol. 6). Yet this posture at once elevates his identity into the ranks of his authorities and separates him from the tradition now relegated to the past, in gestures like Higden's magisterial opening *Post* and his repeated description of his work as the *present* chronicle, written at an identifiably English locale.

A constant conversation with a contemporary national readership about the past is implied in such an identification of himself as an English, contemporary writer, and is implied whenever he interrupts his authorities (as he frequently does) to adjudicate on their merits or explain the cultural and material limits of their perspectives. This is a function of his emphasis of his own distinctive cultural location. A. J. Minnis has valuably traced the persona of a commentator in late medieval *compilationes* from late-twelfth-century commentaries on Peter Lombard's *Sentences* through the thirteenth-century Continental encyclopedist Vincent of Beauvais (Minnis, "Discussions"); but *R,* presenting a stance at once intellectually critical and historically and geographically located, speaks with a much different voice from that of Vincent's *actor.* Vincent's *actor*—a word that (unlike the unrelated word *auctor*) refers to a legal representative of a group, and thus does not constitute some personal views of Vincent's—remains uninterested in the reasons for conflicting historical opinion, seeking to remain detached from any conflict between the sources that his *Speculum Maius* collates: "not, therefore, to have by great labor endeavored to draw the sayings of philosophers into concord, but to recite as much about each matter as each of them has perceived or written," as Vincent declares his goal.[14] These principles lead Vincent's *actor* mostly to adopt the bland role of summary and transition, his voice as passionless and detached as his name for its function suggests.

  R does not forcefully reconcile his *auctores,* but he also does not let discrepant versions lie quietly. Rather, he is always deeply involved in their discrepancies or implausibilities, and often especially concerned with how their settings—temporal and geographic—account for these conflicts. Chester had since the Conquest been a county palatine (that is, with prerogatives equal to those of the Crown), and inscribing such a locale as an author's locus therefore speaks from a position of distinct independence and authority (as too might Higden's observation that it began as a Roman "city of legions"). But Chester was of course also a county of England, prominently so listed in all chronicles. Higden's act of displaying his authorial identity in a map of the English countryside— the prototype for Trevisa's locating the origins of English schooling in Cornwall—thus has generalizable significance for a posture of English identity and national readership. Such nationally geographic self-identification also has generalizable significance for historical vision, because of the importance Higden puts on geography as, literally, the fundamental basis of historical perspective.

  In recounting the history of Bath, for example, Higden presents a characteristically empirical and geographical criticism of his source, which leads directly to Trevisa's assertion of personally and nationally located experience. Using Trevisa's translation here makes the connection more visible:

> Bladud, Leyl hys sone, a Nigromauncer, was the nyþe kyng of Britons [Higden states, summarizing Geoffrey of Monmouth's *Historia*]. He bulde Bathe and clepede hyt Caerbadun. Englysch men clepede hyt afterward Athamanus hys cyte, bote atte laste a ys ycleput Bathonia þat ys Bathe. Willelmus, *De pontificibus,* libro secundo. Yn þis cite welleþ up and springeþ hoot bathes, and me weneþ þat Julius Cesar made þar such bathes. R. But Garifre Monemutensis yn hys brittysch book telleþ þat Bladud made þulke bathes. Apon caas William *De pontificibus* þat hadde noȝt yseye þat brittysch book wroot so by tellyng of oþere men, oþer by hys oune gessyng as a wroot oþere þinges somdel onwyslych. Þerfore hyt semeþ more soþelych þat Bladud made noȝt þe hote bathes noþer Julius Cesar dude such a dede, þey Bladud bulde and made þe cite. Bote hyt acordeþ betre to kundelych reson þat þe watre eorneþ undur erthe by veynes of brenston, and so ys yhat kundelych in þat cours and springeþ up in dyvers places of þe cite, and so þer buþ hoot bathes þat wascheþ of tettres oþer soores and schabbes. *Trevisa.* Þeyȝ me mygȝte by craft make hoot bathes for to duyre long ynow, þis acordeþ wel to reson and to philosophi þat treteþ of hoot welles and baþes þat buþ in divers londes, þey þe watre of þis bathe be more trouble and hevyer of smyl and of savour þan oþere hoot bathes þat ich have yseye at Okene in Almayn and at Eyges in Savoy. Þe bathes at Eyges in Savoy buþ as fayr and as cleer as eny cold welle streem. Ych have asayed and ybaþed þerynne. (2:59–61; fol. 42)

This sequence of views is virtually a summa of historiography from the twelfth-century to the late Middle Ages. *R*'s compilation of the previous accounts of Bath is guided by his interest in an underlying historical "real" that is physical, geological, and closer than his authorities to what we would call materialist and socially oriented. William of Malmesbury had not seen "þat brittysch book," and so he must have learned his version by some other socially and physically mediated means. (And Higden is often interested in what books were consulted by previous historians:

Bede, he once conjectures, must have himself used the book on "holy places" that Bede describes Bishop Arnulphus as writing [7:172].) William's historical methods are then cast into general doubt; since he did not see the "brittysch book," he "wroot so by tellyng of oþere men, oþer by hys oune gessyng as a wroot oþere þinges somdel onwyslych." Higden then ventures his empirical, geological explanation for the hot waters of Bath.

By elaborating an ellipsis in Higden's text, Trevisa gives this empiricism the quasi-scholastic name "kundelych reson," where *R* simply mentions that this is *magis verisimile* ("videtur magis verisimile quod licet rex Bladud hanc urbem construxerit, non propter hoc ipse aut Julius haec calida balnea construxerit; immo quod aqua originalis transiens per venas sulphureas"). Trevisa thus elevates Higden's vague criterion of verisimilitude into a category of innate understanding—a natural power of reasoning that is in principle noninstitutional and universal, and at the same time deeply personal and particular. Trevisa's "kundelych reson" thus, in the most fundamental sense, makes a claim to the authority of vernacular knowledge.[15] This empirical principle is then taken as a directive by Trevisa, who carries the search for historical explanation further into "reson and to philosophi þat treteþ of hoot welles and baþes þat buþ in divers londes," and, as a final test of such authority, into repeated assertions of his own experience: "Ych have asayed and ybaþed þerynne." In arriving at this point, Trevisa parallels the views of a more famous fourteenth-century literary pilgrim from Bath. Higden later refers back to his speculation on Bath as one of his own opinions: "*R*. Nevertheless William Malmesbury says that Julius Cesar conceived of those baths, which I think not true *[quod non puto verum]*, as is said above in the section on cities" (3:26).

Yet although most readers would not realize it, as clearly Trevisa did not, Higden has derived the point of his materialistic refutation of William of Malmesbury on the hot waters of Bath from Bede, who in turn took it from Saint Basil's fourth-century writings. In the first chapter of the *Ecclesiastical History*, Bede states:

> The land [of the English] possesses salt springs and warm springs and from them flow rivers which supply hot baths, suitable for all ages and both sexes, in separate places and adapted to the needs of each. For water, as Saint Basil says, acquires the

quality of heat when it passes through certain metals, so that it not only becomes warm but even scalding hot. The land also has rich veins of metal, copper, iron, lead, and silver. (17–19)

This textual lineage for his materialism does not alter its provocative effect, which appears because in Higden (unlike Bede) the physical context is used to refute the mere hearsay or "gessyng" of a major monastic historical authority, William of Malmesbury. Perhaps because of the leverage against past authorities it offers, Higden always displays interest in geology as the fundamental basis of history; even if such views depend on earlier authorities, and even if this approach sometimes reveals Christian implications, his sense of history and hence of culture emphasizes the material location of events and thoughts.

Describing the moment of the Crucifixion, for instance (a description that is as astonishing for its lack of detail concerning the event itself, as for its startling induction from the one detail it does present), Higden declares that the splitting of the stones marked the first splitting of *all* stones—although it is possible that this remark too is not original:

> Christ suffered on the eighth calends of April, on which day according to Cassiodorus was so great a diminishing of the sun as had never occurred before, so that the stars were visible in the heaven; and by means of great earthquakes the cities of Bithynia were overturned. *R.* Then also the stones were split, whence it seems likely *[unde verisimile est]* that the veins and fissures that now appear in stones and rocks came about from that earthquake, since before that time the rocks were unsplit. (4:345–47)

To the extent that it accounts for "the veins and fissures that now appear in stones and rocks," this is empiricist and materialist, though it retains the Christian location of the Crucifixion as the moment of supreme importance. His pervasive passion for historical geography—for a physical location and basis for historical perspective—implies a sense of culture that in turn subtends his sense of himself writing a present chronicle in a specific location of England the nation.

This is perhaps why geography particularly organizes his associations and research in the context of English matters. Thus, summarizing Bede's account of St. Birinus under the year 636, he records Bede's

assertion that Birinus died at Dorchester and was then translated to Winchester (*Ecclesiastical History,* 3.7). *R* then offers an updated contradiction to that statement, and follows that by surveying the terrain carefully:

> *R.* But the canons of Dorchester deny this, and they say that it
> was a different body from Birinus's that was moved, and that
> those moving it were deceived in this. Whence a bier of mar-
> velous workmanship is seen today above the place of his first
> grave. Now, Dorset or Dorking stands six miles to the south
> of the city of Oxford, situated between the two rivers of the
> Thame and the Thames. It is also found in chronicles that King
> Kingilsus assigned the whole land in a circumference of seven
> miles around Winchester to an episcopal seat in Winchester and
> to sustain his ministers, but because the king, prevented by a
> fatal illness, was not able to fulfill this, he commanded that his
> son Kenwalcus fulfill it. William, *De pontificibus,* book two. This
> city from that time until the coming of the Normans remained
> under the bishops of Mercia, but at the time of the Conquest
> the bishop's see was translated to Lincoln. (6:4–6)

R's comment on the canons at Dorchester indicates that Higden has
paused in his compilation and made some inquiries or remembered
some current information at this point. He researches the precise location and the tangle of religious rights in the area before proceeding with
Bede's chronological narrative.

This example demonstrates one reason why Higden contextually
grounds his English sources in particular: so that he can present an accurate picture of the present territorial rights of various English religious entities, as here those of Winchester, Dorchester, and Lincoln. Yet
while this concern governs a large proportion of Higden's opening survey of the English landscape (including a lengthy discussion of the relations between Canterbury and York), it is also linked to a more general
interest in how the physical environs of the world condition historical visions, often leading Higden to refute Benedictine authorities along with
all other authorities. Just as William of Malmesbury must not have seen
Geoffrey of Monmouth's book, so (Higden reasons) Bede must never
have been to Ireland, or he would not have claimed that there is good
hunting of roebucks there (1:336). Similarly, Dido and Aeneas could not

have known one another, since Aeneas died three hundred years before
the building of Carthage (2:432)—a comment Higden found in John of
Salisbury, but whose prominent place in Higden's account is of a piece
with his approach to history as a matter of local perspectives, best as-
sessed by one who defines his local point of view overtly.

Many such declarations have sources in other authors. Yet Higden
collects such views with a carefulness that shows his concentration on
critical historiography—at least of an armchair variety.[16] Like Osbern
Bokenham, who in the fifteenth century translated Higden's opening
survey of England in order that such settings may provide "þe more
clerere vndirstandynge" of the accounts of English saints that Bokenham elsewhere provides, Higden seeks to illuminate individual accounts
and actions by placing and interpreting them within the world's physical
settings (Horstmann, "*Mappula*," 6). Fourteenth-century theologians'
interest in *originalia* provides a parallel to this interest; but Higden takes
the concern further, since the theologians seek merely to recover complete textual contexts.[17]

Higden's awareness of the importance of setting and context is also
directly responsible for his construction of one of the first "nationalist"
world maps in the Middle Ages. The word "nationalist" must always be
defined: in this case, it means displaying the world carved irregularly
into labeled nations (*Flandria, Francia,* etc., with *Anglia, Scotia,* and *Wallia*
resting out in the perimeter of the ocean) but with almost no other geographic detail, with Jerusalem at the center and Adam and Eve at the top.
It has been suggested that Higden's oval map is in the shape of Noah's
Ark, as Hugh of St. Victor had suggested that maps be made (Woodward, "Medieval *Mappaemundi*," 313); indeed, the only other illustration
in the autograph manuscript is of the Ark (fol. 48). However, there the
Ark appears as a labeled cross section of a square building (human beings on top, various animals below), and apart from the similarly
schematic and textual emphasis, this Ark does not resemble Higden's
map, nor are there other indications that his map is meant to resemble
the Ark. More pertinent is Kathryn Lavezzo's observation that the position of *Anglia* in the margin of the world in all the maps of the *Polychronicon* corresponds with Higden's assertion that "England is so called
from 'corner of the world' *[ab angulo orbis]*" (2:4; Lavezzo, "Angels," chapter 2), a statement Higden cites as from Isidore but that is not recorded
in manuscripts of the *Etymologies* (perhaps from a gloss in an English

manuscript of that work). The especially clear correspondence of this statement with the position of England in Huntington MS 132, where *Anglia* is even further outside the mass of countries than in most other *Polychronicon* maps, floating out beyond the oval perimeter at the north-western edge of the world, seems to confirm the view (corroborated by abundant other evidence of revision of R's comments and the letters of the acrostic) that this manuscript and this copy of the map is an auto-graph (for a reproduction, see Woodward, "Medieval *Mappaemundi*," plate 15, and other copies of Higden's maps in figs. 18.21, 18.22, 18.67, 18.68, and 18.69; he disputes, unpersuasively, the authorial connection to the Huntington copy [312]). At any rate, most of the early *Polychroni-con* maps follow this emphasis on national labels: like the map in HM 132, their concern is typically focused on distinguishing national areas with looping lines and twisting borders that trace not the simple ordered globe found in the venerable but still common "T-O" maps (where Asia, Europe, and Africa separate an ordered "T" within a circular world), but a maze of border relations of nations, with England's placement beyond the oval world making it the epitome of eccentricity.

While his historiographical geography emphasizes territorial nation-alism, Higden also uses literalism to probe and unsettle central tenets of vernacular nationalist ideology. Like most monastic chroniclers, Higden carefully intercalates into his chronicle materials from the Brut story, so important to late medieval nobility and kings; as Peter Brown notes, Higden's consideration of discrepancies in these accounts, and his out-right challenges against them, persistently undermine the claims of the Brut tradition to unquestionable authority: Higden "poured cold water on one of Edward III's cherished myths, the Arthurian legend" ("Hig-den's Britain," 114). Higden's critiques are subtle as well as sweeping. For instance, just when he notes Brutus's occupying of the island of Britain for the first time—the moment of all Brut histories' and nearly all aristocratic lineages' ultimate foundation claims—he lingers on a discrepancy in the accounts of Brutus's lineage. His intense and intri-cate consideration quietly demolishes the most important claim of the myth in terms of nationalistic ideology: its connection of the founding of Britain, via Brutus, Ascanius, and Aeneas, to the founding of Rome.

> The third Silvius Posthumus of the Latins, the son of Aeneas
> and the brother of Ascanius, born from Ascanius's stepmother

Lavinia, began to reign, and he reigned thirty-nine years. In this year Brutus, son of Silvius, son of Ascanius, occupied Britain, according to historians. *R.* Concerning the father of this Brutus the histories seem dissonant. For [Geoffrey of Monmouth's] *History of the Britains* says that this Brutus was the son of Silvius, the son of Ascanius; but [Paul the Deacon's] *Roman History* says that Ascanius bore Julus, from whom the family of the Julians arose, making absolutely no mention about Silvius. Therefore unless this Julus had two names, and was also called Silvius, one or the other of the said histories wavers from the truth *[Nisi ergo iste Iulus fuerit binomius, et dictus Silvius, altera dictarum historiarum vacillat]*. For since this Brutus is asserted to have killed his father while hunting when fifteen years old, and since Silvius Posthumus according to all the historians was the son of Aeneas not the son of Ascanius, and for a long time afterwards he [Silvius Posthumus] lived and reigned, not having been killed, it is therefore clear that this Silvius Posthumus is not the father of Brutus—unless perchance because, since the *Roman History* says that Ascanius after the death of Aeneas brought up Silvius Posthumus with the greatest tenderness, on that account he would be thought to be his father *[nisi forsan quia historia Romana dicit Ascanium post mortem Æsilvium Posthumum summa pietate educasse, ob hoc patrem ejus putandum fore]*. Which indeed I might accept without doubt, if one did not read that Silvius Posthumus was killed by his son Brutus. (2:442)

This is tortuous, but the situation is complex, and Higden's courage lies in *being* tortuous in his pursuit of such a sensitive matter. In one tradition derived from the twelfth-century founder of the Arthurian stories, Geoffrey of Monmouth, the *Historia Brittonum* (the "Vatican" version), the father of Brutus is Ascanius; this is followed by some medieval chronicles, such as the first three versions of Henry of Huntingdon's twelfth-century *Historia Anglorum*. But Geoffrey's main prose work, the *Historia Regum*, calls Brutus the son of Silvius and he the son of Ascanius, a view Henry of Huntingdon followed in his final version (Geoffrey of Monmouth, *History* 1.3, 4.1 [pp. 55, 107]; Henry of Huntington, *Historia*, 25 n. 40). The uncertainty about this among medieval chroniclers ultimately springs from Livy, who admits doubt about whether he has the right Ascanius and mentions no fewer than three Silviuses, one the son of Ascanius and the rest grand- and great-grandsons. But Livy calls none "Posthumus," a tradition Higden derived from Paul the Deacon's history, possibly by way of the thirteenth-century compiler Martinus Polonus whose condensation of Paul the Deacon (whom Martinus [*Chronicon*, 399] is drawing on directly here) and of other chroniclers was popular in late medieval England. Finally, Higden, seeking to square the lineages in Paul the Deacon against those in one of Geoffrey of Monmouth's works, arrived at the original and humanizing suggestion about how the mistake might have derived: it was from a misunderstanding of Ascanius's tender ministrations of his young stepbrother. But Higden ends by dismissing this hypothesis because the Galfridian text flatly contradicts it. He allows the key source of Arthuriana to render insecure any effort, no matter how imaginatively immediate, to recuperate the whole tradition.

This series of doubts ending in self-doubt does not attack the authority of Arthuriana with a hachet but a thin blade, identifying a discrepancy and proposing a directly social basis for the historical misunderstanding. With a grosser instrument, Higden elsewhere refutes outright the likelihood of King Arthur's existence: "moreover, concerning this Arthur, whom Geoffrey alone among all chroniclers so extolls, many men marvel how the things that are said about him might be able to smack of truth, to the extent that if Arthur, as Geoffrey writes, acquired thirty kingdoms, if he subjugated the king of the French, if he killed Lucius the procurator of the republic in Italy, why all histories of the Romans, French, and Saxons should have omitted to mention such extraordinary things about so great a man, histories that tell so many smaller things about lesser men."[18] For Trevisa, this is a matter to be counterattacked as would be doubts about Scripture's inconsistent presentation of Jesus (see Waldron, "'Celtic Complex'"). For Higden, belief in Arthur is a species of uncritical nationalist ideology that all *nationes* (and the modern notion of "nation" is clear as he moves from antiquity to the present in his assessment of this) tend to produce:

> Finally, Geoffrey marvels that Gildas and Bede made no mention of Arthur in their writings; but I think it is more to be marvelled at why that Geoffrey extolled so much he whom all ancient, veracious, and famous historians left almost utterly unmen-

tioned. But perhaps it is customary for each nation to extoll one
of their own with excessive praise *[sed fortassis mos est cuique nationi aliquem de suis laudibus attollere excessivis]:* just as formerly
the Greeks did their Alexander, the Romans their Augustus Caesar, the English their Richard the Lionhearted, and the French
their Charlemagne, so the British cry up their Arthur. (5:334–36)

What matters in Higden's approach is less its specific claims than
the way in which his questioning keeps central a national field of concerns, and a sense of "culture" that must subtend such concerns. To
raise questions *about* national myths might cast cold water on belief in
simplistic aristocratic foundation claims; it also deepens the nature of
and engagement with nationalism as such. Active disenchantment (in
Weber's sense) or deconstruction (in Derrida's sense) increases fascination in the object of inquiry. Higden's unsettling approach to the bases
of national ideology inscribes its claims more deeply on attention, more
fully naturalizing nationalism as an "empirical" category in a materialist
view of culture with engrossingly complex misperceptions and disunities.

In keeping with such debate in and concerns with English historical
identity, Higden concludes his opening geographic survey of the world
by focusing intensely on the social "variety" *(varietas)* of the contemporary
English, whose social instability offers the most insoluable and hence
fascinating problem of national unity of all—a fascination evident at
the most immediate level in Higden's spontaneous series of national
insults, and evident more broadly as Higden, in revision, uses this moment to structure his entire history:

> R. This people [the English] squeamishly despise their own
> things, and commend those of others; hardly ever content with
> the rank of their own estate, they freely transfigure themselves
> into what pertains to others. Wherefore it is that a servant *[ver-
> naculus]* represents in himself what is proper for a squire, a
> squire what is proper to a knight, a knight what is proper to a
> duke, a duke what is proper to a king. Indeed, some circum-
> venting every rank are in no rank, and seeking every order are
> of no order. For in mannerism they are cheap entertainers, in
> talking Ciceros, in banquets worthless scoundrels, in decoration
> and get-up novices, in profiting many-eyed Arguses, in labors

Tantaluses, in cares Daedaluses, in bed-activities Sardanapaluses, in temples idols, in courts thunderers, and by privileges and prebends alone do they call themselves clerics *[Nam in gestu sunt histriones, in affatu Cicerones, in convictu nebulones, in quaestu caupones, in apparatu sunt tirones, in lucris Argi, in laboribus Tantali, in cures Daedali, in cubilibus Sardanapali, in templis simulacra, in curiis tonitrua, solis privilegiis et praebendis clericos se fatentur].* But indeed among all the English everywhere is spread so great a variety of clothing and multiformity of decoration that almost no one can be counted of any social order [or "of either sex": *Sed et in cunctis passim Angligenis tanta vestium varietas et apparatus multiformitas inolevit, ut neutri jam generis quilibet paene censeatur].* Concerning which thing a certain holy anchorite prophesied in the days of King Egelfred in this manner: *Henry of Huntingdon,* book 6: The English, because they are prodigal, drunken, and given to negligence to the house of the Lord, will be conquered, first by the Danes, next by the Normans, thirdly by the Scots, whom they reckon most vile; and to such an extent then will the age be varied, that the variety of mind will be represented by the multiple variety of clothing *[adeoque tunc varium erit seaculum, ut varietas mentium multimoda vestium variatione designetur].* (2:169–75)

This energetic condemnation of English *varietas* is the larger context for Higden's comments on the diversity of the English language, the moment that in turn provided Trevisa such fodder for announcing the end of English disunity. Higden's remarks should be read in the first instance, however, as evidence of his own fascination with the impossible stability and unity of Englishness, and an epitome of the physical and cultural variety of all history. These two matters explain why he made his comments on English language, identity, and clothing so architectonically and thematically crucial. Placed just before the account of history proper beginning with book 2, the section provides a neat transition from the geographical contexts of history in book 1 to the human points of view that emerge in and are shaped by those physical, temporal, and cultural environments. And over time Higden deepened the structural and topical significance of this discussion of *varietas:* it becomes both an encompassing principle of all history and a broadening "now" in his

locatably English act of writing (a far more powerful assertion of such a
"now" than Trevisa's, it might be added). For while generally following
Augustinian tradition by dividing his history into six ages, Higden has
here superimposed on this—following the prophecy recorded by Henry
of Huntingdon—a nationalist periodization based on increasing English
varietas of minds and clothing and three major conquests of the English,
the third yet to come (book 6.1, Henry of Huntington, *Historia,* 338–40).
Higden has anticipated this with a suggestion that English social type,
and even sexual gender, are not stable.[19]

His increasing attention to this nationalist eschatology as a unifying
principle of his history is clear in his revisions, as the autograph manuscript shows. He mentions the prophecy again at the Norman Conquest
and also when King Edward I first attacks the Scots; both cases have
cross-references to the end of the first book, and in the autograph manuscript all three passages show signs of revision. The first passage has
been fit tightly onto the bottom of folio 43v, its intrusion into the marginal date columns showing that it was added to the original page. The
second passage's cross-reference to the first passage is a supralinear insertion—"Circa hos dies quidam vir dei predixit anglis insperatum a
Francia dominium venturum quod eos deprimeret <et cetera, sicut in
fine primi libri>" ("Around these times a certain man of God predicted
to the English that an unexpected domination would come from France
which would crush them, <*inserted above the line:* etc., as in the end of
the first book>": fol. 214r; 7:114)—and at this point the earlier, shorter
texts of the *Polychronicon* include a version of the complete prophecy (in
the Rolls Series sigla, "C" and "D" at 7:114). These changes show that in
his final revisions, Higden moved the prophecy from his discussion of
the Norman Conquest, where it would appear chronologically from Henry
of Huntingdon's history, to the more prominent and thematically comprehensive position at the front of the entire narrative, leaving a cross-
reference at its former location. He recognized in this succinct definition of unstable Englishness something that belonged at the head of his
entire work.

The third passage, during an account of Edward I's war on the Scots,
suggests that Higden is aware that the prophecy had some popular currency. Arguably drawing on the living memory of those from regions
closer to the Scottish border than Chester, Higden here recounts that
during the war on the Scots there was widespread fear that the prophecy

might be about to come true. In this passage too he inserts over an era-
sure the cross-reference to the end of the first book, again directing the
reader to consider the comprehensive importance of Englishness, if Englishness as a problem that cannot be solved: "Nonnulli vero vindici dex-
tre dei hoc ascripserint, iuxta prophetiam illam que tempore regis Egelredi
predixit gentem Anglorum per dacos, francos et Scotos fore extermi-
nandos, <quemadmodum superius tactum est in fine primi libri>"
("But some people ascribed that [misfortune] to the vengeance of the
hand of God, according to the prophecy that in the days of King Ethelred
predicted that the people of the English would be exterminated by the
Danes, the French, and the Scots, <inserted above the line: in the way that
is mentioned above in the end of the first book>": fol. 276r; 8:286).

In the anti-Scottish element of the prophecy, Higden may well be
drawing on what were originally local, border-country feelings; yet he el-
evated such nationalist sentiments to a central position in history and in
his work. By means of careful cross-referencing, the prophecy gives the
work a "finished," tightly bolted, and decisively "English" focus, even as
it documents the successive corruptions of English culture, language,
and morality with each invasion. (And as the Normans brought in greater
pride, social diversity, and national disorganization by introducing a
caste split between those who speak French and those who are reduced
to strange gruntings comprehensible only in local environments, so the
Danes introduced drunkenness and gluttony to the English [2:166]—a
remark that literary scholars might recognize as the progenitor of Hamlet's comments on the Danes in *Hamlet*.)[20]

Such a use of cross-references helps focus English national unity, if
only by way of its absence, as a central fascination of Higden's history
and its implied and explicit "now." Higden's intense and self-consciously
textual debate *about* England keeps and deepens the focus *on* England;
and the topoi of problems in English unity that he chose spawned truly
national responses and remained for decades the center of what may
well be called a discourse of nationhood. To be sure, his carefully orches-
trated prophecy of the Scots' final attack was almost entirely ignored by
his followers, probably as a frightening prospect of national annihilation
that they did not want even to engage (only Sir Thomas Gray, who used
Higden for his *Scalacronica*, writing in a Scottish prison after being captured in battle, has anything to say on the Scottish threat, and he leaves
such questions to "lez deuynes" [3]). But Higden's views on fashion as

an instance of national disorder or *varietas* strike a widespread concern that could be adapted to less apocalyptic arguments and endeavors—and that was certainly amenable to the increasingly anxious maintenance of caste gradations (Galloway, "Authority"). In 1363, eleven years after Higden was ordered for unknown reasons to appear "with all his chronicles" before Edward III (Edwards, "Ranulf"), the king issued England's first detailed clothing regulations, made necessary because "Garceons usent Apparaill des gentz de Mestire, et gentz de Mestire Apparaile des Valletz, et Valletz Apparaile des Esquiers, et Esquiers Apparaill de Chivalers; l'un et l'autre Pellure que seulment de reson appertienent as Seigneurs et Chivalers" (*Rotuli Parliamentorum* 2:278; Baldwin, *Sumptuary Legislation*, 34–47). The stair-step progression of this rhetoric recalls if not draws from Higden's prophecy.

Clearly, the period was alive to this topic. At least two of the monastic continuators of the *Polychronicon* have something to add to Higden's fears about fashion. The author of the *Eulogium historiarum* repeats the prophecy and declares that such variety of vestiture is to be feared for a host of associated ills: the corruption of law, the perversion of truth, and the worsening of all circumstances, just as in Dunstan's time—whence it might happen that tailors and suitors who are employed one year may well be attacked by the entire people the next (2:171). The chronicler of Leicester abbey, Henry Knighton, rephrases Higden's warnings under the year 1388, stating that these days there is so great a presumption *(elatio)* among the common people in dress and apparatus that one status can hardly be distinguished from another: "Non pauper a potente, non egens a divite, non servus a domino suo, non sacerdos ab alio de populo"; each one imitates the other *(unusquisque imitabatur alium)*.[21] Adam Usk, the Welsh secular clerk who continued Higden's history as, he states, an explicitly private act of history writing, probably has the same passage in mind when he describes the dress of the Greek emperor, Manuel II Palaeologus, who arrived in England in 1400. Usk chooses to emphasize the emperor's *lack* of *varietas,* putting into the emperor's mouth precisely the criticisms of the English that Higden has used:

> This emperor always and his men always went about dressed uniformly in long robes cut like tabards which were all of one color, namely white, and disapproved greatly of the fashions and varieties of dress worn by the English, declaring that they

signified inconstancy and fickeleness of heart [*animarum incon-stanciam et uarietatem significari*]. (Usk, *Chronicle*, 118–20; trans. Given-Wilson)

No doubt there was substance to the charge about fashion. As the emergence of the "new guise" in the 1340s suggests, a courtly fashion springing from changes in the design of the tunic (from two flat "t"s sewn together, to a torso-tube with sleeves sewn on; see Galloway, "Clothing"; and Newton, *Fashion*). Indeed, fourteenth-century clergy were themselves notorious offenders in matters of dress, threatening in their fashionable clothing to obliterate the professional and caste boundaries between them-selves and the laity. It may be that Higden's fellow monks of St. Wer-burgh's, who had been told by the bishop of Lichfield on his visitation in 1315 and again in 1323 to cease from buying new clothes or from wear-ing "belts and knives unnecessarily ornamented" (qtd. Burne, *Monks*, 66–71), were abashed when Higden put their tastes in the context of na-tionalist apocalypse. But there is no reason to suppose that monks in the Chester and Lichfield area—or anywhere else in England—stopped cul-tivating such personalizing, worldly ornamentation. In 1338 at Darley in Lichfield, monks were wearing "pleated tunics" *(rochetas plicatas);* in 1347 at Baswich, also in Lichfield, a complaint was made that it was hard to distinguish monks from laity because of the short tunics and pointed shoes that both wore (Swanson, "Visitation," 99 and n. 39). By 1363, the General Chapter of Benedictines—perhaps in support of Edward III's sumptuary laws—issued a complaint about the destruction of tradi-tional divisions by means of colorful clothing; the president sharply re-minded his order: "We are not called red, or brown, or blue, but *black* monks" (Pantin, *Documents*, 67).

But the rhetorical structures and ideological scope of Higden's for-mulation exerted a power that can be seen beyond the history of fashion as such. From the echoes just presented, one is led to posit that Higden made a trope about English instability in social identity into a set feature of national ideology, emitting varying implications in a variety of con-texts. The proliferation of comments in this vein shows how late me-dieval national ideology was profoundly indebted to Higden's act of framing the possibility of English cultural unity, if one whose difficulties they often cast as more soluble than he had. His pessimistic proposal spurred others to imagine solutions in the form of nationalisms that they would not otherwise have conceived, or at least encouraged more complacent repetitions of his passage that in themselves acknowledged as he had a national "culture."

The penchant for personalized, caste-breaking fashion is like the pro-liferation of personal voices in fourteenth-century history writing that Higden more directly fostered: both tendencies define an idea of indi-viduality in opposition to an increasingly impersonal social and political domain. Yet there was also a principle of community in such admissions of individual unpredictability and variability. Fourteenth-century individ-ualizing trends both in fashion and in historical narratives are remark-ably imitative of other contemporaries—if not of tradition. They bespeak present-looking rather than past-looking collectivity. Henry Knighton, writ-ing in the 1390s, emphasizes the imitations of "new dressers," *(unusquisque imitabatur alium);* the same notion and almost the same phrasing ap-pears in Knighton's discussion of how Lollards spread their seditious teachings (Martin, *Knighton's Chronicle,* 302–03; see Hudson, "Vocab-ulary?"). Like the personal voice of fourteenth-century vernacular "public poetry" that Anne Middleton has described, the dissenting personal voice of fourteenth-century monastic Latin chronicles is another trope for a collective contemporary English voice, capable of addressing a "common" audience "now" whose limits are implicitly national (Middleton, "Idea").

It can be shown that both before and after Trevisa's translation in 1387, the *Polychronicon* made popular among English writers of many kinds the posture of a personal relation to received historical materials. Indeed, if the twelfth century in England was, in R. W. Southern's phrase, the age of "intimate" biography (*Saint Anselm,* 329–36), the fourteenth century was the age of "intimate" historiography—as the proliferation among so many of Higden's continuators and adapters of various uses of his acrostic, compiler's identification, and personal commentary on historical authorities shows. But intimacy in these terms implies alien-ation from the past—and, paradoxically, also from those who are seen to be betraying tradition. An implication of contemporary, nationally locat-able identity, of the dissident Higdenian sort, inheres in most of Higden's followers. Among these, the least appreciated in these terms are his Latin monastic followers—and detractors. Thus the monk of Leicester abbey, Henry Knighton, who explicitly relies on Higden for the early portions of his history, includes an acrostic inscribing his own name across its opening chapters, presents material that he has collated from sources

other than the *Polychronicon* under his own sign, "Leicestrensis," and inserts a rather touching note under the year 1336: "The seventh and so the
last book of Chester's having come to an end, Leicester goes on alone,
pursuing the work that he has begun *[solus procedit Leycestrensis prose-
quens inceptam materiam]*" (Martin, *Knighton's Chronicle,* xxiv–xxv, 2–3).
A more complicated case is the author of the *Eulogium historiarum,* who
uses Higden's information extensively, inserts his own signature *(D* instead of *R)* to indicate the compiler's comments, and repeatedly scolds
Higden for disrespecting traditional *doctores et auctores.* "The Chester
monk reproves authorities and teachers *[Monachus Cestriae reprobat doctores et auctores],*" one heading in the medieval index of the *Eulogium historiarum* states, guiding the reader to a passage where Higden's criticisms
of William of Malmesbury are condemned; but the passage is both preceded and followed by the *Eulogium* author's extensive use of the *Polychronicon (Eulogium* 3:324). Moreover, the *Eulogium* author presents his
own authority in the preface by means of a first-person persona whose
views are little more than animations of Higden's more impersonal opening remarks.

The resulting tone of the preface is peculiar. The *Eulogium* author's
refocusing of Higden's most stentorian claims for the value of history
onto an entirely personal point of view grants those claims an unpredictable and perhaps unintentional wryness, since the *Eulogium* author
personalizes Higden's modesty topoi of general human insufficiency.
Thus Higden's oratorical opening declares that "in the historical literature passed down to us by the diligence of chronographers shines more
clearly the standard of morals, the proper way of life, the incentive for
probity, the trivium of the theological, and quadrivium of the cardinal
virtues, neither the knowledge of which nor the ability to follow the foot-
steps of which *our* mediocrity could possess, if the efforts of writers had
not suffused *our* ignorance with the remembrance of things past";[22] the
Eulogium narrator opens with a personal redirection of these statements,
asserting "the proper way of life, the incentive for probity, the trivium of
the theological, and quadrivium of the cardinal virtues, render no savor
to *my own* dullness, since I am so far from clever and so inadequate."[23]
Where Higden declares (following John of Salisbury's *Policraticus [Opera,*
col. 385b]) that "shortness of life, dullness of sense, torpor of soul,
lapsing of memory, and unfruitfulness of labor impede us *[nos]* from
much knowledge, but divine mercy has provided a remedy in writing,"

the *Eulogium* author declares that all these things impede him personally *(me)* from gaining much knowledge.

The *Eulogium*'s nineteenth-century editor, Frank Haydon, sees these
transferred allusions to the *Polichronicon* as deliberately demoting Higden's grand reasons to write history into seeming "insipid," a way of
"sneering" at Higden "under a thin disguise of humility" (1:xlv, xlvi). Certainly, the immediate interests of the *Eulogium* author in denouncing Higden are not difficult to surmise; his affiliation with Malmesbury Abbey
is clear from many of his comments, and Higden's rejections of William
of Malmesbury (as in the discussion of the hot baths of Bath) draw the
Eulogium author's sharpest criticisms. A monastery's tradition of historical authority often subtended its immediate legal and economic claims,
thus encouraging home-defenders; and there were other reasons for
monastic defensiveness, especially the arguments for dispossession taken
up by the laity.[24] And from one point of view, the *Eulogium* narrator's
attack is not wholly a stylistic and moral failure, however jarring to modern (or at least Victorian) aesthetics. By out-Higdening Higden in self-
abasement, the monk of Malmesbury does implicitly criticize Higden's
hypocrisy in claiming to be modest while in fact attacking traditional
Benedictine *doctores et auctores.* At the least, the *Eulogium* author registers
the scandal and disruption of tradition that Higden—that *novus chrono-
graphus,* as the *Eulogium* author once calls him (2:130)—has accomplished, even if the *Eulogium* author is an additional if less willing instance of Higden's disruptive influence.

The bathos of the *Eulogium* preface is probably best seen as the result of expressing all of Higden's points about the greatness of the past
and the meanness of the present in entirely personal terms. Whatever
the intention, the irony is a structural effect of refocusing Higden's impersonal reasons for human modesty onto intimately personal circumstances. Even the *Eulogium* author's detailed description of his reasons
for compiling a history may not be the historically accurate details that
Haydon and John Taylor take them to be (Taylor, *Historical Literature,*
13 n. 28, 106), but rather a rhetorical refocusing of the condition of
human frailty from Higden's impersonal rhetoric to an entirely personal
referentiality. Where Higden magisterially recounts the problems in
sustaining the past's greatness—shortness of life, dullness of wit, torpor, weak memory, and futile occupation—the *Eulogium* author's "self-
portrait" fully personalizes these circumstances. "Seated, utterly wearied,

in his monastic cell, with dulled senses and frustrated in his efforts for
virtue, assailed frequently by the worst kind of thoughts—now because
of lengthy reading or weariness of praying, now because of past vain
boastings and foul labors in the secular world, with all their pleasure
and consent and, worst of all, their multitudinousness," the author per-
sonifies everything Higden laments in the human condition. Their descriptions of their decisions to write a history are similarly related. Higden
is "provoked by such examples of the past"; neither boasting of himself
nor attacking others, he has decided, as he might, to hammer out a treatise about the circumstance of the island of the British, for the knowledge
of those to come.[25] The *Eulogium* author is "provoked by his own feeble-
ness and torpor, and the memory of his own boasts and vain worldly
labors," by which he has decided, as he might, to hammer out, as his su-
periors had asked, some kind of treatise *(aliquem tractatum)* excerpted
from the labors of various authors for the knowledge of those to come.

By taking Higden's provocative personalizing gestures one step further, the *Eulogium* narrator stands yet more alienated from the praise of
tradition that he at the same time invokes. Collapsed entirely into the
trope of the personal voice, tradition loses all *auctoritas*. Were this a
Chaucerian narrator, we would not hesitate to credit this strategy with
literary genius. But that would be more than it deserves, just as to see it
as simple "sneering" at Higden offers less credit than it deserves. The
Eulogium author's daring underlining of Higden's personalizing rhetorical strategy mainly shows how authoritative was Higden's model for
present, personal identity and perspective, locatable within a national
geography. This for the *Eulogium* author is not an overt nationalist ideology, but it is implicitly connected to a sense of alienated national community, partaking in and assailing others for the English vice of *varietas*.

Higden's utility for vernacular writers seeking to establish a novel
and widespread authority against the past is easier to see, and his specific influence here has been more studied (see Edwards, "Influence").
But the general impetus Higden provided vernacular writers to forge a
contemporary, English voice of dissent may still be underappreciated.
The voice of narrator-poets such as Will in *Piers Plowman* or Geffrey in
Chaucer's works of the 1370s and 1380s, climaxing with *Troilus and
Criseyde* and the *Legend of Good Women,* show how the personal relation
to historical texts and compilation may easily turn into a direct if slightly
gloved assault on "what so myn auctor mente" (*Legend* F 470)—and

Chaucer's *Legend* opens with a metaphor of "gleaning" texts that depends on Higden's preface, one of several signs that Chaucer's posture draws from Higden's. Even beyond Higden's explicit indications of a nationalist framework, his critical, materialistic inquiry into Latin authority and his culture's fractured cohesion made his a voice that spoke from a contemporary national culture that vernacular writers could easily—indeed more easily than he—assimilate as their own.

Chaucer's Wife of Bath is a compiler very much in Higden's vein, even if much of her narrative is cast as an *anti*compilation (see Hanna, "*Compilatio*"). Indeed, her voice reciting, while rejecting, Jankyn's misogynist compilation "the boke of wikked wyves" probably finds direct inspiration in Higden, as corroborated by at least one sign of direct use. The Wife warns the Pardoner, "Whoso that nyl be war by othere men, / By hym shul othere men corrected be. / The same wordes writeth Ptholomee; / Rede in his Almageste, and take it there" (III.180–83). Thus, as often, the Wife applies a text to herself and puts forth her bodily presence as proof of the text, paradoxically providing a textual reference for the need to use others' experience as an authoritative model; and she later reassures a jealous husband by quoting from the same named source, with a similarly wry application of such wisdom to her own physical and social experiences and activities:

> Of alle men yblessed moot he be,
> The wise astrologien, Daun Ptholome,
> That seith this proverbe in his Almageste:
> "Of alle men his wysdom is the hyeste
> That rekketh nevere who hath the world in honde."
> By this proverbe thou shalt understonde,
> Have thou ynogh, what thar thee recche or care
> How myrily that othere folkes fare? (III.323–30)

Both passages have raised wide speculation as to actual source, since neither is in Ptolemy's *Almagest* but instead closely follow proverbs cited in the introduction of the Latin translation by Gerard of Cremona (a summary of the scholarship's errors is in North, *Universe*, 147–48 n. 11). But it may not be necessary to look further than Higden in Trevisa's translation, where a passage places the two proverbs together in phrasing that the Wife follows almost exactly:

And Ptholomeus, a konnyng man of þe sciens of mathematik,
was in his floures; he made more of astronomy þan was al þat
he fond ymad tofore hys tyme. Þes [man] was of strong wreyth
and of lytel mete and hadde a swete breþ; he made meny bokes
þat buþ *Almagestus perspectiva* and *In judiciis quadripartitum, Cen-
tiloqium.* Among hys proverbes tweyne buþ famous and nobel:
"He ys hey3este among men þat rechcheþ nevere þat who haþ
þe world on honde"; and, "Oþer men buþ no3t amended by
hym þat ys no3t amended by oþer men." (5:27–29; fol. 147)

Such specific connections underline a more general one. In her personal,
oppositional voice, the Wife partakes in what Higden's work helped establish as a trope of fourteenth-century national identity, if one much
more effectively mobilized by vernacular writers than by Latin, monastic
ones.[26] The paradoxes of authority in Higden's effort to speak personally
to and about a national community that he acknowledges he cannot directly speak for, are shifted in the *Wife's Prologue* to different and more
studied paradoxes: a textually steeped demolition of clerical compilation
and clerical guidance. The paradox of her involvement in the textual traditions she rejects, while an endless source of fascination for critical
commentary, may be seen in a broader perspective as a reprise with different self-authorizing purposes of the latent paradox in Latin, clerical,
national compilations by Higden and other clerical writers, who cannot
speak for the national entity they acknowledge, define, and speak to.

Variable identity, a troubling feature of Englishness as Higden overtly
states, is seized on by many late-fourteenth-century vernacular writers as
their common bond. It may thus be no accident that the one quotation
from Higden in William Langland's *Piers Plowman* (found in Langland's
first version only) is to Higden's peroration on the restless elusiveness
of the English between traditional estates: as Langland's Wit declares,

> I haue lernid how lewid men han lerid here children
> þat selde moseþ þe marbil þat men ofte treden,
> And ri3t so be romberis þat renen aboute
> Fro religioun to religioun, reccheles ben þei euere;
> Ne men þat cone manye craftis, clergie it telliþ,
> Thrift oþer þedom with þo is selde ysei3e:
> *Qui circuit omne genus in nullo genere est.* (A.10.103–08a)[27]

Langland's later versions of his poem make such "recklessness" and elusive identity the most persistent features of the narrator's own identity (in his final version, the narrator's own longest speech is even attributed to Recklessness): the background in Higden suggests again that the problem of identity within this terrain where "romberis...renen aboute" is a badge of national identity.[28] Wit, the Wife of Bath, and many other vernacular voices register the lay-clerical social and linguistic division as a central paradox of a broadly communal identity. They thus contribute to Higden's project of defining an inclusive contemporary cultural entity of "England," in terms of the very problem of national identity that Higden so steadily contemplated. Yet only Higden articulated the nationalism implicit in this critical outlook; the vernacular writers only intermittently and fragmentarily respond to his powerful and paradoxical outlook, either resolving his view of English disunity or not seeing its intriguing and, for them, enabling paradoxes of authority as extending as far as a national scope.

In bequeathing so much to a culture that was increasingly opposed to the Benedictine order, and in taking so strong an interest in the problems of social and intellectual unity of that culture, Higden is unique among fourteenth-century monks. Yet he was but one of many Benedictines who were, as Christopher Cannon has shown, concerned with the laity, especially in pastoral roles ("Productions," 331–36). Indeed, Higden's pastoral contributions are the direct source of his signature and a clue to the more obscure and particular social experiences behind his vision of English and universal history. His insertion of the acrostic in the *Polychronicon* dates from the period when he wrote manuals for preachers, a genre in which such acrostics are common, as in Robert of Basevorn's manual, which may well represent Higden's specific contact with the device (first noted by Caplan, *Artes Praedicandi,* 27). Such manuals are normally associated with academic spheres, and preaching itself was directly forbidden English cloistered monks during most of the Middle Ages (see Jennings, "Monks," and Jennings, *Sermones*). But Higden includes a remark in the *Polychronicon* that Pope Boniface IV granted to monks the right of preaching, baptizing, and remitting sins (5:418), and fourteenth-century monks were sometimes encouraged to learn this university art with licences to study at university. Yet no other Benedictine is known to have written a manual for preaching (Jennings, "Monks," 119–28, Murphy, *Rhetorical Arts,* xvii–xx). Two of Higden's manuals are dated to 1340, just when he began his final revisions on the *Polychroni-con* that include the acrostic and a marked increase in *R*'s comments; both manuals spell across the first letters of the chapters Higden's name and the date (see Pantin, *English Church,* 203). Higden undertook a literary activity that crossed professional boundaries and presented explicit guidance for vernacular culture; moreover, he went on to transfer that genre's presentation of individual authorship to universal history.

In such ambition to write beyond his professional order, Higden seems yet again an instance of the *varietas* he condemns—as the *Eulogium* author clearly implies he was. Yet it is finally impossible to determine whether Higden's motives in asserting and constructing his powerful personal authority were remarkably presumptuous or unusually charitable, or simply compelled by a context of widening lay authority or ecclesiastical counterefforts to maintain economic and intellectual authority. In 1348, the abbot of St. Werburgh's wrote Pope Clement VI asking that the exemption he had obtained for St. Werburgh's be extended to the local parish churches, including the altar of St. Oswald "under the roof of the monastery church, to which the cure of souls attached" (qtd. Burne, *Monks,* 91). The monks' unusual allowance to these parishioners to worship in the abbey church, as well as their responsibility for these parishioners' *cura animarum,* apparently extended back to pre-Conquest times and ended only when the abbey nave had to be repaired in the 1350s, when they were moved to a new chapel (Burne, *Monks,* 91–92). Monasteries in the late Middle Ages frequently appropriated benefices, but usually without making provisions for the cure of souls in the areas appropriated; Higden's pastoral manuals may be seen in tandem with St. Werburgh's ancient, more recent, and soon forthcoming appropriations. The St. Oswald parishioners, whose inner parish territory lay in the block just across Northgate Street from the cathedral precincts but whose outer territory stretched in a wide triangle for over a mile north of the city walls (Dunn, *Ancient Parishes,* 39 n. 23, and maps on 36 and 37), may have been the first intended beneficiaries of Higden's unusual manuals.

While this unusual intimacy between worlds normally separated in medieval culture is notable, it cannot explain Higden's constructions of national inquiry. Broad shifts of institutional opportunity and pressure along with social and pastoral vision and other factors that we can never see led to Higden's pastoralia, his concern with *varietas* and with vernacular culture, and his own authorial signatures. But Higden's intimate contact with vernacular parish culture within his own abbey may very well have shaped the extent to which the *Polychronicon* emphasizes clerical and lay English *varietas,* and thus contributed to the influence his work exerted on so much of late medieval English literature and life.

IMPERIALISM AND THE SPIRIT OF '76: THOMAS WALSINGHAM'S HISTORIA MAJORA

Nearly every Latin chronicle in the later fourteenth century was designed to be, or is now in fact found as, a continuation of Higden, just as nearly every French and English chronicle is designed or found to be continuation of the prose *Brut* (in one of its many forms in French and English). Just as the *Brut*—that is, the aristocratic, Arthurocentric history from Brutus's entry into Britain on, governing English poetic histories like Layamon's and Robert of Gloucester's—provided an overtly "nationalist," usually vernacular tradition (apart from a few Latin translations), so Higden provided an overtly "universal" clerical and Latin tradition. To be sure, in political detail and English administrative focus, the later fourteenth-century continuations of either of these traditions tend to resemble one another more than they differ. Either model is simply accepted, remains implicit, in the often brilliant and wry political histories that constitute late-fourteenth-century continuations of Higden or the *Brut*. But in gross, these were the twin models for late-fourteenth-century shapers of the history of "England the nation": the one premised on a belated yet individuating and personal engagement with sources whose harmony, considered with Higden's materialistic and geographic bent, fissures into a *variatio* like that of English identity itself; the other structured as a lineage of English kings after Brutus and allowing increasingly larger pockets of political history. Perhaps it was not accidental that Chaucer joined the Arthurocentric *Wife of Bath's Tale* to the compilational, Higdenian *Wife of Bath's Prologue.*

Among late-fourteenth- and early-fifteenth-century Latin chroniclers, only Thomas Walsingham, monk of St. Albans, offered a true third way for conceiving "England the nation." But this claim needs careful qualification, like nearly any claim about Walsingham's work. In a career as precentor at St. Albans, probably preceded by a stint as a student at

Oxford and followed by a period as prior of Wymondham in 1394, after which he returned to St. Albans, Walsingham wrote and compiled many chronicles and versions of chronicles—a body of work that is still being defined amidst the works of his more dimly visible contemporaries at St. Albans (see Clark, "Thomas Walsingham," esp. 838–48). He, along with other monks of St. Albans, excerpted compilations of universal history from John of Tynemouth and others, compressed others' continuations of Higden, and carried forward various continuations of the great chronicle tradition of St. Albans begun by Matthew Paris in the thirteenth century, producing, as Vivian Galbraith remarks, an output "of ceaseless experiment and change" (Walsingham, *St. Albans Chronicle,* lxiii), which James Clark recently has shown puts Walsingham's varied historical scope and other writings, from musicology to hagiography to classical studies, amidst a central range of late-fourteenth- and early-fifteenth-century intellectual culture.

Walsingham produced his most original and elaborate narrative as a continuation to 1420 of Matthew Paris's world chronicle, and of Matthew Paris's house-history, the *Deeds of the Abbots of St. Albans,* for roughly the same period; but Walsingham's relationship to Matthew's work is not always obvious from the manuscripts. Walsingham seems to have wanted in some measure to stand as a comprehensive historian on his own merits. While the *Deeds of the Abbots* reads continuously from Matthew Paris on, the fullest copies of Walsingham's English chronicles appear in manuscripts like London, British Library, MS Royal E IX, which covers world geography, including a Latin translation of John of Mandeville, before moving rapidly through universal history from several sources (especially John of Tynemouth, whose works might have been known to Walsingham through the abbot of St. Albans, Thomas de la Mare, who spent three years as prior of Tynemouth where he surrounded himself with a circle of masters and other clerks to coach him in preaching and other learning [Walsingham, *Gesta Abbatum,* 2:380]), then finally setting forth the long, original sections of his *Chronica Majora.* The status of this large project is complicated by the fact that no one modern edition includes its entire text, but this fragmentary modern condition was encouraged by Walsingham's own interruptions and changes. For example, he excised several leaves from the Royal manuscript that include a severely critical view of John of Gaunt during the Good Parliament of 1376 and that is recoverable only from a copy of his earlier version of this event. And he ended the effort to produce the *Cronica Majora* in the Royal manuscript at 1392, with an entry stopping mid-page, only much later continuing that endeavor to 1420. At the same date, evidently just before his death, Walsingham also wrote another history of purely English affairs from 911 to 1419, the *Ypodigma Neustrie* ("paradigm of Normandy"), which draws on and compresses his other writings into a structure, not of conquests of England, but of English conquests modelled on the Conquest itself.

Sprawling as this corpus is, some passages across it display remarkably more dramatic passions and affective power in their assessments of history and society, and more than justify any view Walsingham might have had of his independent creation as a distinctive chronicler. His most powerful sections access into his notions of English community. Walsingham's account of the Good Parliament, which he repressed when he recopied his chronicle for the Royal manuscript, for example, posits passionate criticisms of corrupt aristocratic power in the form of John of Gaunt; his account of the Rebels of 1381 in his continuation of the St. Albans *Deeds of the Abbots* presents a sustained, bitter, and parodic criticism of the abbey's rebellious tenants in a nation-wide rebellion; his final continuation of his *Cronica Majora* triumphantly and exuberantly posits a view of England's military victories in France as that of a new conquering empire. How can these three notably powerful and explicitly national considerations be linked, and their interwoven issues of community and authorial identity explicated?

Walsingham's first ambitions to be a historical writer may have been expressed in or provoked by 1376, with the Good Parliament, for his original writing begins with that, and this account was evidently later connected back to Creation and universal history by a series of compilations. At some later point, that narrative was cancelled and rewritten, possibly in 1394, when BL MS Royal E IX was completed, when Walsingham assumed his role as prior of Wymondham, and when Walsingham made other changes to his chronicle reflecting a deteriorating view of Richard (see Stow, "Richard II"). That first narrative of the Good Parliament is less useful to historians than, for example, the *Anonimalle Chronicle* (a *Brut* continuation) in providing political and legal detail (see Holmes, *Good Parliament,* passim); but it has other interest for considering nationalist ideologies. For Walsingham defines the parliament as a conflict between a satanic John of Gaunt and the true interests of the "community" (communitas), an entity whose meaning remains vague but pregnant throughout Walsingham's writings in the 1370s and 1380s. In his account, the effort by a group of knights to demand an answer to their general grievances about corrupt government before they will pay a new tax from the senile Edward III's councillors is structured as a series of stages in the creation of what we would call representative government, but which Walsingham defines at each stage of its representational progress as divine inspiration—as if mere political representation were not enough to ensure sustained purity of purpose.

At the first stage, a handful of parliamentary knights, who themselves act on behalf of the *commune plebs*, the common people, and are said to be *de comitatibus* (from the commons), are driven "as it is believed by divine inspiration" (*Chronicon Angliae*, 68) to mount their first resistance to the magnates of Parliament. They act *commune decreto* ("by common decree" [70]), and one and all they ardently seek royal honor, the kingdom's well-being, and the people's peace ("cum omnes et singuli honorem regium, regni commodum, pacem populi ardentissime affectarent"). One of their members even has a vision while the parliament is underway that demonstrates how pious, holy, and commendable their endeavor was: he dreams he finds himself in the chapter hall of St. Paul's Cathedral (where the negotiations were in fact taking place) where, casting his eyes down to the pavement, he discovers seven gold florens. After gathering them and inquiring among all the negotiators to see who has lost them, he finally enters the cathedral choir where he finds among some Benedictine monks a particularly holy monk who tells him that the coins are really the seven gifts of the Holy Ghost, granted to him and his companions for the reform of the realm. "For gold denotes the wisdom granted to you, by which you might be able to carry out the necessary reforms and to speak more eloquently when facing the princes of this kingdom."[29] We again meet such tokens of communal binding, and on another religious floor, in Walsingham's work, in a parodic scene from his account of the Rising of 1381 when he recounts that the rebels seized pieces of their confiscated mill-stones that the abbey had had imbedded in its pavement; the rebels break them up and hand them out "as if they were pieces of the consecrated Host" for each of the rebels to bring home and remember that day.[30] That this second instance is a nightmare vision shows how unstable Walsingham's vision of the nation's "commons" is, a point to pursue below.

In the dream-vision during the Good Parliament, the gold coins function on a more serious parallel with the socially binding pieces of the consecrated Host; for the "seven gifts of the Holy Ghost" are literally manifested in the next stage of representative government. This is when the first speaker of the commons in England, Peter de la Mare, is elected to represent the knights before John of Gaunt. Peter is chosen because God had inspired Peter's heart and filled him with abundant wisdom, boldness to speak what is in his mind, inspired eloquence, along with perseverance and constancy in the face of danger; God finally infused him with a sense of justice and truth to endure anything (72). Here all the "gifts of the Spirit" are woven in: wisdom, boldness, eloquence, perseverance, constancy, justice, and truth; "so that upon a firm rock [petra] in accord with his name he might lay his foundation" (72–73). The pun on "Peter" as petra follows the famous Gospel pun about the founding of the Church (Matthew 16:18) used throughout medieval culture to describe the evangelical origins of the papacy. That Walsingham shifts this claim to a secular leader of a secular communitas shows how far he is willing to go to embrace and sanctify a vernacular and secular culture for which he, like Higden, can never speak. Here and elsewhere, Walsingham's approbation goes significantly further than Higden's, but leads to a more tensely poised outlook.

It is possible that Peter de la Mare is praised so extravagantly in part because of some relationship to Walsingham's abbot, Thomas de la Mare, although evidence points away from their being the same branch of the family.[31] Whatever distant relationship they had should probably not be considered the chief reason for Walsingham's praise of Peter. For Peter is far from the only secular hero here. What is notable about Walsingham's historical vision and historiographical vocation even here in this early writing is that it remakes the secular realm, the commons, and even the lowest commoners—properly inspired by God and refracted into the knightly representatives, who indeed eclipse in Walsingham's account any mention of the clergy or the burghers who actually were among the commons of the 1376 parliament—into the true Church. The allusive pun on Peter de la Mare's name only makes this explicit; and from this, the vilification of John of Gaunt when he opposes these endeavors follows directly. He becomes a figure of tyranny and pride. In Walsingham's vivid account (recoverable only from one of the two early copies of this cancelled chronicle), Gaunt coarsely tries to deny the knights' power in dismissive and vain terms that resemble the Herod of the cycle plays:

> "Why," he asked, "are these degenerates and serpent-knights riled up? Do they think they are kings or princes of this land, or where does so great a swelling-up and pride come from? I think they do not know my power. I, therefore, at the height of the day tomorrow will appear before them so glorious, and I will set in motion among them such power, and I will terrify them with such great severity, that neither they nor anyone like them will dare henceforth to assault my majesty." While he gloried and made empty promises about himself with such words, a certain retainer of his is said to have responded as follows: "Lord," he said, "it is not hidden to your majesty by whom and with how much help these knights, not commoners as you have claimed, but hardy warriors, are supported. For they possess the favor of the lords, and especially of the lord prince Edward, your brother, who supplies to them efficacious council and help. Indeed, the Londoners, one and all, and the common people are so stirred on their behalf that they would not allow them to be burdened with abuse or assaulted by the least injury. Indeed these knights, if affronted, would be driven to try every last thing against your person and those of your friends, which perhaps otherwise they would hardly undertake."[32]

In late medieval culture the type is instantly recognizable. As Herod says in the Towneley play of the "Offering of the Magi," before he is thwarted by the birth of the baby Jesus,

> Vnder my feete I shall thaym fare,
> Those ladys that will not lere my lare;
> For I am myghty man aywhare
> Of ilka pak;
> Clenly shapen, hyde and hare,
> Withoutten lak. (1:159)

Yet there are significant details in Walsingham's portrayal. Gaunt's interlocutor, his "certain retainer," emphasizes (unlike Herod's minion) that these knights are far from powerless or socially humble, and he goes on to include the Londoners, "one and all," even the *plebs,* at the heart of the notion of a community of the realm. A hierarchy of middling knights is important in Walsingham's ideal, and Gaunt's elision of this is a central part of his tyranny. The knights' representation of the lower social spheres remains a theme throughout Walsingham's account; for example, the outrageous behavior of Alice Perrers in meddling in law cases leads to Peter de la Mare again speaking up on their behalf, as Walsingham describes in a careful emphasis on the sequence of pure transmission of what and whom Peter represents: "Therefore the aforesaid knights of the commons, on the part of the community, through the mouth of Peter de la Mare, petitioned the duke and his fellow judges that they establish a remedy of correction for so great excesses...."[33] The rock that is Peter de la Mare functions as a truer pope than the pope himself, his church the *communitas regni,* and his cardinals and bishops the knights of the commons.

Readers of Walsingham's wry and contemptuous account of the popular Rising in 1381 will perhaps be surprised by the eulogy in 1376 for a divinely inspired, yet secular, representational *communitas.* Yet what an American might consider Walsingham's ideal of '76 figures throughout his life's work, even in the parodic account of the popular community in the Rising. Of course it is not surprising that a monk, from a world that typically had greater affinity to the aristocracy than the laboring classes, would be more pleased with the disruptive actions of a group of knights who are, as Gaunt's unknown retainer remarks, "not commoners as you have claimed, but hardy warriors," than with a group of craftsmen and tenants of the monastery. What is striking in the account of the Good Parliament is that an abstraction of the will of the commoners themselves, along with evidence of divine sanction, ultimately legitimates what the knights do. And the Rebels of 1381 embody not a viewpoint wholly alien to this ideal of the commons, but its evil twin. As Walsingham states repeatedly in his house-history, the *Gesta Abbatum (Deeds of the Abbots),* where his account is most biting, especially describing the rebels' efforts to recover or forge an ancient charter from King Offa granting them the liberties they claim, the rebels defined themselves as the "true commons."

This self-definition is recorded by all of the accounts of the Rising, but Walsingham focuses his special anger and satire on it. For instance,

just after they burn down a hospital on the way to London, they reaffirm
their oath to adhere "Regi Ricardo et communibus" ("to King Richard
and the commons" [*Gesta Abbatum*, 3:298]). "Who could desist from
weeping, perceiving that the noble head of the realm, I mean the city of
the Londoners, was utterly destroyed both day and night and subject to
the will of the commons?" (3:309). It is Walsingham alone who declares
that the rag-tag band still at St. Albans displayed a banner of St. George,
"as is done in war" (a treasonable offense after 1352), and that they entered
the abbey of St. Albans demanding that the abbot emerge and treat with
"the commons." He adds, "for so at that time they gloried in that name,
such that they judged no name more honorable than the name of the
commons, nor moreover did they believe that anyone ought to be considered a lord, according to their own stupid judgment, except only the
king and the commons [*nisi Regem solummodo et communes*]" (3:305).

Walsingham's ideal of 1376 appears here in a parodically inverted
form, and the resemblance is the source of his outrage. His discourse of
a *communitas*, which lauds secular lordship as supported simultaneously
by divine inspiration and representation of the common people, has
been usurped by rebels who claim it with unprecedented energy and
emphasis, and with their own historical arguments for its legitimacy. It
is precisely because their ideal is in competition with his own that Walsingham misses no opportunity to declare that the form it takes in their
mouths and hands is diabolical and depraved. Their view, as he rehearses
it, elides intermediary lords, "according to their own stupid judgment,
except only the king and the commons": not a naive assessment of their
agenda, evidently, since they both rely on the pardon from King Richard
(to their own destruction) and bend all their efforts at St. Albans on se-
curing a "certain charter among the monastery's ancient liberties" issued,
they claim, by King Offa in the seventh century to all the laborers who
built the monastery, whose descendents they claim to be, but hidden
away in the monastery's muniments (3:311). This endeavor "to recuperate an unrecuperable charter" (3:311) was not new in 1381, and Walsingham and other St. Albans's writers had recorded stages of its endeavor
(Faith, "Class Struggle," and Galloway, "Making," 31–39). But like Walsingham, they espouse an ideal of representation, as Walsingham clearly
shows he realizes, even emphasizing it in the account of their breaking
up confiscated mill-stones and distributing them to all the tenants "like
pieces of the consecrated Host" (*Gesta Abbatum*, 3:309), and the account

of their hideous, diabolic cry "which the Londoners taught them in de-capitating the archbishop [Simon Sudbury]" (3:304). In his view mere imitation and specious commemoration are their mode of political rep-resentation, thus they lack any guarantee of righteousness in what they represent. But it is a fine line between the principle of communal repre-sentation they espouse in 1381 and that which he espoused in 1376.

In general terms, Walsingham moves much further than Higden along the general trajectory of monastic writers in the later fourteenth and fifteenth centuries who positioned themselves progressively closer to secular power, Lydgate being the best known to literary scholars (see Cannon, "Productions," 340–48). Higden's journey to Edward III's coun-cil perhaps marks an important moment in this trend. But Walsingham pays a heavier ideological price for intimacy with and adulation for sec-ular power than did Higden, in the inconsistencies and paradoxes lurk-ing in his vision of English secular community. Walsingham's horror of both Gaunt's and the St. Albans's rebels' elision of intermediary "lords" between laborers and king displays (like Higden's concern with *varietas*) a nervous affirmation of the unstable and increasingly fine caste grada-tions typical for the period, but this is incoherently joined to his equal insistence on an ideal of a perfectly transparent representation of the good of the community of the realm, and an unpredictable divine plan for the leadership of the true, secular English community. In theory, the elaborate secular hierarchy he persistently supports would be subject to flux and reorganization depending on wherever the divine efflatus hap-pened to breathe forth, and from wherever the true pope of the lay com-munity might be called. In practice, a principle that appears redemptive in one instance becomes demonic in another. If in 1376 a divinely in-spired representative politics unsettling the hierarchy was good, in 1381 a claim to representative politics was sheer horror. If in 1376 exclusive reliance on hierarchical power was monstrous, in 1381 such reliance was almost the only hope for Walsingham's and many other institutions whose tenents found an opportunity to rebel. If in 1376 the plebs legiti-mated the knights who legitimated Peter de la Mare, in 1381 Thomas de la Mare was besieged by a plebian rabble of the "true commons" acting and speaking on their own behalf. The demons generated by Walsing-ham's own ideology of a rigidly hierarchical yet divinely inspired and representationalist Latin England—the fear that anyone could be cho-sen by God to represent the best interests of the people, but the equal if irreconcilable fear that the strength and authority of hierarchy might allow any Herod to come along—create energies and tensions that contribute all the more to the problem and the obsessive interest of secular national power.

These inconsistencies and tensions are expelled in Walsingham's narrative in the form of satire, but they leave him standing centrally within a new arena of secular nationalism, for which he is the most paradoxical but also most articulate spokesman. The rebellious peasants, who by the principle of unpredictable divine inspiration might claim a vision of reformation no less legitimately than the knights of the Good Parliament, are ridiculed as provincial sad-sacks and fools; Gaunt, who by the principle of hierarchy might claim legitimate power in the parliamentary conflict, is savaged as a would-be Herod unable even to convince his retainers of his legitimacy. The terms of the satire, and the underlying conflicts it derives from, emphasize the secular English community as the focus of all his historical fascination and his narrative energy and craft.

In his last writings, Walsingham pursues this goal on a still larger scale, and indeed with a larger map of "England." Rather than premising his national history on and structuring it by the successive conquests of England—and its successive degeneration—like Higden, Walsingham in his final years exalted the English re-conquest of Normandy, or "Neustria," as he persistently calls it in both his late continuation of the *Chronica Majora* in Oxford, Bodleian Library, Bodley MS 462 and the *Ypodigma Neustrie* that he dedicated to Henry V, using a name for Normandy from Geoffrey of Monmouth's founding Arthurocentric history, the *Historia regum Britanniae* (e.g., 9.12: "Neustria nunc vocata Normannia"). The eccentricity of Walsingham's re-naming of Normandy in these late writings can be registered by noting that even *Brut* continuations, based on Geoffrey of Monmouth, call it Normandy. It is as if Walsingham were aggressively antiquating Normandy in order to find in ancient English nationhood some resolution to the questions about the legitimacy, structure, and meaning of secular national community in which his other narratives engage him. For he addresses aggressively the fundamental problems of any notion of the secular nation in the later Middle Ages: a nervously maintained secular hierarchy; an uncertain status and uncertain intentions of the "true" national community; an unprovable claim to extension into France; and an unknowable presence of divine control

throughout these crucial national issues of representation, social organization, and territorial scope.

Walsingham's fullest development of the promise of Neustria for
settling these matters is found in his last portion of the *Cronica Majora,*
(printed now as *The St. Albans Chronicle*), especially with the Battle of
Agincourt. Here a royal figure, Henry V, at last allows Walsingham to
endow secular history with a structure of redemptive rather than degen-
erative typology, and with the king's direct representation of lower social
realms in a way that does not threaten any of the intermediary hierarchy.
Here at last Walsingham can shift from satirist to heroic bard, weaving
fragments of Statius, Lucan, Virgil, and other heroic Latin verse into a
prose that outdoes all further eulogies of Agincourt's muddy field:

> But therefore first the thundering steeds of the French were
> transfixed by arrows, the riders, whipping the reigns around,
> rushed headlong into their own ranks, and all the knights who
> had escaped the battlefield gave ground. Whereupon as the
> armies clashed, an enormous din of our men ascends to the
> stars and the vast air is, so to speak, filled up by cries. Then
> again fly from every side clouds of missiles, and metal resounds
> on metal while arrows, continually sent forth, pelt helmets,
> plate armor, and corselets. Accordingly, hords of the French fall,
> riddled with arrows, on one side fifty, on another sixty. The king
> himself, displaying the roles not only of king but also soldier,
> flies first into the enemy, inflicts and receives cruel blows, offer-
> ing to his followers powerful examples of boldness in his own
> person, by dissipating the opposing ranks with an unsheathed
> axe. Nor otherwise did the soldierly men, emulating the king's
> deeds, labor together with all their powers to level with their
> blades that opposing forest of screaming Frenchmen, until fi-
> nally with a path having been created by force, the French did
> not so much give ground as drop dead. And truly the French,
> when they perceived those they had considered unconquerable
> lying in the fray of battle, soon "Their hearts were dazed, and a
> cold shudder ran through / their innermost marrow" [*Aeneid,*
> 2:120–22], such that motionless and senseless they stood while
> our men wrenched their weapons from their hands and sent
> them falling to the ground with the others like beasts. "Unlim-

ited slaughter followed, and nothing like resistance occurred, but rather throats are offered up to the battle: nor are our men strong enough to lay low as many as are able to die on the enemy side" [cf. Lucan, *Bellum civile*, 7.532–33]. Thus all the glory of the French perished by the hands of a few whom they had scorned just a little while earlier.[34]

Walsingham's account, while less detailed than some others (like the eye-witness account in the *Gesta Henrici Quinti*), is independent of the main contemporary narratives of Agincourt and relies on what has been judged "good second-hand information" (*Gesta Henrici Quinti*, xxxv). Its importance, however, is not its details but how it exceeds any other account in supercharging the event with a combination of emphatic hierarchy yet perfect social representation, and a sense of historical redemption. Its portrayal of the English king is one who both represents the force of divine history and allows his royal identity to be subsumed into that of an exemplary soldier, thus socially representative in a unidirectional way that invokes the ideal of 1376 but protects it from the nightmare of 1381. Typology and historical parallel enrich the scope and the violence of the event: Agincourt as antique Roman battle; the new English claim as a realization of its ancient possession of Neustria; the contemporary Benedictine as classical poet-historian. The gaps and slippage between these representations and parallels—and the troubling way in which using Virgil, Lucan, and especially the dubious history of Geoffrey of Monmouth to define the bloody English seizure of territory closely resembles what the St. Albans tenants did with their territorial myth of Offa—are potential anxieties that seem merely to incite the narrative to further hyperbole. As often, Walsingham's engagement with yet evasion of his ideological demons elevates the boundaries of the secular nation into a new religious kingdom, a new city of God, just as it is also potentially a new city of the plains. Thus his account of Agincourt portrays total slaughter of the stunned, passive French in the course of the battle (rather than only a particular if large contingent, and rather than the killing of the prisoners ordered by Henry V, as eye-witness accounts report) as if to suppress, by overemphasizing the successful and divinely authorized outcome, the dubious legitimacy of the territory and ideal of community thus offered.

This is simultaneously an expansion of English national claims to community and territory beyond any previous limits, and of Walsingham's own writerly authority beyond any traditional monastic ideology. It requires continual exclusion of communities that might generate local political representives from below; but it maintains a claim to its own capaciously representational status of the nation as a whole, ancient past and pregnant present. It is finally an outlook that identifies Walsingham's historical perspective with that of the imperialist king claiming a new world on the grounds of mythic right. Such an identification of a monk with secular imperialism on such dubious historical grounds (he had only to read Higden on Brutus or Arthur) risks an utter emptying of legitimacy from both national community and writerly vocation. But Walsingham's simultaneous definitions of vast English community and his own deep historical authority are sharpened rather than blurred by these threats of bad faith, which Walsingham spent a career risking and fending off. His final words in his chronicle offer his most triumphant claims to national ideology, if also his most defensive, sharing in the nervousness of the king surveying his new and ancient territory:

> Our most glorious king solemnly celebrated the birth of the Lord in a certain very well fortified spot, which is called the fortress or castle of St. Anthony; this location rises up from one side of the city in a wall both subtly and solidly crafted, overlooking the town, such that whatever rulers take this position, they may easily repress all citizens from rebellion.[35]

This final paragraph in Bodley MS 462 on Henry's celebration of Christmas at Paris in 1420, perhaps the last paragraph of English history Walsingham wrote, positions the king at a high vantage-point looking back over all of Paris, sweeping his gaze over France back toward England in order to encompass the full territory of his new realm. But it is also a perspective framed by and literally constructed against the danger of rebellion by citizens, whose local loyalties speak to a level of representation and sub-groups against which any more abstract notion of national representation rings hollow and oppressive. Satire has no place in Walsingham's last writings. Yet in the midst of epic imperialism, the anxiety of rebellion figures large, just as in the midst of all his affirmations of his visions of English secular community his doubts and paradoxes remain to assail him, not soluble by his simply embracing the royal position any more than by his cutting out the leaves presenting his account of 1376.

Late medieval Latin monastic historians faced more than one paradox. To maintain their literary and historical authority they needed to commit their energies to defining an English secular community, yet this commitment resisted and undermined the authority that the monastic tradition embodied. When they seized this challenge directly, as they did from the mid-fourteenth through the early fifteenth century, they contributed to the most emphatically "nationalist" period of pre-Reformation England—if with nationalist visions fraught with self-contradictions. But these contradictions in turn served to involve their work and their writerly vocations the more deeply with such national visions. Just as Higden's fascination with a dangerous *varietas* that his own endeavor resembles etches the boundaries and the importance of the secular nation more deeply, so Walsingham's ideological paradoxes reflect but also contribute to the engulfing narrative and intellectual obsession with defining a sanctified secular nation. When monastic chroniclers after Walsingham retreated from this challenge, nationalist formulations in many spheres withered, until the Reformation gave them a new impetus. It is not a simple path for the monastic chroniclers to follow or us to appreciate. By engaging intractable problems in ideals of secular English community as well as in their own relationship to that community, Higden and Walsingham committed the resources of Latin monastic historiography to an ultimately self-destructive trajectory. In doing so, they enriched the definition of secular nationalism to a degree that vernacular and secular culture alone could never have accomplished, and to which that culture was more profoundly indebted than has perhaps ever since been adequately acknowledged.[36]

NOTES

1. Many of those further "chapters" appear in a pan-European form in Allmand, *Cambridge Medieval History*; others are in the excellent collections of Smyth, ed., *Medieval Europeans*, and Forde, Johnson, and Murray, eds., *Concepts*.

2. Gellrich, *Discourse*, 134–50; see my review. Study of earlier chronicles in "literary" or narratological terms has yielded significant results as well: see especially Otter, *Inventiones*, and Spiegel, *Romancing* (I discuss the latter in "Narratology").

3. On such royal interest, see (for Edward I) Clanchy, *Memory*, 152–54; for Edward III's summoning of Higden to his council, see Edwards, "Ranulph."

4. Bale's *Index* lists five of Wyclif's works "ex additionibus polychronici" (267–70), and numerous citations to the *Polychronicon* can be found in the works of the Oxford Lollards and other Lollards: see Talbert, "Chronicle," 173 and n. 48, Edwards, "Influence," 114, Embree, *Chronicles*, 223–44. Another vernacular Lollard compilation, called the *Floretum* or the *Rosarium Theologie*, uses Higden for an account of the origin of tithes (Hudson, "Lollard Compilation," 73).

5. Walsingham's phrase "rustic tragedy" comes from his *Ypodigma Neustriae*, 335. For discussion of it, see Justice, *Writing*, 203–04. However, I do not hold with Justice's views that "Walsingham became a historian only in response to 1381" (202) or that Walsingham was largely oblivious of the strategic efforts and perspectives of the rebels he describes; for discussion, see Galloway, "Making," 31–39.

6. On the long odds against the wide dissemination of Trevisa's work if his patron Thomas, Lord Berkeley, had not sponsored it in London, see Hanna, "Sir Thomas Berkeley," esp. 910, 912.

7. References to Higden are to the Rolls Series edition by volume and page; the text printed there is checked throughout against Higden's autograph manuscript, San Marino, CA, Huntington Library MS HM 132 (see Galbraith, "Autograph Manuscript"). Generally the differences are slight, and thus quotation is typically made from the Rolls Series edition; when readings from the manuscript are used, additional folia references are given. Citations of Trevisa are also given to the Rolls Series edition but the text is quoted entirely from the superior manuscript, London, British Library, Cotton MS Tiberius D VII, with all contractions expanded, modern punctuation added, and (as here) the folia noted after the Rolls Series citations; on this manuscript, see Waldron, "Manuscripts," 281–317, esp. 308. I thank The Huntington Library for permission to quote and reproduce a leaf from HM MS 132, and the British Library for permission to quote from BL Cotton MS D VII. All translations of Latin writers into modern English unless noted are mine, including Higden, since Trevisa's translation does not always present the literal sense of the Latin with which I am concerned.

8. Holkot, *Super Sapientiam Salamonis*, cap. I, lec. x; see Smalley, *English Friars*, 162–63, and Galbraith, "Nationality," 121–27.

9. "Post praeclaros artium scriptores, quibus circa rerum notitiam aut morum modestiam dulce fuit, quo adviverent, insudare, illi merito, velut utile dulci commiscentes, grandisonis sunt praeconiis attollendi, qui magnifica priscorum gesta beneficio scripturae posteris derivarunt" (1:2).

10. Vincent of Beauvais, *Speculum Maius*. For a discussion of this aspect of Vincent's work, see Minnis, "Discussions," esp. 389.

11. For discussion of Trevisa's translation of Bartholomeus, see Lawler, "Properties."

12. For some examples among later Latin writers, see Gransden, "Silent Meanings," 234; among vernacular writers, only Thomas Usk has been shown to have used the acrostic device: see Skeat, "Thomas Usk."

13. "Ubi praesens chronica fuit elaborata, sicut per capitales hujus primi libri apices clarius patet" (2:76–77).

14. "Ideoque non magno opere laborasse dicta philosophorum ad concordiam redigere, sed quantum de unaquaque re quilibet eorum senserit, aut scripserit, recitare" (Vincent of Beauvais, *Speculum Maius*, Gen. Prol., cap viii).

15. Some discussion of this term is provided by Quirk, "Langland's Use," Davlin, "*Kynde Knowyng*," and Harwood, "Langland's *Kynde Wit*." The equation to a distinctively vernacular mode of knowledge is my suggestion.

16. For the first statement, see Gerald of Wales, *Topographia Hibernica*, dist. I, cap. 6, p. 29; the second is in John Ridevall's commentary on the *Civitate Dei*, which Taylor believes Higden to have used for this point (*Universal Chronicle*, 77).

17. See Ghellinck, "*Originale*," Trapp, "Augustinian Theology," and Minnis, "'Authorial Intention.'"

18. "Ceterum de isto Arthuro, quem inter omnes chronographos solus Gaufridius sic extollit, mirantur multi quomodo veritatem sapere possint quae de eo praedicantur, pro eo quod si Arthurus, sicut scribit Gaufridus, terdena regna acquisivit, si regem Francorum subjugavit, si Lucium procuratorem reipublicae apud Italiam interfecit, cur omnes historici Romani, Franci, Saxonici tot insignia de tanto viro omiserunt, qui de minoribus viris tot minora retulerunt" (5:332–34).

19. The sense of *genus* as "gender," a sense Trevisa wholly misses or avoids (he renders it "of what degree"), is common from classical times in grammatical contexts especially (see *Oxford Latin Dictionary*, s.v. 8a) and is here reinforced by *neuter* ("neither"), a word applicable to "social degree" only if a binary social scheme is assumed (viz., "clerical/lay"). Yet just above Higden has used *genus* as "social type," so the word appears to shift in sense in the passage.

20. Shakespeare, *Hamlet*, I.iv.17–39. The passage is found only in the Second Quarto and its presence has often perplexed scholars.

21. Knighton, *Chronicle*, 508–09. For the suggestion that this passage may represent some contact with the lost preamble to the Statute of Laborers reissued at Cambridge in 1388 (which Knighton goes on to quote), see Galloway, "Making," 30 n. 42; in any case the resemblence to Higden is striking.

22. "In historico namque contextu chronographorum nobis diligentia delagato relucet clarius norma morum, forma vivendi, probitatis incentivum, trivium quoque theologicarum virtutum et quadrivium cardinalium trabearum, quorum notitiam aprehendere seu vestigium imitari *nostra* modicitas non sufficeret, nisi sollicitudo scriptorum *nostrae* transfunderet imperitiae memoriam transactorum"; emphasis added (1:4).

23. "Forma vivendi, probitatis incentivum, theologicarum virtutum norma, et quadrivium cardinalium trabearum *mihi* hebeti saporem non reddit, quia minus idoneus et insufficiens"; emphasis added (1:1).

24. Knowles (*Religious Orders*, 64–65, 97–101) still offers a useful beginning point for studying these developments. Some particulars of the defensive atmosphere of late medieval chroniclers at Westminster Abbey are given briefly but evocatively in Harvey, *Westminster Abbey*, 12–18. Further contexts for the debate are provided by Aston, "'Caim's Castles,'" and Kerby-Fulton, *Apocalypticism*, 172–77.

25. "Horum nempe merito provocatus et exemplo, non mea jactanter jaculans nec aliena joculanter jugulans, decrevi, ut potui, geniale solum meum profusioribus extollere laudum titulis, ac sic tractatum aliquem, ex variis auctorum decerptum laboribus, de statu insulae Britannicae ad notitiam cudere futurorum" (1:6).

26. At least three other likely uses of Higden by Chaucer are described, cumulatively, in Dwyer, "Some Readers," Galloway, "Chaucer's *Legend*," and Galloway, "Authority." The cumulative evidence is very strong for Chaucer's close knowledge of Higden, probably by way of Trevisa's translation, as the verbal echoes in the present instance suggest.

27. Identified by Alford, *Piers Plowman*, 61; see Higden 2:170, from the passage on *varietas* discussed above.

28. On Langland's persona and its representativeness, see Middleton, "'Kynde Name'"; Galloway, "Making," 28–31.

29. "Auro sapientia designatur vobis collata, qua indagare possitis reformanda et exprimere gratiosius in conspectu principum hujus regni" (*Chronicon Angliae*, 71).

30. *Gesta Abbatum*, 3:309; see Justice, *Writing*, 169; and cf. Galloway, "Making," 36–38, where I discuss Walsingham's presentation of this scene, opposing Justice's reading of it as merely the chronicler's unwitting reportage.

31. The main branch of the de la Mare family held lands in Wiltshire, Oxfordshire, Gloucestershire, and Hertfordshire, where St. Albans is located; many of their members had the name "Thomas," both points suggesting that this was the abbot's family. However, this branch was different from Peter de la Mare's family whose holdings were in Herefordshire; see Roskell, Clark, and Rawcliffe, *History*, 3:686–87.

32. "'Quid,' inquit 'isti degeneres et sepium milites moliuntur? Num putant ese terrae istius reges sive principes; vel unde eis tantus tumor et superbia? Puto cujus sum potestatis ignorant. Ego itigur summo mane eis tam gloriosus apparebo, et tantam inter illos excitabo potentiam, et eos tanta severitate terebo, quod nec ipsi nec illis similes audebunt majestatem meam de cetero lacessere.' Taliter glorianti et vana sibimet pollicenti quidam ex suis armigeris dicitur respondisse: 'Domine,' ait, 'non latet vestram magnificentiam quibus et quantis auxiliis isti milites, non plebei, ut asseruistis, sed armipotentes et strenui, fulciuntur. Namque favorem obtinent dominorum, et in primis domini Edwardi principis, fratris vestri, qui illis consilium impendit efficax et juvamen. Londonienses etiam omnes et singuli et commune vulgus tantum penes eos afficiuntur, quod non permitterent eos vel probris praegravari vel minima injuria molestari. Set et ipsi milites, accepta cotumelia, cogantur contra personam vestram et amicorum vestrorum cuncta extrema moliri, quae forsitan alias minime molirentur'" (*Chronicon Angliae*, 74–75).

33. "Supradicti igitur milites comitatuum, ex parte communitatis, per os domini Petri de la Mare, petierunt ut dux et sui conjudices apponerent correctionis remedium tantis ejus excessibus" (ibid., 96–97).

34. "At ergo primum sonipedes [Gallorum] ferro transfixi sunt, sessores, conversis fresis, in sua agmina precipites corruere, omnesque equites qui evaserant campo cessere. Exhinc ut acies convenere ingens nostratum clamor ad sidera tollitur et impletur quodam modo vocibus vastis aer. Tunc iterato volat undique telorum nubes, et ferrum ferro sonat dum iacula constanter emissa cassides feriunt, laminas et loricas. Cadunt proinde plurimi de Gallis sagittis terebrati, hinc quinquageni, hinc pariter sexageni. Rex ipse, non tantum

regis, quantum militis, exponendo vices, primus in hostes advolat, crudeles ictus infert et recipit, exempla suis audendi forcia prebens in persona sua, stricto securi oppositas acies dissipando. Nec secus militares viri emulantes acta regia totis viribus collaboraverunt oppositam illam silvam Francorum fremencium ferro prosternere, donec tandem via vi facta, Galli non tantum cessere quantum mortui cecidere. Et revera Galli, cum prostratos in acie beli cernerent quos autumabant insuperabiles, eorum mox

> Obstupuere animi; gelidusque per yma cucurrit
> ossa tremor

tantum ut immobiles et sine sensu starent dum nostri secures ab eorum extorquerent manibus et eos velut pecudes prosternerent cum eisdem. Perdidit inde modum cedes et velut nulla secuta est pugna. Sed iugulis bellum geritus nec valent nostrates tot prosternere quot possunt perire de adversa parte. Sic ergo Francie perijt omne decus per manus paucorum quos despectui habuit parum ante" (Walsingham, *St. Alban's Chronicle*, 95–96).

35. "Inclitissimus rex noster natale domini Parisius solemniter celebravit in quodam loco munitissimo quod municipium seu castrum sancti Antonii appellatum est: erigitur idem locus ex uno latere civitatis in muro subtili pariter et solidissimo artificio tantam villam prospectans ita ut qui in eo loco principatum suscipiunt leviter cives omnes a rebellionibus poterunt cohibere" (ibid., 126).

36. Two forthcoming essays, brought late to my attention, suggest that attention to pertinent aspects of this question is increasing on several fronts: see Beal, "Mapping Identity," and Larkin, "Suggested Author."

REFERENCES

Alford, John A. *Piers Plowman: A Guide to the Quotations*. Binghamton, NY: Medieval and Renaissance Texts and Studies, 1992.

Allmand, Christopher, ed. *The New Cambridge Medieval History*. Vol. 7, *c. 1415–c. 1500*. Cambridge: Cambridge University Press, 1998.

Anderson, Benedict. *Imagined Communities: Reflections on the Origin and Spread of Nationalism*. Rev. ed. London and New York: Verso, 1991.

Aston, Margaret. "'Caim's Castles': Poverty, Politics, and Disendowment." In *The Church, Politics, and Patronage in the Fifteenth Century*, ed. Barrie Dobson, 45–81. Gloucester: Sutton, 1984.

Baldwin, Frances Elizabeth. *Sumptuary Legislation and Personal Regulation in England*. Baltimore: n.p., 1926.

Bale, John. *Index Britanniae Scriptorum*. Ed. R. L. Poole and Mary Bateson. Oxford: Oxford University Press, 1902.

Beal, Jane. "Mapping Identity in John Trevisa's English *Polychronicon*: Chester, Cornwall, and the Translation of English National History." In *Fourteenth-Century England*, vol. 3, ed. William Mark Ormrod. Woodbridge: Boydell and Brewer, forthcoming.

Bede. *Ecclesiastical History of the English People*. Ed. Betram Colgrave and R. A. B. Mynors. Oxford: Clarendon Press, 1969

Brown, Peter. "Higden's Britain." In *Medieval Europeans*, ed. Smyth, 103–18.

Burne, R. V. H. *The Monks of Chester: The History of St. Werburgh's Abbey.* London: SPCK, 1962.

Cannon, Christopher. "Monastic Productions." In *Cambridge History,* ed. Wallace, 316–48.

Caplan, Harry. *Medieval Artes Praedicandi: A Hand-List.* Cornell University Studies in Classical Philology 24. Ithaca: Cornell University Press, 1934.

Chaucer, Geoffrey. *The Riverside Chaucer.* 3rd ed. Ed. Larry D. Benson et al. Boston: Houghton Mifflin, 1987.

Clanchy, M. T. *From Memory to Written Record: England 1066–1307.* 2d ed. Oxford: Blackwell Publishers, 1993.

Clark, James G. "Thomas Walsingham Reconsidered: Books and Learning at Late-Medieval St. Albans." *Speculum* 77 (2002): 832–60.

Danbury, Elizabeth. "English and French Artistic Propaganda during the Period of the Hundred Years War: Some Evidence from Royal Charters." In *Power, Culture, and Religion in France, c. 1350–c. 1550,* ed. Christopher Allmand, 75–97. Woodbridge: Boydell Press, 1989.

Davlin, Mary Clemente. "*Kynde Knowyng* as a Major Theme in *Piers Plowman* B." *Review of English Studies,* n.s., 22 (1971): 1–19.

Dunn, F. I. *The Ancient Parishes, Townships and Chapelries of Chesire.* Chester: Cheshire Record Office and Chester Diocesan Record Office, 1987.

Dwyer, R. A. "Some Readers of John Trevisa." *Notes and Queries* 202 (1967): 291–92.

Edwards, A. S. G. "The Influence and Audience of the *Polychronicon:* Some Observations." *Proceedings of the Leeds Philosophical and Literary Society: Literary and Historical Section* 17, pt. 6 (1980): 113–19.

Edwards, J. G. "Ranulf, Monk of Chester." *English Historical Review* 47 (1932): 94.

Embree, Dan, ed. *The Chronicles of Rome: The Chronicle of Popes and Emperors and the Lollard Chronicle.* Woodbridge: Boydell Press, 1999.

Eulogium historiarum sive temporis. Ed. Frank Scott Haydon. 3 vols. Rolls Series 9. London: Her Majesty's Stationery Office, 1858.

Faith, Rosamond. "The Class Struggle in Fourteenth-Century England." In *People's History and Socialist Theory,* ed. Raphael Samuel, 50–60. London, Boston, and Henley: Routledge and Kegan Paul, 1981.

Forde, Simon, Lesley Johnson, and Alan V. Murray, eds. *Concepts of National Identity in the Middle Ages.* Leeds Texts and Monographs 14. Leeds: University of Leeds Press, 1995.

Galbraith, V. H. "Nationality and Language in Medieval England." *Transactions of the Royal Historical Society,* 4th series, 23 (1941): 113–29.

———. "An Autograph Manuscript of Ranulph Higden's *Polychronicon*." *The Huntington Library Quarterly* 23 (1959): 1–18.

Galloway, Andrew. "Chaucer's *Legend of Lucrece* and the Critique of Ideology in the Fourteenth Century." *English Literary History* 60 (1993): 813–32.

———. "Narratology and the Pursuit of Context: Three Recent Studies of Medieval Narrative." *Humanistica* 21 (1994): 111–26.

———. Review of Jesse Gellrich, *Discourse and Dominion in the Fourteenth Century: Oral Contexts of Writing in Philosophy, Politics, and Poetry. Studies in the Age of Chaucer* 18 (1996): 213–22.

————. "Writing History in England." In *Cambridge History*, ed. Wallace, 255–83.

————. "Authority." In *Blackwell Companion to Chaucer*, ed. Peter Brown, 23–39. Oxford: Blackwell Publishers, 2000.

————. "Making History Legal: *Piers Plowman* and the Rebels of Fourteenth-Century England." In *William Langland's "Piers Plowman": A Book of Essays*, ed. Kathleen Hewett-Smith, 7–39. New York and London: Routledge Press, 2001.

————. "The Literature of 1388 and the Politics of Pity in Gower's *Confessio Amantis*." In *The Letter of the Law: Legal Practice and Literary Production in Medieval England*, ed. Emily Steiner and Candace Barrington, 67–104. Ithaca: Cornell University Press, 2002.

————. "Clothing and Fashion." In *The Chaucer Encyclopedia*. Norman: University of Oklahoma Press, forthcoming.

Gellrich, Jesse. *Discourse and Dominion in the Fourteenth Century: Oral Contexts of Writing in Philosophy, Politics, and Poetry*. Princeton: Princeton University Press, 1995.

Geoffrey of Monmouth. *The History of the Kings of Britain*. Trans. Lewis Thorpe. London: Penguin Books, 1966.

————. *Historia regum Britannie*. Ed. Neil Wright. Cambridge: D. S. Brewer, 1985.

Gerald of Wales. *Topographia Hibernica*. Ed. James F. Dimock. Rolls Series 21.5. London: Longman, 1867.

Gesta Henrici Quinti: The Deeds of Henry the Fifth. Ed. and trans. Frank Taylor and John S. Roskell. Oxford: Clarendon Press, 1975.

Ghellinck, J. de. "*Originale* et *Originalia*." *Bulletin du Cange* 14 (1939): 95–105.

Gransden, Antonia. "Silent Meanings in Ranulf Higden's *Polychronicon* and in Thomas Elmham's *Liber Metricus de Henrico Quinto*." *Medium Ævum* 46 (1976): 231–40

Gray, Sir Thomas. *Scalacronica: A Chronicle of England and Scotland From A.D. MLXVI to A.D. MCCCLXII*. Ed. Joseph Stevenson. Edinburgh: Maitland Club, 1836.

Hanna, Ralph. "Sir Thomas Berkeley and His Patronage." *Speculum* 64 (1989): 878–916.

————. "*Compilatio* and the Wife of Bath: Latin Backgrounds, Ricardian Texts." In *Pursuing History: Middle English Manuscripts and Their Texts*, 247–57. Stanford: Stanford University Press, 1996.

Harvey, Barbara. *Westminister Abbey and Its Estates in the Middle Ages*. Oxford: Clarendon Press, 1977.

Harwood, Britton J. "Langland's *Kynde Wit*." *Journal of English and Germanic Philology* 75 (1976): 330–36.

Henry, Archdeacon of Huntingdon. *Historia Anglorum (History of the English People)*. Ed. and trans. Diana Greenway. Oxford: Clarendon Press, 1996.

Heywood, Thomas. *The Rape of Lucrece*. Ed. Allan Holaday. Illinois Studies in Language and Literature 34, no. 3 Urbana: The University of Illinois Press, 1950.

Higden, Ranulph. *Polychronicon, together with the English Translations of John Trevisa and of an Unknown Writer of the Fifteenth Century*. Ed. Churchill Babington and Joseph Lumby. 9 vols. Rolls Series 41. London: Her Majesty's Stationery Office, 1865–86.

Holkot, Robert. *Super Sapientiam Salomonis*. Basil: Johannes Amerbach, 1489.

Holmes, George. *The Good Parliament*. Oxford: Clarendon Press, 1975.

Horstmann, Carl, ed. "*Mappula Angliae* von Osbern Bokenham." *Englische Studien* 10 (1887): 1–34.

Hudson, Anne. "A Lollard Compilation and the Dissemination of Wycliffite Thought." *Journal of Theological Studies*, n.s., 23 (1972): 65–81.

———. "A Lollard Sect Vocabulary?" In *So meny people longages and tonges: Philological Essays in Scots and Mediaeval English Presented to Angus McIntosh*, ed. Michael Benskin and M. L. Samuels, 15–30. Edinburgh: M. Benskin and M. L. Samuels, 1981.

Jacob, E. F. "Verborum florida venustas: Some Early Examples of Euphuism in England." *Bulletin of the John Rylands Library* 17 (1933): 264–90. Reprinted in his *Essays in the Conciliar Epoch*, 2d ed., 185–206. Mancester: Manchester University Press, 1953.

Jennings, Margaret. "Monks and the 'Artes Praedicandi' in the Time of Ranulph Higden." *Revue Bénédictine* 86 (1976): 119–28.

———. *The Ars Componendi Sermones of Ranulph Higden OSB*. Leiden: E. J. Brill, 1991.

John of Salisbury. *Opera. Patrologia Latina*, ed. J.-P. Migne, vol. 199. Paris: J.-P. Migne, 1844–64.

Justice, Steven. *Writing and Rebellion: England in 1381*. Berkeley and Los Angeles: University of California Press, 1994.

Kerby-Fulton, Kathryn. *Reformist Apocalypticism and "Piers Plowman."* Cambridge: Cambridge University Press, 1990.

Knighton, Henry. *Knighton's Chronicle, 1337–1396*. Ed. and trans. G. H. Martin. Oxford: Clarendon Press, 1995.

Knowles, David. *The Religious Orders in England*. Vol. 2, *The End of the Middle Ages*. Cambridge: Cambridge University Press, 1955; reprint, 1979.

Langland, William. *Piers Plowman: The A Version*. Ed. George Kane. Rev. ed. London: Athlone Press; Berkeley and Los Angeles: University of California Press, 1988.

Larkin, Peter A. "A Suggested Author for *De ortu Waluuanii* and *Historia Meriadoci*." *Journal of English and Germanic Philology*, forthcoming.

Lavezzo, Kathryn. "Angels on the Edge of the World: The Geography of English Identity from Ælfric to Chaucer." Ph. D. diss., University of California, Santa Barbara, 1999.

Lawler, Traugott. "On the Properties of John Trevisa's Major Translations." *Viator: Medieval and Renaissance Studies* 14 (1983): 267–88.

Martinus Polonus. *Chronicon*. Ed. Ludwig Weiland. *Monumenta Germaniae Historica*, Scriptores 22. Hannover: Hahn, 1872.

Middleton, Anne. "The Idea of Public Poetry in the Reign of Richard II." *Speculum* 53 (1978): 94–114.

———. "The Audience and Public of *Piers Plowman*." In *Middle English Alliterative Poetry and Its Literary Background*, ed. David Lawton, 101–23; 147–54. Cambridge: D. S. Brewer, 1982.

———. "William Langland's 'Kynde Name': Authorial Signature and Social Identity in Late Fourteenth-Century England" In *Literary Practice and Social Change in Britain, 1380–1530*, ed. Lee Patterson, 15–82. Berkeley and Los Angeles: University of California Press, 1990.

Minnis, A. J. "'Authorial Intention' and 'Literal Sense' in the Exegetical Theories of Richard Fitzralph and John Wyclif: An Essay in the Medieval History of Biblical Hermeneutics." *Proceedings of the Royal Irish Academy* 75C (1975): 1–31.

————. "Late-Medieval Discussions of *Compilatio* and the Role of the *Compilator*." *Beiträge zur Geschichte der deutschen Sprache und Literatur* 101 (1979): 385–421.

Murphy, James J., ed. and trans. *Three Medieval Rhetorical Arts*. Berkeley: University of California Press, 1971.

Newton, Stella Mary. *Fashion in the Age of the Black Prince*. Suffolk: Boydell Press, 1980.

North, J. D. *Chaucer's Universe*. Oxford: Clarendon Press, 1988.

Otter, Monika. *Inventiones: Fiction and Referentiality in Twelfth-Century English Historical Writing*. Chapel Hill and London: University of North Carolina Press, 1996.

Oxford Latin Dictionary. Ed. P. G. W. Glare. Oxford: Clarendon Press, 1982.

Pantin, W. A. *Documents Illustrating the Activities of the General and Provincial Chapters of the English Black Monks, 1215–1540*. Camden Society 47. London: Camden Society, 1933.

————. *The English Church in the Fourteenth Century*. Cambridge: Cambridge University Press, 1955; Toronto: University of Toronto Press, 1980.

Pearsall, Derek. "The Idea of Englishness in the Fifteenth Century." In *Nation, Court and Culture: New Essays on Fifteenth-Century English Poetry*, ed. Helen Cooney, 15–27. Dublin: Four Courts Press, 2001.

Quirk, Randolph. "Langland's Use of *Kind Wit* and *Inwit*." *Journal of English and Germanic Philology* 52 (1953): 182–88.

Roskell, J. S., Linda Clark, and Carole Rawcliffe. *The History of the House of Commons, 1386–1421*. 4 vols. Stroud: Alan Sutton, 1992.

Rotuli Parliamentorum; ut et Petitiones et Placita in Parliamento. Ed. J. Strachey. 7 vols. London: House of Lords, 1767–83.

Shakespeare, William. *Hamlet*. Ed. Harold Jenkins. London: Methuen, 1982; Surrey: Thomas Nelson, 1997.

Skeat, W. W. "Thomas Usk and Ralph Higden." *Notes and Queries*, 10th series, 1 (1904): 245.

Smalley, Beryl. *English Friars and Antiquity in the Early Fourteenth Century*. Oxford: Basil Blackwell, 1960.

Smith, Anthony D. "National Identities: Modern and Medieval?" In *Concepts of National Identity*, ed. Forde, Johnson, and Murray, 21–46.

Smyth, Alfred P., ed. *Medieval Europeans: Studies in Ethnic Identity and National Perspectives in Medieval Europe*. Houndmills and London: Macmillan; New York: St. Martin's, 1998.

Southern, R. W. *Saint Anselm and His Biographer: A Study of Monastic Life and Thought, 1059-c. 1130*. Cambridge: Cambridge University Press, 1963.

Spiegel, Gabrielle. *Romancing the Past: The Rise of Vernacular Prose Historiography in Thirteenth-Century France*. Berkeley and Los Angeles: University of California Press, 1993.

Stow, G. B. "Richard II in Thomas Walsingham's Chronicles." *Speculum* 59 (1984): 68–102.

Swanson, R. N. "Episcopal Visitation of Religious Houses in the Diocese of Lichfield in the Early Fourteenth Century." *Studia Monastica* 29 (1987): 93–108.

Talbert, Ernest William. "A Lollard Chronicle of the Papacy." *Journal of English and Germanic Philology* 41 (1942): 163–93.

Taylor, John. *Universal Chronicle of Ranulf Higden*. Oxford: Oxford University Press, 1966.

————. *English Historical Literature in the Fourteenth Century.* Oxford: Clarendon Press, 1987.

The Towneley Plays. Ed. Martin Stevens and A. C. Cawley. 2 vols. EETS s.s. 13–14. Oxford: Oxford University Press, 1994.

Trapp, D. "Augustinian Theology of the Fourteenth Century: Notes on Editions, Marginalia, Opinions and Book-Lore." *Augustiniana* 6 (1956): 146–274.

Turville-Petre, Thorlac. *England the Nation: Language, Literature, and National Identity, 1290–1340.* Oxford: Clarendon Press, 1996.

Usk, Adam. *The Chronicle of Adam Usk, 1377–1421.* Ed. and trans. C. Given-Wilson. Oxford: Clarendon Press, 1997.

Vincent of Beauvais. *Speculum Maius.* 4 vols. Duacus, 1524. Reprint Graz, Austria: Akademische Druk-u. Verlagenstadt, 1964–65.

Waldron, Ronald. "Trevisa's 'Celtic Complex' Revisited." *Notes and Queries* 36 [234] (1989): 303–07.

————. "The Manuscripts of Trevisa's Translation of the *Polychronicon:* Towards a New Edition." *Modern Language Quarterly* 51 (1990): 281–317.

Wallace, David, ed. *The Cambridge History of Medieval English Literature.* Cambridge: Cambridge University Press, 1999.

Walsingham, Thomas. *Gesta Abbatum Monasterii Sancti Albani.* Ed. Henry Thomas Riley. 3 vols. Rolls Series 28.4. London: Longman, Green, 1867–69.

————. *Chronicon Angliae, 1328–1388.* Ed. Edward Maunde Thompson. Rolls Series 28. London: Longman, 1874.

————. *Ypodigma Neustriae.* Ed. Henry Thomas Riley. Rolls Series 28.7. London: Longman, Green, 1876.

————. *The St. Albans Chronicle, 1406–1420.* Ed. V. H. Galbraith. Oxford: Clarendon Press, 1937.

Woodward, David. "Medieval *Mappaemundi.*" In *The History of Cartography.* Vol. 1, *Cartography in Prehistoric, Ancient, and Medieval Europe and the Mediterranean,* ed. J. B. Harley and David Woodward, 286–370. Chicago and London: University of Chicago Press, 1987.

"As Englishe is comoun langage to oure puple": The Lollards and Their Imagined "English" Community

Jill C. Havens

In her article "Lollardy: The English Heresy?" Anne Hudson argues that Lollardy and its promotion of the English vernacular was not propelled by a "nationalistic" movement: "To attempt to show that the single major heresy known in medieval England arose from a concatenation of peculiarly insular factors would be, I think, a forlorn enterprise. Nor does it seem right to discern nationalism as a major force in the origin of lollardy or in its continuance" (143). Hudson defines "nationalism" here as a catalyst, not an end result. She is right in asserting that nationalism had little to do with the emergence of the Lollard heresy; the reforming fundamentalism of the Lollard movement arose at the end of the fourteenth century because it satisfied groups of laymen and priests who were disillusioned by the corruption of the ecclesiastical hierarchy and the lack of true spiritual guidance provided by the Church.

When this causal relationship put forth by Hudson is reversed, and we consider the Lollard heresy as a possible catalyst or a contributing factor in the emergence of English nationalism at this time, our efforts prove more fruitful. There is evidence in the many vernacular texts produced by the Lollards to suggest that they saw themselves as part of a changing nationalistic perspective in England. But the relationship between Lollardy and English nationalism is far more complex than such a simplistic relationship implies, and many of their ideas about nationalism are deeply entangled with their polemic in texts about church reform.

In contrast to Hudson's conservative stance about the relationship between nationalism and the Lollard heresy, Adrian Hastings argues more strongly for the role of Lollardy in his book *The Construction of Nationhood*—but his approach is equally limited. He argues that an ethnicity or culture develops into a nation at the very moment that culture's language makes the leap from a strictly oral form to a written form, and "is being regularly employed for the production of a literature, and particularly for the translation of the Bible" (12). Though the literature he is thinking about here is particularly relevant to a discussion of the Lollards and their use of the English vernacular, it is disappointing that their translation of the Bible and their advocacy for the vernacular is minimalized by Hastings, especially when their case so strongly supports his theory. He briefly mentions Wyclif and the Bible, and his discussion stresses that its importance "has been unduly played down" (47), but he does little more to bring it to our full attention.[1]

How the Lollards defined their own "Englishness," their sense of themselves as English, is another manifestation of spreading nationalistic sentiment that characterized the decades of the later fourteenth and early fifteenth centuries. An exploration into the Lollard translation debate, witnessed in the Prologue to the Wycliffite Bible, the collection of tracts about translation in Cambridge University Library MS Ii.6.26, and texts and testimonies elsewhere, reveals the Lollard belief in the authority of the vernacular as a sacred language and an awareness of their unique English identity. Though their texts present a Lollard ideal of an "English" identity, by studying their well-established book trade, the expansive and strictly controlled sermon cycles, and the documentary and trial evidence for the existence of actual groups of Lollards throughout England, these ideals are realized.

This evidence in the Lollard texts becomes even more compelling when examined in conjunction with the theories about language and nationalism put forth by Benedict Anderson, in his book *Imagined Communities: Reflections on the Origin and Spread of Nationalism*. Here Anderson demonstrates that literature, especially literature written in the vernacular, creates nationalisms, a sense of a culturally and historically

linked community, when the author imagines his audience and anticipates their expectations of shared experience rooted in shared cultural
and historical identity (37–46).

While Anderson has some compelling arguments that are persua-
sive for a colonial and postcolonial age, the transfer of his theories onto
medieval England is not without its difficulties. I do not propose to argue
here that the Lollards helped to shape English nationalism or that Lollardy was a nationalistic heretical movement similar to the Hussites in
Bohemia. But the language of their texts suggests that the Lollards were
at some level conscious of their role in the emergence of an English nationalism; at the same time, the language of their texts seems reliant
upon a preexistent idea of an English national identity. What I wish to
do here is let the Lollards speak for themselves in the many texts they
produced. The Lollards, through the language of their texts, construct
their own national identity in the way they imagined their religious community: an identity that is defined by its shared heterodox beliefs, its
shared cultural heritage, and its shared use of the English vernacular.

There is no single term used by the Lollards to describe their Englishness, and this makes defining the Lollards' concept of an English
nation problematic; yet, this ambiguity also suggests how varied and
changeable the concept of nationhood was for a medieval people. With a
close examination of a number of Lollard vernacular texts, a "vocabulary
of nationalism" emerges from them, and the expressions the heretics
use, such as "þe pepel of Englond," "we English men," "Englische
nacioun," "oure rewme," "þe comoun pepel," and "þe comountee of
cristyn peple," seem to imply an idea of nation compatible with other
contemporary texts. That Lollards would use this "vocabulary of nationalism" without attention to the connotations such words have seems
unlikely. Their keen sensitivity to the semantic power of words and language is seen in their own adaptation of the vernacular into a "Lollard
idiom," a particular group of expressions that the heretics used to identify themselves and to help them express their beliefs.[2]

Many of the Lollards' texts and testimonies reflect how known individual heretics perceived their community. At the beginning of his written testimony that records his interrogation by the archbishop of Canterbury around 1407, the Lollard heretic William Thorpe discusses the
inspiration for his work:

> And so þanne I, *ymagynynge þe greet desire of þese sondir and*
> *diuerse frendis of sondri placis and cuntrees,* acoordinge alle in
> oon, I occupiede me herwiþ diuerse tymes so bisili [in] my wittis
> þat þoruȝ Goddis grace I perseyued, bi her good mouynge and
> of her cheritable desir, sum profit þat myȝt come of þis writing.
> (Hudson, *Two Wycliffite Texts*, p. 25, lines 41–45, my emphasis)[3]

Supposedly imprisoned at the time, Thorpe found himself physically and
spiritually removed from the company of his fellow Lollards (xlv–liii).[4]
In a way similar to that suggested by Anderson, Thorpe images his audience and its expectations. He shares his experience and boosts the
morale of his followers and supporters by imagining their "desire" for
edification and encouragement. Though some he knew and some he
could only imagine, their shared belief in the goals of a new and radical
doctrine, including the use of the English vernacular, connected them
despite the distance and persecution Thorpe knew only too well. Most
importantly for my argument, Thorpe imagines in his text an audience
made up of Lollards who were "sondir and diuerse frendis" he could
reach through his text despite the faraway "placis and cuntrees" where
they lived. For Thorpe, the many Lollard diasporas were linked by the
English vernacular. Through their use of English texts and translations
circulated in quires and books, these separated communities could maintain contact. By writing his testimony in English, Thorpe saw himself as
part of a diverse "English community": Lollards spread out across vast
spaces and counties in England who could be unified through the dissemination of a text written in their own language, English.

Other testimonies echo Thorpe's strong sense of belonging to an
English Lollard community, a priesthood of all believers. During her
trial for heresy in Norwich in April 1429, Margery Baxter proclaimed
that "omnis homo et omnis mulier qui sunt de opinione eiusdem Marg-
erie sunt boni sacerdotes, et quod sancta Ecclesia est tantum in locis
habitacionum omnium existencium de secta sua" (Tanner, *Heresy Trials*,
49). Margery, an illiterate housewife from Martham, gave her statement
in English, which was then translated for the official record into Latin,
the language of the Church Universal. For Margery, to participate in a
popular heresy was understood as participation in the congregation of
the elect, the homes where all of her sect were gathered together. But

the Lollards were not just bound by their belief in themselves as part of a larger, ideologically linked community. They were connected by their belief in an English community, a people bound by their use of a single language that distinguished them from their Continental neighbors and a pride in their cultural identity as an emerging English nation.

THE LANGUAGE OF AN
IMAGINED COMMUNITY

The polemic of Middle English Lollard texts sets up an ideal of an imagined community, united by a belief in the ability of the English language to convey sacred truth. Benedict Anderson refers to this as a "vernacularly imagined" community (*Imagined Communities*, 79). The exclusivity of the medieval church and the control of its members through the use of Latin was challenged and subverted by the Lollards in their translation of the accepted sacred language into that of their "nation": English. Other beliefs of the Lollards further define them as "English": their condemnation of the primacy of the church in Rome over the English church and their proposals to disendow alien priories on English soil.[5] But the Lollards' greatest achievement is their support of the English vernacular and their circulation of vernacular texts. In any complete discussion of an emerging national identity in Late Medieval England, the Lollard movement must be considered. While Lollardy was not necessarily an outgrowth of a nationalistic trend in late-fourteenth-century England, its appearance at this time is an indication that the *peoples* occupying the island of England were ready to think of themselves as separate, linguistically and spiritually, from the Continent.[6]

English was not the strict domain of the Lollards; their concern for the vernacular was equally represented by orthodox writers such as John Trevisa and Geoffrey Chaucer, two great translators contemporary with the Lollards.[7] Richard Ullerston's tract defending vernacular translation, written in Latin, somewhere between 1401 and 1407, has suggested that the debate over the vernacular was still an open topic, at least in Oxford (Hudson "Debate," 82–83). Though the Lollards were mainly preoccupied with the translation of sacred texts, their interest can be seen as part of a larger vernacular trend that sought to produce a vast amount of vernacular literature, a change that arguably harkens the dawning of nationalism.

But what claims did the Lollards make to justify their translation of Scripture and other devotional materials into English? Moreover, how do these arguments fit within their perception of an English community? The arguments used by Lollards found in several tracts, including Chapter 15 of the Prologue to the Wycliffite Bible and the various tracts in CUL MS Ii.6.26, seem to fall into three main categories: translation for practical purposes, translation based on historical precedent, and translation into the vernacular by other nations.[8] While the first does not seem particularly connected to nationalism, the other two are in many ways symptoms of a growing national self-consciousness, and further arguments used reveal a developing patriotism and pride in the English identity.

For the Lollards, the most pragmatic reason for texts in translation was to enable the common person, the "simple" or "lewid" man, to have access to God's law and the Truth, a truth that, as far as the Lollards saw it, was the same in any language.[9] For years, only the Catholic Church and its hierarchy had exclusive access to Scripture and certain other religious texts written in Latin, a monopoly that subsequently resulted in ignorant shepherds and an ignorant flock. One text that argues for the practicality and legality of Scripture in English is found in the collection of vernacular treatises in CUL MS Ii.6.26 all of which make claims for English translation.[10] The seventh tract in this manuscript begins confidently: "þis trett[yse] þat folewþ proueþ þat eche nacioun may lefully haue holy writ in here moder tunge" (1–2); the author contends that God's law can be written in any language, but its most important purpose is to "edifie þe commen pepel" (6) so they "knowe þe riȝt and redi weye to þe blisse of heuene" (20–21). The author of the first tract in the same manuscript shares this concern: he believes that Christ's command to his disciples to "preche þe gospel and his lawe to alle men and women and to alle naciouns" (139–40) makes it necessary that God's law is in the vernacular, and in this case specifically English.[11] Again, a practical point is made here that the law should be translated into the vernacular, "in here langage" (143), because most English people do not know Hebrew, Greek, or Latin (164–68). The author's quotation of Deuteronomy 32:29 suggests a particularly English audience; he translates "Utinam saperent, et intelligerent, ac novissima providerent" as

"Wolde God þat men, *þe pepel of Englond*, kowden Goddis lawe and vnderstonden it, and aviseden hem and token heede in here doynge allewey of þe laste eende..." (577–79, my emphasis), including the appositive phrase, "þe pepel of Englond," that further specifies his audience as English. The Lollards believe that the translation of religious texts, especially the Bible, into the English language is necessary for true Christians in England to follow their faith.

Another reason frequently found in Lollard arguments for authorizing the vernacular is historical precedent that takes the form of a glance back to earlier texts, particularly the translations of the Anglo-Saxons. This move also shows the Lollard author's sense of historical continuum; that his audience is culturally linked to their ancestors and the vernacular intertwined with their English identity. Arguably, Hastings considers the Anglo-Saxon period to be the earliest age of evolving national consciousness and refers specifically to the writings and translations of Bede and King Alfred as indicative of this awakening (Construction, 38–39). The Lollards seem aware or conscious of this and invoke these same authors. Two texts in particular refer back to Anglo-Saxon times: the Prologue to the Wycliffite Bible and a vernacular treatise on translation in Cambridge, Trinity College, MS B.14.50.[12] For example, in Chapter 15 of the Prologue the author proclaims that it is sensible to translate into English, just as the Anglo-Saxons translated into Old English "þat was English eiþer comoun langage of þis lond in his [Bede's] tyme" (162–63). As Jerome and Augustine in their day translated into Latin "a comoun langage to here puple aboute Rome and biȝondis," so now "as Englishe is comoun langage to oure puple" (142–43), translation into English is only reasonable. And a shared cultural and historical past is alluded to in this author's explication of Luke 19:40: "And we English men ben comen of heþen men, þerfore we ben vndurstonden bi þese stoonis þat shulden crie holi writ" (15–16). The author directly links his contemporary English audience to their historical and cultural ancestors, exploiting their shared national past. Though these ancestors were mostly pagan, lived in distinct and separate kingdoms, and were generally illiterate, excepting only a privileged and small portion of the population, the Lollards argue that they still had the practical sense to write their texts in their own tongue, Anglo-Saxon.

The tract in the Trinity manuscript cites not only Bede (131–40) and Alfred (146–51), but also more recent English translations such as John

Gaytrick's of Archbishop Thoresby's catechism (189–95) and Richard Rolle's Psalter (182–87). The emphasis is, however, not only on the fact that these translations exist but that they have already edified many an English person:

> Also a nobil hooly man Richerde E[er]myte drewe oon Englice þe Sauter with a glose of longe proces & lessouns of dirige & many oþer tretis, *by wiche many Engliche men han ben gretli edified,* and he were cursed of God, þat wolde þe puple schulde be lewder eiþer wors þan þei ben. (182–87, my emphasis)

Whether the Anglo-Saxons ever perceived that their use of the vernacular was nationalistic is not my point.[13] My argument here is that the Lollards saw their own use of these Anglo-Saxon and earlier English precedents in those terms. The Lollards believed, as these examples given above suggest, that the Anglo-Saxons were pragmatic in their faith and their use of the vernacular.

An argument used by the Lollards in support of vernacular translation most relevant to my discussion here is their reference to other nations that already possess vernacular translations of the Bible. Chapter 15 of the Prologue to the Wycliffite Bible argues that because the French, the Bohemians, and the "Britons" have their own translations in their mother tongue; "Whi shulden not English men haue þe same in here modir langage?" (165–68). This argument is repeated in the Trinity manuscript where the author mentions that the Spanish, French, Germans, and Italians have their own vernacular Bibles (113–17). In the seventh tract of CUL MS Ii.6.26, the author mentions Bibles in Latin, French, and German (40–42), for Christ commanded at his ascension that the disciples must preach "in þat langage þat þe pepel vsed to speke" (38). By comparing themselves with other nationalities, the Lollards see themselves as different, with a cultural identity separate and different from their Continental cousins, yet equal in national status. The Lollards also show us how they equate each country's use of its own vernacular language, in the form of the Bible, to each country's national identity: that the population of each country is united by its shared language. The Lollards also seem to be intimating that a country's vernacular legitimizes its status and identity as a nation. This view of the Lollards provides us with the strongest example of how they equate national identity to vernacular language. Though this is for us now a highly debatable issue, their texts demonstrate that the Lollards saw this connection as far more clear and direct.

To Lollards, translation was a necessity, a practical and utilitarian means to an end; but, in choosing the mother tongue of their nation, they also supported that idea of the nation as united by a common language. Of course, England was at the time a polylingual community. But the Lollards never choose to write in any other vernacular apart from English. Though some of the early Lollards wrote in Latin, those texts were intended for a much smaller, exclusive audience at a stage when the heresy was primarily an academic one. The appropriation of English by the Lollards as their language of discourse might be seen not only as a challenge to the Latinate community of the Church, but also the Latinate community of the government and other elements of Medieval English society that were Latinate. While we can now challenge this perspective with evidence that there was more functional literacy in Latin at the time, and that it wasn't the strict domain of the Church, what is more important here is that the Lollards perceived it as the exclusive language of an oppressive, hierarchical institution. To them, as their texts make clear, the English tongue is the language of the "common people."

The Lollards were more concerned with spreading their message than necessarily promoting themselves as distinctly English. Yet, there is an unconscious tendency toward national pride expressed in the arguments that have been discussed above. Their choice showed how Lollards perceived their cultural identity and their use of the English vernacular as intrinsically linked, and that their shared "Anglo-Saxon" heritage and their shared spiritual identity as "true Christian men" shaped them as English too. For example, the Trinity manuscript makes reference to the fear that the English would "be holden barbarus" (162) by other nations if its vernacular lacked authority and was declared not suitable as a medium for the Truth in the Bible. The end of the Trinity text refers to an incident in Parliament when a bill against biblical translation was presented,

> wiche wanne it was seyn of lordis and comouns, þe good duke
> of Lancastre Jon, wos soule God asoile for his mercy, answered
> þer-to scharpely, seying þis sentence: *we wel not be þe refuse of*

alle men, for siþen oþer naciouns han Goddis lawe, wiche is lawe
of oure byleue, in þer owne modir langage, we wolone haue oure in
Engliche, wo þat euere it bigrucche; and þis he affermede with a
grete oþe. (283–90, my emphasis)

It is not surprising that the Lollard author places this declaration in the
mouth of John of Gaunt, duke of Lancaster, an early advocate of Wyclif's
reforms. Yet, if he even made this statement, Gaunt expresses anxiety
that the reputation and honor of the English nation would be deemed
inferior in the European political arena if it did not authorize and endorse the translation of the Bible in English.

The Lollards also appear in their polemic to support translation as a
benefit for the English nation, and refer frequently to England as a "nacioun" as some of the examples above have already shown and as seen
here in the first tract of the Cambridge manuscript:

For what holy chirche rediþ opunly to þe pepel, it may be tauȝt
hem opunly, *as wel on Englische to Englische folk* as to þe Romayns
in Latyn corrup, or to Duchemen in Deuche, or to Frenschemen
in Frensch; or let hem telle cause whi þat Englische folk schulde
nouȝt as wel be tauȝt Goddis lawe and þe gospel and holy writte
as wel as oþere naciouns, and whi *Englische naciouns schulde*
more be excludid from þe blessynge of Goddis lawe more þan oþere
naciouns. (397–405, my emphasis)

The author sees England as a nation of "Englische folk" who share the
same tongue, and he clearly believes that national identity and language
are closely connected. It unifies the Italians, the Germans, and the
French. The identity of each nation is equivalent to the use of their
respective vernaculars and, more importantly, the writing of the Gospel
and holy writ in that vernacular. Therefore "þe pepel of Englond" are as
worthy as any other nation to have God's law in their mother tongue.[14]

The people of England are united under the titular head of the English king, a position that is both the symbol of England the "nation"
and the political heart of the country. The author of the first tract of CUL
MS Ii.6.26 recognizes the king as head of the English nation whose
people are connected not by French or Latin, but by the English language
with the following hypothetical example:

> 3if þe kynge of Englond sente to cu[n]trees and citees his
> patente on Latyn or Frensche and not [on Englische] to do crie
> his lawis, his statutes, and his wille to þe peple, and it were
> cried oonly on Latyn or Frensche and not on Englisch, it were
> no worschip to þe kynge, ne warnynge to þe peple, but a greet
> desseyt. (150–55)

The people, over whom "þe kynge of Englond" rules, are tied together
by their use and understanding of the English language; the king of
England is also joined to these people by that same language. It is the
king's duty to communicate with his people in that language, otherwise
he deceives his own realm. Therefore, the king's honor and his legitimacy
depend on the people's understanding of his law and will.

Interestingly, this statement seems to disregard, at least in the Lollards' eyes, the fact that most English kings, up until this point, were
speakers of French. This would certainly be true of Richard II, a king en-
amored with French culture, though the patronage of vernacular authors
such as Gower, Hoccleve, and Chaucer show that Richard was just as
interested in English literature as in French. The Lollards seem to be
making a claim for legislative and administrative changes here too. It
was common practice that laws, decrees, and other documents were
written in French or Latin; the documents would be understood by those
few who would then interpret them for the illiterate populace—much in
the way the Church worked in informing congregations about God's
law. The Lollards are making a claim here that a king must rule in English so that all can understand and interpret for themselves the justice
of their ruler.

Chapter 15 of the Prologue to the Wycliffite Bible sets out a distinct
and determined Lollard purpose to "saue alle men in oure rewme" (24–
25) through the translation of the Bible into English. The author expresses, with what appears to be patriotic fervor, a belief that all people
of the realm need an English Bible and can only be saved through this.
Through the knowledge of God's law in English, the language of the
English people as understood throughout the realm of England, Christians can live a good life and be spiritually saved from sin and eternal
damnation. Knowledge leads to salvation, but that knowledge can only
be attained through access to the law in the language of the land. The
Prologue to the Wycliffite Bible reinforces this belief by also claiming a

strong separate identity for the English nation by equating that nation to its church as separate from the Church in Rome. The text consistently refers to the Church not as simply "The Church," but as "þe chirche in Engelond." And it is only the Church in England that needs to approve the English translation to serve only its members (114–16). Additionally, the Prologue expresses a sense of pride in the quality of the English Bible; the author argues that many Latin Bibles are in need of correction, far more than the English Bible (74–75).

While the welfare of the English nation is, according to the Lollard texts, dependant upon the knowledge of God's law, the texts seem to imply that the suppression of the English tongue leads as well to the loss of English identity. England, the nation, through the spiritual guidance of a vernacular Bible is a strong, stable, and unified country. Similarly, when God's law is not available in the language of the people, the peace and stability of the English nation are at risk. The first tract in CUL MS Ii.6.26 poetically proclaims: "And so Goddis worde and Goddis lawe is neʒ forʒeten in þis lond: vertu is forsaken, and vice is taken; truþe is in dispit, falshed is in worschip; pees and charite ben exilid, synne and malice, baat and dissencioun regnen; for wiþouten kepynge of Goddis lawe is no pees" (90–94). The Lollard author of this tract argues that because God's law is not known of the people in their native tongue, the country has fallen apart. The author continues in this vein, asserting "And so þe lond, for defaute of techynge and kunnynge of Goddis lawe, is in poynt to be vndon" (545–47). The implications of this ignorance are not only on a personal, individual level, but also threaten at a national level to bring about political upheaval, subsequently making the mother tongue imperative to national security. The Lollard author here connects personal salvation among his Lollard community to the greater interests of the English nation and its continuity and stability.

The text continues to argue for this causal connection:

> For ignoraunce of Goddis lawe is cause of alle meuynge and vnsta-bilte in þe comoun pepel, þat þei dreden neiþer God ne man as þei schulden do, false and vnstable, redi to rebelle aʒens here souereyns, redi to mordre and manslauʒter. And so it is to drede, þat for ignoraunce of Goddis lawe and falsnesse and schrewidnesse, þe lond schal be moued and chaungid from oure nacion to anoþer nacion, but we amende us. (568–75, my emphasis)

The causal claim here is now made more explicit: because God's law is not in English, "þe comoun pepel" are ignorant and therefore "redi to rebelle" against their king. Because the common people do not know God's law in their own tongue, and therefore cannot live good Christian lives, those common people are becoming restless and disorderly. When the people are difficult to rule, the nation's stability is weakened and the land becomes vulnerable to more stable nations. Therefore, the lack of an English Bible makes the English nation vulnerable to attack from foreign powers because it is internally weakened by the absence of true spiritual guidance. With ignorance of God's law comes a loss of English identity as England would then be "moued and chaungid" from "oure nacioun" to another nation. Thus the suppression of the English tongue becomes associated with the loss of English identity and the possibility that England could be conquered by another country.

In the second tract of the Cambridge manuscript, a similar causal chain is discussed. The argument used by opponents of the Lollards holds that "holy writt in Englische wolde make men at debate, and sougitis to be rebel aȝens here soueryns" (68–70) because they would have at their disposal a text that also challenges accepted institutions.[15] But the author responds "þat þe comountee of cristyn peple" (74), the English people, are far worse off because they are wallowing in their sins, unable to know how they sin due to their ignorance of God's law, and that is a greater threat to the health of the English nation. The knowledge of God's word can only be known by the people in their native tongue, the English language. Of course, the Lollards believed in spreading God's law through vernacular preaching, but their desire for those preachers and the people to have access to the actual text of the Gospel and God's law in the vernacular was necessary because it enabled individuals to teach and learn for themselves. As I will discuss later, preachers were not always able to preach, so the written form of a text had more permanency. Practically speaking, the written form of a text was, quite simply, portable, unchanging, and more personal when used for individual reading.

The sense of community conveyed by these Lollard vernacular texts reveals in the heretics not only a sense of their "Lollardness," but also a strong awareness of their Englishness and their place within the larger English nation. The frequent reference in these texts to the laity as the "comoun puple," to the language they speak as the "comoun langage," and to their shared identity as a "comounity," all bind the Lollards with their neighbors as part of an English community that bases its identity on a shared common language: English. Benedict Anderson discusses how in the literature of nationalism, the use of the collective pronominal adjective "our" and the connection of the author to his audience through other pronouns like "us" and "we" connects the author, his subject, and the audience into a "collective body," an "imagined community" (*Imagined Communities,* 32). We find ample occurrences of such collective bodies in the writings of the Lollards. One instance occurs in "Fifty Heresies and Errors of the Friars" a text written around 1384: "And þus þei [the friars] pursuen prestis, for þei reproven hor synnes as God biddes, bothe to brenne hom, and þo gospels of Crist written in Englische, to moost lernyng of *oure nacioun*. . . . And so freris neden *oure lond* to be dampned wiþ fendis in helle" (Arnold, *English Works,* 3:393, my emphasis). The author claims that the gospels in English are beneficial and educate the nation, but the friars' attempt to burn the Wycliffite Bible plunges the land into chaos. Significantly, the phrases used by the author equate the geography of England, "oure lond," with the political and cultural identity of the English nation, "oure nacioun."

By writing in English and collectively referring to the audience as "oure nacioun," the Lollard author already assumes his audience has a sense of what that "nacioun," and especially "oure nacioun," means. Paradoxically, the author is not only trying to relate to his audience a sense of community and shared Englishness, he is also dependant upon a preexistent idea of national identity that he calls forth in his text. In some sense, all of these texts described here work in this contradictory way, not only constructing new ideas of nationhood and an English community, but also reliant upon a sense that this English identity already exists in the mind of the English reader.

By writing in English, "oure langage," Lollards made a very deliberate decision to exclude from their audience anyone who did not speak or read English (Turville-Petre, *England,* 20–21). In doing so, they excluded non-English speaking Britons such as the Anglo-French, Welsh, Scots, Cornish, and others. This makes an even stronger claim that the Lollards saw the use of language equivalent to national identity: if you speak English as your native tongue, you are English, but if you live in England and speak some other tongue, you are not English. Accordingly, the author of the Prologue to the Wycliffite Bible consistently refers in Chapter 15

to England as "oure rewme" and to his audience as "we English men"
(15) not only connecting himself with his audience as Lollards but sharing with them their cultural heritage as people of the English nation
who speak the English language. By writing in English, Turville-Petre
argues—though with reference to earlier orthodox works—"author and
audience became united in their nationality, and the clerical [or in this
case Lollard] writer was able to appeal to the laity through a sense of nationhood, through a perception of shared social values, and in a commonly understood language" (*England*, 27). The relationship between a
nation and its shared social values and language is epitomized in the Lollard texts; the Lollard author shares with his audience the fundamental
tenets of the Christian faith, a cultural heritage, and a shared belief in
the importance of God's law and its accessibility to all of the faithful.
The author, by writing in English, also assumes that this is the only language his audience understands.

The use of the word "comoun" in these texts also embodies the idea
of the imagined community for the Lollards. The phrase "comoun langage" appears several times in Chapter 15 of the Prologue to the Wycliffite Bible: "Saxon, þat was English eiþer comoun langage of þis lond"
(162–63), and earlier at line 143, "as Englishe is comoun langage to oure
puple"; "comoun langage" is here directly equated to the English vernacular. And the use of the phrase "comoun langage" is distinguished
from "modir langage" or "moder tunge" in the Prologue. The author uses
these expressions when discussing the vernaculars of other countries,
whereas the "langage" of English is that of "þe comyn puple." There are
two ways to read or understand "comoun" in this context. The word
could refer to class and the likelihood that the greatest portion of the
population that spoke English was the commons. The other use, and the
one I believe is implied here, is the sense of the English language as
shared—as the language that is known or common to all English people.

The texts dealing directly with the translation debate in CUL MS
Ii.6.26 also refer to the English language as the language of "þe comoun
pepel," a language shared by all who are English. The first tract is more
explicit in its meaning and directly associates the English tongue as the
language of the English people: "Wu[n]der I haue whi þei ben so looþe
to teche Englysche pepel Goddis lawe in Englische tunge, for wiþowten
Englische tunge, þe lewed Englische pepel <mowen not knowe> Goddis
lawe" (514–17). Also in the first tract, the text refers to the common peo-

ple—both literate and illiterate: "al prechinge in Englisch þat is ordennt for þe comoyn pepel, b[oþ] letterid and lewid" (376–77), expressing a belief that a group of people are bound by their language, more so than by their class or education; it is their ability to understand English here that ties them together.

Unlike these other texts in CUL MS Ii.6.26, the expressions "comoun langage" and "moder tunge" are used interchangeably in the seventh tract. Both expressions refer to the vernacular, though the implications of these phrases differ. Again, the expression "moder tunge" is used more generally to describe the natural or native language of a nation or people. The opening lines to this tract indicate that each nation has its own mother tongue or native language into which Scripture should be translated: "þat eche nacioun may lefully haue holy writ in here moder tunge" (1–2). The text frequently defines "comoun langage" as "þat langage þat þe pepel vsed to speke" (38) or "ony oþer langage after þe pepel haþ vnderstondynge" (42). Consistently, these definitions speak of "þe pepel" and argue that the vernacular is the language of the people, of "þe comoun pepel," or the community of common people joined by their faith and their language: "cristyne folke of what langage so euere þei be" (39). This expression of "comoun langage" speaks to the general nature of the Lollardy heresy whose ranks were composed of many unremarkable, "comoun pepel" and whose doctrine has been popularly portrayed, both then and now, as attractive to the common man or woman.[16] But how did the Lollards' message reach this community of common folk? Though they place an emphasis on the vernacular in their writings, that role did the vernacular play in their daily lives? While their texts speak of a "community," what was the actual shape of that community?

BOOKS AND THE
DISSEMINATION OF NATIONALISM

This linguistic evidence from these Lollard texts and polemical tracts about their use of the terms "nacioun" and "comoun" is suggestive, but it is still problematic because it mainly expresses an ideal and an imaginary construct in the minds of the Lollard writers. Additional manuscript evidence, however, seems to endorse the linguistic and textual evidence discussed above, and reinforces the theory that the Lollards were,

in actuality, a closely connected and complex community. Evidence discussed below confirms that the vernacular, in the form of Middle English
texts written in quires and books, played a significant role in the daily
lives of the heretics. Books were used in many ways: to proselytize, to
teach, and to reaffirm the faith of the Lollards. And books, more importantly, became the vehicle through which Lollard communities defined
themselves for both their adherents and their opponents.

Because a direct and unmediated relationship with God was at the
heart of their belief, Lollards valued books highly as a way to facilitate
this relationship. Through the translation into English of the Gospels,
Epistles, and other parts of the Bible "the written word could stay when
the persecuted preacher could not."[17] There is sufficient evidence provided in the heresy trials and the books themselves that this was often
the case. When a Lollard preacher was forced to move on, he would leave
the written version of his sermon or text, in quire or book form, with the
local conventicle to which he had been teaching and preaching. The book
preserved his words and could be easily passed among the members of
the local Lollard community, and easily hidden if necessary. Books were
so important that even illiterate members of the sect took great pains to
acquire copies of texts that they would then have read to them.[18] When
money was not sufficient, trial testimony provides numerous examples
of groups of Lollards pooling their money together to purchase a book,
which was subsequently passed among members of a conventicle or
family.[19] When books were not available, memorization of texts was then
employed (McSheffrey, *Gender*, 72; Aston, "Lollardy," 201).

Since quires and manuscripts could be relatively easily reproduced,
passed around, and hidden, "therefore written materials become the
object of official destruction as well as, or even in preference to, the individual heretic" (Hudson, "*Laicus litteratus*," 233). They were used as
evidence for heresy, sometimes alone and sometimes as merely confirmation of heterodoxy, and abjurations frequently make specific mention of the ownership and use of books.[20] Despite the attempts by the
Church to suppress and destroy the Lollards' written materials, "The
large number of manuscripts of their literature which still survive . . . is
itself a tribute to the vitality of the heretics' literary activity" (Aston, "Lollardy," 206).

With the knowledge we have of the number of Lollard manuscripts
that have survived despite decades of destruction by fire and the assault

of time, few scholars acknowledge how impressive these manuscript witnesses are, especially when we compare them to Middle English manuscripts that contain more popular secular literature. But there is a danger with using manuscript evidence for any type of scholarship on the Lollard heresy. Lollards, for obvious reasons, hid their identity so ownership notes rarely occur in the manuscripts; likewise, some manuscripts fall into an ambiguous category that contains both heterodox and orthodox materials (Hudson, "Lollard Book Production," 135–37). A significant number of Lollard manuscripts have been confidently identified as heterodox, primarily those that contain the Early and Later versions of the Wycliffite Bible and the vernacular sermon cycle.

The most important text produced by the Lollard heretics was their translation of the Bible into English. The Bible was translated in two stages: an earlier, literal, and awkward translation produced in the 1380s and then a later, more readable, and confident version produced somewhere between 1395 and 1397 (Hudson, *Premature Reformation*, 238–47; Hunt, "Edition," 50–56). What is most staggering about this Bible is that, though it was declared illegal to possess one by 1407, over 230 copies, ranging from complete versions of the Old and New Testaments to copies of the Gospels alone, have survived to the present day.[21] This is a remarkable number when compared to other vernacular productions, both secular and religious, of the time. Even copies of the most popular literary texts, Chaucer's *Canterbury Tales* (eighty-two known complete or fragmentary copies) and Langland's *Piers Plowman* (all versions—fifty-two known copies), survive in much smaller numbers. The only vernacular text that even comes close in number is the *Pricke of Conscience* that survives in 117 known copies. Of course, such comparison is risky; greater efforts would have been made to preserve a sacred text like the Bible. Literary texts, such as Caxton's copies of *The Canterbury Tales*, were more apt to have been discarded or destroyed. But the Wycliffite Bible was an illicit text that was confiscated and destroyed on numerous occasions, though perhaps many were hidden, and these are the copies that now remain. Those copies of the Wycliffite Bible that have survived "vary in type and quality a good deal less than might be expected given the history of the text" (Hudson, "Lollard Book Production," 131).

Another production of the Lollards that has survived in large quantities is the English sermon cycle edited by Pamela Gradon and Anne Hudson. Again, the survival rate is impressive: thirty-one manuscripts of the cycle that contains a total of 294 sermons. This is nearly double the number of surviving copies of another popular secular text, Chaucer's *Troilus and Criseyde* (sixteen known copies). Like the Bible manuscripts, the sermons too vary little from each other and significantly contrast to the surviving copies of orthodox sermons that are typically small and amateur.[22] But the critical edition of these sermons has offered additional information about this cycle. Basing her argument on the complex textual relationships between the surviving copies, Hudson has concluded that there were probably a much larger number of copies produced than has survived ("Some Aspects," 183; "Lollard Sermon-Cycle," 150–51). Additionally, it appears that the sermons actually came in a selection of "packages" that offered different orders in which the sermons could be presented (Hudson, "Some Aspects," 187–88); and evidence also suggests that at least forty different hands contributed to the collection (Lambert, *Medieval Heresy*, 249).

While the numbers of surviving Lollard manuscripts is impressive, what is equally remarkable, if not more so, is the uniformity and imposed "standardization" that these manuscripts of both the Wycliffite Bible and the sermon cycle exhibit. Simon Hunt, in his study of prologue material that accompanies parts or the whole of the Wycliffite Bible, examined the size, layout, rubrication, decoration, and scribal hands of nearly two hundred of these manuscripts and concluded:

> It is difficult to convey in words the impression created by such a high degree of unity of layout and decorational features between the manuscripts. The care involved in the presentation of the text extends to the accuracy of the text itself.... It is clear that thought was given to all aspects of the production of the manuscripts of the revised translation, and that the production of those manuscripts was carefully controlled. ("Edition," 45–46)

Hudson, based on the Bible manuscripts she has seen and the sermon manuscripts she has worked with, finds too that they must have been produced under tight supervision with no expense spared. The manuscripts of the Wycliffite Bible are professional and lavish (some, like London British Library MS Egerton 617 and 618, are illuminated) and follow a standard layout, while the manuscripts of the sermon cycle offer a selection of "patterns" and are consistently corrected.[23] What can be concluded here is that the Lollards had money and used a central location that provided a center for the supervised production of these texts. Where this money came from and where this center was located is another problem altogether.[24]

One suggested location for this center from which Lollard texts were produced and distributed can be made on the basis of the content of the texts themselves. The vast, scholarly undertaking represented by the translation of the entire Bible and the composition of the sermons hints at a location where these scholars were congregated and had access to a well-stocked library (Hudson, *Premature Reformation*, 246; "Wyclif," 98–99). The obvious place is Oxford, the birthplace of the heresy. Ralph Hanna argues in support of Oxford as the locale for a center of Lollard book production in his examination of Lollard material that, he proposes, was circulated in booklet form ("Lollard Codices," 59). He argues, first, that booklets would have easily facilitated the production of subversive texts, providing a lending library of sorts from which a scribe could borrow materials in small quantities (56). But this is an arrangement that was already in place, as Hanna suggests, evolved from a sort of *pecia* system, a quick, cheap, and easy method that was used among scholars at Oxford (59).[25]

Despite the fact that the authorities concentrated their efforts on eradicating books, there is little evidence that they ever sought out the source for these books. Based on the manuscripts that survive in such quantities and of such quality, however, such a source would seem most likely. Other proposed locations, especially after Oxford may have become no longer safe or feasible, are the manor of Braybroke in Northamptonshire, Kemerton in Gloucestershire, and London.[26]

So what does all this information about a Lollard "book trade" tell us about the Lollards' community and its role in the emerging nationalism in late medieval England? One of Benedict Anderson's main arguments in support of his theory that nationalism is an imaginary construct is the importance of "vernacular print-capitalism" and how it is through printed texts that a nation can imagine its members (*Imagined Communities*, 37–46). However, I find myself here in agreement with Hastings, who counters Anderson on this point. He does not disregard the fact that circulated forms of literature, which to Anderson are printed texts like newspapers, are vital to growing national consciousness, but his contention is that this can and should include the vast book trade in

earlier preprint Europe (*Construction*, 22–23). I would add to Hastings'
claim, with regard to England, that this should also include the especially
complex and well-organized book trade of the Lollards, which, as evidence given briefly here about the number of manuscripts still surviving
and the quality control imposed upon their production should show,
was as well organized as the later print trade.[27] This is in radical contrast
to the other evidence we have of the "book trade" in England at the time
that, for works by such notable Middle English authors as Chaucer and
Gower, seems to have been organized very differently.[28]

Vernacularity and textuality were at the heart of the heresy; as Rita
Copeland has argued, Lollardy "organizes itself through textuality, with
reading communities and textual transmission among all social levels of
its adherents, whether those members are literate or not" ("William
Thorpe," 210). Hastings argues that "a community, political, religious,
or whatever, is essentially a creation of human communication and it is
only to be expected that the form of the communication will determine
the character of the community" (*Construction*, 20). That communication came in the form of the various quires and books produced and distributed by the Lollards, and these various modes helped determine the
shape of the Lollard community, a widespread, but organized and well-
connected movement.[29]

LOLLARD COMMUNITIES

Quite recently, several Reformation historians have argued that adherents to the Lollard heresy were not united as a "community" at all. In his
The Stripping of the Altars, Eamon Duffy all but erases the Lollards from
the history of pre-Reformation England, blaming Reformation historians who in the past have "overestimated their numbers and their significance" (6). Similarly, R. N. Swanson has asserted that "In England Lollardy was always fragmented . . . its adherents were scattered and its
beliefs lacked coherence" (*Religion*, 274); like Duffy, he argues that later
historians "may have made Lollardy a greater problem than is warranted
by the evidence" in an attempt "to find a national movement against
Catholicism before the Reformation" (*Catholic England*, 36). A scholar of
the Reformation, Patrick Collinson, has also belittled the Lollard movement with his suggestion that Lollard conventicles centered more around

"the idle gossip which might otherwise have accompanied the eating and drinking which was perhaps the chief business on such occasions," than any true discussion of religious reform ("English Conventide," 236). And in an in-depth study of the Lollard communities in Buckinghamshire, Richard Davies shows how geography limited the movement of Lollards and even restricted contact between relatively close groups ("Lollardy," 206–07).[30] These historical perspectives pose an interesting contrast to the progress of research in literary studies. Existing textual and documentary evidence, like that explored in the sections above, challenges the conclusions of these Reformation historians and argues for a more coherent and widespread group.

Another important resource to determine the shape and character of the Lollard community is the numerous trial proceedings recorded by ecclesiastical authorities. Trial records, however, must also be used cautiously, because they record Lollard belief and ideas as the threatened hierarchical institution perceived them.[31] Based on the extensive surveys by Charles Kightly for the early period and J.A.F. Thomson for the post-Oldcastle period, Lollard communities appear to have been most widespread in the south of England, where there is evidence for communities in Kent, the Chilterns, the Mid-Thames valley, Bristol and the West Country, Coventry and the Midlands, Essex and East Anglia, and, most importantly, London.[32] Supporters of the Lollard heresy in these areas would have met in "secret conventicles and illicit congregations" where they read from the many vernacular books they shared and discussed the tenets of their belief (McHardy, "Bishop Buckingham," 138). That these gatherings were important to the Lollards and the welfare of their existence as a community can be ascertained by the reactions of the authorities. Not only would Lollards during their trial have to list those they had met during these conventicles, but they also had to swear in their abjurations never to do so again (Fines, "Heresy Trials," 169; Hudson, *Premature Reformation*, 156–57):

> Y shal never aftir this tyme be no recettour, fautour, consellour or defensour of heretikes or of ony persones suspect of heresie. Ne Y shal never trowe to thaym. Ne wittyngly Y shal felaship with thaym, ne be homly with thaym, ne geve thaym consell, yeftes, sokour, favour or confort. (Abjuration of Richard Knobbyng of Beccles, qtd. in Tanner, *Heresy Trials*, 117)

The authorities realized the extent to which "felaship" between Lollard communities was a major contributor to the spread of their beliefs.

The actual makeup of the communities we find at these locations seems to work in two spheres: those inside the household, where relationships within the family represented strong, close ties, and those outside the household, who provided the weaker ties between other groups (McSheffrey, *Gender*, 47–48). The core of a local conventicle was the family bond, but that family bond could also extend through marriage beyond one particular household into others some distance away.[33] There is significant evidence, too, that marriages were arranged within Lollard circles to keep dissent in the family (Hope, "Lollardy," 11; McSheffrey, *Gender*, 95–96). In some locations, it appears that heresy was passed down through many generations, even down to the Reformation and beyond (McSheffrey, *Gender*, 100). Outside the immediate family were other members of the household (servants, apprentices, lodgers) and beyond the household, close friends and neighbors (Davies, "Lollardy," 197; McSheffrey, *Gender*, 103). Further beyond was the village or town, and Shannon McSheffrey's research has found that in some locations where the Lollards may have represented the majority, such as Amersham in the Mid-Thames Valley, there was significant peer pressure to join the heretics (73–74). Where the heresy did not dominate, towns seemed to tolerate them (McSheffrey, *Gender*, 135–36; Plumb, "Spread," 129). Interestingly, the authorities very rarely used non-Lollards to accuse members of the heresy; charges of heresy always seemed to come from within the church, not from the Lollards' orthodox neighbors (McSheffrey, *Gender*, 73; Tanner, *Heresy Trials*, 9).

Because of the nature of the Lollard heresy and its markedly strong belief in the role of itinerant preachers, the spread of the heresy would inevitably go further afield and provide the connections between isolated and disparate communities throughout the country. While some scholars, like Richard Davies, have argued that the role of the wandering preachers was limited because they were only preaching to the converted ("Lollardy," 200–02), others have acknowledged that their place within the heresy as leaders, teachers, and book-carriers was fundamental to the survival of the heresy (Plumb, "Gathered Church?" 134). The names of these men, William Swinderby, William Smith, William White, Walter Brute, and Thomas Man (whose career brought him from Colchester to Newbury with many stops on the way), appear several times in the trials of geographically distant towns.[34] In some areas, particularly the towns of the Chiltern Hills where Lollardy flourished, the communities appear to have been connected "in some sort of association through travelling evangelists" (Cross, "'Great Reasoners,'" 368). Trial evidence provides numerous examples of visitors from other distant Lollard communities, like "missionaries" coming to share their knowledge and beliefs (McSheffrey, *Gender*, 76; Hudson, *Premature Reformation*, 137–39). Heretics who were being persecuted would often flee to a less hostile location (Hudson, *Premature Reformation*, 157), suggesting that Lollards must have had some communication with other groups in order to know where they would be welcome (139–41).

CONCLUSION

The Lollards, through their widespread communities, their vigorous book trade, and the language of their texts, constructed for themselves a community that embodied God's law; they were a community of English folk who desired to spread the good news in the common language, the English vernacular, and who identified themselves by that common language. But they were also self-righteous in their belief that their interpretation of God's law was the true path to salvation. The testimony of Joan Washingby of Coventry in 1511 so aptly portrays this arrogance: "my belief is better than theirs, save that we dare not speak it . . . I care not, they cannot hurt me, my Lord knoweth my mind already" (qtd. in Cross, "'Great Reasoners,'" 367). And Margery Baxter proclaimed that the members of her sect were all "boni sacerdotes," good priests or true priests who together represented on earth the "priesthood of all believers." Though this seems like an exaggerated sense of purpose in the popular Lollard movement, this idea was based on Wyclif's earlier theory of the "congregatio omnium predestinatorum," the congregation of the elect (Hudson, *Premature Reformation*, 169).

By positing themselves as "true men" against the false Antichrist in Rome, Lollards saw themselves as the saviors of England. William Thorpe even refers to himself and his fellow Lollards as "Goddis chosen peple" (Hudson, *Two Wycliffite Texts*, line 551) and pleads, at the end of his testimony, for his audience to pray to God that he "graunte to vs, and to alle oþere þat in þe same wyse and for þe same cause specialy or for ony oþer cause ben at distaunce, to ben oonyd in trewe feiþ" (2252–54). But how should we interpret this self-righteous attitude of the "congregation of the true believers"? Towards the end of his book, Hastings explains that "the root of the more extreme wing of European nationalism lies precisely here, in a widely held Christian assumption that there can only be one fully elect nation, one's own, the true successor to ancient Israel" (*Construction,* 198). The Lollards genuinely saw themselves and their nation as chosen. With the translation of the Bible, the Bible became to them the *liber vitae Anglicanae* in which the English were the *populus Dei,* the chosen people of Israel. The Lollards promoted their Bible "to convince the English, not only that God was an Englishman, but also that England was itself the inheritance, the *haereditas Dei,* the promised land and a new Jerusalem of which the scriptures had spoken" (Wilks, "Royal Patronage," 148).

The Lollards' belief that England was the promised land carried over into their belief that the English language was a suitable medium for theological exploration and debate, as well as for the law and the word of God. While the various tracts discussed here reveal the insecurity of the Lollards in doing so, they also show how the Lollards looked to their own nation and its solidarity under the English tongue to lend authority to the vernacular, usurping the longstanding reign of the Latin of the Church Universal. The Lollards turned to their audience's sense of patriotism and their anxiety that the English people were considered less than their Continental neighbors, and appealed to their belief in an English identity and its connection through the English language to give the vernacular sacral authority. This belief manifested itself in the many vernacular texts and translations and the sheer number of manuscript copies produced; yet, even these manuscripts can only be a portion of their original output. Likewise, through books, the Lollards literally bound themselves together with the ties of their faith, language, and national identity, creating their own England, an England that came to its fruition with the Reformation.

The Lollards were an "imagined community" in the truest sense because they did not exist in a single geographical location, but were widely spread throughout England in various conventicles from Bristol to Essex. Because they could not exist together in a physical unit, but had to survive underground as a persecuted heresy, the Lollards had a much more developed sense of themselves as a community. Though separated by many miles, the Lollards through their strong faith, expressed in their texts, realized in their books, and shared with their immediate family and neighbors, maintained a strong sense of themselves as part of a large community and constructed for themselves in their texts a larger imagined community of "trewe men." For them the Church existed wherever they were "in cubili vel in campo" (qtd. in McHardy, "Bishop Buckingham," 143). Writers of Lollard texts imagined their audience as English readers and part of, in Hastings's words, a "historico-cultural community" (*Construction*, 25) that had a history of personal testimonies, such as Thorpe's, and their own pantheon of "national" saints like Richard Fitzralph and John Wyclif, and martyrs for their cause such as Sir John Oldcastle, William Sawtry, Richard Wyche, and William White; men who were willing to die for their community whose breadth they could only imagine.

Notes

I would like to thank Anne Hudson, Elizabeth Scala, Majorie Woods, and Glenn Davis for reading an earlier draft of this essay and their many ideas and suggestions. I would also like to thank the editor, Kathy Lavezzo, for her helpful advice and astute editing of my work. Any errors here are entirely my own.

1. Hastings uses dated sources, focuses mainly on Wyclif, and seems completely unaware of the evidence of the vernacular Lollard writings I discuss below (*Construction*, 15–17, 24–25).

2. For a discussion of the Lollards' development of their own "discourse," see Hudson, "Vocabulary?".

3. The use of the term "cuntrees" here is potentially ambiguous, so ambiguous that it was omitted in a later sixteenth-century printed edition. "Cuntrees" here should be glossed as "counties" (Hudson, *Two Wycliffite Texts*, 25 [see variant for line 42]). Though two surviving copies of the Latin translation of this testimony made it to Bohemia, the surviving Middle English witness that descends from a Middle English text Thorpe undoubtedly wrote was intended for Lollards in England (xlv).

4. Hudson debates the historicity of this scenario, arguing that it is perhaps closer to reality that Thorpe modeled his testimony on the Letter of Richard Wyche which was also supposedly written from prison (ibid., liii–lix). But even if this is not the case, Thorpe is still able to imagine himself removed from this "community."

5. The Lollard Disendowment Bill, presented to Parliament in 1410, was in itself an attempt to cut ties with the church in Rome for the "profyte of the rewme" (Hudson, *Selections*, 135–37, line 84). This very calculated "manifesto" was not just targeting the members of Parliament as its audience, but was obviously playing upon England's relatively recent economic crises—the ongoing involvement in the Hundred Years War and the earlier

problems of the Peasants' revolt—that left English people vulnerable and desirous to expel the financial drain of alien priories and other monastic orders (Aston, "'Caim's Castles,'" III). Other texts, like the "Tractatus de Regibus," express a fear that through these orders, the pope could gain political control of nations: "As, if alle þo freris of Yngelonde hadden howses and godes in þo rewme of Yngelonde, and maden þo pope lord of hem, þo popis lordschipe were to myche ande regale were lessid; and þus, by processe of tyme, my3t þo londe be conquerid al into þo popis honde as oþer rewmys bene" (Hudson, *Selections*, p. 131, lines 127–31).

6. Tension between the English church and the papacy has a long history in the medieval period; for a general overview see Hay, "Church of England," and Brooke, *English Church*. But closer to the time of the Lollards, Edward III's reign was marked by a particular legislative bias against papal intervention in the workings of the English church. The passing of the Statute of Provisors in 1351 and the Statute of Praemunire in 1353 significantly limited the papacy's control over appointments to ecclesiastical benefices and the papal court's jurisdiction in England, especially over cases that also fell under royal jurisdiction; see Harper-Bill, *Pre-Reformation Church*, 3; Hay "Church of England," 40–43; Wilks, "Royal Patronage," 147. The problem between England and Rome seems to stem from the papacy's belief that it represented the "Church Universal" and could hold authority over churches in other countries that were all part of this Universal Church. When that Universal Church, as represented by the Avignon papacy, became associated with France, the situation "fostered a nationalistic view of the English church" (Harper-Bill, *Pre-Reformation Church* 9).

7. Chaucer deals with the issue of translation in several of his texts, such as both the F and G Prologues to the *Legend of Good Women*, and John Trevisa in his debate *Dialogus inter Dominum et Clericum*, the preface to his translation of Higden's *Polychronicon*. Hudson declares that "more interesting...is the evidence that Wyclif's ideas inspired others to turn to the medium of English and to use that language to express notions of a complexity unattempted in the vernacular at least since the time of Alfred's translation of Boethius" ("Wyclif," 90).

8. Hudson comments that the scholar who refers to the Prologue should do so with caution because, despite the extensive number of Wycliffite Bibles, only six include the Prologue and are therefore unlikely to have been "widely influential" (*Premature Reformation*, 238). Hunt explores the specifically Lollard arguments in favor of translation ("Edition," 225–40), and he also breaks them down into categories: pragmatic, precedents in the Bible, earlier translations, other countries' translations, connecting preaching and the written word, and grammar. His focus is, however, very different from mine here.

9. As the author of the "Tractatus de Regibus" argues: "Sythen witte stondis not in langage but in groundynge of treuthe, for þo same witte is in Laten þat is in Grew or Ebrew, and trouthe schuld be openly knowen to alle manere of folke" (Hudson, *Selections*, p. 127, lines 1–3).

10. Quotations from the seventh tract in CUL MS Ii.6.26 are taken from the critical edition in Hudson, *Selections*, 107–09, and are cited by line numbers in the text.

11. Quotations from the first tract in CUL MS Ii.6.26 are taken from the critical edition in Hunt, "Edition," 256–78, and are cited by line numbers in the text.

12. Quotations from Chapter 15 of the Prologue to the Wycliffite Bible are taken from the edition in Hudson's *Selections*, 67–72; quotations from the tract in Cambridge, Trinity College, MS B.14.50 are taken from the edition by Bühler, "Lollard Tract," 170–79. Both are cited by line numbers in the text.

13. Nationalism in the Anglo-Saxon culture is a contentious issue because, historically, Anglo-Saxon England comprised a disunited group of smaller kingdoms, and the texts produced during this period were written and read by a small, exclusive audience while a large majority of the country was illiterate. See Janet Thormann's essay "The Anglo-Saxon Chronicle Poems," in which she explores the fiction of the nation created in the chronicle.

14. It is interesting to note here that the author has used the plural form "naciouns"; while this could be a scribal error or variant reading, it might also suggest that the author sees the English nation as a collective grouping of nations: Scotland, Ireland, Wales, and England.

15. Quotations from the second tract in CUL MS Ii.6.26 are taken from the critical edition in Hunt, "Edition," 282–84.

16. For example, Chaucer's humble parson from his *Canterbury Tales* has been often interpreted as a Lollard poor priest as in Loomis, "Was Chaucer a Laodicean?" and Ives, "Man of Religion," but more recent scholarship has shown that the social status of Lollards varied considerably; see Plumb's "Spread" and Hudson's *Premature Reformation*, 128–33.

17. Hudson, "*Laicus litteratus*," 231. Hudson discusses the occurrence at the end of a sermon in London, British Library, MS Egerton 2820 of a note from the author asking the reader to note any points or questions, stating that the author will deal with these when he returns; see her "Lollard Book Production," 127 and "Wycliffite Scholar," 301–02. The text has been printed in Hudson, *Selections*, 96.

18. McSheffrey, *Gender*, 70–71; Hudson tells of John Claydon, the illiterate skinner who commissioned quires containing the "Lanterne of Liȝt" which, once he was certain the text was correct, had them bound, despite his illiteracy; see "Lollard Book Production," 125–26.

19. Hudson, "Lollard Book Production," 132; Hudson suggests that this could account for the paradox presented by the elaborate manuscripts and the generally economically humble Lollards; see *Premature Reformation*, 205–06, 233.

20. Hudson, *Premature Reformation*, 166–68. The register of Richard Mayew, bishop of Hereford, recording the trials in 1505, offers the standard clause in the abjuration: "that I have had in my ward and keeping divers books containing heresies and errors against Christian faith and the determination of all holy church, which books I have read and declared oftentimes privily and openly, on holy days and feast days, before many divers persons, reading, declaring and teaching against the blessed sacrament of the altar otherwise than I ought to have done" (qtd. in Harper-Bill, *Pre-Reformation Church*, 115). There are also letters from various bishops to one another that warn of the dangers of Lollard books in sowing the seed of heresy amongst the diocese. A letter from Bishop Blythe of Coventry to the bishop of Lincoln between 1511 and 1512 encourages the searching out of heretical books: "I p(ra)ie god ye may cu(m) to the seid books / ffor by such ther be many corrupted" (qtd. in Fines, "Heresy Trials," Appendix I, 172).

21. For the most comprehensive catalogue of these manuscripts see Lindberg, "Manu-scripts," and more recently Hunt, "Edition," Appendix III, 557–63.

22. A catalogue of these manuscripts is found in *English Wycliffite Sermons*, ed. Hud-son and Geradon, 1:51–97.

23. Hudson discusses these manuscripts in a number of places, including "Lollard Sermon-Cycle," 150, "Lollard Book Production," 131–34, *Premature Reformation*, 197–99, and her more detailed analysis of individual manuscripts in *English Wycliffite Sermons*, ed. Hudson and Geradon, 1:8–207.

24. Hudson, *Premature Reformation*, 233–34; Aston, "Lollardy," 203–05; Andrew Hope has suggested that some of this money must have come from the gentry because, once re-form became acceptable in the later sixteenth century, many Wycliffite Bibles resurfaced in gentry families; see "Lollardy," 10.

25. For a fuller discussion of this type of system, see Parkes, "Influence."

26. The manor of Braybroke in Northamptonshire was held by Sir Thomas Latimer, one of the infamous Lollard Knights, and Kemerton in Gloucestershire was held by Sir William Beauchamp, another possible associate of the Lollard knights; see Hudson, *Prema-ture Reformation*, 90–91. For more on Latimer and Beauchamp, see McFarlane, *Lancastrian Kings*. The most concrete evidence about these locations comes from a manuscript copy of Wyclif's *De Dominio Divino* and *De Ecclesia*, preserved in Vienna, Österreichische National-bibliothek MS 1294; in this manuscript, a note records that in 1407 the two Hussites Mikuláš Faulfiš and Jiří Knĕhnic copied these texts at Braybroke and Kemerton (Hudson, *Premature Reformation*, 90–91). In "Lollard Book Production," Hudson also asserts that by Oldcastle's rebellion, "Braybrooke was known as a centre for the dissemination of sedi-tious and heterodox pamphlets" (129). Another possible location is London; during the proceedings against Sir John Oldcastle, tracts belonging to him were found in an illumi-nator's shop in Pater Noster Row, and while a fugitive he was hidden in the home of a London stationer, one William Parchemyner, see Lambert, *Medieval Heresy*, 252–53 (who mistakenly names Oldcastle's protector "William Fisher"); Hudson, *Premature Reforma-tion*, 206–07.

27. Far more information about Lollard manuscripts is available than can be covered in this brief article; for more detailed and extensive evidence see Hudson's *Premature Re-formation*, and *English Wycliffite Sermons*, ed. Hudson and Geradon. My work here rests heavily upon these monumental contributions to the field, though my interpretation of the data might differ from Hudson's conclusions.

28. As Doyle and Parkes have shown ("Production," 237–41), the evidence of earlier Chaucer and Gower manuscripts indicates that these texts were produced using a sort of bespoke system through which each manuscript was custom made to suit the individual patron's wishes.

29. Hudson even shows how communication through books could account for the occurrence of unusual beliefs shared by communities that were very distant from each other, particularly the case of Thomas Bikenore from Salisbury whose beliefs were remarkably similar to the beliefs of Lollards in East Anglia (*Premature Reformation*, 141–42).

30. Though he argues against a connection between geographically disparate groups, Davies still believes that these smaller local groups were well organized and stable ("Lollardy," 211–12).

31. Hudson, *Premature Reformation*, 32–42; Kightly is also cautious, convinced "that groups of lollards in several areas succeeded in altogether avoiding detection" ("Early Lollards," v).

32. Both Thomson and Kightly organize their chapters by region. Kightly, unfortunately, makes no general conclusion about the extent of the heresy or its spread, though the evidence he has amassed speaks for itself. See also Lambert, *Medieval Heresy*, 274–75, and his Map 8 on 276–77; he attributes the lack of surviving bishop's registers from the northern counties to explain why no evidence exists for Lollard communities there. Thomson suggests on this point that the rural economy and lack of a mobile artisan class could account for this (*Later Lollards*, 200–01).

33. Plumb, "Gathered Church?" 152–53; McSheffrey, *Gender*, 106. A number of scholars discuss the importance of the nuclear family unit; see Hudson, *Premature Reformation*, 135–36; Cross, "'Great Reasoners,'" 360; Hope, "Lollardy," 10; McSheffrey, *Gender* 81; Davies, "Lollardy," 195.

34. Plumb, "Gathered Church?" 144; Hudson, *Premature Reformation*, 140–41. Kightly lists twenty known itinerant preachres who "between them . . . are known to have visited nearly every part of the country in which lollardy subsequently flourished" ("Early Lollards," 581).

REFERENCES

Anderson, Benedict. *Imagined Communities: Reflections on the Origin and Spread of Nationalism*. London and New York: Verso, 1983.

Arnold, T., ed. *Select English Works of John Wyclif*. 3 vols. Oxford: Oxford University Press, 1869–71.

Aston, Margaret. "Lollardy and Literacy." In her *Lollards and Reformers: Images and Literacy in Late Medieval Religion*, 193–217. London: Hambledon Press, 1984.

———. "'Caim's Castles': Poverty, Politics, and Disendowment." In her *Faith and Fire: Popular and Unpopular Religion, 1350–1600*, 95–131. London: Hambledon Press, 1993.

Brooke, Z. N. *The English Church and the Papacy: From the Conquest to the Reign of John*. Cambridge: Cambridge University Press, 1989.

Bühler, Curt F. "A Lollard Tract: On Translating the Bible into English." *Medium Ævum* 7 (1938): 167–83.

Collinson, Patrick. "The English Conventicle." *Studies in Church History* 23 (1986): 223–59.

Copeland, Rita. "William Thorpe and His Lollard Community: Intellectual Labor and the Representation of Dissent." In *Bodies and Disciplines: Intersections of Literature and History in Fifteenth-century England*, ed. Barbara Hanawalt and David Wallace, 199–221. Minneapolis: University of Minnesota Press, 1996.

Cross, Claire. "'Great Reasoners in Scripture': The Activities of Women Lollards 1380–1530." In *Medieval Women,* ed. Derek Baker, Studies in Church History, Subsidia 1, 359–80. Oxford: Blackwell, 1978.

Davies, Richard. "Lollardy and Locality." *Transactions of the Royal Historical Society,* 6th series 1 (1992): 191–212.

Doyle, A. I., and M. B. Parkes. "The Production of Copies of the *Canterbury Tales* and the *Confessio Amantis* in the Early Fifteenth Century." In *Medieval Scribes, Manuscripts, and Libraries: Essays Presented to N. R. Kerr,* ed. M. B. Parkes and Andrew G. Watson, 163–210. London: Scolar Press, 1978.

Duffy, Eamon. *The Stripping of the Altars: Traditional Religion in England 1400–1580.* New Haven: Yale University Press, 1992.

Fines, John. "Heresy Trials in the Diocese of Coventry and Lichfield, 1511–12." *Journal of Ecclesiastical History* 14 (1963): 160–74.

Hanna, Ralph. "Two Lollard Codices and Lollard Book Production." In his *Pursuing History: Middle English Manuscripts and Their Texts,* 48–59. Stanford: Stanford University Press, 1996.

Harper-Bill, Christopher. *The Pre-Reformation Church in England, 1400–1530.* Seminar Studies in History. London: Longman, 1989.

Hastings, Adrian. *The Construction of Nationhood: Ethnicity, Religion and Nationalism.* Cambridge: Cambridge University Press, 1997.

Hay, Denys. "The Church of England in the Later Middle Ages." *History* 53 (1968): 35–50.

Hope, Andrew. "Lollardy: The Stone the Builders Rejected?" In *Protestantism and the National Church in Sixteenth Century England,* ed. Peter Lake and Maria Dowling, 1–35. London: Croom Helm, 1987.

Hudson, Anne. "A Lollard Sermon-Cycle and Its Implications." *Medium Ævum* 40 (1971): 142–56.

———. "A Lollard Compilation and the Dissemination of Wycliffite Thought." *Journal of Theological Studies,* n.s., 23 (1972): 65–81. Reprinted in her *Lollards and Their Books,* 13–29.

———. "Some Aspects of Lollard Book Production." *Studies in Church History* 9 (1972): 147–57. Reprinted in her *Lollards and Their Books,* 181–91.

———. "The Debate on Bible Translation, Oxford 1401." *English Historical Review* 90 (1975): 1–18. Reprinted in her *Lollards and Their Books,* 67–84.

———. "A Lollard Sect Vocabulary?" In *So meny people longages and tonges: Philological Essays in Scots and Mediaeval English Presented to Angus McIntosh,* ed. Michael Benskin and M. L. Samuels, 15–30, Edinburgh: M. Benskin and M. L. Samuels, 1981. Reprinted in her *Lollards and Their Books,* 165–80.

———. "Lollardy: The English Heresy?" *Studies in Church History* 18 (1982): 261–83. Reprinted in her *Lollards and Their Books,* 141–63.

———. *Lollards and Their Books.* London: Hambledon Press, 1985.

———. "A Wycliffite Scholar of the Early Fifteenth Century." In *The Bible in the Medieval World: Essays in Memory of Beryl Smalley,* ed. Katherine Walsh and Diana Wood, 301–15. Oxford: Blackwell for the Ecclesiastical History Society, 1985.

————. "Wyclif and the English Language." In *Wyclif in His Times*, ed. Anthony Kenny, 85–103. Oxford: Clarendon Press, 1986.

————. *The Premature Reformation: Wycliffite Texts and Lollard History*. Oxford: Clarendon Press, 1988.

————. "Lollard Book Production." In *Book Production and Publishing in Britain, 1375–1475*, ed. Jeremy Griffiths and Derek Pearsall, 125–42. Cambridge: Cambridge University Press, 1989.

————. "*Laicus litteratus*: The Paradox of Lollardy." In *Heresy and Literacy, 1000–1530*, ed. Peter Biller and Anne Hudson, 222–36. Cambridge Studies in Medieval Literature 23. Cambridge: Cambridge University Press, 1994.

————, ed. *Selections from English Wycliffite Writings*. Cambridge: Cambridge University Press, 1978.

————, ed. *Two Wycliffite Texts: The Sermon of William Taylor, 1406; The Testimony of William Thorpe, 1407*. EETS. OS 301. Oxford: Oxford University Press, 1993.

Hudson, Anne, and Pamela Gradon, eds. *English Wycliffite Sermons*. 5 vols. Oxford: Clarendon Press, 1983–96.

Hunt, Simon. "An Edition of Tracts in Favour of Scriptural Translation and of Some Texts Connected with Lollard Vernacular Biblical Scholarship." Ph.D. diss., University of Oxford, 1994.

Ives, Doris V. "A Man of Religion." *Modern Language Review* 27 (1932): 144–48.

Kightly, Charles. "The Early Lollards: A Survey of Popular Lollard Activity in England, 1382–1428." Ph.D. diss., University of York, 1975.

Lambert, Malcolm. *Medieval Heresy: Popular Movements from the Gregorian Reform to the Reformation*. Oxford: Blackwell, 1992.

Lindberg, Conrad. "The Manuscripts and Versions of the Wycliffite Bible: A Preliminary Survey." *Studia Neophilologica* 42 (1970): 333–47.

Loomis, R. S. "Was Chaucer a Laodicean?" In his *Studies in Medieval Literature: A Memorial Collection of Essays*, 255–74. New York: Burt Franklin, 1970. Originally printed in *Essays and Studies in Honor of Carleton Brown*, 129–48. New York: New York University Press, 1940.

McFarlane, K. B. *Lancastrian Kings and Lollard Knights*. 1972; Oxford: Oxford University Press, 1998.

McHardy, A. K. "Bishop Buckingham and the Lollards of Lincoln Diocese." *Studies in Church History* 9 (1972): 131–45.

McSheffrey, Shannon. *Gender and Heresy: Women and Men in Lollard Communities, 1420–1530*. Philadelphia: University of Pennsylvania Press, 1995.

Parkes, Malcolm B. "The Influence of the Concepts of *Ordinatio* and *Compilatio* on the Development of the Book." In *Medieval Learning and Literature: Essays Presented to Richard William Hunt*, ed. J. J. G. Alexander and M. T. Gibson, 115–41. Oxford: Clarendon Press, 1976.

Plumb, Derek. "The Social and Economic Spread of Rural Lollardy: A Reappraisal." *Studies in Church History* 23 (1986): 111–29.

————. "A Gathered Church? Lollards and Their Society." In *The World of Rural Dissenters,*

1520–1725, ed. Margaret Spufford, 132–63. Cambridge: Cambridge University Press, 1995.

Swanson, R. N. *Catholic England: Faith, Religion and Observance Before the Reformation.* Manchester Medieval Sources Series. Manchester: Manchester University Press, 1993.

———. *Religion and Devotion in Europe, 1215–1515.* Cambridge Medieval Textbooks. Cambridge: Cambridge University Press, 1995.

Tanner, Norman P., ed. *Heresy Trials in the Diocese of Norwich, 1428–31.* Camden 4th series 20. London: Royal Historical Society, 1977.

Thomson, John A. F. *The Later Lollards, 1414–1520.* Oxford: Oxford University Press, 1965.

Thormann, Janet. "The Anglo-Saxon Chronicle Poems and the Making of the English Nation." In *Anglo-Saxonism and the Construction of Social Identity,* ed. Allen Frantzen and John Niles, 60–85. Gainesville: University Press of Florida, 1997.

Turville-Petre, Thorlac. *England the Nation: Language, Literature, and National Identity, 1290–1340.* Oxford: Clarendon Press, 1996.

Wilks, Michael. "Royal Patronage and Anti-Papalism from Ockham to Wyclif." In *From Ockham to Wyclif,* ed. Anne Hudson and Michael Wilks, Studies in Church History, Subsidia 5, 135–63. Oxford: Blackwell, 1987.

PART III
CHAUCER'S ENGLAND

Chaucer Imagines England (in English)

Peggy A. Knapp

> SEVEN OF NINE: *You do not know what it is to be Borg.*
> CAPTAIN JANEWAY: *No, I don't, but I can imagine.*

When Benedict Anderson argued that the nation is "an imagined political community," his phrase seemed so apt, even obvious, that it made its way into many facets of analysis in the human sciences. It also meshed with the current elevation of imagination as the most interesting, most effective, mental power we humans have—Captain Janeway must make a remarkable leap to find any continuity between her self-enclosed mental landscape and the collective intelligence of the Borg.[1] More particularly, the idea of imagined communities forged an important link between political and literary theories, since the mutual effects of imaginative constructs and "real world" social practices have been a focus of literary scholarship for some time now. By pointing out that an imagined entity like the nation can elicit the sacrifice of life on a large scale, Anderson elevates the status of imagining and renders socially symbolic acts freshly relevant to historical study. Although Chaucer's career lies well before the full establishment of nationhood Anderson describes, his is the figure that later generations associate with the beginnings of a specifically English sensibility. This association is all the more arresting when we consider how many of Chaucer's productions were in fact translations from Latin, Italian, and French "originals." I want to investigate the extent to which Chaucer is and ought to be credited with imagining an emergent and distinctive Englishness by looking at his and his era's apprehension of imagining, his handling of the linguistic and religious affiliations that mark off communities, and his treatment of citizenship (rather than subject-hood) informed by a shift from a consciousness of time as cyclic and typological to time as linear and "empty," enabling *national* communities.

Chaucer's pilgrims have been thought of as making up an imagined community—the nine and twenty in a *compaignye* assembled at the Tabard and on the road to Canterbury—for centuries. In one sense, this is a matter entirely different from Anderson's assertion, since the members of this community are themselves imagined, first by Geoffrey Chaucer and then by each of his interpreters, in contrast with the apparently simultaneous recognition of communion living "in the minds of each" member of a nation even though they do not know one another (Anderson, *Imagined Communities,* 15). One might say that the community the pilgrims form is *only an imaginary* one—nobody will fight a war for it. But then again, people who will fight wars have to encounter images of those of their fellows whom they have not met, and those images must resonate with their sense of those they have in order for a community to form. Without erasing the difference between Chaucer's fiction of community and Anderson's posited political community, we might consider Richard Helgerson's comment: "We think more easily of people as agents and of the things they make or imagine as structures. But people themselves, whether individually or in groups, are made and imagined. Their identity—*our* identity—is a structure, a cultural construct" (*Forms,* 13). Helgerson seems a bit too certain of this, a bit too neglectful of natural and constitutional elements in our sense of ourselves, but the insight that collective identity is culturally constructed in large part and inheres in people's imaginations, often through the cultural objects they attend to, cannot be gainsaid.

I will begin by investigating the nature of imagining. Anderson objects to the claim that the invention of nationhood should be linked with fabrication rather than imagination more broadly considered; his definition of imagining, therefore, must involve bringing forth something previously in existence, though differently experienced. I will conduct a brief tour of some medieval and modern senses of imagination to see how we might understand a specifically Chaucerian imaginative act. Then I intend to argue that Chaucer did indeed imagine an English community in the *The Canterbury Tales* and that he was able to do so because in some measure such a community was already in existence. Finally, I will argue that there are many features of his fiction that allow it to be read (and thus imagined) as concerned with national identity—that is, with the modern sense of language, power, and time that Anderson identifies with nationalism. This third point must, of course, be marked by considerable nuance. Sponsored by influential writers like John Foxe, the large-scale construction of the imagined community of saints continuous with an ancient past awaited England's Calvinist conception of itself in the sixteenth century,[2] but Chaucer's English imaginings may point to some conditions of possibility for that later moment.

"RESOUN YMAGINATYF"

Murray Wright Bundy finds "faculty psychology," the broadest strand of medieval thinking about imagination, compartmentalizing mind into imagination (*imaginatio* or *phantasia,* often not distinguished, the storehouse of received sensations, a capacity shared with animals), intellect (which shapes sensations into ideas), and memory. In this scheme, imagination figured as the opposing pole to reason and was consequently distrusted as fostering illusion. This description is behind the sense, often expressed by modern scholars, that "medieval people did not value originality or creativity" since they accorded imagination the lowly place of "a sort of draught-horse of the sensitive soul, not even given intellectual status," as Mary Carruthers puts it.[3]

The mystic tradition, concerned to produce communion of the mind with God rather than to classify the faculties of mind, accounted imagination the "handmaiden of reason" and an indispensable feature of spiritual contemplation, relying on a somewhat different division of the faculties (sensation, imagination, reason, and intellect). For Hugo (Hugh) of St. Victor, "Viewed as an aggregate of material parts, it [the universe as a whole] is merely a matter for the senses; but, when brought within the domain of man's understanding, it becomes the subject matter of imagination—the imagination not of the brute, but of the man of reason" (qtd. Bundy, *Theory*, 383). Aquinas wrote of imaginings inspired by angels, but also of demonic visions, some revealing or seeming to reveal the future. These are especially likely to occur during sleep, when the rational faculty is not able to exert its wonted control (Bundy, *Theory*, 403–06). What various theories have in common is that in ethical domains, reason or intellect must control imagination. These mainstream, though not altogether reconcilable, descriptions of the imaginative function were not materially challenged by later thinkers like Gianfrancesco Pico. His *De Imaginatione* (1501) makes use of both analytic and mystical traditions, though he stresses more than others the indispensable power of imagination to suggest what is not present to sensation (29) and minister to "both the discursive reason and the contemplative intellect" (37). Although "apparently, no deed or action at all can be performed without it," the purest minds must seek to dominate it and recede from it (83).

Medieval assessments of imagination, perforce, presented a challenge to poetics and to the creation of fictional text. Much as Dante has been likened to Aquinas in his range and his tendency to subdivide and categorize, his implied theory of the role of vision and imagination in spiritual enlightenment more strongly resembles that of the mystics, who attempted to use rather than bypass concrete, earthly experience, including mental experience, to effect communion with God. Bundy regards the *Divine Comedy* as "perhaps the greatest conscious attempt in the history of art to express, to make intelligible, a vision" (*Theory*, 410). Moreover, like so many medieval writers—Langland, the *Pearl*-poet, Chaucer—he casts that vision as a dream, in spite of the fact that most mainstream philosophy saw in dreams the dangerous potential for fantasy uncensored by conscious intellect.

It is likely that Chaucer was pondering the two aspects of medieval tradition while he was working on *Troilus and Criseyde* and *The Knight's Tale* since he was at that time translating the Boethius's *Consolatione Philosophie*, with its synthetic theory of imagination in Book V. In *Boece*, the usual stress on the control of imagination by the "higher" faculties of reason and intellect is clear, but the treatise keeps imagination in the realm of judgment throughout cognition. Chaucer phrases the point thus:

> Also ymaginacioun, albeit so it takith of wit [sense impressions] the bygynnynges to seen and formen the figures, algates al- thoughe that wit ne were nat present, yit it envyrowneth and

comprehendith alle thingis sensible, nat by resoun sensible of demyng, but by resoun ymaginatyf. (V, prosa 4, 200–10)[4]

"Resoun ymaginatyf" seems to me a resonant locution for considering Chaucer's practices in relating observed reality, especially social reality, to authorial creation.

I hope to show, however, that more is implied by Chaucer's textual practice than he could have found directly presented by Boethius or any of the received theorists of his time, haunted as they are by suspicion that imagination occludes the ethical judgment needed for rational society. More modern notions, like Hume's assertion that imagination has the propensity "to turn ideas into living impressions, to arouse actual passions and to experience them" (qtd. Warnock, *Imagination*, 200–01) match the emotional aura of images used to aid memory discussed by Carruthers (*Book of Memory*, 60) and seem highly relevant to Chaucer's method. Particularly useful for understanding Chaucerian imaginative projection is Wittgenstein's tenet that imagination both forms pictures in the mind *and* interprets the world actually before us, causing us to see something *as* an aspect of something (*Investigations*, 115 and 213). He then plays with the idea that someone could be "aspect-blind," able to see, but without the normal intervention of imagination that recognizes forms and classes of things. Before *Philosophical Investigations* appeared, Jorge Luis Borges had played with a similar idea in "Funes the Memorious," the story of a boy whose fall from a horse rendered his memory so acute that each impression was separate, and he was therefore "disturbed by the fact that a dog at three-fourteen (seen from in profile) should have the same name as the dog at three-fifteen (seen from the front)."[5] Later, Annie Dillard also wrote about cases of "aspect-blindness" caused by the surgical cure of life-long blindness. On their sudden entrance into the world of the sighted, most people's new vision, "pure sensation unencumbered by meaning," presented itself "as a dazzle of color-patches." They found that world "tormentingly difficult" and sometimes defeating ("Sight," 248). What they had to do much later in life and more quickly than other people was to develop the function of imagination that recognizes images. As Mary Warnock says, "images themselves are not separate from our interpretations of the world; they are our way of thinking of the objects in the world.... The two are joined because forms have a certain meaning, always significant beyond themselves.

We recognize a form as a form *of* something [as the newly sighted could not], as Wittgenstein said, by its relation with other things" (*Imagination*, 194–95). This last point may be, of course, what certain medieval thinkers meant by bringing imagination into the domain of reason. It certainly seems to be Anderson's way of using the term "imagination"[6] and may be what Chaucer gestured toward in his phrase "resoun ymaginatyf."

Forming figures through "resoun ymaginatyf" is further signaled by Chaucer's occasional use of "engyn" for the imaginative faculty. In *The Second Nun's Tale* a traditional reference is made to the three faculties of mind, man's "sapiences three— / Memorie, engyn, and intellect" (VIII.338–39). Cecile is explaining how God can be single yet in three persons by likening him to the triune composition of human minds. The Parson also uses the "engyn" as an aspect of mind.[7] He lists "subtil engyn" among the gifts of soul bestowed by nature, along with "vertu natural" and good memory. Chaucer's narrator in the *House of Fame* invokes Thought to unlock the dream images in his mind and present them (to "every maner man / That English understonde kan") aright, displaying his "engyn and myght" to do so (II.509–10, 28). In *Troilus and Criseyde*, Pandarus has all he can do with "engyn" and "loore" to keep love-sick Troilus from dying (II.565), in this case clearly "engyn" implies ingenuity. Pandarus's second use of "engyn" reveals even more fully the range Chaucer allowed the terms. In this passage in Book III, Pandarus is swearing Troilus to secrecy about the love affair, in part to protect Criseyde's name (which currently is "halwed") and partly because the charge of treachery would be brought against him if it were known that the affair had come about through his "engyn" (275). The added implication here is that of a contrivance, like that of the lover standing outside the garden in the *Romaunt of the Rose* trying to come up with an art or "engyn" to admit him. Even more fully contrivances, although not employed stealthily, are the astrolabe, which the modest Chaucer does not want Lewis to think his own invention ("myn engyn," *Treatise on the Astrolabe*, Prologue 61), and the catapult whose stone makes such a noise in the *House of Fame* (III.844). The range of "engyn" from an exact synonym for imagination as a faculty of mind to clever mental planning and then to physical machines suggests that Chaucer could think of imagination as an active, even an aggressive, intellectual process rather than a passive repository for sensations given by the "real world" or by the angels and devils.

The picture-forming aspect of imagination is vividly presented in the Merchant's account of January thinking about womanly beauty as *like* setting a mirror in the market place. "Heigh fantasye and curious bisynesse" (note the activeness implied by "bisynesse") characterized the first phase of his search as he watched "many a figure pace / By his mirour" (IV.1576, 1584–85), allowing his willed plan to marry work through imagination "to arouse actual passions and to experience them," as in Hume's assertion. His passion lights on May, and his love ("blynde alday"—"always," but a nice pun on daytime reality) portrayed in his bed at night her imagined beauties of body and deportment. Boethius presents this aspect of imagination as a first step in cognition, that faculty of mind that "comprehendith oonly the figure withoute the matere" (*Boece*, V, prosa 4, 150–60). In January's case, little is done to modify by reason or intelligence the "fantasye" (the word itself appears twice in thirty-five lines) in which he revels. *The Merchant's Tale* might be read as an account of willful fantasizing unmasked, a misuse of imagination out of touch with its ordinary references to the world outside the self. Chaucer does not involve the word "imagination" in this account. He does use it, however, to achieve a pointed satiric effect in *The Nun's Priest's Tale*. The col-fox burst through the hedge to plot against Chauntecleer by "heigh ymaginacioun forncast" (VII.3217), the dignified phrasing suggesting foreknowledge, perhaps even a reference to Dante (see *Riverside*'s note), but moving the tale forward by indicating that the fox had imaged a long-range plan to dine on the rooster. This mental picturing was less sealed off from rational observation than January's, and it almost succeeded.

Imagining as "seeing as" is foregrounded in the reaction of the lord in *The Summoner's Tale* to the task of dividing the fart twelve ways.

> How had this cherl ymaginacioun
> To shew swich a probleme to the frere?
> Nevere erst er now herde I of swich mateere.
> I trowe the devel putte it in his mynde.
> In ars-metrike shal ther no man fynde,
> Biforn this day, of swich a question. (III.2218–23)

The humor of this response lies in the lord's trance-like absorption in the problem of imagination, rather than the outrage the friar expects.

How could a simple villager like Thomas mentally represent an interesting *mateere*—the higher of Boethius's levels in the scholarly venue further suggested by *shew* ("set"), *probleme, ars-metrike, question, demonstra-
cion,* and *inpossible*—to himself and then carry out the plot? How could
he refigure his earthy joke as a challenge to the friar's vaunted intellectual superiority? The lord can only conclude that the devil sent him
the vision, and Thomas has therefore become "demonyak," a common
medieval reaction to unusual imaginative feats.

A glancingly presented example of the "seeing as" use appears in
The Clerk's Tale: The sergeant leaves Griselda after taking away her baby
boy, ostensibly to be killed, to report to Walter, "ful faste ymaginyng /
If by his wyves cheer he myght se / Or by her word aperceyve, that she /
Were changed" (IV.598–601). *Riverside* glosses "ymaginyng" as "considering" and Donaldson as "pondering," but neither Fisher's edition nor
Robinson's gives it a gloss and there is little reason not to take it to
mean "interpreting through imagination." The sergeant is bringing reason and experience to the image of Griselda's behavior he has seen, trying to picture it *as* either obedience to Walter's will or veiled rebellion.
He concludes that it is obedience.

Even more substantial evidence that Chaucer's text could use imagination in its Wittgensteinian sense of "seeing something *as*" is found in
the Knight's account of Palamon objecting to Arcite's seeing his shocked
loss of color (his *bleynte*) and his "A" as distress over his imprisonment.
He resents Arcite's lecture on enduring what seems to have no remedy.
"Thou hast a veyn ymaginacioun," he says, and discloses the real cause
of his suffering as the wound of love.

> This prison caused me nat for to crye
> But I was hurt right now thurghout mine ye
> Into myn herte, that wol my bane be.
> The fairnesse of that lady that I see
> Yond in the gardyn romen to and fro
> Is cause of al my criyng and my wo. (I.1094–1100)

Beyond Chaucer's imagining his Knight and the Knight imagining Palamon, we have two acts of imagination here. Arcite imagines Palamon's
suffering *as* an effect of his imprisonment, and Palamon imagines the
effect of seeing Emelye *as* the construct familiar to courtly culture: an

arrow has entered through his eye and pierced his heart, undetected by the outside world. What Arcite sees (quite understandably) as an enactment of the complaint against Fortune, Palamon sees as a spontaneous reaction to Venus's aggressive attack. Which form the perception takes has consequences, since "forms have a certain meaning, always significant beyond themselves (we recognize a form as a form *of* something, as Wittgenstein said, by its relation with other things)" (Warnock, *Imagination*, 194–95). An immediate consequence is that Palamon conflates Venus's influence over his seeing Emelye with thinking of Emelye *as* Venus herself ("soothly"), thereby putting himself at a disadvantage rhetorically when Arcite claims he loved her first *as* a woman.

The picture-forming mode of imagining is also apparent in *The Knight's Tale*. The "derk ymaginyng / Of Felonye" is figured on the wall of the temple of Mars. This is a passage relevant to the dramatic thesis in general, since the Knight says "Ther saugh I" (I.1995–96) when he is presumably retelling a story from the distant past and might therefore be taken as a lapse in the impersonation of the Knight. H. Marshall Leicester makes an important distinction, however, between *presence* and *voice*, and regards, as I do, the Knight's voice as that being characterized as the tale proceeds (*Disenchanted Self*, 8–10). That voice suggests a teller working to endow Theseus with heroic stature and his story with expansive scale through its "epic formality of language and clarified largeness of gesture" (226). This voiced impulse is appropriate to the gentle Knight of *The General Prologue*, someone for whom the text has created the expectation of dignity in filling out the demands of his estate and presenting them to the *compaignye* without irony. Yet the descriptions of the temples, particularly the temple of Mars, suggests a voice not altogether able to project the idealized knightly estate without an undertow of horror and chagrin born of his own experiences in battle. Little of what he reports seeing in Mars's temple recalls the clean image of Theseus riding to the aid of the Theban women and defeating Creon in "pleyn bataille"; instead he describes "the smylere with the knife under the cloke," the suicide, the leveled town, the babe in his cradle eaten by a sow. Who sees these things? Within the Knight's fiction, the "soutil pencel" (I.2049) of the artist commissioned by Theseus is responsible. On that level, either the Knight or Chaucer may be remarking on the propensity of art to escape its institutional warrant and say disturbing things. Within the Canterbury frame tale, they may contribute to the

Knight's further characterization: intent though he is on presenting chivalric heroism, he cannot keep the images he has seen from infecting his account of Mars's domain. His attempt to see military violence *as* heroic resistance to Fortune cannot in this passage be sustained.[8] The conscious wish is imposed on by a too richly remembered reality, too vividly present to imagination. Here the picture-forming aspect of imagination is deeply fused to the Knight's seeing battle *as* something, as in fact horrifying results of violence in their less-than-epic formulations.

But, like other medieval texts, *The Canterbury Tales* also recognizes that imagination lies close to fantasy, especially in visions experienced in sleep. When Mercury appears to Arcite in a dream, his image and message are tinged with threat. His "slepy yerde" is held upright, in power over the prone Arcite, and Arcite recognizes that he looks as he did when he killed Argus (I.1387–90). Nonetheless, Arcite reads his instruction to end his woe by going to Athens as helpful advice, though he acknowledges the risk. Imagination in this case is seductive and potentially destructive: "men may dyen of ymaginacioun."

But it is the Miller, not the Knight, who says so. Commenting on how eagerly John the Carpenter entertains the fiction of the flood Nicholas is predicting, the Miller comments:

> Men may dyen of ymaginacioun,
> So depe may impressioun be take.
> This sely carpenter bigynneth quake;
> Hym thynketh verraily that he may see
> Noees flood come walwynge as the see
> To drenchen Alisoun, his hony deere. (I.3612–17)

Here is the picture-making imagination on a grand and comically portentous scale. John's simplicity and distrust of scholarly learning notwithstanding, he falls as easily into Nicholas's trap as the sleeping man deceived about the future by demons in Aquinas's account (Bundy, *Theory*, 404). In a way, Nicholas *is* a demon producing fantasies in someone else's imagination, which is a beautiful irony considering that John thought the elves and wights had cast a night-spell on Nicholas (I.3479–86). There is great economy in Nicholas's appeal to John's imagination; he provides few details about the destuctiveness of the flood. It is worse than that of Noah's day and will drown everyone in less than an hour—

John fills in the specific "Allas my wyf." Nicholas then concentrates on detailed directions for equipping the kneading tubs. The appeal to imagining the unfamiliar is Nicholas's description of the bliss the three of them will share "when that the greet shour is goon away":

> Thanne shaltou swymme as myrie, I undertake,
> As dooth the white doke after hire drake.
> Thanne wol I clepe, "How, Alison! How, John!
> Be myrie, for the flood wol passe anon."
> And thou wolt seyn, "Hayl, maister Nicholay!
> Good morwe, I se thee wel, for it is day."
> And thanne shul we be lordes al oure lyf
> Of al the world, as Noe and his wyf. (I.3574–82)

John's ambition to be a lord does not seem to be stirred by this vision; his mental pictures are driven by fear that harm will befall Alison and by pleasure in the serenity of their floating together after the storm (perhaps faint suggestion of the postcoital)—throughout the tale he demonstrates that he loves his new wife "moore than his lyf" (I.3222). He creates his own mental picture of the giant waves wallowing. The point here is that imagination is working with reason (such as John's capacities allow—he *is* practical and consistent) to produce the particular mental picture that drives his actions.

The Knight's description of the temple is derived from images stored in memory, Arcite's image of Mercury comes to him in sleep, and the feared flood is a mental picture for John the Carpenter, formed under Nicholas's inspiration. What these examples are intended to show is the synthetic way Chaucer is using medieval psychology in its most positive and assertive aspects—that imagination stores sense impressions, receives them from supernatural agents through dreams, and creates them from ideas (Hume's "living impression") through "resoun ymaginatyf." Such pictures have consequences—Arcite's return to Athens, John the Carpenter's lashing himself to the ceiling in a kneading tub—that may prove either positive or negative. But once they are formed, they influence the "real world," become real, one might say, as Anderson does. In addition, Chaucer seems to have understood imagination as the set of forms in or through which the real world is apprehended. Arcite sees Emelye *as* a goddess, the Knight sees battle *as* a ravaged town. The connection

Chaucer makes between "imagination" and "engine" merely furthers the sense of craft and craftsmanship, active rather than passive, he bestows on the creation of the image.

COMMUNITY

Bundy regards Dante's role in the long line of thinkers who shaped the medieval tradition on imagination as pivotal in raising the status of imagination and imaginative works. Certainly, *The Divine Comedy* makes remarkable claims for the intellectual and spiritual incisiveness of the imagination's power to call up situations that are not present to direct observation (Pico, *De Imaginatione*, 29). As Chaucer's predecessor, Dante also uses imagination to see "real world" situations *as* involved with transcendent, meaning-bearing forms. What his work does not offer Chaucer is the vision of a human *community*. Dante's powerful characters inhabit isolated circles and pouches of hell and few are presented as having interacted communally when they were alive, even those from Dante's Florence. Chaucer's people are *together* on the pilgrimage. The stakes for which Dante's characters play are spiritual, moral, and ethical perfections, set in postapocalyptic worlds from which local custom has receded. Even Boccaccio's *Decameron,* whose realism is celebrated as a break with medieval practice, gives its ten young storytellers very little of the local distinctiveness and personal interaction that would make them appear as a community. Chaucer's crew is far more motley and far more contentious, but also more engaged with one another. They are assembled on and competitive over the distinctive social and economic terrain of late medieval England. To contend this way, they use the varied registers available to Middle English and disclose their various takes on English controversies. To present them this way Chaucer's text both creates what is not in being and interprets what is. In turning from *how* Chaucer regarded imagination to *what* he imagines, we come first to the issue of language.

Anderson argues that a condition of possibility for nationalism arises with the waning of the idea that "a particular script-language offered privileged access to ontological truth, precisely because it was an inseparable part of that truth" (*Imagined Communities*, 40). As long as Latin bound the linguistically adept of the Christian West together in a transnational conversation, local communities were slow to form vertical ties. In this matter Chaucer's work registers a particularly strong element in the loosening of the prestige of Latin, but that prestige was "regularly contested by other languages of real or putative authority," as Christopher Baswell puts it ("Latinitas," 123). The substitution of the international script-language Latin by English took centuries and was by no means complete when Edmund Spenser wrote to Gabriel Harvey in 1580, arguing for "the kingdom of our own language" (Helgerson, *Forms*, 1). The trials of Bible translators like Tyndale in the fifteenth century are too familiar to rehearse here, and only sixty of the sixty thousand books in the library at Oxford in 1600 were English language volumes. Queen Elizabeth, denied the right to speak to the faculty of Cambridge in English, was able to deliver a graceful and well-received address in Latin. The "kingdom of our own language" is a resonant phrase, fusing the sense of entitlement to a national identity with the right to be heard in one's vernacular. Helgerson asserts that it "govern[s] the very linguistic system, and perhaps more generally the whole cultural system, by which their own identity and their own consciousness were constituted" (3). That access to printing and expanded capitalism worked together to establish the vernaculars seems as true for England as for the other cases Anderson examines (*Imagined Communities*, 47), but acceptance of the vernacular as able to transmit sacred truths rested heavily on the particulars of the Reformation in England as well.

Early modern debates over the authority of an English Bible were pre-figured in the Wycliffite controversies of the 1380s and 1390s.[9] Anderson asserts that the transhistorical, transterritorial sodalities are communities of signs, not spoken language, signs that were regarded as "emanations of reality, not randomly fabricated representations of it," and notes that this view of language itself—"the non-arbitrariness of the sign"—is distinctly unmodern. But in the West, this nonarbitrariness was a political rather than a philosophical/theological construct even in the early Middle Ages, since Latin was the original language of neither the Old nor the New Testament. Jerome's Latin Bible was no doubt a convenience for stabilizing the still unfixed canon and phrasing of sacred text for the far-flung Christian empire, but it could not be defended as the uniquely delivered Word.[10] It was, nonetheless, the institutionally sanctioned language, the language that made the sacraments efficacious, the one in which knowing your neck-verse could save you from hanging.

Most English priests knew only enough Latin to announce their membership in that community, not enough to participate in its controversies. Latin was not so much the actual currency of religious teaching[11] as the sign of connection with the long-standing community of believers dead and living. Lollards were not the only proponents of vernacular presentations of devotional and doctrinal matters, although they are, of course, the best remembered. On the one hand, in 1362, Parliament ordained all pleas "at the barre schulde be in Englisch tunge, and in no othir tunge" according to Capgrave's chronicle of 1464 *(MED)*. On the other, there was the proliferation of vernacular *escrowez* or broadsides posted for public consumption that, as Steven Justice asserts in *Writing and Rebellion* "embodied a claim as well as a message: merely by existing, it asserted, tendentiously or not, that those who read only English—or even could have only English read to them—had a stake in the intellectual and political life of church and realm" (30).

Chaucer is a great translator, and therefore contributes to the debates about the competence of English in his own time and wins consistent praise from early modern poets like Spenser, who seemed to understand how difficult a task was faced by a poet working within a language considered neither "sacred" nor "literary." Chaucer's decision to use English for his poetry was, as Derek Pearsall remarks:

> an extraordinary decision for a writer attached to the English court of the 1360s. At least it must have seemed extraordinary at the time. . . . English, though it may have lacked the finesse in polite discourse of French and the abstract and conceptualizing vocabulary of Latin, was, after all the mother-tongue, with more immediate access to the deeper well-springs of emotional experience. (*Life*, 73)

From this vantage point, it would seem that Chaucer's consistent use of English was consciously calculated to by-pass some of the more obvious chances for recognition in the international intellectual community in order to touch a more local "well-spring," that of specifically English "core consciousness" (in Helgerson's term). If this is so, it suggests that Chaucer saw his readers *as* in some important ways English, and that he desired to appeal to some sort of communal consciousness by using a local vocabulary and referring to more local understandings. I say a "more local" rather than simply "a local" understanding because Chaucer is fully aware of the unsettled matter of which, if any, dialect will become the standard: "for ther is so gret diversite / In Englissh and in the writyng of oure tonge, / I prey God that non myswrite the [the "litel book"], / Ne the mysmetre for defaute of tonge" (*Troilus* V.1792–96). Varied as its pronunciation and written forms might be, it is "oure tonge." And he introduced into English usage many of those elegant French phrases and Latin abstractions (the latter role shared with Wyclif) that expanded the range of Middle English so quickly in this period. One might say that Chaucer speaks *for* English, as well as *in* English.

It seems clear that Chaucer staked his career on the expressive potentialities of English. In presenting his fictitious English community, he often refers explicitly to the pilgrims' linguistic modes and habits. The narrator fears the "gentles" may object to the Miller's coarse language (I.3169), Harry Bailley is concerned that the Clerk should speak intelligibly, without the terms, colors, and figures of the high style (IV.15–20), and the Franklin apologizes for his "rude" speech (V.718). It may even be possible to infer something about Chaucer's attitudes toward the competing claims of Latin and English for authoritative teaching. *The General Prologue*'s description of the Parson calls him "lerned" (I.480), doubtless in the technical sense of "literate in Latin." This places him as part of the "bi-lingual intelligentsia mediated between heaven and earth," in Anderson's phrase (*Imagined Communities,* 22–23), typical of the prenational social formation. But he is described as speaking to his congregation in the plainest English possible (I.499–504) and refuses to supplement his income by reciting Latin prayers at Saint Paul's in London. He does have the power of excommunication, but he uses it sparingly, relying instead on setting an ethical example and "snybbing" his parishioners sharply in English. He is presented, therefore, as both a performer of efficacious sacraments and an instructor in the ethics of daily life. The Friar has the power of confession and is slyly accused of misusing it, as well as his pleasant "*In principio,*" to bilk poor widows out of their farthings. Chantecleer's "*In principio*" is also false dealing, this time a mistranslation from Latin that achieves the double effect of impressing Pertelote with his command of a tongue reserved for men and flattering her female vanity by attributing "joye" and "blis" to her influence

instead of *confusio*. The Summoner knows a bit of Latin too—he speaks
nothing but Latin in his cups—using it occupationally for extortion, like
the summoner depicted in *The Friar's Tale*. (Carruthers makes a somewhat different critique of that summoner's Latin, contrasting his inert
phrases with the Man of Law's ability to fuse his Latin learning with
other kinds of knowledge and thus use in practice what he knows [*Book
of Memory*, 20].) The Pardoner's bulls are not likely to be authentically
papal (since some are credited to the patriarchs), but how will the simple people recognize this, if the proofs are in Latin? These instances
suggest that what Chaucer saw when he looked at his cultural world
was familiarity with Latin, but not necessarily as the sole repository of
"emanations of reality," nor was such reverence what he seems to have
supported by his narrative choices.

Anderson nicely catches the paradox of the hold on imagination of
the transterritorial sodalities when he writes, "Christendom assumed
its universal form through a myriad of specificities and particularities:
this relief, that window, this sermon, that tale, this morality play, that
relic" (*Imagined Communities*, 29). The specificities, at least for the laity,
all incorporate an element of the local, which under the right conditions
could mobilize imaginative loyalties to the local as well as unite the seer
with the transcontinental communion of the faithful, like Chaucer's
Parson. In other words, I find Anderson's sharp distinction between an
identity imagined as commitment to Christianity (even Latin Christianity) and an early form of nationality too stark. I am positing a Chaucerian
text that dips into both identities. Certain textual gestures look like appeals to national identity. For example, the Pardoner is associated with
Rounceval, near Charing Cross but a daughter house of Roncesvalles in
Navarre; his chicanery over the papal bulls is directly associated with
Rome. The archdeacon's courts, which come off so badly in the Summoner's portrait and *The Friar's Tale* are opposed in part because the presiding archdeacon is so often not an Englishman. Parliament, meantime, was hearing Wyclif's argument for withholding England's tribute
to Rome.

Linguistic issues melt quickly into religious issues, as we have seen.
The Prioress tells a tale about a boy just beginning his studies, who
praises the Virgin by singing a song he has learned by heart and understands only as homage to Mary, "Noght wiste he what this Latyn was to
seye" (VII.523). His failure to understand the text he sings is, of course,

immediately attributable to his being such a young scholar, but, as Eamon Duffy has written,

> In a culture where the whole liturgy was celebrated in Latin most lay people would pick up a wide range of phrases and tags, with a depth of understanding perhaps not more profound than Chaucer's Summoner's grasp of legal Latin. (*Stripping*, 221–22).[12]

The boy's fascination with Mary arises in the first place from his seeing her image. Once again, there is an immediate *English* controversy stirred up by Wycliffites over the efficacy of images and the value of lay literacy and an English Bible. The boy's piety and claim to martyrdom when the Jews, offended by his song, cut his throat is both aroused and expressed by works of art, imagination touched by sculpture and song, rather than ethical or intellectual appeals. Dominant discourse ideas accorded "learning by heart" a higher status than moderns do, stressing the emotional tagging of the memory-image, as well as its rational content, often associating it with "desire and fear, pleasure or discomfort." Such personal storing away of learning was regarded as "morally virtuous in itself" (Carruthers, *Book of Memory*, 60, 71), certainly by the Prioress, who expresses herself in her *Prologue* in a similar rehearsal of poetry learned by heart. She places herself in the medieval mainstream by joining those who held that the power of Scripture, the liturgy, and even the primers were, as Duffy puts it, "full of 'vertue' which 'availed' by God's grace, independently of the reader's or hearer's comprehension" (*Stripping*, 218). As late as the motto on Henry VIII's coins, Mary was imagined as preferring certain phrasings of praise, "this prayer shewed our lady to a devoute persone, sayenge that this golden prayer is the most swetest and accepablest to me" (218). This sort of appeal to religious imagination is replicated in the fact that the boy's memorized Latin is almost completely opaque to him beyond its association with Mary's statue.

Both the Prioress's self-presentation and her presentation of the boy suggest the world of the unquestioning faithful, those who grasp spiritual themes through precisely worded prayers and songs and affecting statues—Anderson's "myriad of specificities and particularities" (*Imagined Communities*, 29). This is the world of most lay piety, as Duffy sees the matter, and would have continued to be had it not been for the divisiveness of the Lollards and later the rapaciousness of the Reformers.

The General Prologue suggests, however, the shortcomings of a markedly nonintellectual Prioress whose ethical sense conflates manners with morality and squeamishness with compassion. Her inert piety contrasts with the vigorous struggles to understand spiritual and ethical ideas in characterizations and performances like those of the Clerk, Parson, Knight, Franklin, and even the Pardoner and the Wife. These gestures would seem to undermine a straightforward sponsorship of the tale and its teller's "take" on her story. They suggest that the Prioress is imagined as the representative of a well-populated circle of nuns whose appeal to pathos is still widely felt by lay listeners (on the pilgrimage, "Whan seyd was al this miracle, every man / As sober was that wonder was to se" [VII.691–92]), but not immune from critique. The community I am positing among the pilgrims is not one of unanimous agreement, but one that shares distinctive beliefs and distinctive controversies over belief.

If it can be granted that Chaucer evokes an English community, at least in part as the result of his *seeing* certain phenomena *as* indicative of an English community, it remains to be asked how great a likeness to modern national communities his image of it bears.

TIME AND THE CITIZEN: THE "SHOCK OF THE POSSIBLE"

I have argued that Chaucer's commitment to the English language leads him to depict the pilgrims' linguistic modes and habits explicitly, to give them very specific locations in the discursive systems of the late fourteenth century, compared, once again, with Dante's characters, who inhabit the timeless world of salvation history. The fact that a well-known genre, estates satire, is called upon in *The General Prologue* does not interfere with the creation of characters who in the course of the fiction grow larger, more complex, than their social roles require and demand attention in a variety of modern ways. Steven Justice concludes that, in *The Canterbury Tales,*

> Individuals—even when created to represent a class—still speak and act, from moment to narrative moment, as individuals; the impression that their actions emerge from psychologies and personal histories proscribes even the possibility of mentally substituting the class for its representative. (*Writing*, 230)

I agree with the reasoning that leads (and has led for many commentators) to that conclusion, and I think what it means is that Chaucer imagined his pilgrims as citizens rather than as either subjects or exegetical types. There is, of course, no overt antimonarchical gesture in *The Canterbury Tales*.[13] What there is, though, is a nuanced sense of entitlement for each of the pilgrims, especially with respect to "the kingdom of [their] own language." They are presented as speaking as they are inclined to by a complicated network of affiliations like constitution (Martian and Venusian for the Wife, sanguine for the Franklin), gender, estate, age, religious profession, and the like. I am going to speculate that Chaucer presented them this way because he imagined his community—both in the sense of creating mental pictures and in the sense of reading the world he saw—as consisting of citizens. The increasing rates of vernacular literacy, the use by villagers themselves of charters and documents, the fact that communication and record keeping were increasingly set down in English, the quick response to the Wycliffite Bible and the teaching of the "poor priests," and of course the Rising itself may have been among the signs he was interpreting. These signs are not to be taken as indications that fourteenth-century society generally understood itself as a nation of citizens; it is likely that Chaucer's fiction produced, in its time, "the shock of the possible," in Paul Ricoeur's striking phrase (*Time*, 1:79).

There is a great deal to be said in favor of the thesis that Chaucer's pilgrims are best read as citizens, but it has been said very ably elsewhere. I would like to examine another of Anderson's preconditions for the emergence of the modern nation: the apprehension of time. So much in the English Middle Ages conforms to Anderson's description of typology, the sense that what is seen by moderns as a causal chain, as sequential and temporally separated, is actually the shape of an event recurring in salvation history. Markers of this apprehension of time, resembling Auerbach's "omnitemporal" occurrence "which has always been, and will be fulfilled in the future" (*Mimesis*, 64) are everywhere in medieval record. Saints and visionaries saw the Holy Family in their own houses; Margery Kempe was offered soup by the Virgin. Even Wyclif, so modern in many ways, writes as if the biblical term Antichrist specifically referred literally to the fourteenth-century popes. Peter Haidu comments on the narrative form of this sense of time, the exemplum: "exemplary narrative continued to function as a predominant fictional mode, even in vernacular literature, throughout the Middle Ages" in spite of the contradiction between its mode as fiction and its role in ideology.[14] Such stamina in exemplary writing suggests that it was a deeply rooted feature of imagination in the Middle Ages. Apparently no Fredric Jameson was saying "Always historicize"—instead Berthold Brecht "It always happens that way." Anderson contrasts this typological thinking with the modern conception of the "homogeneous, empty" time that finds "a precise analogue of the idea of a nation," in which a citizen does not know what his countrymen are up to at any given time, yet "has complete confidence in their steady, anonymous, simultaneous activity" (*Imagined Communities,* 30). He links this secular conception of time with print culture as a contributing cause for the establishment of the modern state, but long before print other predisposing causes were in motion.

Two of the predisposing causes bear particularly on the design of *The Canterbury Tales.* The first is embedded in Western Christianity. From the earliest meditations on it, theological time is described both as an island in the vast sea of eternity—consider Bede's beautiful image of the sparrow who flies into the meeting hall, as into time, from the undelineated reaches of the air outside—and as the mundane arena in which a person's faith and conduct must be tested. Jacques Le Goff puts it thus: "the Christian must simultaneously renounce the world, which is only his transitory resting place, and opt for the world, accept it, and transform it, since it is the workplace of the present history of salvation" (*Time,* 31).[15] In Le Goff's analysis, the secularization of time, indicated by clocks that measured and rang out hours, was motivated by mercantile and urban concerns and marked the transition from the agrarian "natural" day to the closely measured time of the urban working day. And it began earlier than Anderson's shift toward the modern nation, its pressures being felt from the end of the thirteenth century. From this point of view fourteenth-century Christians were taught by their faith *and* by their economic lives, especially in cities, to think of time as both cosmic recurrence and linear sequence.

The second pressure comes from the structures of narrative itself. As Ricoeur says, emplotment draws "a configuration out of simple succession" (*Time,* 1:65), which must presume succession and "meanwhile" understandings of time in the first place. The strongest version of the typological attitude needs no precise succession.[16] Incidents are isolated and repeated in an undifferentiated history: Moses and the unburnt burn-

ing bush is restated in the unviolated virginity of Mary, and Wyclif's sermons, in explicating the gospel, refer to the friars of his own day as
"oure pharisees" or "modern pharisees." But narrative as Aristotle describes it, draws events toward "the linear representation of time," both
because it causes readers to wonder what is coming next and because,
in retrospect, it allows its episodes to be seen as leading toward this particular ending, suggesting that time can be read either forward or backward toward its "thought" (Ricoeur, *Time*, 1:67). Even more directly relevant to *The Canterbury Tales* is Ricoeur's comment that "[p]eregrination
and narration are grounded in time's approximations of eternity, which,
far from abolishing their difference, never stops contributing to it" (29).
A pilgrimage is a traditional typological figure, but each separate pilgrimage and each stage in it is an episode enacted sequentially. Chaucer's
pilgrims are wandering through time, some perhaps toward "Jerusalem
celestial," but the "wey" they must take is measured in incidents, hours,
and days that unfold in familiar places in England and occupy mundane,
measurable time—the Friar remarks about the "long preamble" of the
Wife's performance (III.831) and the Knight expresses impatience with
the temporal extension of the Monk's store of tragedies (VII.2767–68).

For Chaucer's frame story and many of the stories his pilgrims tell,
Anderson's modern "complex gloss upon the word 'meanwhile'" (*Imagined Communities*, 31) is directly apposite. The trip to Canterbury is charted
against clock time, Anderson's "empty time" (37), indicated every now
and again by the position of the sun (which may be read both as a real-
istic detail and a nod to the still agrarian habits of the era). Paul Strohm
argues that as Chaucer's career moves from the providential early poems
to *The Canterbury Tales*, "his treatment of time and narrative becomes, in
a word, progressively more social," marked by more modern time schemes
(*Social Chaucer*, 112). Strohm also stresses the mixed, even "awkward,"
signals in Chaucer's unfolding of events throughout his work.[17] I will
argue that the individual *Canterbury Tales* are varied in their handling of
the temporal, the strongly "exemplary" *Monk's Tale*, for example, at one
end of a spectrum, and the strongly "modern," like *The Miller's Tale*, at
the other. Other tales exhibit a mixed sense of narrative time within themselves. This internal oscillation and the contrast between one tale and
another suggest the text's consciousness of the problem of apprehend-
ing narrative time. As with other features of the sign systems at his disposal, Chaucer fashions a storytelling instrument that registers both old

and new understandings of the world; in this case the mix tilts toward the "modern," the "meanwhile."

The privilege given to the modern system is fully evident in the frame tale.[18] There both sequence and the "empty time" of each day's passing are insisted on. The narrator-Chaucer acquaints himself with the other pilgrims at the tavern, describes them, and relates their conversation on the road. The Miller responds to the Knight, the Reeve to the Miller, the Friar to the Wife, in what we would now call a "real time" representation of people's interactions. Many of the tellers make a point of locating their narratives, old or contemporary, in time, as with the Knight's "Whilom, as olde stories tellen us" (I.859), the Wife's "In th' olde dayes of the Kyng Arthour" (III.857), the Clerk's elaborate footnotes on the source of his tale, and the Physician's "as telleth Titus Livius" (IV.1). Even the fable setting of *The Nun's Priest's Tale* is located temporally: "For thilke tyme, as I have understonde, / Beestes and briddes koude speke and synge" (VII.2880–81). The Reeve, on the other hand, begins, "At Trumpyngtoun, nat fer fro Cantebrigge, / Ther gooth a brook" (I.3921–22), suggesting both a recent time setting and a place that corresponds to the Oxenford of the *The Miller's Tale,* further locating his telling of his tale as a response to the pilgrimage conversation. The Franklin introduces his story in terms of its venerable age and generic type. As events in it unfold, he seems particularly aware of the double time sense Ricoeur alludes to: his story arrives at a nearly intolerable existential situation for the characters when Arveragus tells Dorigen to go to the garden, but he lets on that he knows the ending:

> Paraventure an heep of yow, ywis,
> Wol holden hym a lewed man in this
> That he wol putte his wyf in jupartie.
> Herkneth the tale er ye upon hire crie.
> She may have bettre fortune than yow semeth;
> And whan that ye han herd the tale, deemeth. V.1493–98

Without explicitly claiming providential intervention, he undermines the open-ended, "real time" sense of his tale at this point, suggesting that he intentionally invokes both time schemes. It might be said that a level of awareness about the modes of presenting time is part of the characterization the poet-Chaucer builds into the tellers of *The Canterbury Tales.*

Some tales, of course, are not introduced or nuanced with this attention to time and sequence, and many of them—the Man of Law's, the Prioress's, the Second Nun's, the Monk's, Chaucer's *Melibee*—seem in one way or another fitted to the allegorical mode with its link to typology. Each seems a largely unhistoricized exemplum whose outlines might be repeated in any generation and whose crisis does not depend on intricate timing.[19] In each of these tales narrative seems designed, as "an historical anecdote employed in a rhetoric of persuasion," an instrument of edification, which is the way Le Goff defines the genre in *Medieval Imagination.* Yet Le Goff remarks that the form depended on calling up a historical image and served "a vogue for narrative. . . . new importance [began to be] attached to narrative time, that is, historical time" (78). Its venue was often sermons, and particularly the sermons popularized by the mendicants and so openly satirized by the performance of the friar in *The Summoner's Tale,* who lines up historical tales at odd angles to his avowed didactic purpose.

The Monk's Tale is perhaps the most striking example of unhistoricized storytelling, its scriptural, historical, and modern examples related without differentiation, the same "moral" attached to all of them, seemingly without regard to the telling differences in their patterns of detail. The Monk has no sooner introduced his series of object lessons against trusting Fortune than he has to veer away from it to account for Lucifer, "nat a man" (VII.2000) and therefore not able to be harmed by Fortune. He does not explicate Adam's trust in Fortune, although he does blame his fall on "mysgovernaunce" (VII.2012). He credits Cenobia and Julius Caesar, for example, with uncommon moral strengths and nowhere indicates their failings. He gets sidetracked by Dalida into drawing an entirely different moral from Sampson's story (*The Nun's Priest's Tale* revisits the mis-applied exemplum in general and this one in particular). Whatever failings the Knight may be taxed with as a Boethian philosopher, his tale surely outbids the Monk's, and his objection to the Monk's performance is apt in this way as well as in others. When "omnitemporality" is treated most seriously, no sampling from the whole range of history is needed or proper; the very fact that the Monk is impelled to tell so many stories weighs against him. The narrative logic in his failure to please might be stated as a recognition that no two anecdotes will ever produce quite the perfect match with each other or with the timeless lesson they are intended to illustrate. In spite of the long reign of privilege the exemplum enjoyed in the Middle Ages, Peter Haidu claims, "it is a type of writing which contained its inherent contradiction, a contradiction whose effects become more pronounced until their flagrant display in the Rabelaisian disjunction between verbal invention, and the continually implicit presupposition of the serious, perhaps even allegorical, intent and structure of writing" ("Repetition," 886). Whether by authorial design or not, *The Canterbury Tales* everywhere displays this contradiction.

Within the other tales, "meanwhile" is a linchpin in the storyline. *The Miller's Tale* is the most obvious example. Anderson's chart and discussion of a hypothetical novel is precisely relevant to *The Miller's Tale* in concluding that "all these acts are performed at the same clocked, calendrical time, but by actors who may be largely unaware of one another" (*Imagined Communities,* 31). Moreover Chaucer's tale *only works because* Alison, Nicholas, John, and Absolon act in the same time frame unaware of each other's plots. That John is generally ignorant of Nicholas's wooing is a stock feature of fabliau plotting, but that he waits for the second flood in his own kneading tub lashed to the ceiling of his own house while Nicholas enjoys his bed raises the ante. Absolon's first serenade crowds the meantime still further. It is, however, the finale that allows the tale to be read as an attempt to push the idea of meantime as far as it will go. Nicholas's cry "Water!" signals the culmination of Absolon's successful plot against him, the disclosure of his adultery with Alison, and the crumbling of John's delusion about the flood. On the grounds of narrative timing, *The Miller's Tale* may be the most modern of *The Canterbury Tales.*

Although in many ways *The Knight's Tale* presents a direct contrast to *The Miller's Tale,* in this matter the constrast is more nuanced. It is true, of course, that time passes more slowly for Palamon and Arcite, that an epic sense of range over both time and space obtains. And it is true that the Knight/teller seems bent on invoking a Boethian patience in the face of long time spans, justified by frequent references to *destiny* and *purveiaunce.* The Knight may strive to make an allegory or parable out of his narrative through his commentary, but the deeper logic of the story depends almost as much on "meanwhile" as the Miller's. For example, *The Knight's Tale* turns from the adventures of Arcite in exile to Palamon in prison, basing the *debat* that concludes Part I on the simultaneity of Arcite's freedom and distance from Emelye and Palamon's incarceration and nearness to her. The Knight stresses *destiny* and *purveiaunce* in Theseus's turning up during the battle between the cousins, digressing rather heavy-footedly about both external occurrences and internal inclinations as "reuled by the sighte above" (I.1672), but the plot need not explain why "Duc" Theseus might have gone hunting in his own domain. What accounts for this development in the plot is that the cousins have arranged to fight and simultaneously the duke to go hunting. The fateful appeals to deities made by Palamon, Emelye, and Arcite are carefully timed (Palamon's two hours before daybreak, Emelye's at daybreak, and Arcite's shortly after that at Mars's hour). Each of these nearly simultaneous appeals is made in ignorance of the others, laying the groundwork for the outcome of the plot. Even though the teller's every ploy in *The Miller's Tale* suggests his insistence on the intricate play of human agency and those of *The Knight's Tale* teller consistently stress destiny, the plots themselves both manifest "a complex gloss on the word 'meanwhile'" (Anderson, *Imagined Communities*, 31). In *The Knight's Tale* it just takes longer.

The Pardoner's Tale would seem the most exemplary tale (in both the generic and the hortatory modern sense) in Chaucer's collection. The misguided youths who seek Death as if he were a person might have played out their story with only minimally altered details any time, any place (and indeed its *sentence* has been dramatized many times, for example in films like *The Treasure of Sierra Madre* and recently *A Simple Plan*). Two details, though, stress the idea of "meanwhile," and they deeply inflect the plot. First is the precipitating death of the rioters' friend *while* they (and he) were drinking, and second the poisoner's purchase of ratsbane while the two conspirators plan his murder. Of all the exempla related in *The Canterbury Tales*, the Pardoner's is the one that most clearly participates in the various time frames Le Goff discusses: the "segment of narrative time—historical, linear, and divisible" within the fiction, the shape of the whole plot that "drew upon and nourished the time of private memory," and the ultimate, timeless lesson that "pointed toward eternity" (*Medieval Imagination*, 79–80). Le Goff links this complication in the history of moral teaching to the practice of auricular confession mandated by the Fourth Lateran Council (1215) requiring "introspective self-examination" and memory of a personal sort. A long logic would link such capacities with citizenship.

Like most successful exempla, the Pardoner's offering makes a surprising turn with considerable emotional impact. Unlike Custance's or Cecilia's story or that of the "litel clergeon" of The Prioress's Tale, though, pathos is not its mode, nor is visceral repugnance; the tale works intellectually. No emphasis is given to any suffering the young men might have experienced as they died, and there are no wicked mothers-in-law or Jews to execrate. What the story enacts is exactly what biblical and Augustinan tenets have to say about the intrinsic connection between the lust for gold and the death of body and soul. Linear time unfolds for the characters in the tale and for the pilgrims as they listen and respond, but the point of the exemplum resides in a timeless present. This tale, therefore, strikes one as both deeply medieval and subversively modern, looking to eternity but also to citizenly responsibility and intellectual acumen.

In imagining and presenting his compaignye as proto-citizens, but framing their presentation with pilgrimage, estates satire, and in some cases typology, Chaucer blunts the "shock of the possible," sneakily allowing his fiction to be seen in traditional terms, and often making good on those terms. With Haidu, we might conjecture that medieval authorities paid too little attention to the consequences of verbal play in allowing fiction to flourish, with the result that deep mental structures undergo subtle changes:

> We may even guess that the belief in free variation was one of those magnificent inventions of self-deception which enable historical change to take place without the awareness that it is taking place, an awareness that if present, might have impeded that historical development. ("Repetition," 884)

I will let the Canon's Yeoman have the last word, since he is the character most like a modern citizen—especially a citizen under capitalism. The Yeoman is free of feudal encumbrances through his own offense to the Canon, who would not stay to hear his mystery disclosed, much as Seven of Nine is free of the collective, but as yet uncomfortable in Federation culture. His freedom is both exhilarating, as his telling shows, and tragic, since now he has only his labor to sell, but he has seized the kingdom of his own language:

> Syn that my lord is goon, I wol nat spare;
> Swich thyng as that I knowe, I wol declare. (VIII.719)

NOTES

In writing this essay, I have benefitted from the learned advice of James F. Knapp and Michael Witmore.

1. Catherine Janeway is the captain of the Federation Starship Voyager, the latest of the Star Trek heirs. The Borg is a predatory cosmic force, a collective intelligence that acts through bodies "assimilated" from other species and enhanced with mechanical parts that strengthen them for combat. Seven of Nine had been a human child when she was assimilated, and the captain gradually returns her to human habits of mind.

2. Helgerson chooses a somewhat different address to an emergent nation by treating a group of writers whose texts seem more "secular" (*Forms*, 2).

3. Carruthers, *Book of Memory*, 1. Medieval writers offered much greater respect to memory. Carruthers documents and examines estimates of memory and in doing so stresses the enormous role images played in aiding feats of memory and the ideas well-stocked memories produced.

4. All references to Chaucer's work are cited from *The Riverside Chaucer*.

5. The narrator concludes that, although Funes had learned five languages, "I suspect, nevertheless, that he was not very capable of thought. . . . In the overly replete world of Funes there were nothing but details, almost contiguous details" (Borges, "Funes," 114–15).

6. It would account for his response to Gellner's contrast between awakening to self-consciousness and inventing nationhood that does not exist. Anderson replies by insisting that invention be linked to imagining and creativity rather than fabrication and falsity (*Imagined Communities*, 15).

7. In the Parson's discourse, imagination can figure as a benign gift of nature or as a deadly sin when "malice ymagined" arises from pride (X.445–50).

8. Leicester suggests yet another meaning for "ymaginyng" here: the planning being done by Felony, rather than the artist or the Knight imagining Felony (*Disenchanted Self*, 277).

9. Anderson notes the Wycliffite "vernacular *manuscript* Bible" translation, but consigns it, along with the English used in courts and in opening Parliament to state, rather than national interests, and notes that this state encompassed some non-English-speaking terrain (*Imagined Communities*, 45).

10. Augustine discusses translation in Book II of *On Christian Doctrine*, even going so far in his defense of the Septuagint (the translation of the Hebrew Old Testament into Greek) as to claim that its reading should be preferred to the Hebrew where the two conflict, since the Holy Spirit guided the translators (II. XV.22).

11. Christopher Baswell observes that from the thirteenth century on "growing emphasis was placed on clerical ability not only to use the Latin liturgy but also to explain it in the vernacular. . . . By the late 1250s, Matthew Paris reports, Archbishop Sewald of York resisted papal candidates for bishoprics if they did not have good English" ("Latinitas," 147). Baswell's work also suggests that Latin in England is itself "an array of increasingly disparate, specialized language practices" (123).

12. Duffy does not read this distance between the words and the worshiper's grasp of them as reducing in any way the efficacy of the prayers and sacraments for the spiritual well-being of the laity.

13. Anderson includes among his criteria for "the specific origins of nationalism" shedding the belief that "society was naturally organized around high centers . . . human beings who ruled by some form of cosmological (divine) dispensation" (*Imagined Communities*, 40). Although I am not arguing that England's social organization in the fourteenth century was that of a nation, I would argue that the monarch's divine warrant was not well established or unchallenged and that the people were felt to have some rights protecting them from his power.

14. Haidu's fuller claim is that "even where intentionally established to function in subordination to an ideological superstructure, [a Neoplatonic Form or Idea] is inherently subversive of such vehiculation, and betrays that externally imposed purpose by its very nature. It must immediately be acknowledged that, in spite of this constitutive contradiction, exemplary narrative continued to function as a predominant fictional mode, even in vernacular literature, throughout the Middle Ages" ("Repetition," 886).

15. Le Goff writes of an "economy dominated by agrarian rhythms, free of haste, careless of exactitude, unconcerned by productivity—and of a society created in the image of that economy, *sober and modest*, without enormous appetites, undemanding, and incapable of qualitative efforts" (*Time*, 44).

16. "Before Abraham was, I am" is Wyclif's rendering of John 8:58.

17. "Mixed" I hope to show, but I disagree with Strohm that the handling of temporality in *Troilus and Criseyde* is "awkward." It is just such tension between a narrator who knows the story (and readers or hearers at least partly aware of the outcome) and the characters in suspense of the outcome that makes the circle of reading both forward toward and backward from the conclusion a healthy rather than a vicious circle. See Ricoeur, *Time*, 1:67–68 and passim.

18. The fact that surviving manuscripts offer conflicting orders does not detract from this conclusion. A meaning-bearing sequence can be based on either of the likeliest orders and the fact that discussion of the issue has been so vigorous suggests that modern readers consider the frame to be dependent on a modern sense of "empty time."

19. *The Physician's Tale* is especially interesting here, since it is so difficult to see what general point is being made. If tragic irony is intended in that Virginius acted too quickly and the people might have saved his daughter if he had let them, the expository section on Virginia's moral excellence is wasted. If Virginius is to be seen as a noble Roman, able to sacrifice for principle, the specifically Christian moral edge of the plot is blunted. The puzzling moral of this tale may, of course be part of the characterization of the Physician.

REFERENCES

Anderson, Benedict. *Imagined Communities: Reflections on the Origin and Spread of Nationalism.* London and New York: Verso, 1983.

Auerbach, Erich. *Mimesis: The Representation of Reality in Western Literature.* Trans. Willard Trask. Garden City, NY: Doubleday, 1957.

Augustine, Saint. *On Christian Doctrine.* Trans. W. W. Robertson, Jr. Indianapolis: Bobbs-Merrill, 1958.

Baswell, Christopher. "Latinitas." In *The Cambridge History of Medieval English Literature,* ed. David Wallace, 122–51. Cambridge: Cambridge University Press, 1999.

Borges, Jorge Luis. "Funes the Memorious" (1942). Trans. Anthony Kerrigan, in *Ficciones,* 107–15. New York: Grove Press, 1962.

Bundy, Murray Wright. *The Theory of Imagination in Classical and Medieval Thought.* Urbana: University of Illinois Press, 1927.

Carruthers, Mary. *The Book of Memory: A Study of Memory in Medieval Culture.* Cambridge: Cambridge University Press, 1990.

Chaucer, Geoffrey. *The Works of Geoffrey Chaucer.* Ed. F. N. Robinson. Boston: Houghton Mifflin, 1957.

———. *Chaucer's Poetry.* Ed. E. T. Donaldson. New York: Ronald Press, 1975.

———. *The Complete Poetry and Prose of Geoffrey Chaucer.* Ed. John H. Fisher. New York: Holt, Rinehart and Winston, 1977.

———. *The Riverside Chaucer.* Ed. Larry D. Benson et al. Boston: Houghton Mifflin, 1987.

Dillard, Annie. "Sight into Insight." In *Popular Writing in America,* ed. Donald McQuade and Robert Atwan, 247–51. New York: Oxford University Press, 1977.

Duffy, Eamon. *The Stripping of the Altars: Traditional Religion in England 1400–1580.* New Haven: Yale University Press, 1992.

Haidu, Peter. "Repetition: Modern Reflections on Medieval Aesthetics." *Modern Language Notes* 92 (Dec. 1977): 875–87.

Helgerson, Richard. *Forms of Nationhood: The Elizabethan Writing of England.* Chicago: University of Chicago Press, 1992.

Justice, Steven. *Writing and Rebellion: England in 1381.* Berkeley and Los Angeles: University of California Press, 1994.

Le Goff, Jacques. *Time, Work, and Culture in the Middle Ages.* Trans. Arthur Goldhammer. Chicago and London: University of Chicago Press, 1980.

———. *The Medieval Imagination.* Trans. Arthur Goldhammer. Chicago and London: University of Chicago Press, 1985.

Leicester, H. Marshall. *The Disenchanted Self.* Berkeley and Los Angeles: University of California Press, 1990.

Middle English Dictionary. Ed. Hans Kurath et al. Ann Arbor: University of Michigan Press, 1952–2001.

Pearsall, Derek. *The Life of Geoffrey Chaucer: A Critical Biography.* Cambridge: Harvard University Press, 1992.

Pico, Gianfrancesco. *De Imaginatione* (1501). Latin text with trans. and notes by Harry Kaplan. New Haven: Cornell and Yale University Press, 1930.

Ricoeur, Paul. *Time and Narrative*. Trans. Kathleen McLaughlin and David Pellauer. 3 vols. Chicago and London: University of Chicago Press, 1983.

Sartre, Jean-Paul. *Imagination: A Psychological Critique*. Trans. Forrest Williams. Ann Arbor: University of Michigan Press, 1962.

Strohm, Paul. *Social Chaucer*. Cambridge: Harvard University Press, 1989.

Warnock, Mary. *Imagination*. Berkeley and Los Angeles: University of California Press, 1976.

Wittgenstein, Ludwig. *Philosophical Investigations*. Trans. G. E. M. Anscombe. Oxford: Blackwell, 1984.

Hymeneal Alogic: Debating Political Community in *The Parliament of Fowls*

Kathleen Davis

Woman as trope, displacing historical
women, consolidating hybridity into totality,
[erases] the doubled border into a single sign.
——Alarcón et al. 6

At the end of the dream vision in *The Parliament of Fowls,* just after Nature has given the common fowl their mates "by evene acord," the birds sing a departing song in Nature's honor. "The note," the narrator explains, "imaked was in Fraunce, / The wordes were swiche as ye may heer fynde, / The nexte verse, as I now have in mynde" (677–79).[1] The multivalenced "heer" in this context refers most obviously to the written page, to the "nexte verse" of the poem; however, "heer" must also refer to England, the geographical source of these "wordes," in counterpoint to "Fraunce," the source of the "note." These two spatial references intersect at the point of language: *here* words are English.[2] This collocation of English land, language, and text at the moment the poem reflects on its own literary matter suggests an English specificity to its well-recognized contemplation of political community and attests to the interrelation of such contemplation and textuality. Indeed, the suggestion of an unspoken Englishness in this "heer" is perhaps obvious for a poem that has been read in connection with England's parliamentary struggles, with Richard II's bride-quest, and with the issues of sovereignty and consent circulating during Richard's reign and Henry's usurpation. Even as the numerous readings of this poem's engagement with late-fourteenth-century English politics and class conflict have demonstrated its interest in the English political community, their varied interpretations signal the difficulty of identifying the poem's political stance.[3] My aim in this essay is not to adumbrate a specific political agenda in Chaucer's *Parliament*, but to examine its method of establishing the geopolitical grounds for debate—a "here" that can refer to a polity as well as to a page. This method must negotiate the aporia of identification necessarily entailed in presenting (spatially and temporally) a unity comprised of differences. I wish to consider the terms and implications of the relation between this poem's invocation of an English identity, in a time it labels "now," through the conjunction of land-language-polity and its production of textual, social, and geographic space.

The lines of the *Parliament* quoted above clearly invoke a sense of spatiotemporal immediacy, as they refer to the here and now of the manuscript page, to England's complicated cultural relation with France, and perhaps even to a particular poetic performance.[4] This immediacy connects the English present of the poem's composition to the atemporality of the dream, but only through a startling rupture of the vision's temporal order. Throughout the dream, the narrator consistently distances the description of the garden, the temple of brass, and the events of the parliament through the use of past tense and spatial markers such as "there" and "that place." After the initial portrait of Nature, for instance, we read, "For this was on Seynt Valentynes day, / Whan every foul cometh there to chese his make" (309–10), and later, "Of foules every kynde / . . . Men myghten in that place assembled fynde" (365, 367). The only uses of "here" and of the present tense are in the dream characters' direct references to their situation. In an important way, then, the dream events are *not* fourteenth-century English, but timeless and universal.

Moreover, the dream maintains its transcendent status as well as its sense of cyclic, cosmic time—first instantiated with the connection to the *Dream of Scipio*—through the repeated "fro yer to yeere," as in Nature's "This is oure usage alwey, fro yer to yeere" (411; cf. 236, 321). The lines introducing the song immediately follow just such a temporal marker: before departing, birds are selected to sing in Nature's honor, "As yer by yer was alwey hir usaunce" (674). Given the cosmic status thus attributed to the song, the narrator's ensuing comment that "The note, I trowe, imaked was in Fraunce / The wordes were swiche as ye may heer fynde, / The nexte verse, as I now have in mynde" breaks with the time and space of the dream and—with its shift to present tense and direct address to the reader—performs a sudden and remarkable shrinkage to the immediate time and space of its own literary performance. The fowl of this *locus amoenus* apparently know contemporary French tunes, which, moreover, they adapt to English. A live performance of this scene would effect a paradoxical chiasmus, simultaneously placing Nature and her garden in the English court, and the performers and their audience in the transcendent dream world. Thus it is not so much an allusive link but a textual rupture that directly connects the dream parliament to England.

The productive rupture effected by the song's introduction is both intensified and complicated by the inconsistent manuscript tradition of the song itself, which I will discuss in the final section of this essay. Whatever its words and form, however, the song functions as a hymeneal for the newly betrothed birds. Its paradoxical conflation of Nature's timeless scene of reproduction and the immediate scene of English literary (re)production vis à vis France, in a poem concerned with political community, sets up an interchange between the processes of Nature's and England's sociosexual bodies politic. As such, it points to the text's method of imagining a space that is simultaneously natural and political. The occurrence of this interchange at the moment of the hymeneal—and in the space of poetic rupture—points toward the gendered, sexed logic of the *Parliament's* spatiotemporal representation of community. The alogical presentation of this community, which appears as *both* immutable, timeless object *and* as performative, reproductive subject, signals its inescapable conceptual ambivalence. As recent investigations have shown, writing political community is always a conflicted project, in that it must claim to transcend—even as its meaning depends upon—the local and the contingent.[5] This ambivalence is of a different nature than the unresolved tensions of the *Parliament's* sociopolitical conflict, which, as a staging of the community's governance issues and power struggles, must presuppose the existence of the "community of the realm" within which such conflicts arise.[6] My approach to the *Parliament* in terms of political community, then, does not suggest that it argues for a particular political ideal or that it exemplifies a polemical nationalism; rather, I examine how it manages to carry on a conversation about what David Aers, for instance, calls "a discordant political realm" ("*Vox populi*," 449). The *Parliament's* foray into political debate is a project set against itself in that it must keep aloft both a conceptual (necessarily ambivalent) grounding for community and the historical contingency of particular communal ideals—all of which is cut across, of course, by the limits of Chaucer's own historical situatedness. The importance of the hymeneal to this project indicates the degree to which "Woman as trope," as my epigraph suggests, negotiates the doubled border of political community; because this representational role constitutes a crucial aspect of women's historical conditions, its operation demands our attention.[7]

MAKING TIME

The *Parliament* foregrounds the problem of contradiction, of course. As often noted, its entire poetic matter proceeds from contradictions, the most obvious of which is the split inscription "of ful gret difference" (125) posted over the gate to the dream vision garden. This *fin amor* caveat presents love as a paradox, leading both to "the welle of grace" and to "the mortal strokes of the spere" (129, 135). Nevertheless, the ideal garden into which the narrator initially walks manifests neither contradiction nor any of the differential markers that constitute the movement of history; indeed, by definition this *locus amoenus* must transcend history. Nothing happens here because there is no difference, no time as marked by changing seasons, aging, or passage of the sun:

> Th'air of that place so attempre was
> That nevere was grevaunce of hot ne cold.
> There wex ek every holsom spice and gras;
> No man may there waxe sek ne old;
> Yit was there joye more a thousandfold
> Than man can telle; ne nevere wolde it nyghte,
> But ay cler day to any mannes syghte. (204–10)

As the narrator passes by the silent allegorical figures of Cupid and his attendants, we view the means of love's contradictions, but get no narrative. Since our dreamer is ostensibly exempt from love and there are no lovers here, we see the weapons of love but not their effect. Desire is the effect of difference, and in Cupid's realm desire is sexual, but here there is no desire, and thus no history, no political narrative.

The potential for historically relevant political narrative begins as the dreamer crosses the threshold of the "temple of bras," often called the temple of Venus, where he is immediately surrounded by sighs of desire:

> Within the temple, of sykes hoote as fyr
> I herde a swogh that gan aboute renne,
> Whiche sikes were engendered with desyr,
> That maden every auter for to brenne
> Of newe flaume. (246–50)

He first encounters the fertility god Priapus, to whom I will return, but the focal point of this temple is Venus, who seems both to act upon desire as she reclines "in disport" with her porter Richesse and to incite desire as an object viewed, apparently arousing even the nonlover narrator: "naked from the brest unto the hed / Men myghte hire sen / The remenaunt was wel kevered to my pay, / Ryght with a subtyl coverchef of Valence" (269–72). Commenting upon this passage, Lynn Staley notes that "Venus embodies the site of desire itself" ("Chaucer," 193), an assessment that equates the goddess with the desire-filled temple within which she reclines. The poem and its source for this section, Boccaccio's *Teseida*, support the equation of Venus with the physical structure of the temple of brass, a metal, as Boccaccio explains, "born of the planet Venus."[8]

The alogical thought of Venus as having birthed that which contains her well suits her contradictory space/time function in the poem as a whole, for she figures not only at the center of the dream, as its "core of sexuality" (Pearsall, *Life*, 125), but also as the outside and transcendent cause of the dream narrative. Just after the narrator has begun telling his dream, and has quoted his guide Affrican's announcement that the dream is reward for his laborious reading, he interrupts himself for an invocation that contradicts both the words of Affrican and the previous suggestion that his own reading elicited the dream:

Cytherea, thow blysful lady swete,
That with thy fyrbrond dauntest whom the lest
And madest me this sweven for to mete,
Be thow myn helpe in this, for thow mayst best!
As wisly as I sey the north-north-west,
Whan I began my sweven for to write,
So yif me myght to ryme, and endyte! (113–19)

The narrator's gaze directly connects this stanza, in which he looks upon the transcendent goddess/planet in a remote corner of the sky, with the dream passage in which he looks upon a very carnal, sexual Venus "in a prive corner" of her temple.[9] Moreover, the invocation to Venus—who has caused and will help to "endyte" the dream—not only interrupts the start of the dream and simultaneously provides a connecting sight line between the frame and dream narratives, but, like the paradoxical "heer," conflates the linking of the atemporal and the historical with the immediate time and space of literary production.[10] The doubleness of Venus becomes a means of linking the two conflicting "times" necessary to the conceptualization of community.

The temple passage makes quite explicit Venus's function as the site of temporal rupture. In contrast to the garden's ceaseless daylight, Venus's chamber is "derk," with scarcely enough light to see that "on a bed of gold she lay to reste, / Til that the hote sonne gan to weste" (265–66). Thus the introduction of Venus and female sexual activity coincides precisely with the introduction of temporal movement in the dream. David Lawton notes that this element of time, "inserted" into the depiction of Venus, is not just a forgetting, but a subversion of the garden's timelessness. His further observation that "Venus here is not the Cytherea to whom Chaucer's brief invocation is addressed; but both are aspects of one goddess, who expresses in herself the two possibilities represented on the gates" (*Chaucer's Narrators*, 41) nicely delineates her paradoxical linking of two mutually exclusive "times," as well as the role of this linking in both mediating and containing the narrative.[11] This process—this "erasing the doubled border into a single sign"—turns on the ambivalence of Venus's sexual activity/nonactivity in these lines. "Reste" (*MED* 553–57) can mean, most obviously, "repose" in the sense of sleep, inaction, death, or a temporary cessation of action. This meaning would imply that Venus lay inactively on the bed, but would do so only *until* the sun began to set, when, presumably, she will begin sexual activity. However, being at "reste" with another person can also imply "sexual intercourse," and we have already been told that Venus is "in disport" with her porter Richesse. Venus's (in)action in this line is and must be undecidable, because her paradoxical doubleness presents the opening of time.[12]

The change in Venus's state, whether from action to inaction or vice versa, also disrupts the vision's temporal pattern, which keeps to the continuous past tense (except for the previously discussed break contextualizing "heer" in lines 678–79). The change in Venus's activity cannot be observed by the narrator, but is accessible only through the temporal slippage embedded in the future implication of "til," which, combined with the past tense "gan," amounts to a future perfect construction. In the interval of this slippage time both stands still, while Venus's body is continually at "reste," and began/will begin to move as her body engages or disengages sexual activity. Time begins where sex is/not yet. This interstitial paradox—the simultaneous presence and absence of "Woman's" sexual activity—subtends, I suggest, the political capacity of the entire poem.

The difference of Venus from herself is the spacing that makes signification, time, and therefore narrative possible. Timeless goddess even as she both causes and is the site of the rupture that initiates time, she marks temporality and opens story.[13] The nature of Venus's connection to narrative becomes apparent as the narrator, having passed her bedroom, ventures further and for the first time encounters "story":

> And ferther in the temple I gan espie
> That, in dispit of Dyane the chaste,
> Ful many a bowe ibroke heng on the wal
> Of maydenes swiche as gonne here tymes waste
> In hyre servyse; and peynted overal
> Ful many a story, of which I touche shal
> A few, as of Calyxte and Athalante,
> And many a mayde of which the name I wante. (280–87)

This beginning of story required a breaking open, a breaking into—quite explicitly here the breaking of hymens of women who resisted. The symbolic "broken bows" that lead to stories correspond to the thinly veiled genitals and legs of Venus, through which these stories are also born, just as the only sound in the temple, hot sighs, "were engendered with desyr" (248). The time these maidens spent serving Diana is "wasted" not only because their conscription into sex/narrative is inevitable, but also because their period of resistance—an undifferentiated virgin time—is necessary to the conceptualization of community, even though it obtains meaning through the thought of its violation, of already temporalized story. Like Venus, these "broken" would-be-virgins conjoin conflicted "times."

This structural alogic of the feminine corresponds precisely to the "heer" introducing the hymeneal at the dream's end, which, also through rupture, contradictorily links Nature's atemporal garden to the contemporary English political community. The *Parliament*'s "time" operates according to the alogic of the hymen, a signifier that, like other undecidables such as *supplément* and *pharmakon,* have a double, contradictory value. Thus, as Derrida puts it, they operate "in two absolutely different places at once, even if these are only separated by a veil, which is both traversed and not traversed, *inter*sected" ("Double Session," 221). Like Venus, hymen "produces the effect of a medium (a medium as element enveloping both terms at once; a medium located between the two terms). It is an operation that *both* sows confusion *between* opposites *and* stands *between* the opposites 'at once'" (212).[14] I am not suggesting through this reading that hymeneal alogic is an essential or inevitable aspect of thinking political community, a complex issue that I cannot adequately address in this essay.[15] My argument at this point is that according to the structure of the *Parliament*, the contradictory linking of "times" not only *does*—but can *only*—occur at the (non)moment of the hymeneal.

MAKING SPACE

Unsurprisingly, the *Parliament*'s dreamer emerges from the sexual experience of the temple into differentiated, social and political space. This "is the same garden as before, but now the goddess Nature is there" (Pearsall, *Life,* 125–26)—and so it is both the same and different, its previously homogeneous ground now mapped by the hierarchized bodies of Nature's realm. In contrast to the garden where "Ne nevere wolde it nyghte" (209), here the lower class birds cry out when the eagles' speeches last "from the morwe... / Tyl dounward went the sonne wonder faste" (489–90). This temporalization, already initiated through Venus, allows the poem's *locus amoenus* suddenly to become crowded, noisy, politicized space. The poem's social differentiation of the birds according to their attitudes toward the passage of time, which is also an attitude toward love and politics, has been often noted. While the debate of the royal eagles "wastes" time, "spends time magnificently," the uncourtly birds "refuse to wait" (Fradenburg, "Spectacular Fictions," 500–01).[16] This socially variable time is directly at odds with Nature's unchanging cyclic time, which fully encloses difference as stable hierarchy and reifies this hierarchy as *place:*

> This noble emperesse, ful of grace,
> Bad every foul to take his owne place,
> As they were woned alwey fro yer to yeere,
> Seynt Valentynes day, to stonden theere. (319–22)

The hierarchal propriety of one's "owne place" is, quite literally here, grounded in the immutability of repetitive time. Moreover, Nature's community literalizes the spatial metaphor of hierarchy, and rank becomes a geographical feature:

> That is to seyn, the foules of ravyne
> Weere hyest set, and thanne the foules smale
> That eten, as hem Nature wolde enclyne,
> As worm or thyng of which I telle no tale;
> And water-foul sat lowest in the dale;
> But foul that lyveth by sed sat on the grene,
> And that so fele that wonder was to sene. (323–29)

Despite the apparent immutability of Nature's order, this parliament, as David Aers observes, is not left "quite as free from the pressures of history as the assembly's initial order suggests" ("*Vox populi*," 447). Once set "in motion," it clearly engages the political tensions and rivalries occupying England in the 1380s. My interest here is in *how* history breaks in to Nature's absolutism, and how this can occur without dissolving the transcendent reference point necessary for the very thought of the community whose problems it debates.

Nature's process as presented here entails routine mating, which is also the maintenance of social hierarchy and a political stability that would seem to preclude change and thus history. Males choose their females "by ordre" (400), with the stipulation that the female consent, thus ensuring harmonious closure. The elite female beauty on Nature's hand, a formel eagle, will be the first to go, and her successful mating would signal the untroubled continuance of this order. The dispute over the formel, however, interrupts Nature's process, opening an indeterminate space in which history can occur. Even though this interruption proceeds from a conflict between elites, it also suspends the control keeping the lower classes—indeed, all of Nature's order—in "place." With Nature's rigid order in abeyance a multivoiced, volatile debate becomes possible, which destabilizes both "natural" and bookish authority. The ground of this debate, then, is *not*-Nature's, but rather a spatiotemporal rupture of her grounding power.

How is that rupture figured here? All the while, Nature holds the formel aloft on her hand. The formel's marriageability, which corresponds both to her hymenal intactness and to the inevitability of her violation, constitutes the possibility and the premise of the debate. The temporal extension of this bodily condition provides the (non)space for historical argument, in this case an argument over how a divided political community can proceed. The formel both syntaxes this argument, in that she gives meaning to the exchanges *between* individuals and groups, and she holds open the space—here a void in Nature's totalizing time—that allows for meaningful exchange. As Derrida remarks of the hymen, "*Neither purely syntactic nor purely semantic,* it marks the articulated opening of that opposition" ("Double Session," 222). As long as the formel keeps up the suspense, history can signify but can never totalize.[17]

Both the debate and the well-recognized irresolution of the *Parliament*'s politics, then, require the deferral of the formel's hymeneals. The hymeneal that eventually does occur for the lower birds and reinstates the parliament's bond with Nature remains incomplete, thus qualifying the closure and harmony suggested by their mating and by its lyrics. Nature's time resumes in the sense that the formel defers *to* it by promising to choose her mate the next year, but it simultaneously remains suspended by her one-year deferral *of* it, which holds open history. If, as David Lawton suggests, the poem implies that "the next year's debate will be just as abortive as the one we have now overheard" (*Chaucer's Narrators,* 42), it is not because Nature's fixity ultimately prevails, but because in the idiom of communal debate it continues/interrupted.

By depicting this doubled deferral as the formel's *choice* (in that she chooses not to serve Venus "as yit," but promises to choose a mate the next year), the *Parliament* uses her (non)consent to tell of an ongoing political community that cannot agree on how to *be* a community.[18] We must remember that it is precisely at the time and place of its incomplete hymeneal, made possible by this (non)consent, that the poem is chiasmatically spliced into the English court. The *Parliament* may, as David Aers suggests, represent the temple as "an erotic domain which has set aside any concern for the common good or any conception of the political" ("*Vox populi,*" 445–46), but the doubleness by which its eroticism achieves this representation *is* the conception of the political. Moreover, when in this poem time—which opens through the figuration of hymenal (non)space—suddenly becomes the prerogative of the female and community quickly ensues, we must suspect that "Woman as trope" displaces the doubled border that I have been exploring here. As Gayatri Spivak notes, "the continuity of community or history . . . is produced on (I intend the copulative metaphor—philosophically and sexually) the dissimulation of [woman's] discontinuity, on the repeated emptying of her meaning as an instrument" ("Subaltern Studies," 31). Insofar as this poem bears importance to the understanding of the narrative techniques of late-fourteenth-century English political discourse, analysis should attend to its sexed and gendered logic or risk complicity with it.

SOVEREIGNTY AND CONSENT

While the formel's marriageability provides the possibility and the premise of the parliament's debate, its "condicioun" is female consent. Nature's stricture "That she agre to his eleccioun, / Whoso he be that shulde be hire feere" (409–10) underwrites the possibility of the formel's (non)consent and the eagles' competition for her favor, as well as the other birds' reaction to this competition. The debate itself expatiates upon the possibility of various, sometimes mutually unintelligible attitudes toward sexual/political processes, and its conclusion leaves these differences, like the formel's marriage plans, unresolved. The moment of the debate's concluding irresolution, when the *Parliament* perhaps most clearly invokes the contemporary political strife of the 1380s, also points up the instability of the sexual logic underwriting the poem's conception of community. If there are several models of love, or sexual/political relations, operating in the parliament, then the female consent governing its procedure must also carry multiple meanings. When "To every foul Nature yaf his make / By evene acord" (667–68), the "evene acord" repeated with each mating (as well as that assumed but absent in the case of the eagles) must repeat differently, according to differently constituted assumptions. Thus the ritual repetition that ostensibly confirms communal harmony at the dream's end also marks its own instability, as well as the instability of its sexual paradigm. As Judith Butler notes of the destabilizing gaps and fissures opened by reiteration: "This instability is the deconstituting possibility in the very process of repetition, the power that undoes the very effects by which 'sex' is stabilized, the possibility to put the consolidation of the norms of 'sex' into a potentially productive crisis" (*Bodies*, 10). The birds' departing song may suggest a harmonious closure that reifies a "natural" repeating process, but the difference in their repetition as they take their mates demonstrates the impossibility of a harmony so complete that it assimilates difference.

Whether one believes that Chaucer intended to show that "all versions of Nature are mediated in specific human discourse" (Aers, "The *Parliament*," 14), or that a "natural" harmony should prevail, the poem's (a)logic belies the impossibility of an unproblematic communal synthesis. If it seems that the *Parliament* achieves the unity in plurality so desired in one of its sources, Alain de Lille's *De Planctu Naturae*, we should recall that the condition of the hymeneal's possibility is the self-difference of the formel's (non)consent.[19]

Before further investigating the instability of the sexual relations based on female consent in the *Parliament,* it would be useful to consider some of the narrative strategies in which female consent, particularly in reference to marriage, works to mediate the concept of polity. While the analyses discussed below differ from each other and from this essay in their method and conclusions, they consistently demonstrate the political necessity of an ambivalent female consent. Exchange stories perhaps offer the most direct access to this topic, in that they overtly narrate, in Gayle Rubin's phrase, the "traffic in women" that forms a basis of social organization. Stories of "traded" women demonstrate in their very plot lines the function of women in forming social bonds, and suggest that the female consent upon which they invariably insist is a social demand and a narrative necessity. As Carolyn Dinshaw puts it in reference to Criseyde, "if patriarchy is to perpetuate itself, the woman exchanged between men must adapt her desire to the desire of the man who has received possession of her" (*Sexual Poetics,* 57–58). Narrative consummation in these stories depends upon the closure of consent, not the breach of rape, but their gender asymmetry as well as their narrative priorities suggests the equivocal status of the female consent they require.

In a different context, Elizabeth Fowler has shown how the well-developed contractual relations of fourteenth-century marriage doctrine, along with its gender inflections, helped to shape a contractual analysis of economic regulation and constitutional monarchy. Marriage provided a model for exchange that stressed intention and consent, yet the uneven conditions under which a woman gave consent compromised its meaningfulness. Under the doctrine of "unity of person" and the legal structure of "coverture," a woman's will, "covered" by her husband's, is voided, and the voluntary nature of her consent extinguished. Still scripted as representative of her husband, she becomes a dangerous "agency without intentionality," and is ultimately excluded from the social contract—despite its dependency upon her "consent" (Fowler, "Civil Death"). The paradox of an asymmetrical social or political contract, Fowler argues, disappears from the space of male relations, and reappears within the now dangerous "woman" whom the contract excludes.

In her work on women and sovereignty, L. O. Aranye Fradenburg has examined the implications of woman's conflicted consent for the unity of "nation" or "people," the conception of which requires "the (ritual) refashioning of captivation as an experience of freedom." Fradenburg particularly focuses on the role of the queen, who in this process

> becomes the paradigm of the subject's impossible identification with the sovereign. For woman, subject, nation, should not exclusively be imagined as "the Other" to the sovereign: woman, subject, nation, must in relation to the king be theorized both as sovereign Subject *and* object, both capable of choice *and* bound, made captive, by consent ("Sovereign Love," 81).

The erotic conceptualization of political bonds across a hierarchized community likewise cannot fully efface the volatility of the female consent that this conceptualization attempts to posit as a stable category.

Susan Crane investigates women's "paradoxically erased and powerful will" in late medieval marriage through an examination of the Griselda story, which she reads alongside the 1396 ceremony at Ardes, when Richard II and Charles VI sealed their alliance and transferred Charles's seven-year-old daughter Isabel to Richard, her new husband. Arguing for a revision of an exchange-of-women model that sees women as fully objectified and powerless, she suggests that marriage is one among many types of personal exchange in which people "objectify" themselves strategically. Crane finds that the Griselda story, and particularly Chaucer's *Clerk's Tale*, imagines "that women can undertake marital subordination intentionally and even powerfully" (*Performance*, 29).[20] She suggests that this interplay of subjection and agency corresponds to the complexity of women's position in "the patriarchal, largely arranged, but also bilateral and consent-driven marriages of the late Middle Ages" (32). The complexity of this interplay and of women's position in such instances must be understood, I suggest, in relation to the already gendered (a)logic of political bonds.

In order to consider the conflicted nature of female consent in the *Parliament*, I want to return to the temple passage, which quite specifically raises the issue of male sovereignty and female consent at the same moment that it introduces sexual desire. In the temple, the dreamer first encounters the god Priapus, in "sovereyn place":

> The god Priapus saw I, as I wente,
> Withinne the temple in sovereyn place stonde,
> In swich aray as whan the asse hym shente
> With cri by nighte, and with hys sceptre in honde.
> Ful besyly men gonne assaye and fonde
> Upon his hed to sette, of sondry hewe,
> Garlondes ful of freshe floures newe. (253–59)

Priapus in these lines is depicted as in Ovid's *Fasti*, at the moment when, having slipped the coverlet off the sleeping nymph Vesta (who had earlier rejected him), he was poised to rape her. The emphasis on the "sovereyn place" of Priapus—especially in such a politically charged poem—underscores the double entendre of the "sceptre" in his hand, which is not only the symbolic phallus, but, quite literally here, his erect penis.[21] The violence of this figure is disavowed both by the humor in Ovid's telling and, in Chaucer's addition, by men scurrying to place garlands "Upon his hed"—"whether of the god or of his organ scarcely matters,"

A. C. Spearing wryly observes, "since Priapus here is an embodied erection" (*Medieval Poet*, 215). This ambiguity does matter, however, in that it not only collapses his regal and his "natural" functions, but suggests that the power of the sceptre signals a constant readiness to rape.

This ambiguity between the king's symbolic function and his physical body recalls the much discussed thesis of "the king's two bodies" put forth by Ernst Kantorowicz. As a crowned god in "sovereyn place" with sceptre in hand, Priapus suggests the king's sacred "body politic," which transcends the physical concerns of sex and death. On the other hand, as the instrument of sexual regeneration, Priapus is all "body natural," and manifests the very issues of sex and death. Kantorowicz's thesis has been advanced and complicated by suggestions that the king's two bodies can never exist as simple dichotomy. Slavoj Žižek notes that the distinction "between king as a symbolic function and its empirical bearer" misses the paradox of their chiasmic interrelation, which effects the redoubling of the king's body (*They Know Not*, 254–55). He cites Claude Lefort's observation that:

> . . . it is the natural body which, because it is combined with the supernatural body, exercises the charm that delights the people. It is insofar as it is a sexed body, a body capable of procreation and of physical love, and a fallible body, that it effects an unconscious mediation between the human and divine. (255, citing Lefort, *Democracy*, 244)

Caught in the embarrassing, yet humorously narrated position of sexual readiness, Priapus would seem to epitomize this mediating charm. Moreover, heterosexual rape certainly can work to form bonds between men. In a discussion of this topic, Carolyn Dinshaw traces the connections between rape and the logic of a social structure ordered according to a gendered hierarchy of power. Far from an anomalous act of violence, rape is structurally similar to other gender-asymmetrical acts, such as marriage, that are always potentially "violations or evacuations of women's wills" whenever a society's power relations are "between men" ("Rivalry," 144).[22] Priapus makes sense as an image of rape that effects such homosocial bonds, but his conflation of sovereignty and rape is not sufficient to mediate the reciprocal, differentiated bonds of political community that I have sketched above. For that matter, the king's redoubled body as discussed by Žižek is never itself sufficient to incarnate the body of the "people" through a symbolization that fully forecloses the feminine.[23] Conceiving political community in these eroticized terms requires, and must therefore risk, the instability entailed in women's "paradoxically erased and powerful will."

In his chapter "Queens as Intercessors," Paul Strohm studies several cases of female mediation that exemplify the fundamental role of conflicted feminine will to the king's political viability. Examining chronicle descriptions of Queen Philippa's and Queen Anne's intercessory pleas—for the burghers of Calais in the case of Philippa and for London itself in the case of Anne—Strohm finds that even though both women are scripted as sexed bodies intervening from outside the official space of authority, they are also described as having voices capable of critique. Anne, for instance, mediates between Richard and the people of London "by enacting the city's eroticized abjection in a form that will mollify Richard's manly anger" (*Hochon's Arrow*, 109). Yet, she is aligned with biblical women (Judith and Esther) who, within certain limits, speak and act independently, and she provides pragmatic counsel that ostensibly checks regal authority. As the king's sexual consort, a role particularly emphasized in Richard Maidstone's *Concordia*, Anne sexualizes Richard's regal body, limning its potential for physical love as well as physical force. However, the unassimilable corrective of her counsel, which conflicts with her otherwise abject position, prevents the collapse of love and force through a self-difference that enables the writing of political community.

Another, perhaps more emphatic example of female mediation between the king's two bodies with reference to Richard occurs in the Wilton Diptych. The left panel of this complex painting portrays a very youthful Richard, flanked by John the Baptist and the sainted English kings Edmund and Edward. Richard kneels as he adores and/or is presented to the Virgin and Child on the right panel. In an observation that recalls the issue at hand, Caroline Barron notes, "Richard is represented as a king, yet kneels as a man before Christ, who in His turn is represented as a child yet rules the world" ("Introduction," 17).[24] Richard's hands extend in a gesture of supplication or adoration, while the Child's similarly extended hands point toward Richard in blessing. The Virgin mediates this chiasmus not only as the "bearer" of the Christ Child, whom she holds out toward Richard, but also through her exchange with Richard of a standard (a white banner with red cross) topped with an orb. Microscopic examination of the orb has revealed a painting of an island with trees and a castle, and a ship under sail in the foreground. Dillian Gordon argues that the orb represents England as the dowry of the Virgin, based on two descriptions of a very similar (now lost) altarpiece with the inscription "*Dos tua Virgo pia haec est, quare rege Maria* ('This is your dowry, Holy Virgin, wherefore rule over it Mary')" ("Wilton Diptych," 24). He further suggests that Richard has offered the orb to the Virgin and that after giving his blessing the Christ Child "will then return the banner to Richard, who waits with hands open to receive it, in token of the fact that he rules Britain with Divine blessing" (25). In such a complex exchange, Richard's body would become sacralized through the association of marriage with the Virgin—a marriage that, despite its spiritual, symbolic nature, is grounded in the physical reciprocity suggested by a "dowry," which here corresponds to the bodily transfer of England across the space between panels. Both uniting and dividing the spiritual and the mundane, this space—like the "rule" of the Virgin over the orb of England—marks the possibility of divine access and simultaneously disappears, as England becomes Richard's, sexually and spiritually.

In Chaucer's *Parliament*, the dreamer leaves the "sovereyn place" of Priapus and immediately encounters the figure of women's paradoxical will in the shape of Venus, or more specifically, in the "subtyl coverchef of Valence" that does and does not "cover" her genitals:

> And naked from the brest unto the hed
> Men myghte hire sen; and, sothly for to say,
> The remenaunt was wel kevered to my pay,
> Ryght with a subtyl coverchef of Valence—
> Ther was no thikkere cloth of no defense. (269–73)

Venus in this scene has been routinely interpreted as unambiguous enticement, and debate has focused on the moral charge of that enticement. Even J. A. W. Bennett, who insists that her portrait contains no "sensual or prurient suggestion" (*Parlement*, 94; qtd. *Parlement*, ed. Brewer 20–21), considers her "attraction" and "allure" as the important issue. The question is whether she is "wanton," never whether she is consenting.

But Venus's "coverchef" speaks otherwise about the simplicity of this portrait. Offering "no thikkere cloth of no defense," Venus would seem on the one hand to invite sex, indeed to be the very model of volition, a "Subject" who willingly consents and therefore negates the suggestion of sovereign power as rape. It is as though the repressed coverlet slipped off Vesta in the Ovidian text reappears elsewhere in the Chaucerian text, only to become an invitation to sex rather than a signal of resistance. On the other hand, the description of the cloth as "no *defense*" (unique to Chaucer) defines sex from the female vantage as a matter of defending oneself, thus exposing the conflicted nature of consent enacted only as "no defense." Venus's "coverchef," like the legal structure of "coverture," both insists upon the active presence of her will and voids that will as an act of self-erasure. Like—or as—the hymen, it is both presence and absence, a self-difference that syntaxes relations of power and opens the semantic place of inscription. It is worth noting that this is the only place in the poem where the narrator, who seeks "mater of to wryte" (168), considers himself "paid."

Before returning to the strange spatiotemporality of the dream's closing hymeneal, I want to explore the implications of the relation between the paradoxical (non)space of the hymeneal and the instability of sexual relations entailed in its repetition differently. We can glimpse these implications by taking up some critical hints.

In his reading of Venus, A. C. Spearing, who wants to maximize the erotic possibilities of this voyeuristic scene, notes that Chaucer adds to Boccaccio the detail that Venus is "in disport" with her porter Richesse. He takes the "implication of 'in disport'" to be "that Venus and Richesse are engaged in erotic play—the kind of wrestling that Africanus promised [the dreamer] he could watch" (*Medieval Poet*, 216). Spearing does not identify Richesse as either male or female, and his pattern of quotation manages to avoid Chaucer's description of Richesse as "ful noble and hautayn of hyre port" (262). Bennett, who wants to keep Venus as untainted as possible and therefore reads no sensuality into this scene, has no trouble identifying Richesse as the "portress" whom Boccaccio borrowed from de Lorris. In the *Roman* she is "Une dame de grant hautece," translated in Chaucer's *Romaunt* as "An high lady of gret noblesse" (99). In reading Chaucer's reworking of the *Dream of Scipio* in the *Parliament*'s frame, Bennett also notes that medieval readers might find the suggestion of sodomy in Cicero's condemnation of those who succumb to *libido,* as well as in the "likerous folk" of Chaucer's version:

> Whether Chaucer gave *libido* the classical meaning of "sensual passion" is a nice question. By the time of Prudentius the word denoted "sodomy"; and nothing in the context—or in Macrobius, who practically ignores the passage—would prevent a medieval reader from taking this as Cicero's meaning; whilst anyone familiar with Alain's *De Planctu Naturae* would certainly be inclined to identify the transgressors of human and divine law with the perverts there castigated for hindering the perpetuation of the species and the operation of the principle of plenitude. (*Parlement,* 41–42)

If (to bring Spearing's and Bennett's implications together) Affrican in the frame condemns sodomy, while Affrican in the dream offers glimpses of same-sex "wrestlyng," this sequence simply bears out what the poem already implies. For if, as seems obvious, political order in this poem rests on the order of sexual relations, then the parliament's destabilization of Cicero's and Nature's closed model of politics in order to open debate *must* unhinge the sexual relations grounding their "Natural," non-contingent community. The degree to which it seems not to do so is the degree to which Woman as trope successfully effaces the poem's hymeneal alogic.

(NOT) "HEER"

The simultaneous continuance and rupture of Nature's order, which is figured in the formel and which supports a stable concept of political community even as this community is set "in motion," parallels the spatiotemporal break of "heer" in the introduction to the dream's closing roundel, or hymeneal. As I have suggested, this disjunctive linkage negotiates—but can never close—the difference between the conflicting "times" necessary to imagining community. This ineradicable difference appears in the song itself, which on the one hand suggests harmony and immutable repetition from "yer to yeere," particularly if we consider the

"Now welcome, somer" lyric attested in some of the best manuscripts. On the other hand, the song's manuscript tradition demonstrates the contingency of the English community invoked by the introduction, "The wordes were swich as ye may heer fynde." The words, it seems, were never "heer," never *present*, in the sense that the following line, "The nexte verse, as I now have in mynde," would suggest. As Julia Boffey has shown, even though the "narrator's careful introduction to [the song] is preserved in all surviving copies. . . . no surviving manuscript preserves in its original layer of copying the roundel which editorial tradition has persuaded us to associate with the poem" ("Lyrics," 31). The manuscripts vary widely, three giving different versions of the song printed in *The Riverside Chaucer,* several supplying stanzas from other sources, and some giving a line from a French proverb (presumably indicating the "note"). The most complete version of the song (in CUL MS Gg.4.27) was clearly not "heer" at the "now" of the manuscript's inscription. It consists of nine lines, squeezed by a later hand into a seven-line space left by the primary scribe.[25] At the very point when the narrator's direct address to the audience would seem to provide an immediate connection to Nature's transcendent community, the words are *not* "heer," not on the manuscript page, at least, and would therefore need to be supplied.

This spatial disjunction simply confirms the alogic of the temporal conjunction that these lines imply: a verse that is "now" in the "mynde" of a poet cannot already be "heer" on the manuscript page. Furthermore, a verse with words in England and music in France actually has no "heer" at all. Just as the letter of the text requires an animating consciousness, a "mynde," that can never fully control or coincide with it, so too a political community exists only when its "here" and "now" are also elsewhere, at another time. The fullness of the hymeneal's void therefore has a two-fold effect. It creates a sense of community by conscripting its audience, redactors, readers, players into a double *performance* of the hymeneal: they become actors in Nature's garden, producing and performing material to close the debate and to confirm communal harmony. Yet, as each manuscript attests, one must "repeat" the hymeneal anew each time, differently, thus demonstrating the radical contingency of this community. Like—or as—the hymen, the hymeneal is both "here" and "not here." Its presence as absence yields the space of writing community that must for its legitimacy always be elsewhere, but at the same time can only be viable if it is "heer."

NOTES

I wish to thank Susan Crane, Carolyn Dinshaw, David Lawton, D. Vance Smith, and Peter Travis for reading and commenting on earlier versions of this essay.

1. All references to Chaucer's works are to *The Riverside Chaucer*, ed. Benson, cited by line number.

2. Thirteen of the fourteen manuscripts of the *Parliament* read "here (or heer) fynde" in line 678. One important manuscript, Cambridge University Library MS Gg.4.27, omits "here" and Brewer, following this manuscript in his edition, finds it metrically unnecessary, although quite plausible (*Parlement*, 127). The consistency of the manuscripts indicates that it made good sense to the poem's redactors. For discussion of the manuscripts and variants, see the notes in Chaucer, *Riverside*, and *Parlement*, ed. Brewer.

3. For various opinions of the political significance of the poem, see Olson "*Parlement*"; Fowler, "Hard Cases"; Fradenburg, "Spectacular Fictions"; Staley, "Chaucer" and "Gower"; and Aers, "The *Parliament*." David Aers uses the *Parliament* to exemplify Chaucer's response to "revolutionary forces and ideas in his society" in his contribution, "*Vox populi* and the Literature of 1381," to *The Cambridge History of Medieval English Literature*.

4. For discussions of the roundel as indicating a court performance, see Quilligan, "Allegory"; Dean, "Conclusiveness"; and Boffey, "Lyrics."

5. Scholars such as Homi Bhabha ("DissemiNation"), Anne McClintock (*Imperial Leather*), and Julia Kristeva ("Women's Time") have investigated and detailed the conflicted temporalities supporting concepts of political community. On the one hand, a claim to political community depends for its credibility upon the supersession of the everyday, with its glaring multiplicities, contingencies, and competing voices. Hence we find ubiquitous appeals to *another* time or to timelessness—to a national mythic past, to a lost ideal past, or to a transcendent political order, all of which can work to reify not only the community, but a particular conception of political community itself. On the other hand, the enunciation of this appeal can only be a singular, context-dependent performance subject to, and effect of, the very contingencies that it seeks to escape; indeed its very recognizability requires its inscription in immediately relevant terms. As the editors of *Between Woman and Nation* (ed. Alarcón et al.) point out, sexualization and genderization are most often the means of negotiating the inherent contradictions of such presentation. Important critical predecessors to thinking the "time" of the nation are Anderson, *Imagined Communities*; Hobsbawm, *Nations*; and Nairn, *Break-Up*.

6. See Aers, "*Vox populi*," for discussion of the focus on centralized government in the 1380s, and Staley, "Gower," for the focus on the "community of the realm."

7. As Carolyn Dinshaw puts it, the causal relations between "gendered representation and actual social relations . . . have real, and negative, effects on lived lives" (*Sexual Poetics*, 11–12). We must recognize, for instance, that the condemnation of rape as political tyranny and, conversely, respect for women's consent as representation of ethical rulership does not diminish but redoubles the significatory burden of women. Political discourse in these eroticized terms does not simply employ a time-worn sexual metaphor, but redoubles and obscures the already contradictorily sexed, gendered, and temporalized conceptualization of community. It thus replicates, as today's nationalisms do more and more violently,

a dangerously sexed logic of representation that plays itself out on women's bodies. I have discussed this issue and its effect on women in terms of contemporary medievalism in "Time Behind the Veil." Paul Strohm documents cases of gendered representation playing itself out on the bodies of medieval women in chapter 6 of *Hochon's Arrow.*

8. In Boccaccio the temple is copper, but in his *choisa,* a long explanatory note to the *Teseida,* Boccaccio says that copper and brass are essentially the same metal "born of the planet Venus" (see the note to lines 230–31 in Chaucer, *Riverside*).

9. This reference to Venus in the "north-north-west" has provided an interminable exercise for scholars interested in interpreting Chaucer's astrological details. For an overview of the debate and an attempt at its conclusion, see Benson, "Occasion."

10. Staley suggests that Venus in the temple, with a "remenaunt" of her body covered, is described as a text that, like Cicero's *Dream of Scipio,* demands exegesis ("Chaucer," 193–94). This interpretation further underscores the connection I draw between Venus and the narrator's "endyting," although I question the positive valence that Staley seems to give it. Carolyn Dinshaw provides a thorough discussion of the figure of woman as veiled text in her *Sexual Poetics.*

11. Elizabeth Salter (*English Poetry,* 139) also notes that the movement of the sun is introduced with Venus. I want to thank David Lawton for suggesting that I reexamine the implications of "to reste" in these lines.

As Bennett (*Parlement*) and Salter ("Medieval Poetry") also observe, medieval literature provides plentiful material for contradictory depictions of Venus. Critics who argue that she serves a purely negative function in this poem foreclose the role of her ambiguity here (see, for example, *Parlement,* ed. Brewer, 21–22; Olson, *Parlement,* 54–57).

12. This opening must not be thought as a simple temporal or spatial break, but as the interval that enables presentation, as Derrida has described it: "An interval must separate the present from what it is not in order for the present to be itself, but this interval that constitutes it as present must, by the same token, divide the present in and of itself, thereby also dividing, along with the present, everything that is thought on the basis of the present. . . . this interval is what might be called *spacing,* the becoming-space of time or the becoming-time of space *(temporization)*" ("*Différance,*" 13).

13. Some of the contradictions of Venus in the *Parliament* have been read as Chaucer's subversion of the monolithic, and masculine, political agenda presented by Scipio in the dream frame. Elaine Hansen, for instance, argues that Chaucer subverts Macrobius's account of male authority transmitted through the suppression of female presence by staging the return of what Scipio repressed in the form of Nature and Venus, "undefeated." She is careful to note, however, that this subversion does not lead to the abolishment of gender assymetry (*Chaucer,* 114–16). Likewise, Lynn Staley suggests that by placing Venus in the same frame as Scipio, Chaucer disrupts any unitary interpretation of political community ("Chaucer," 193–94). I agree that Chaucer may have intended to subvert a single-minded political view, or at least, as Staley says, to present the unresolvable tensions inherent in social groupings. However, my aim here is not to demonstrate Chaucer's response to Scipio, but to tease out the sexed and gendered underpinnings of political narrative that complicate any such response and its implications for women.

14. *Hymen* has a contradictory value in that it signifies marriage (archaically), and is thus what disappears at its own consummation. Derrida also comments, with specific reference to the hymen and time: "Thanks to the confusion and continuity of the hymen, and not in spite of it, a (pure and impure) difference inscribes itself without any decidable poles, without any independent, irreversible terms. Such difference without presence appears, or rather baffles the process of appearing, by dislocating any orderly time at the center of the present" ("Double Session," 210).

15. For a discussion of the arguments regarding the inevitability of "Woman's place" in signification, particularly with regard to Derrida's arguments in relation to those of Lacan and Žižek, see Cornell, "Where Love Begins."

16. Fradenburg elaborates a complex argument regarding the sovereign "body of perpetual desire" that "transcends history and the bourgeois time of the clock" ("Spectacular Fictions," 501 and passim), to which I cannot do justice here.

17. Fradenburg suggests that this respect for female choice indicates a nonabsolutist political discourse. She argues that Dunbar's revision of the *Parliament* in *Thrissill and the Rois* refuses accommodation of the discourse of the Other (whether in the form of "olde bokes" or the female rose); it is thus a "rewriting of difference by absolutist discourse" ("Spectacular Fictions," 509).

In a similar vein, James Simpson argues that Gower's *Confessio*, like the *Parliament of Fowls*, represents an Ovidian modification of the Neoplatonic and imperialist Latin traditions that they address by reinstating sexuality at the heart of the political, thus "transgressing the jurisdiction of the apparently irresistible power of a tyrannical Cupid" ("Breaking," 340), and effecting a critique of political absolutism. However, Simpson reinscribes Woman as trope when he suggests that the Lucrece story, when "told as an exemplum against tyranny in sexual and political practice," indicates "an alternative, fully ethical and political exercise of the imagination." For a discussion of the implications of this representational logic, see note 7 above.

18. As Susan Crane observes of Dorigen's ambivalent refusal in her study of feminine resistance in *The Franklin's Tale,* not only does the formel's resistance in the form of deferral reveal "that there is no vocabulary of refusal in this generic context" (*Gender,* 65), but it also "configures woman as a ground" of masculine accomplishment (63; see generally her chapter 2).

19. Unity in plurality and its disruption by human perversion is a constant concern in the *De Planctu.* Alain's Nature declares: "For just as concord in discord, unity in plurality, harmony in disharmony, agreement in disagreement of the four elements unite the parts of the structure of the royal palace of the universe, so too, similarity in dissimilarity, equality in inequality, like in unlike, identity in diversity of four combinations bind together the house of the human body" (*Alain of Lille: Plaint,* 118–19). For discussions of the normative heterosexuality and its self-contradictions in *De Planctu Naturae,* see Scanlon ("Unspeakable Pleasures"), Kiser ("Alain de Lille"), and Dinshaw (*Getting Medieval,* 120). A. J. Minnis also doubts that the differences and disjunctions of the *Parliament* can be resolved in the idea of *discordia concors* advocated by Alain (*Oxford Guides,* 311)—a position somewhat at odds with his insistence that the poem offers "little space for 'dissident

reading'" regarding normative heterosexuality (305). He does acknowledge in this context, however, that literature can textualize far more than the sum of its determinations (ibid).

20. Forthcoming. I want to thank Professor Crane for allowing me to read her work in manuscript.

21. In comparing the temple passage to its source in Book VII of Boccaccio's *Teseida,* A. C. Spearing notes that one significant shift "is that in the *Parliament* we are never told that the temple is dedicated to Venus; thus the impression given by the lines just quoted is that Priapus 'in sovereyn place' is the presiding deity, with Venus 'in a prive corner' not just because love is private but because she is subordinate to him" (*Medieval Poet,* 215).

22. For a useful discussion of the political, social, and imperial functions of rape in some medieval texts, see Finke and Shichtman, "Mont St. Michel Giant." For an extended analysis of the literary and legal history of rape in the Middle Ages, see Gravdal, *Ravishing Maidens.*

23. For a critique of Žižek's exclusion of the feminine from political signification, see Butler, *Bodies,* chapter 7. We could take as a rather literal example of this exclusion Žižek's observation regarding the effect of Ceauşescu's execution: "when confronted with the picture of his bloodstained body, even the greatest enemies of his regime shrank back...but at the same time a strange fear flashed across their mind, mixed with incredulity: is this really *him?*" (*They Know Not,* 255–56). Reading this account, one would never know that Ceauşescu was executed with his wife: that there were two bloodstained bodies in that picture.

24. I want to thank Vance Smith for suggesting that I consider the relevance of the Wilton Diptych to this argument.

25. Boffey provides detail from several manuscripts. M. C. Seymour provides a thorough description of each manuscript's treatment of the roundel ("Manuscripts," 194–95). CUL Gg. 4.27, generally considered the "best" manuscript, was used by Brewer for his edition of the poem and is the basis of the *Riverside* edition.

REFERENCES

Aers, David. "The *Parliament of Fowls:* Authority, the Knower and the Known." *Chaucer Review* 16 (1981): 1–17.

———. "*Vox populi* and the Literature of 1381." In *The Cambridge History of Medieval English Literature,* ed. David Wallace, 432–53. Cambridge: Cambridge University Press, 1999.

Alain of Lille: The Plaint of Nature. Trans. James J. Sheridan. Toronto: Pontifical Institute of Mediaeval Studies, 1980.

Alarcón, Norma, et al, eds. *Between Woman and Nation.* Durham and London: Duke University Press, 1999.

Anderson, Benedict. *Imagined Communities: Reflections on the Origin and Spread of Nationalism.* London and New York: Verso, 1983; rev. 1991.

Barron, Caroline M. "Introduction." In *The Regal Image,* ed. Gordon, Monnas, and Elam, 9–17.

Bennett, J. A. W. *The Parlement of Foules: An Interpretation.* Oxford: Clarendon, 1957.

Benson, Larry D. "The Occasion of *The Parliament of Fowls.*" In *The Wisdom of Poetry: Essays in Early English Literature in Honor of Morton W. Bloomfield,* ed. Larry D. Benson and Siegfried Wenzel, 123–44. Kalamazoo: Medieval Institute Publications, 1982.

Bhabha, Homi. "DissemiNation: Time, Narrative and the Margins of the Modern Nation." In his *Location of Culture,* 139–70. London and New York: Routledge, 1994.

Boffey, Julia. "The Lyrics in Chaucer's Longer Poems." *Poetica* 37 (1993): 15–37.

Butler, Judith. *Bodies that Matter: On the Discursive Limits of "Sex".* New York and London: Routledge, 1993.

Chaucer, Geoffrey. *The Riverside Chaucer.* Ed. Larry D. Benson et al. Boston: Houghton Mifflin, 1987.

Cornell, Drucilla. "Where Love Begins: Sexual Difference and the Limit of the Masculine Symbolic." In *Derrida and Feminism: Recasting the Question of Woman,* ed. Ellen K. Feder, Mary C. Rawlinson, and Emily Zakin, 161–206. New York and London: Routledge 1997.

Crane, Susan. *Gender and Romance in Chaucer's Canterbury Tales.* Princeton: Princeton University Press, 1994.

———. *The Performance of Self: Ritual, Clothing, and Identity during the Hundred Years War.* Philadelphia: University of Pennsylvania Press, 2002.

Davis, Kathleen. "Time Behind the Veil: The Media, the Middle Ages, and Orientalism Now." In *The Postcolonial Middle Ages,* ed. Jeffrey Jerome Cohen, 105–22. New York: St. Martin's Press, 2000.

Dean, James. "Artistic Conclusiveness in Chaucer's *Parliament of Fowls.*" *Chaucer Review* 21 (1986): 16–25.

Derrida, Jacques. "The Double Session." In his *Dissemination,* trans. Barbara Johnson, 173–286. Chicago: University of Chicago Press, 1981.

———. "Différance." In his *Margins of Philosophy,* trans. Alan Bass, 1–27. Chicago: University of Chicago Press, 1982.

Dinshaw, Carolyn. *Chaucer's Sexual Poetics.* Madison: University of Wisconsin Press, 1989.

———. "Rivalry, Rape, and Manhood: Gower and Chaucer." In *Violence Against Women,* ed. Roberts, 137–60.

———. *Getting Medieval: Sexualities and Communities, Pre- and Postmodern.* Durham and London: Duke University Press, 1999.

Finke, Laurie, and Martin Shichtman. "The Mont St. Michel Giant: Sexual Violence and Imperialism in the Chronicles of Wace and Layamon." In *Violence Against Women,* ed. Roberts, 56–74.

Fowler, Elizabeth. "Civil Death and the Maiden: Agency and the Conditions of Contract in *Piers Plowman.*" *Speculum* 70 (1995): 760–91.

———. "Chaucer's Hard Cases." In *Medieval Crime and Social Control,* ed. Barbara A. Hanawalt and David Wallace, Medieval Cultures 16, 124–42. Minneapolis: University of Minnesota Press, 1999.

Fradenburg, Louise O. "Spectacular Fictions: The Body Politic in Chaucer and Dunbar." *Poetics Today* 5 (1984): 493–517.

———. "'Voice Memorial': Loss and Reparation in Chaucer's Poetry." *Exemplaria* 2 (1990): 169–202.

———. "Sovereign Love: The Wedding of Margaret Tudor and James IV of Scotland." In

Women and Sovereignty, ed. Louise O. Fradenburg, Cosmos 7, 78–100. Edinburgh: Edinburgh University Press, 1992.

Gordon, Dillian. "The Wilton Diptych: An Introduction." In *The Regal Image*, ed. Gordon, Monnas, and Elam, 19–26.

Gordon, Dillian, Lisa Monnas, and Caroline Elam, eds. *The Regal Image of Richard II and the Wilton Diptych*. London: Harvey Miller Publishers, 1997.

Gravdal, Kathryn. *Ravishing Maidens: Writing Rape in Medieval French Literature and Law*. Philadelphia: University of Pennsylvania Press, 1991.

Hansen, Elaine Tuttle. *Chaucer and the Fictions of Gender*. Berkeley and Los Angeles: University of California Press, 1992.

Hobsbawm, E. J. *Nations and Nationalism since 1780: Programme, Myth, Reality*. Cambridge: Cambridge University Press, 1990.

Kantorowicz, Ernst H. *The King's Two Bodies: A Study in Mediaeval Political Theology*. Princeton: Princeton University Press, 1957.

Kiser, Lisa J. "Alain de Lille, Jean de Meun, and Chaucer: Ecofeminism and some Medieval Lady Natures." In *Mediaevalitas: Reading the Middle Ages*, ed. Piero Boitani and Anna Torti, The J. A. W. Bennett Memorial Lectures, 9th series, 1–13. Cambridge: D. S. Brewer, 1996.

Kristeva, Julia. "Women's Time." In *The Kristeva Reader*, ed. Toril Moi, 187–213. New York: Columbia University Press, 1986. First published in *Signs* 7, no. 1 (1981): 13–35 (trans. by Alice Jardine and Harry Blake).

Lawton, David. *Chaucer's Narrators*. Cambridge: D. S. Brewer, 1985.

Lefort, Claude. *Democracy and Political Theory*. Minneapolis: University of Minnesota Press, 1988.

McClintock, Anne. *Imperial Leather: Race, Gender and Sexuality in the Colonial Contest*. New York: Routledge, 1995.

Middle English Dictionary. Ed. Hans Kurath et al. Ann Arbor: University of Michigan Press, 1952–2001.

Minnis, A. J. (with V. J. Scattergood and J. J. Smith). *Oxford Guides to Chaucer: The Shorter Poems*. Oxford: Clarendon Press, 1995.

Nairn, Tom. *The Break-up of Britain*. London: Verso, 1983.

Olson, Paul A. "*The Parlement of Foules*: Aristotle's *Politics* and the Foundations of Human Society." *Studies in the Age of Chaucer* 2 (1980): 53–69.

The Parlement of Foulys. Ed. D. S. Brewer. London: Nelson, 1960.

Pearsall, Derek. *The Life of Geoffrey Chaucer: A Critical Biography*. Oxford: Blackwell, 1992.

Quilligan, Maureen. "Allegory, Allegoresis, and the Deallegorization of Language: The *Roman de la rose*, the *De planctu naturae*, and the *Parlement of Foules*." In *Allegory, Myth, and Symbol*, ed. Morton W. Bloomfield, 163–86. Cambridge: Harvard University Press, 1981.

Roberts, Anna, ed. *Violence Against Women in Medieval Texts*. Gainesville: University Press of Florida, 1998.

Rubin, Gayle. "The Traffic in Women: Notes on the 'Political Economy' of Sex." In *Toward An Anthropology of Women*, ed. R. R. Reiter, 157–210. New York: Monthly Review Press, 1975.

Salter, Elizabeth. *Fourteenth-Century English Poetry: Contexts and Readings.* Oxford: Clarendon, 1983.

Scanlon, Larry. "Unspeakable Pleasures: Alain de Lille, Sexual Regulation and the Priesthood of Genius." *Romantic Review* 86 (1996): 213–42.

Seymour, M. C. "The Manuscripts of Chaucer's *Parlement of Foules*." *Scriptorium* 47 (1993): 192–204.

Simpson, James. "Breaking the Vacuum: Ricardian and Henrician Ovidianism." *Journal of Medieval and Early Modern Studies* 29 (1999): 325–55.

Spearing, A. C. *The Medieval Poet as Voyeur: Looking and Listening in Medieval Love-Narratives.* Cambridge: Cambridge University Press, 1993.

Spivak, Gayatri Chakravarty. "Subaltern Studies: Deconstructing Historiography." In *Selected Subaltern Studies*, ed. Ranajit Guha and Gayatri Chakravarty Spivak, 3–32. New York and Oxford: Oxford University Press, 1988.

Staley, Lynn. "Chaucer and the Postures of Sanctity." Chapter five of David Aers and Lynn Staley, *The Powers of the Holy: Religion, Politics, and Gender in Late Medieval English Culture*, 179–259. University Park: Pennsylvania State University Press, 1996.

———. "Gower, Richard II, Henry of Derby, and the Business of Making Culture." *Speculum* 75 (2000): 68–96.

Strohm, Paul. *Hochon's Arrow: The Social Imagination of Fourteenth-Century Texts.* Princeton: Princeton University Press, 1992.

Žižek, Slavoj. *For They Know Not What They Do: Enjoyment as a Political Factor.* London and New York: Verso, 1991.

PART IV

LANGLAND'S ENGLAND

King, Commons, and Kind Wit: Langland's National Vision and the Rising of 1381

Larry Scanlon

The Poem of Piers Ploughman is peculiarly a
national work.

—Thomas Wright

Erich Auerbach is not generally associated with postcolonial theory. Yet open up that postcolonialist urtext, Benedict Anderson's *Imagined Communities,* and you will find that Auerbach is the very first thinker Anderson mentions: "As will be apparent to the reader, my thinking about nationalism has been deeply affected by the writings of Erich Auerbach, Walter Benjamin and Victor Turner" (ix). On its face, this grouping seems unlikely; but what is most surprising, given the predominantly Marxist orientation of Anderson's project, is that it is Auerbach who proves to be the most important of the three. Turner gets cited only once, as a brief theoretical gloss on the semiotics of pilgrimage (53). Benjamin appears more often, but in the most substantive citation, Anderson interprets him through Auerbach, rather than the other way round, rather drastically misreading him in the process. Anderson quotes Auerbach's explanation of Christian typology, focusing on the eternal, "omnitemporal" character that for Auerbach typology imposes on the historical present. He then suggests this notion of Christian temporality as continuous and

unchanging is analogous to the idea of "Messianic time" Benjamin
introduces in "Theses on the Philosophy of History" (23–24; Auerbach,
Mimesis, 73–74). In fact, Benjamin himself presents the notion as specifically Judaic, and he concentrates on its capacity for rupture: it is precisely the Messianic that will enable the historical materialist "to blast
open the continuum of history" ("Theses," 262–63).[1] Anderson's misappropriation of Benjamin shows just how important Auerbach actually
is to him. Auerbach supplies the book's chronological metanarrative.
Anderson uses Auerbach's omnitemporal present to define a global apprehension of time underlying the two premodern forms of "sacral" community the modern nation will displace, the world religion, such as Christianity, Islam, or Buddhism, and the dynastic realm. He contrasts this
notion with Benjamin's "homogeneous, empty time," characteristic of
modernity, a notion of the present that is "transverse, cross-time, marked
not by prefiguring and fulfilment, but by temporal coincidence, and
measured by clock and calendar." This sort of present is antithetical to
the sacral temporality of the premodern and insures that the modern
idea of the nation constitutes a radical break with all that has gone before
(*Imagined Communities*, 12–26).[2]

What are we to make of Auerbach, one of the premier medievalists
of the century just past, in this role of intellectual midwife at the birth of
postcolonial theory? At the very least, it suggests that medieval studies
may have a good deal more to offer postcolonial theory than is generally
recognized. Anderson's reductive opposition between premodern and
modern temporality has been severely criticized by subsequent postcolo-
nialists, as we might expect in an emergent, volatile field (e.g., Bhabha,
Location, 157–60; Spivak, *Critique*, 368–69). Yet these critiques tend to
be mainly theoretical, and, while they call into question the neatness of
Anderson's temporal divide, they do not reopen the question that his
initial articulation foreclosed—that is, what does modern nationhood
owe to the past? Traces of this banished past recur everywhere in Anderson's argument. He defines the nation as "an imagined political community—and imagined as both inherently limited and sovereign" (*Imagined Communities*, 6). Two of the key terms in this definition, *community*
and *sovereign*, have strong etymological connections with the religious
and dynastic modes that modern nationhood ostensibly leaves behind.
Of the many other instances I could cite, one more will suffice. Anderson
quotes, with modified approval, Tom Nairn's observation that "The ar-

rival of nationalism in a distinctively modern sense was tied to the political baptism of the lower classes." Nairn makes a metaphorical appeal to
the notion of "baptism" at exactly the moment he is attempting to define
nationalism "in a distinctively modern sense." The metaphor recalls not
simply the older religious worlds from which modern nationalism is to be
distinguished but Christianity specifically. By it he means to suggest a
process of initiation that is participatory without necessarily being democratic, as a more abstract gloss in a succeeding sentence makes clear:
"Although sometimes hostile to democracy, nationalist movements have
been invariably populist in outlook and sought to induct lower classes
into political life" (Anderson, *Imagined Communities*, 47–48; Nairn, *Break-
up*, 41). The metaphor of baptism brings something to Nairn's description
lacking in the gloss: the sense of a profound and irreversible ethical
commitment that initiation into the community of Christian believers
demands. Nairn clearly wants to assign a similar sense of profound commitment to modern nationalism as a way of illustrating its overwhelming ideological power. Could it be that this ideological power, that is, the
"imaginary" aspects of modern nationalism, is itself not fully imagin-
able except as a derivative version of Christian spirituality?

Anderson accepts Nairn's definition in regard to European nationalism, but questions it in regard to nationalism elsewhere, especially in
the Americas, where nationalist movements actively sought to exclude
the lowest of potential classes, that is, indigenous peoples and slaves of
African descent (*Break-up*, 48). The point is a crucial one, both for
Anderson's own argument, and for the subsequent course of postcolonial theory. Anderson notes that for the most part European nationalism
emerges only after successful nationalist movements in the Americas.
From this fact he argues, against older, more evolutionary models, that
the colonial context is modern nationalism's key determinant. Obviously,
this assertion serves as one of postcolonial theory's most basic axioms.
However, what is most noteworthy for my purposes is that as Anderson
proceeds to elaborate this point, his reliance on religious metaphor grows
even more acute than Nairn's. Through a series of complicated argu-
mentative turns he appeals to the notion of the pilgrim. The upper-class
creole, that is, the colonist of European descent but American birth, cut
off by the fact of that birth from the highest circles of power in the home
country, develops an imaginative relation to the colonial capital that
Anderson argues is best understood as that of pilgrim to holy center.

This imaginative relation to the "imperial administrative unit" of Britain or Spain will then combine with the sense of community generated by emergent print-markets (especially those of the newspaper) to produce a nationalist consciousness. As Anderson concludes, "In accomplishing *this* specific task, pilgrim creole functionaries and provincial creole printmen played the decisive historic role" (*Imagined Communities*, 65).

The persistence of these religious metaphors strongly suggests an unacknowledged medieval legacy within modern nationalism. This essay will reexamine Anderson's definition of nationalism, focusing particularly on the notion of *community*. In a slightly more vernacular articulation, "the commons," this notion informs certain radical visions of political sovereignty current in later medieval England, and gives them a discernibly nationalist cast. It links one of the period's most important vernacular texts, *Piers Plowman*, "the first English poem to attain a national readership and influence while its author lived," to the period's most radical political event, the Rising of 1381 (Middleton, "'Kynde Name,'" 15).[3] I will argue that this conceptual link provides one of the philosophic rationales for the explicit connection between the two that has long puzzled Middle English scholars. According to the chronicler Thomas Walsingham, in a cryptic letter the radical preacher John Ball urged on his fellow rebels by exhorting them to "biddeþ Peres plouȝman. go to his werk." According to Henry Knighton, the figure of Piers appears in the letter of another rebel, Jakke Carter, along with the Langlandian formula, "do wele and ay bettur and bettur" (transcriptions from Justice, *Writing*, 14–15, 13). Most scholars believe these letters are actually citing Langland's poem, instead of simply drawing on a preexistent stock figure, but most also view these citations as misreadings and misappropriations.[4] My argument works on both sides of the disciplinary divide between postcolonial theory and Medieval Studies. As I offer to postcolonial theory a significant complication to the apparent modernity of nationalist ideals, I also want to suggest, under the pressure of that theory, that Middle English studies has underestimated a radical strain of vernacular thought within its own period.[5] This is not a matter of reinstating some evolutionary model. On the contrary, what is most interesting about the nationalist visions of Langland and his insurgent readers is their counterevolutionary thrust relative to most modern nationalisms: they are more politically radical than these modern counterparts, not less.

At first glance, this claim may seem nothing more than a blatant anachronism: Langland is viewed by many as a conservative, or at best a reformer concerned almost exclusively with ecclesiology. However, matters are not quite that simple. For one thing, the notion of Langland as conservative is actually relatively recent, as is the notion that the 1381 Rising misappropriated him. Both emerged after the middle of this century, displacing a much older and more venerable tradition that viewed Langland as a "visionary spokesman for reform," and "literary father of English dissent" (Middleton, "Introduction," 2, 4, 6). That tradition was already well established in 1550, when the Protestant polemicist Robert Crowley produced the first printed edition of *Piers Plowman*. In his introduction Crowley explains that Langland lived at a time when "it pleased God to open the eyes of many to se hys truth, giving them boldnese of herte to open their mouthes and crye oute agaynste the workes of darckenes," including Wyclif as well as Langland. Crowley goes on to declare that "There is no maner of vice, that reygneth in anye estate of men, whyche thys wryter hath godlye, learnedlye, and wittilye, rebuked." In the passus by passus summary that follows, he notes in the Prologue, which he takes "as an argument to whole boke," that the poem "declareth the great wickednes of the byshoppes," and "some what of the powre and office of kinges and princes, and than secretly in latine verses, it rebuketh their cruelnes and tyranny" (ii, iii; it is worth noting that a copy of this edition was in the library of that later revolutionary, Thomas Jefferson.) Versions of this reading lasted well into the twentieth century, dovetailing with progressivist and Whig interpretations of history. Langland appears frequently in Trevelyan's *England in the Age of Wycliffe*. Comparing him to John Bunyan, Trevelyan classes him among "most democratic supporters" of disendowment (35, 39). As late as 1930, G. G. Coulton describes him as "radical . . . in politics and religion" (*Medieval Scene*, 158), and as late as 1941, the sociologist George Caspar Homans would write that Langland "wrote of Piers Plowman as a left-wing novelist writes of the worker, and for the same reason. His sympathies were with the common man at a time when the conflict between the classes of society was bitter" (*English Villagers*, 307). Although nineteenth-century scholarship had offered other views of Langland as it struggled to understand him in relation to modern political categories, the progressivist view was not really displaced until literary scholars like C. S. Lewis and E. Talbot Donaldson were able to combine arguments about his politics with a formalist-inspired insistence that the central critical concern should be his poetic achievement. Ironically, what is now taken as a historicist commonplace actually began in attempts to set Langland's poem somewhat apart from the exigencies of history. When it comes to Langland's politics, it is profoundly unclear where the burden of anachronism lies.

No Middle English poem puts more pressure on the problem of periodization than *Piers Plowman*. For all the many ways the poem seems indissolubly tethered to a past now long lost, its most fundamental rhetorical motive aims at escaping its own moment of utterance. Its basic mode of address is prophetic. It wants to speak to the future. Moreover, lest we take this prophetic mode as the ultimate sign of the poem's essential medievalness, we need also to note that its prophecy is directed at what it takes as the most urgent needs of its own present. In this regard it resembles modern discourses like Marxism. Although these we call utopian rather than prophetic, they also speak to the present in the name of a yet unrealized future. Can we call *Piers Plowman* utopian? Perhaps, although utopian discourses are self-consciously modern, insistently characterizing their forms of futurity as a definitive break with the mystifications of a premodern past. In particular, they tend to be antireligious.[6] For this reason, the more interesting challenge is understanding how Langland's prophetic mode incorporates aspirations utopian discourses have claimed as theirs alone. Nor is the problem restricted to politics. Under the pressure of his prophetic aims, Langland develops a macaronic, disjunct, visionary poetic that strikes the modern reader, even the professional medievalist, as somehow "unmedieval." Thus, Kathryn Kerby-Fulton suggests that, "the impressions of the earliest readers of the poem, navigating it without modern editorial punctuation and quotation marks, must have been of a compelling contemporary critique of nearly stream-of-consciousness fluidity" ("*Piers Plowman*," 514). At the risk of placing too much emphasis on what may simply be an unguarded remark, I find it striking that one of our most learned Langland scholars, in setting Langland into the closest possible relation to his own contemporary moment, must appeal to the avowedly modernist notion of "stream of consciousness." The analogy puts the problem in a nutshell. Conventional notions of anachronism assume that historical moments possess an ideological unity that is easily identifiable and recuperable. Such notions cannot finally accommodate a figure like Langland. Whatever the putatively conservative tendencies in his thought, his intellectual project comprises a profound argument with his own time. *Piers Plowman* opens up a breach with its own moment, and indeed, with its earliest readers. No subsequent scholarly reconstruction can make that breach disappear.

The Rising of 1381 constitutes another breach in the same historical moment and poses a similar problem. What can be reconstructed of its ideology also contains "conservative" elements, and its own prophetic cast: as John Ball's letter promises, "johan þe mullere haþ ygrounde smal smal smal þe kynges sone of heuene schal paye for al" (Justice, *Writing*, 15). Classical Marxism viewed medieval peasant revolts as reactionary, while older mainstream historians viewed them as anomalous responses to localized excesses. In the past few decades, social historians—led by the magisterial example of Rodney Hilton—have come to understand the Rising as originating in structural tensions endemic to medieval social formations as well as in the more particular problems of the second half of the fourteenth century (Hilton, *Bond Men*; Hilton, *Class Conflict*; Hilton, *Decline*; Hilton and Aston, *English Rising*; Fryde, *Peasants*, 1–75). In spite of the traditional character of many of its ideals, and the ambiguities surrounding its goals, most scholars now recognize the Rising as an authentically radical social movement whose immediate defeat must be balanced against its longer term impact, which was substantial. The implications for Langland scholarship of this shift are significant even if they have gone largely unnoticed. If the Rising was politically meaningful in spite of its traditionalism, then why should Langland's apparent conservatism necessarily signify opposition to the rebels or antipathy to their goals?

Traditional and *conservative* are often treated as synonymous in Middle English studies. In fact, they are not. Although *conservative* is deployed in the name of empirical historical accuracy, it is by no means as neutral as *traditional,* and it is in fact more anachronistic in some respects than a term like *radical*. As the description of a political position, *conservative* signifies much more than simply a resistance to change. It also involves a nostalgic attachment to the premodern, which it understands to exclude everything about modernity it does not like. In this respect, *conservative* is by definition an entirely modern category, and if we are to insist on absolute chronological accuracy, it is one thing a medieval thinker could never be, whatever his or her attitude toward political power and social change.[7] Moreover, the term also tends to be understood as a position at one end of a single ideological spectrum defined by the degree of commitment to social change, with *revolutionary* at the other end, and in the middle terms like *moderate, liberal,* and *reformer.* If by calling Langland conservative, one means only that he critiques the present in the name of a simpler, purer past, then the term would not be inaccurate, merely imprecise. Unfortunately, the term generally means much more, perhaps inevitably, given the course of the Langland scholarship in the past half-century.

E. Talbot Donaldson, like C. S. Lewis before him, presented a politically quietist Langland interested primarily in the literary specificity of his poetry. Lewis had complained, "Scholars more interested in social history than in poetry have sometimes made this poem appear much less ordinary than it really is as regards its kind, and much less extraordinary as regards the genius of its poet." He went on to declare that "As a politician, Langland has nothing to propose except that all estates should do their duty" (*Allegory,* 158–59). Donaldson, whose main concern was to demonstrate the integrity of Langland's authorship across all three versions of the poem, described him as "a political moderate" ("*Piers Plowman,*" 110). Ironically, this more literary approach cleared the way for the exegetical Langland—in spite of the other differences between exegetics and formalism. In their landmark work, *"Piers Plowman" and Scriptural Tradition,* D. W. Robertson and Bernard F. Huppé present a Langland whose commitment to the spiritual is so unwavering he disdains all forms of *temporalia.* In their conclusion, they declare

> To the poet [i.e., Langland] it was of the utmost importance that the system of values which he found symbolized in Jerusalem be maintained, lest the vision fade away entirely from the sight of men. The fears of the poet were justified. What the poet was witnessing and attempting to counteract was the beginning of the great intellectual chaos which produced the Waste Land, a country which has become so much more terrifying than the poet's Field of Folk that the modern reader is apt to overlook as insignificant some of the poem's bitterest portrayals of evil. *Piers Plowman* is the epic of the dying Middle Ages. (236)

In reaction to the long progressivist tradition, Robertson and Huppé have produced a counterprogressive model that is almost a mirror image.

Langland is still a poet ahead of his time, with rare prophetic power. It is just that this time what he sees is neither the Reformation nor modern democracy but Eliot's *Waste Land*. This Langland has already absorbed the modern conservative's nostalgia for the lost premodern, and that proleptic nostalgia constitutes the essence of his poetic.

At the beginning of his study Donaldson wryly notes that tradition seems to have unusual power in Langland scholarship (*"Piers Plowman,"* 1). In spite of a profusion of impressive new work on Langland in the past two decades, it is striking how much the particular question of his politics continues to be structured by the lines of inquiry laid down by Lewis, Donaldson, and Robertson and Huppé. The advent of New Historicism, with its more capacious understanding of the category of history, together with a renewed historiographic interest in the problem of dissent (best exemplified in Anne Hudson's monumental *Premature Reformation*) have meant that most recent historicist studies of the poem have begun to return to the notion of Langland as a reformer, if not necessarily a dissenter.[8] At the same time, almost all of these studies have retained the exegetical school's exclusive focus on ecclesiology. The sixties and the seventies saw the production of a number of important studies aimed at adumbrating the poem's literary complexities. However, more recent "literary" approaches have concerned themselves less with the formal complexities of the poem per se, and have concentrated instead on the contours of Langland's poetic career.[9] In a number of respects, these views remain even more indebted to exegetical criticism than most other current approaches. Most of them regard Langland's reaction to the 1381 Rising as a key development, if not the key development, in his career, expressing his "latent social conservatism" and driving many of the revisions to the B-text he makes in C (Kerby-Fulton, *"Piers Plowman,"* 522).

They have also rehabilitated the longstanding notion of Langland as a London poet. As Derek Pearsall notes, this view goes back to Skeat ("Langland's London," 185). Caroline Barron provides a concise summary: "it is clear that [Langland] intended his poem to speak to people everywhere, yet the poem must have carried most meaning for those who knew London best" ("Williams Langland," 105).[10] The point of departure for my re-evaluation of Langland's politics is an important narrative detail that has always proved something of a loose end to the London thesis. The poem's initial visionary moment occurs not in London but in the West Midlands, specifically in the Malvern Hills. That is where Will finds himself one May morning, after dressing as an unholy hermit and wandering widely in the world to hear of wonders, and where he falls asleep beside a burn. In the B-text, it is also where his body remains for seven full passus, or throughout both dreams of the Visio. Langland emphasizes this continuity in his physical location in the first waking interlude by noting that he fell asleep again before he "hadde faren a furlong" (B.5.5). According to a modern local history,

> The steep and prominent ridge of the Malvern Hills divides Worcestershire from Herefordshire. The hills run due north and south for eight miles rearing "in Pirramidy fashion," as Celia Fiennes described in 1696, a thousand feet above the surrounding plain. From their summit the map of the West Midlands is spread out below. (Smith, *History*, 1)

About thirty miles east of the modern Welsh border, they are the highest western elevation until one reaches the Black Mountains. The Malvern Hills stand between the Severn river and the medieval boundary of the diocese of Hereford, considered the beginning of the Welsh Marshes well into the fifteenth century. It seems more than likely that they suggested to Langland a western boundary.[11] As the dream begins, the dreamer looks eastward. Moreover, this perspective does not waver. His initial focus on the fair field full of folk, a distinctly rural and agrarian figuration of social totality, will give way to the institutional and vocational specificities of estates satire. As it does so, the social geography shifts from the West Midlands to London, first in the profusion of vocations and cacophony of street cries that end the Prologue—a profusion Langland explicitly contrasts with his own location in Malvern (B.Pro.215)—and then with the royal court at Westminster, the setting for both Meed's trial and Reason's sermon. Langland's long opening vision proceeds from a distant standpoint to the west across a good half of the countryside over which London presides. By locating his visionary alter-ego near England's western edge, Langland implicitly invokes the contrast between the more mercantile, more industrialized southeast, and the more traditional, agrarian west, and by extension, the rest of the country. Langland's vision is a national vision, a vision of the nation's center from its periphery.

The C-text renders the representational logic of this fiction more problematic. However, it retains the essential idea of geographical distance. Langland inserts the famous autobiographical passage in the interval between the first and second dreams of the Visio. He begins it with the somewhat surprising declaration that the first dream has transported him from the Malvern Hills to the Cornhill district in London and to a different time in his life: "Thus y awakede, woet God, whan y wonede in Cornehull" (C.5.1). This interpellation disrupts the tidier distinction between physical location and visionary geography that the B-text maintains throughout the Visio. Yet the C-text also acknowledges the disruption, and in so doing does not so much eliminate the Malvern/London distinction as transpose it to a more complex level of figuration. As the autobiographical digression closes, and Will resumes his dreaming, he says,

> Thenne mette me muche more than y byfore tolde
> Of þe matere þat me mette furste on Malverne hulles.
>   (C.5.109–10)

The chronological precision of these two lines installs a double temporality in the center of the Visio. The dream that returns to Will is "matere" that first came to him in Malvern. Yet the exposition to follow will also contain "muche more" of the original matter than he has to this point revealed. Langland's original, national, perspective stays with him even as his dream catapults him from Malvern to London.

Repetition is one of the poem's dominant structural features. One can point to its alliterative line, its oft-noted pleonastic diction, its central penitential triad, *Do-wel, Do-bet, Do-best*, its wildly excessive deployment of its own generic premises (seven dreams, and two dreams within dreams, where most dream-visions offer only one), its extended rehearsals of Christian theology and salvation history. Perhaps because of the poem's many images of pilgrimage, most scholars have seen a major break between the opening Visio and the rest of the poem, a retreat from its opening social concerns to an exclusive focus on Will's own penitential quest. It is important to recognize that even here, the poem never leaves its opening premises behind. As Anne Middleton astutely notes, "The poem is most vividly remembered, and usually explicated, in episodic units whose arrangement seems somehow reiterative rather than progressive" ("Narration," 92). While there is no mistaking the penitential turn of the latter two thirds of the poem, especially in some of the middle passus, there is also no mistaking an equally clear outward turn in the final passus. Moreover, even at its most penitential and autobiographical, the poem rarely retreats from its social and ecclesiological critique. In fact, the poem returns repeatedly, perhaps even obsessively, to the concerns it lays out in its Prologue and the opening Visio. It retains its initial nationalist cast in two ways. First, the brief waking interludes enforce an autobiographical continuity that extends to the very end of the poem, and as one of the few concrete details of that autobiography, the narrator's initial location in the Malvern gives it a specificity that is never superseded. Second, details in the dream-narratives periodically reinforce the initial opposition between the agrarian western periphery and the corrupt London center. The most obvious is Piers himself, the salvific figure anticipated by the poem's very first ethical opposition:

> Somme putten hem to plou3, pleiden ful selde,
> In settynge and sowynge swonken ful harde;
> Wonnen þat þise wastours with glotonye destruyeþ.
>   (B.Prol.20–22)

As the model of uncorrupted agrarian labor Piers necessarily if implicitly maintains the narrator's initial peripheral perspective on the centers of political and ecclesiastical power. It is true that Piers's decision to "cessen" of his "sowying" and make "preieres" and "penaunce" his "plou3 . . . herafter" (B.7.122–24) constitutes one of the strongest markers of the poem's inward turn. Nevertheless, as Lawrence M. Clopper has demonstrated with some precision, it cannot be argued "that Piers, the English plowman, ever entirely disappears from the poem" ("Songes," 185). Instead, the labor that he exemplifies provides a new metaphor through which Langland understands both the apostolic life and his own spiritual quest. Piers's conflict with the priest who disputes his pardon awakens Will, "Metelees and monielees on Malverne hulles" (B.7.147), a state recalling the hunger that marks the dissolution of Piers's briefly improvised society in the previous passus. At the beginning of the Vita (B.8; C.10) Will wanders for an entire summer "yrobed in russet," seeking Do-wel (1–2). After an encounter with two Franciscans, he falls asleep "by a wode," or "By a wilde wildernesse and by a wode side" depending on the textual witness (B.8.63), a peripheral location analogous to the Malvern Hills, and the ensuing dream finds him in a borderland.[12] Wit explains to him that "Sire Dowel dwelleþ . . . noȝt a day hennes," as "duc of þise Marches" (B.9.1, 11).

Three interludes later (two in the C-text), when Will awakes after the Harrowing of Hell (B.18; C.20), his quasi-clerical guise as mendicant or hermit abruptly recedes. He calls out to his wife Kytte and his daughter Calotte and sets off to Church to "reverencen the resurexion" only to slip into another vision that begins with Piers displacing Christ on the Cross (B.18.427–19.11). The vision as a whole concerns Christ's founding of the Church, where Piers plays successively the roles of St. Peter, of subsequent exegetical tradition, and of the source of political community. Grace gives him a team of "foure grete oxen," Luke, Mark, Matthew, and John, and four seeds, the neo-Aristotelian, cardinal virtues of Prudence, Temperance, Fortitude, and Justice. Will's climactic declaration, "Now is Piers to the plow" (338), recapitulates the scene of the Half-Acre in Passus 6, and the opening of the Prologue in a radically ambiguous fashion (cf. Simpson, "*Piers Plowman*," 225). Standard readings of the poem that take the ploughing in this scene to be purely metaphorical, signifying an entirely inward state, simply assume what they set out to prove. In his account of the B-text, James Simpson has argued that Will's long self-examination, which produces "a resounding and optimistic affirmation of the value of human works before God," effectively ends with Passus 17, after which Langland turns in the final passus to the "reformation of the institution of the Church" (139, 161, 203). To this convincing reading I would add only that the Church is not the only object of criticism. Piers Plowman emerges in the Visio in response to the abuses of the nobility no less than to those of the clergy. The impasse with the Priest, which impels Piers to take up his apostolic mission (leaving Will meatless and moneyless on the Malvern Hills), follows the impasse on the Half-Acre, prompted by the knight's complete failure to rule. The re-examination of Christian penance from the perspective of honest labor returns Will to the world to reform not just the Church, but the Christian community as a whole. As the passus ends a king appears and swears by his crown to abide by the *Spiritus Iusticie* (B.18.469–80). The final passus, with its vision of Antichrist, is best known for its antifraternal depiction of Sire Penetrans Domos, yet it also imagines Antichrist infiltrating the "kynges counseille" and the royal courts of Westminster. The geographical specificity of this last detail recalls the Visio, and Will's initial peripheral perspective, albeit faintly.

With its focus on the king's counsel this scene also recalls the poem's initial treatment of kingship. In what will become, many centuries later, one of its most celebrated passages, Langland supplements his national vision with a radically communal notion of political sovereignty:

> Thanne kam þer a kyng; knyghthod hym ladde,
> Might of þe communes made hym to regne.
> And þanne cam kynde wit and clerkes he made,
> For to counseillen þe kyng and þe commune save.
> The kyng and knyghthod and clergie bothe
> Casten þat þe commune sholde hire communes fynde.
> The commune contreved of kynde wit craftes,
> And for profit of al þe peple Plowmen ordeyned
> To tilie and to travaille as trewe lif asketh.
> The kyng and þe commune and kynde wit þe þridde
> Shopen lawe and leute, ech lif to knowe his owene. (B.Pro.112–22)

This passage provides a compelling gloss on the political concerns that occupy the poem throughout. In the discussion to follow I will use it both to illustrate Langland's own beliefs and as a convenient point of comparison with the beliefs of his rebel readers. However, before I can examine it in detail, I need to address its status in the poem's modern critical history, where it has a significance essentially antithetical to the one I want to ascribe to it. From Donaldson onward, it has been, along with its revised counterpart in C, a locus classicus for the illustration of Langland's political quietism. Matters were not ever thus, however. The passage was first brought to the attention of modern scholarship by Thomas Wright, in the introduction to his mid-nineteenth-century edition of the Cambridge, Trinity College, MS B.15.17 (the B-text manuscript that is also the base text for Kane and Donaldson). Wright viewed Langland as a dissenter with populist sympathies and he was so struck by the difference in political valence between this passage and its counterpart in the C-text that, placing the passages side by side, he used the contrast to illustrate a novel theory of multiple authorship. Here is C:

> Thenne cam ther a kyng; knyghthede hym ladde;
> Myght of tho men made hym to regne.
> And thenne cam kynde wytt & clerkus he made

For to conseillen þe kyng and þe commune save.
Conscience & kynde wit and knyghthed togedres
Caste þat þe comune sholde here comunes fynde.
Kynde wytt and þe comune contreved alle craftes
And for most profit to þe peple a plogh gonne þei make,
With lele labour to lyve while lyf on londe lasteth. (C.Pro.139–47)

Calling the passage from B "the statement of popular opinion of the origin and purpose of kingly government," Wright adds that "Nobody... can deny that in this instance the doctrine is stated far more distinctly and far more boldly" in the B-text than the C-text. Although he did not elaborate any further, twentieth-century scholars have noted in particular the change to the second line in the B passage from "Might of þe communes" to "Myght of tho men"; the change of "Plowmen" in line 119 to "plough," along with the complete rewriting of the following line; and the complete excision of B's final two lines. Wright concluded more generally that, "it is my impression that the first [that is, the B-text] was the one published by the author, and that the variations were made by some other person, who was perhaps induced by his own political sentiments to modify passages" (*Vision*, xxxiv–xxxv). This hypothesis never achieved critical consensus. However, J. M. Manly made a fuller case for it in a couple of influential essays published in 1908 and 1909, and in his attempt to refute the hypothesis definitively, Donaldson returns to this passage, making it the point of departure for his argument that Langland was a political moderate (Manly, *"Piers Plowman"* and "Authorship"; Donaldson, *"Piers Plowman,"* 85–111).

Donaldson's argument is curious in at least one respect. It is excessive in relation to the overall purpose of his study, as he freely admits. He notes that Skeat had already answered Wright: "'the poet grew more conservative in his ideas and more careful in his expressions as he grew older; a result so common and natural that it is not be wondered at'" (89; Skeat, *Vision*, lxxix). Donaldson concedes that this "explanation is, in a sense, adequate," but he wants more: "in admitting that C was more cautious and conservative than B, one leaves the door open to further attacks upon the unity of authorship, since not every one will accept C's advanced age as an excuse for his apparent change of heart" (*"Piers Plowman,"* 89). Donaldson clearly wants that door slammed shut, and with this desire he tacitly shifts the grounds of his discussion. In the argument to follow, he attempts to demonstrate not only "unity of author-ship" in relation to the B and C versions of this passage, but also a unity of authorial intention—that is, that both versions mean essentially the same thing. Appealing to the semantic complexities of the term *com-munes,* and citing numerous passages in the poem that use that term or discuss kingship, he will argue that ostensible radicalism of the B version of the passage is atypical and therefore illusory, that its real meaning is virtually the same as the more moderate stance taken by C. He then intro-duces the notion of the rebel misreading as the motivation for what he has now concluded is a minor revision:

> the author, a moderate and a traditionalist, if not a reactionary, could not have approved of this use of his poem and must, indeed, have been considerably embarassed by his unwitting mésalliance with John Ball. The line in B which mentions the might of the *comunes,* even though it is capable of a perfectly innocuous interpretation consonant with the poet's political be-liefs, is also capable by the enthusiastic democrat . . . of an inter-pretation which might, obliquely give support to the participants in an affair like the Peasants Revolt. The C-revision, though made at a certain sacrifice in the breadth of conception, is unequivo-cal. (108)

As far as I have been able to determine, this discussion is the origin of the notion of the rebel misreading. Thus, the notion emerges in the service of another argument, to which it is not strictly necessary. As the larger argument succeeded—the hypothesis of multiple authorship is now viewed as nothing more than a quaint nineteenth-century excess— this originally incidental notion established itself as well. And it retains its status as a plausible historical truth in contexts otherwise at odds with the assumptions of its initial articulation. It is one thing to argue for a rebel misreading when, like Donaldson, one is seeking to minimize the differences between B and C. It is much more problematic to take such a misreading for granted and also hold, as do most current Lang-land scholars (including this one), that the most important thing to rec-ognize about the poem's textual history is its immense variations. From that premise, to argue that rebels misread the B-text on the basis of po-litical views revealed in the C-text seems slightly illogical. Indeed, the

persistence of this notion provides a textbook illustration of a fallacy to
which certain empiricist forms of historicism are especially prone. Sometimes what they claim to be preserving as the immediacy of an original
historical moment is in fact an artifact of the immediately previous moment of their own critical tradition. Without in any way gainsaying the
perspicacity or importance of E. Talbot Donaldson, one of the twentieth
century's greatest medievalists, I feel bound to observe that it seems unlikely that over five centuries of readers (beginning with the rebels themselves) were flatly wrong about Langland's relation to the 1381 Rising,
and the real truth suddenly emerged in 1949. A return to the older tradition may well be in order.

This passage actually raises two distinct questions; part of Donaldson's legacy has been to collapse them into one. The first is what the
passage can tell us about Langland's relation to the rebels; the second is
what it can tell us about the relation between the B-text and the C-text.
The two become the same only if we conclude that in his C-revisions,
Langland was reacting to a rebel misreading. But that conclusion depends
on taking Donaldson's reading for granted. Therefore, I am going to defer
the second question, in the interests of a full re-examination of the first.
I will return briefly to the question of Langland's career at the end of the
essay. Was this passage the work of a political moderate, or indeed "a reactionary"? At first blush, as Wright's reaction illustrates, that does not
seem likely, especially if, as I am suggesting, we ignore the testimony of
C for the time being. But it is unlikely even if we don't. For even the
misreading hypothesis requires us to posit the passage is at some level
potentially radical. Moreover, if we explore the nature of that potential, if
we seek to somehow delimit that potential, to separate it from a putative
actual meaning, we quickly discover such a separation is difficult if not
impossible. For the radical potential of this passage inheres not in some
completely new departure, but rather in a daring combination of old ideas.
Indeed, there is daring in the passage's sheer scope (what Donaldson
justly described as its "breadth"), especially given its brevity. Langland
brings together a number of distinct notions central to medieval political
thought and scholastic tradition, including the theory of three estates (or
the trifunctional theory), the foundation of kingship in popular sovereignty, the problem of royal counsel, and doctrines of natural reason, or
"kynde wit." In framing a study on the currency of notions of universal
salvation in England before the Reformation, Nicholas Watson has argued

that Langland, Julian of Norwich, and others were engaged in the project
of "vernacular theology," that is, that they were committed to making
vernacular writing every bit as adequate a vehicle for theological speculation as the Latin traditions of the Church: "Not only do vernacular
texts derive material from an array of Latin systems, they generate their
own systems" ("Visions," 146). If Watson is right, as I believe he is, it
stands to reason that Langland would have seen his poetry not only as a
platform for vernacular theology, but also for a similarly independent
vernacular political theory.

In fact, this passage is part of the longer elaboration of estates ideology that, as Clopper has argued, constitutes most of the Prologue, and
the Visio as a whole ("*Songes*," 145–79).[13] In his words, "What Langland
has done" with the trifunctional image "is to seize the ideological construct of the ruling classes and translate it into a new moral hierarchy."
Reversing the traditional tendency, he opens the Prologue with the "lowest levels of society." The first specification of the fair field is the ploughman: that is, the initial ethical opposition I have already mentioned,
"Somme putten hem to the plough...." The ploughmen are paired with
"true hermits"; in Clopper's gloss, both "are humble, true workers" (145,
157). This opening leads to a brief survey of true and sham devotional
practices and of the corruption of ecclesiastical offices, working its way
up from the hermits to the papal curia and to grasping cardinals who
presume they have the power to make a pope. With the strong implication that clerical authority has failed, Langland turns to the king. Royal
authority remains the primary focus of the poem until the end of Passus
4, with the ambiguous conclusion of Meed's trial and the King's promise to be ruled by Reason. Inasmuch as Reason's sermon will lead to the
entrance of Piers, one might argue that the survey of the estates ends
where it started, that is with those who put themselves to the plough.
Thus, this passage from the Prologue opens the discussion of kingship
as part of a larger project of reconceptualizing the estates from the perspective of those who labor. It opens that project by reconceptualizing
the notion that a king derives his sovereignty from the people, and the
notion that royal counsel should come from the clergy.

The passage has the character of a concise foundation myth. As
such, it clearly fits Anderson's definition: "an imagined political community—and imagined as both inherently limited and sovereign." The

limitations come first from the specificity of the dreamer's geographical location and his view eastward toward London and Westminster, and second from the specifically lay quality of this newly imagined community, reinforced by the contrast with the papal court from which we have just shifted. There can be only one papal court; here we have a Christian royal court, of which there are necessarily more than one. It is true that sovereignty in this community is not purely imaginary: the king is here in person. While that difference may seem to uphold Anderson's distinction between the modern nation and the premodern dynastic realm, in fact it only makes matters more complicated. There is nothing dynastic in this foundation myth. The king is present, but his sovereignty is still imaginary in that he shares it with everybody else. And that is only where the complications begin.

The King, Knighthood, and Clergy convene with the commons, and arrange that the commons shall be responsible for providing food. Then the commons through their native reason develop crafts. Nevertheless, the originary force of these arrangements is twice complicated, both by its belated occurrence (that is in the middle of the Prologue, after the analysis of the clerical estate), and by the indeterminacy of the adverbs that introduce it. "Thanne kam þer a kyng": this abrupt transition is entirely characteristic of the disjunctive structure of Langland's allegory. The adverbs "Thanne" and "þer" are emphatic: they promise to locate us in a very specific time and place, yet what that time and place might be remains almost entirely unclear. "Thanne" could have a logical rather than a temporal force: having exhausted the possibilities of the clerical estate, Langland is now moving on to lay lordship. But this narrative and temporal resonance is unavoidable, which means the passage's originary significance is vitiated even further. In fact, in this passage Langland splits the difference between two influential notions of a king's moral authority. In most Augustinian formulations, temporal sovereignty is a default made necessary by human sin. Humanity's innate sinfulness would make political community impossible without the arbitrary coercion of a sovereign to keep it in place. In the wake of Aquinas and the rediscovery of Aristotle, later medieval thinkers developed various theories of the autonomy of lay sovereignty based on or analogous to the doctrine of natural law, including Dante's daring claim in *De monarchia* that the temporal monarch draws his authority directly from God (*Monarchy*, 61–

99). From the Augustinian notion Langland draws the superiority of spiritual authority over the temporal; from the Dantean position he draws the adequacy of lay power, which helps support his anticlerical critique.

A similar reappropriation flows from the word "ther." Where does that word place us? Surely not in the papal curia, the locale we have just left with this transition. Are we perhaps back at the fair field? But that would return us to the Malvern Hills and Will's perspective from the periphery. Are we to see this assessment of kingship as proceeding directly from the agrarian viewpoint that both Malvern and the fair field figure? The passage's figural logic strongly suggests the answer to this question is yes. The king it offers us is extraordinarily passive. After his indefinite arrival, the next half-line adds a further temporal confusion. "Knyghthod hym ladde": we have just been told the king has arrived; now we learn that his knights have preceded him, have even, perhaps, led him in. With the next line, "Might of þe communes made hym to regne," Langland articulates a notion of popular sovereignty widely current in the later Middle Ages that can be traced back both to Roman antiquity and to pre-Christian Germanic tradition, the principle that Walter Ullmann called the "ascending thesis" (*Political Thought,* 12–14, 159–222).[14] Langland's articulation formulates this principle in such a way as to nearly reverse its practical significance. As Alan Gewirth explains, the ultimate sovereignty of the people was an almost entirely abstract concept, serving as "the exclusive legitimating principle of the coercive power" (*Marsilius* 2:xxxviii; qtd. in Watt, "Powers," 417). But Langland's use of the word "might" seems to assign coercive power to the commons, an impression the predicated "made hym to regne" only reinforces. We might, for contrast, cite John of Paris's 1302 formulation of Averroes's version of the principle: "The king exists by the will of the people, but while he is king it is natural he should rule."[15] In such formulations, the people are passive and the king is active. In this passage, it is the people who are active.

If anything, Langland's revised notion of royal counsel is even more radical. The proposition that the clergy were the king's proper counselors was not only an abstract ideal, it also reflected a widespread practical reality. Although the later Middle Ages were marked by a progressive laicization of the personnel in the royal household, the Church, as traditionally the major institutional source of both education and textual production, was also traditionally the main source of royal advisors. Clerical advisors continued to play a major role at court in spite of laicizing trends. Langland renders the clergy as derivative as he has just rendered the king. He makes "clerkes" the product of "kynde wit." This characterization, despite its affinity to the Thomist notion of natural law written by God on men's hearts, certainly does not match the medieval church's account of the historical source of its institutional authority, that is, the transmission to the papacy of Christ's charge to Peter. While Langland may not at this point be calling Petrine notions into question, he is certainly anticipating the poem's end, when in Passus 19, he effectively casts Piers as pope. Christ will declare

> Thus hath Piers power, be his pardon paied,
> To bynde and unbynde both here and ellis
> And assoille men of alle synnes bothe here and ellis.
>   (B.19.189–91)

In the Prologue, by making the clerical a function of natural reason, Langland is at the very least suggesting that when clerks counsel kings they bring no special sacerdotal privilege to bear, that their counsel ultimately proceeds from an innate faculty common to all.

The conflation of the commons with political authority continues as the passage goes on. It is true that King, Knighthood, and Clergy "casten" that finding sustenance ("communes") should be an obligation of the "commune." Nevertheless, the word "bothe" at the end of line 116 effectively collapses the category of knighthood back into that of the king, thus making knighthood also an expression of the might of the commons. Moreover "casten" ("arranged," or perhaps, "decided") seems a bit vague and unassertive in this context, where one might expect "commanded" or indeed "ordained," which is what the commons do in line 119. They contrive "craftes" out of kind wit, which, in contrast to most accounts of the three estates, places the function of those who work in the same category as the function of those who pray, and, indeed, above that of those who fight, if the "might of þe communes" still governs royal authority. It is not until the crafts have been contrived that plowmen are assigned their specific obligations of tilling and working, and it is the commons who ordain it. Moreover, this self-ordaining process of

producing sustenance takes a certain pride of place. The shaping of "lawe
and leute" comes after it, and by this point, Knighthood and Clergy have
fallen out entirely, the creation of law coming entirely from the commons, Kind Wit, and the King who expresses the commons' "might."

Langland matches the more dominant role he carves out for the
commons with the authority of royal advisor to which he implicitly lays
claim for himself. By virtue of its substantial redefinition of the source
and nature of royal sovereignty this passage clearly ventures toward the
clerical genre of the *Fürstenspiegel* and its related traditions.[16] The twenty-
eight lines immediately succeeding this passage go even further, consisting of snippets of royal advice drawn from a variety of clerical sources
delivered by an angel, a goliard, and the commons.[17] But Langland's persona is not a cleric; he's only dressed like one: "In habite as an heremite
unholy of werkes" (Pro.2). More significantly, he is also not at court. Instead, he speaks from the kingdom's western periphery. His sole source
of authority is his membership in the national community. Yet that
condition is sufficient, for as his poetry has just proclaimed, it is to the
commons that the king owes his sovereignty, and through the commons
that he makes law. This passage does not conceive of royal authority exclusively, or even primarily, in terms of a superior constraint. Instead, it
conceives of royal authority as the social concretization of a communal
will, responsive to communal counsel.

The point is worth stressing, for it makes emphatic the problem of
periodization I noted above. In Benedict Anderson's formulation: "Kingship organizes everything around a high centre. Its legitimacy derives
from divinity, not from populations, who after all, are subjects, not citizens" (*Imagined Communities*, 19). The hold this view continues to exert
on postcolonial and other postmodern theory has been reinforced by a
subtler formulation from Foucault, who imagines the emergence of medieval kingship as "a principle of right that transcended all the heterogeneous claims, manifesting the triple distinction of forming a unitary
regime, of identifying its will with the law, and of acting through mechanisms of interdiction and sanction" (*History*, 87). Medieval notions of
kingship, especially Langland's, are binary rather than unitary. But the
problem with formulations like Anderson's and Foucault's is not simply
their partial view of the Middle Ages. It is also their foreclosure on possible continuities with the present. One of modern democracy's fondest
ideals is that of an impartial sovereign authority equally responsive to all

members of the community. Indeed, one can find a similar trace of medieval ideologies of kingship even in such a frankly revolutionary notion
as the "dictatorship of the proletariat." The persistence of the ideal in
these modern egalitarian discourses should encourage us to take much
more seriously its radical expression in Langland. The ideal also provides
a compelling link to his rebel readers.

As the rebels made their own drive from the periphery to the center,
what they sought was the sovereign, not in his dynastic role, but precisely
in his embodiment of the entire community. As Rodney Hilton notes,
the rebels envisioned the abolition of lordship, but "clung to the idea of
monarchy," understanding it "as an institution standing above individuals and classes, capable of dispensing even-handed justice" (*Bond Men*,
225–26). Like Langland, the rebels saw themselves as taking an active
role in defining such justice and royal authority more generally. Like
Langland, they understood royal authority as originating in the commons. By abolishing lordship, they expected to eliminate the complex
and proliferating networks of power that stood between them and the
king, and make their constitution of royal authority more immediate
and direct. Derived, like Langland's, from traditional ideals, this new,
more active conception of communal sovereignty had a single if somewhat hazy limit: the English nation.

It is unclear whether the responsibility for this haziness lies with
the rebels or with us. There is no record of those ideals that can be traced
with certainty to the rebels themselves. Everything that survives comes
either from government records or chronicles whose authors are overtly
hostile. Even the letters that purport to be the work of John Ball and
(possibly) other rebels come to us through the mediation of two extremely
biased chroniclers.[18] As Susan Crane puts it, "the rebels remain outside
representation in that they do not represent themselves for the written
record" ("Writing Lesson," 201).[19] This condition constitutes an inescapable qualification of any claim about the aims of the Rising and the
beliefs of its participants. At the same time, all of the accounts of the
Rising, both juridical and historical, concern themselves precisely with
the problem of political representation, and the problem of political representation necessarily involves representation as an ideological and
semiotic issue as well. For this reason, it may be possible to reconstruct
traces of rebel aims and beliefs by concentrating precisely on the biases
of the chroniclers, that is, on those aspects of their accounts where they

seem most fascinated or threatened. In his subtle and suggestive study of the Rising's ideology, Paul Strohm draws on the sociologist Anthony Giddens's notion of "structure," and "interpretative scheme." Giddens argues no social action, no matter how violent or disruptive, can ever take place outside of commonly shared interpretative schemes that give it meaning. Strohm convincingly demonstrates "that some of the very schemes wielded by the chroniclers to stigmatize rebel actions were elements of 'mutual knowledge' available to—and in fact employed by—the rebels for the production of oppositional acts" (*Hochon's Arrow*, 51–52). One of these mutual schemes most important to the rebels was kingship.

The core of the rebel understanding of kingship can be found in their watchword, *With King Richard and the true commons*. A number of claims are implicit in this formula: that the king rules along with the commons, that no intervening authority should stand between the commons and their king, that these are the only true commons. That is to say, in Strohm's memorable explication, they are "an enlarged and regenerated commons," as opposed to "that group of usurping and self-aggrandizing middlemen who ironically claimed the very title of commons, those rural landowners and urban entrepreneurs who were constituted as the commons of Parliament" (41–42). This distinction between the true and false commons is more than a polemical ploy, although it is definitely that too. At a more profound level it also rejoins the prophetic mode we can see in the letters. It asserts a hidden truth that is hard and redemptive, that will displace a false appearance, for all of the appearance's ostensible dominance. The watchword appears as such only in the *Anonimalle Chronicle*, although versions and echoes of the formula recur throughout the other chronicles. As we shall see, it was also explicitly disavowed in the charge Richard gave to the parliamentary session that dealt with the Rising's aftermath. Moreover, the ideals it expresses offer a convincing rationale for many of the rebel actions. Its appearance in the *Anonimalle Chronicle* is itself not without significance. This work is the least overt in its biases of all the chronicles, and historians have long considered it the most reliable according to traditional historiographic standards. If that is true, then the watchword would seem to have a claim to authenticity as strong as that of the five rebel letters.

After noting the rebels had encamped outside of London in Blackheath on Wednesday, 12 June 1381, the chronicler remarks,

les ditz communes avoient entre eux une wache worde en Engleys, "With whom haldes yow?" et le respouns fuist, "Wyth kynge
Richarde and wyth the trew communes": et ceux qe ne savoient
ne vodroient, furount decolles et mys a la mort. (*Anonimalle
Chronicle*, 139)[20]

This moment constitutes one of very few where the *Anonimalle* chronicler quotes rebel speech in English. The departure from the French emphasizes both the authenticity of this rebel notion, and its alienness to
the chronicler's view of the world. Not only is the notion itself alien, but
so is the use to which it is put: "wache worde" appears in English as
well. In the most direct and brutal of senses, this slogan establishes a
community, then murderously polices the community's borders. Here
is Langland's might of the commons put into fairly drastic practice. Yet
the brutality only heightens the chronicler's more general fascination
with the rebel's insistence that the principle of popular sovereignty could
be put in practice at all, especially by the people themselves. Indeed, the
watchword does not even contradict Averroes's principle that while he is
king, the king should rule. On the contrary, it insists that Richard should
rule, with the only qualification that he should rule with the "trew communes," and the "trew communes" alone. It is this qualification that
constitutes the watchword's ideological novelty.

The rebels' aggressive intensification of the notion of popular sovereignty also explains the prominence of another issue in the chronicles. That issue is treason. Not often noted by modern commentators, it
nevertheless features regularly in the *Anonimalle Chronicle* and Thomas
Walsingham's *Historia Anglicana,* and somewhat more sporadically in
the other sources as well. Charges of treason seemed to provide the rebels
with a quasi-legal justification for their violence. The Rising was a response most immediately to the Poll Tax, and like any peasant revolt, to
the underlying structural inequities in the society (Hilton, *Bond Men,* 9–
134, 144–64). But according to both Henry Knighton and the *Anonimalle*
chronicler, violent resistance to the tax did not begin until after the initial collections had been taken, and commissioners were sent back to
track down evaders. According to Knighton one of these commissioners
was corrupt and sparked off the first moment of resistance molesting
young women (*Chronicle,* 206–09). According to the *Anonimalle* chronicler the commissioners were overzealous rather than purely corrupt.

However, in both cases, the immediate cause of resistance was the claim of particular officials to represent the king. The commons took the claim as illegitimate, and therefore treasonous. When Sir Robert Belknap, Chief Justice of the Common Bench followed these commissioners with a commission of trailbaston,

> the commons rose against him and came before him to submit that he was a traitor to the king and kingdom, and that he ill-advisedly and maliciously wished to undo them with the aid of the false inquest taken before him; for which reason they made him swear on the Bible that never thereafter would he hold such sessions again nor be justice of the inquiry; and they made him disclose to them the names of all the jurors. They captured all of these, beheaded and put them to death, and dragged their houses to the ground. (*Anonimalle*, 135)[21]

These commons completely turn the tables on the Chief Justice. They do not simply reject his authority; in accusing him of treason, they claim his authority for their own. They force him to take a juridical oath, then execute his jurors as if they had actually been convicted of high treason. As the Rising ensues, the rebels will claim to be combating treason repeatedly.

After the Essex rebels rendezvous in Rochester with those from Kent, the new group descends on Canterbury cathedral, interrupting mass, and crying "in one voice" to the monks to elect a new archbishop, for the current one "is a traitor and will be beheaded for his iniquity." They then convene an informal inquest of their own, rounding up the mayor, bailiffs, and commons of the city and examining them to see "if they would with good will swear to be faithful and loyal to King Richard and to the loyal commons of England" (137). The next day, when an anxious king sends messengers to inquire why they have revolted, they respond, "for his salvation and to destroy traitors to him and the realm" (138). They will make similar claims when they meet with him in person. At Blackheath they present a petition requesting "the head of the duke of Lancaster, and those of fifteen other lords," including the archbishop of Canterbury, Robert Hales, the treasurer, Robert Belknap, and John Legge (according to the Knighton, the original corrupt commissioner) (139). When he offers them a pardon at the Tower, they cry they will not leave "before they have the traitors within the Tower" and charters of manumission (143). The first meeting at Mile End begins with the crowd kneeling to welcome Richard: "Welcome our lord, King Richard; if it please you, we wish to have no other king than you," and with Tyler's request that he allow them to have "all the traitors against him and the law" (144). According to Walsingham, the rebels wandered about the city speaking of seizing traitors, especially the duke of Lancaster. This idea "so pleased London's lower orders, that, thinking it particularly shameful that any others might inflict losses and injuries on the duke before themselves" they immediately join those burning down his residence, the Savoy (*Historia*, 457).[22]

Wat Tyler's second petition, presented to the king at their second meeting at Smithfield, where Tyler would be murdered and the rebels dispersed, restates the rebel aims in a way that makes the connection between manumission and the resistance to treason completely explicit. After the notoriously cryptic reference to the "law of Winchester," Tyler demands "no outlawry [*ughtelarie*—another Anglicism] in any process of law from now on; and that no lord have lordship except it be divided among all the people, with the exception of the king's lordship" (*Anonimalle*, 147). This demand presents manumission and the abolition of treason as the same thing. When there is no longer any lordship there will no longer be any intervening authority standing between the king and the commons. There will no longer be any opportunity for the sort of treason that from the rebels' perspective touched off the revolt. That is, there will no longer be any "outlawry" offered in the name of the king's justice.

If anything, some chroniclers and governing authorities found this conception of popular sovereignty more unsettling than the demand for manumission. Walsingham breaks off his narration of the invasion of the tower to expostulate:

> Now who would ever have believed that peasants—not just peasants, but peasants of the most abject sort—would dare, not in group, but individually, enter the king's chamber and that of his mother with their vile sticks, not deterred by any of the knights, reaching out and stroking the beards of the most noble of them with their uncouth and sordid hands, and conferring with them in familiar speech, first of consorting with them in

the future, then of faithfully protecting these same ribalds, then of swearing an oath that in common cause with them they might seek out traitors of the realm—when they themselves could not avoid the stigma of manifest treachery, who of course, raising flags and pennants, had not feared to attack, armed in their manner—indeed, in the manner aforesaid. (*Historia*, 459)[23]

Walsingham's frustration threatens to break loose in every phrase, yet even so, he does not forget to mention that in their outrageous invitation to the knights, these prima facie traitors nevertheless attempted to constitute themselves juridically, by asking the knights to swear an oath. The king's charge to Parliament for the sessions of November and December of 1381, while lacking Walsingham's histrionics, is similarly fixated on the rebel claim to have acted in his name. Though the main order of business was to approve his revocation of the charters of manumission, the charge does not mention these at all, but instead is at pains to disavow the rebel notions of sovereignty:

And the king especially wishes to make good ordinance providing for the return of the king and his realm to peace and quiet after the great turmoil and rumor lately moved in certain parts of the said realm because of the rising and insurrection of certain mean commons and others, and their horrible and contemptuous misdeeds against God, the peace of the land, the king's regality, estate, dignity and crown. Although these same commons coloured their misdeeds in another manner by saying that they wished to have no king except our lord king Richard. (*Rotuli Parliamentorum*, 3:99)[24]

As this charge rejects the rebels' claim of loyalty, the characterization "mean commons"—to be repeated throughout the deliberations—also rejects their claim to be "the true commons."

Perhaps the most thorough disavowal of the rebel watchword can be found in the central trajectory of the chronicle narratives themselves. Where the chroniclers do not ascribe the rebels' actions to sheer irrationality and lawlessness, they present the rebels' immediate objective as a direct audience with the king. The rebels achieve that objective and it proves their undoing. After Tyler's death, it is Richard himself who leads the crowd away. In Froissart's memorable portrayal, he rides forth all alone to meet them at the height of their anger, and calls out, "Sirs, what is distressing you? You shall have no other captain but me: I am your king: hold yourselves in peace" (*Chroniques*, 121).[25] Moreover, most of the chroniclers present Tyler's death as the direct result of his inability to observe the protocols proper to a royal audience, or to maintain a dignity suitable to the power he claimed to be wielding. He rinses his mouth and spits before the king, then gets distracted, either by an insult from a valet (*Anonimalle*, 147–48), or by a knight who fails to alight from his horse before approaching (Walsingham, *Historia*, 464), or by a squire who had insulted him earlier (Froissart, *Chroniques*, 119–20); or he seizes the king's bridle (Knighton, *Chronicle*, 220–21), or refuses to remove his hat (Higden, *Polychronicon*, 9:5; *Eulogium*, 3:353–54). Walsingham portrays him as a usurper, declaring he planned to kill the king and then all learned in the law: "In fact it is reported that on the day before these things happened he said with great pride, placing his hands on his lips, that within four days all the laws of England would emanate from his own mouth and lips" (*Historia*, 464).[26] This last image was a common trope for tyranny—one that, ironically, was to be used against Richard himself in his Articles of Deposition two decades later. For the chroniclers, Tyler's quasi-tragic failure illustrates in a more measured and profound way the irrationality of the Rising's goals. The rebels wanted what they could not have: sovereignty in a form different from those actually existing.

Strohm's point that rebel inversions exceeded the purely carnivalesque is especially relevant here (*Hochon's Arrow*, 45–51). For the forms of sovereignty to which the rebels strove to define a more immediate relation were themselves in the midst of a variety of redefinitions. Throughout the century the monarchy had continued its long consolidation and institutional growth, signaled both by its increasing control over the administration of justice and by the steady expansion of its bureaucracy. Yet this expansion did not come simply at the expense of other forms of lordship. The titled nobility, evolving from a baronage to a peerage, "by the second half of the fourteenth century... had emerged as a distinct and privileged group at the top of English lay society" (Given-Wilson, *English Nobility*, 1). The lesser landowners, that is, the gentry, also experienced an increase in power and influence. Both developments were connected to the emergence of Parliament, an institution conceived in constitutional terms as the extension of the king's council (Lyon, *History,*

409). An individual summons to Parliament provided the surest formal definition of a peer (Given-Wilson, *English Nobility*, 55–57). At the same time, the coalescence of a separate House of Commons around mid-century institutionalized the superiority of a group of lesser nobility and the urban patriciate (Strohm's "rural landowners and urban entrepreneurs"). This group also benefited from the expansion of royal justice and the royal bureacracy, for it staffed such offices as sheriff, the Justice of the Peace, coroner, tax collector, and juror. And it staffed the expanding households of the peers (Harding, *Law Courts*, 86–123; Given-Wilson, *English Nobility*, 73–83). All of these new or newly elaborated structures interlocked with royal sovereignty and involved representing or advising the king or both. Thus, with their accusations of treason and their desire to consult the king, the rebels were not simply casting these new forms of power as illegitimate, they were also declaring their right to participate in the political processes that had produced these forms of power to begin with. And they were making this claim in the same ideological vocabulary as their more powerful counterparts. The charge of bad counsel had long been a standard mode for resisting royal power, extending in England as far back at least as the reign of Henry I (Southern, *Humanism*, 206–33). It was to be the dominant rhetorical ground on which Richard's later disputes with his barons would be fought. The rebels also found a precedent in the so-called Good Parliament of 1376, which invented the procedure of impeachment to try a group of Edward III's advisors, including his mistress Alice Perrers.[27]

A new localism complemented the expanding power of the landowning classes to serve as representatives of the king. As Chris Given-Wilson explains:

> In late medieval England, every great lord had his "country." It was here that his chief castle stood, where the core of his estates was concentrated, and where the leaders of local society looked to him to provide a focus for their service and aspirations. (*English Nobility*, 160)

At the same time these local leaders, the lesser landowners, were also enhancing their own power. As members of Parliament, they represented local needs to the Crown even as they represented the Crown to the locality. The consensus among recent historians is "that the increasing political, judicial and administrative responsibilities thrust upon, or assumed by, these leaders of local society tended to enhance the local particularism of the shire communities during the thirteenth and fourteenth centuries, and thus to promote a sense of regional unity" (Given-Wilson, *English Nobility*, 78; see also Saul, *Knights*, 105–67; Maddicott, "County Community," 27–43). Marauding across the countryside to London, seeking a direct audience with the king, the rebels categorically reject this localism. The *Anonimalle* chronicler dramatizes the rejection of the local in the final exchange between Richard and Wat Tyler, which renders their conflict a struggle between a localist status quo and nationalist vision of change. Richard greets Tyler by asking, "Why won't you return to your own country?" (147).[28]

Tyler responds to this appeal to the local with the national. Whatever its substantive meaning, "no law but the law of Winchester" recalls England's ancient capital, and lays claim to a national history prior to the dynastic authority of the current monarchy.[29] Although the demand to redistribute all lordship but the king's refers only to "toutz gentz," in the context of the succeeding demands, this phrase clearly implies all the people in England. Tyler moves from lay lordship to spiritual lordship, demanding disendowment of the Church and a similar reduction in the number of clerical lords to the effect that "nulle evesque serroit en Engleterre fors une." While there is no reason to assume Tyler is envisioning a Reformation-style national church, it is nevertheless clear that *Engleterre* is the term around which the proposed disendowment is ultimately to be structured. Tyler's final demand is that there be no more bond men or women *(nayf)* in England, thus making *Engleterre* the term ultimately structuring manumission as well (147). Like most other aspects of rebel ideology, this nationalist strain remains skeletal, but it is also unmistakable. We can find strong traces of it elsewhere in the *Anonimalle* account, in the vernacularism of the rebel watchword, in the improvised inquest the rebels stage in Canterbury, and in the initial concessions they win from Richard at Mile End. The oath that they require from the mayor, bailiffs, and commons is to Richard and "les loials comunes Dengleterre" (137). This formulation anticipates the watchword and makes the nationalism implicit in its vernacular cast explicit. The Englishness of the commons is part of their truth, is what enables them to assert they are the "true commons," and gives them the authority to presume that they have a direct share in Richard's sovereignty. And the promise Richard makes to them at Mile End contains a similar formula, giving a royal endorsement to the Rising's judicial pretensions:

> ...the king had the commons assemble in two columns and had it announced to them that he meant to confirm and grant to them their freedom and their will generally, and that they might go throughout the realm of England and take all the traitors and lead them to him alone and he will have them executed as the law demands. (145)[30]

This vision of a national inquest, with the rebels as the sole agents of the king, recalls the end of Langland's myth: the king and commons, with the assistance of kind wit, shape "lawe and leute," law and loyalty, or law and justice understood as loyalty. Both visions posit a sovereignty of the commons with a single institutional articulation driven by sheer fidelity to its simple truth. There is a prophetic and exegetical edge to the notion of the true commons, as if in their rejection of royal intermediaries and their crusade against treason, the rebels were stripping away so many dead letters. In laying claim to Langland's protagonist, they were laying claim both to his prophetic authority, and his poem's radical reimagining of political community. Like Langland they were refashioning notions of community out of traditional ideals. Like Langland, their subversion came as much from the act of claiming this refashioned authority as from the content of the refashioning. Langland's poetic persona was a nearly anonymous visionary speaking from the very edge of his newly imagined national community, drawing its authority solely out of its own peripheral enunciations. The rebels were the "mean commons," now suddenly revealing themselves as the true commons, in an act as much symbolic and prophetic as it was insurrectionary, come to claim the sovereignty certain traditions in medieval political thought had always conceded to them all along. While it is true there is little in *Piers Plowman* that can be construed as advocating armed insurrection, it is also true there is much that advocates radical reform, and advocates it urgently. Moreover, it would not be strictly accurate to view the resort to violence as the root of the rebels' self-definition, in the way that it has been for certain modern revolutionary movements. On the contrary, as we have just seen, the rebels understood their violence as an antidote to treason, an instrument for the restoration of proper legal order.

The points of contact between Langland's notion of political and community and that of the rebels are multiple and profound. Both involve a national scope and center on the figure of the king. In both the king draws his power from might of the commons; he is part agent, part embodiment, and part protector of their will; both his counsel and his law come from community's kind wit, the innate reason that defines its commonality. And in both the commons is defined in the broadest terms with the most minimal of requirements; it is associated both with labor and with simple membership in the nation. In the face of these substantial congruences, there seems little point in describing the rebel appeal to Langland's poem as a misreading. Can we really say, for example, that the rebel ideals have less in common with Langland's prophetic urgency than the version of Langland's protagonist Chaucer produces in *The General Prologue?* Chaucer's plowman, who, living "in pees and parfit charitee," working "withouten hire," and contentedly paying his tithes, displays no urgency at all (I.529–41). This portrait is clearly a domestication; yet most scholars would agree that to stigmatize it as a misreading would do little critical work of any value. It is hard to see that the stigmatization of the rebel reading accomplishes any more.

That brings us to the question I deferred: what of Langland's own reading of this issue. For the specific question of the passage from the Prologue we can turn to Susan Crane, who has demonstrated that "it does not necessarily follow" that its C version "censures the rebels of 1381" ("Writing Lesson," 212–13). On the contrary, considered solely in themselves, the changes just as easily support a reading of profound disillusionment with medieval political theory itself. To replace "Might of þe communes made hym to regne" with "Myght of tho men [i.e., the knighthood of the preceding line] made hym to regne," and to replace the image of the commons shaping law with the lines, "And for most profit to þe peple a plogh gonne þei make, / With lele labour to lyve while lyf on londe lasteth" could constitute a bitter assertion that royal sovereignty rests on armed coercion alone, to which the commons have no choice to submit.[31] To speak more generally, the C-text as a whole may constitute a repudiation of the Rising or it may not, but in order for it to serve as evidence of an antithesis between the rebels and the B-text we must posit the intellectual trajectory to Langland's intellectual career assumed by Donaldson. While such a trajectory is certainly possible, it is by no means inevitable, and it is not necessarily even the most plausible.

There are at least two other trajectories one could easily imagine. Both are equally consistent with single authorship. The first is essentially the one offered by Skeat. It would hold that the Langland of the B-text was fully committed to social change, and that his rebel readers were responding to an urgency in his poem that he fully intended. Then in the aftermath of the Rising, he became more conservative, as often happens to aging radicals. Under this possibility, his revisions to the C-text would represent a repudiation of the rebellion, but they would also represent a disavowal of his own former radicalism. We could no longer dismiss the radicalism of the B-text as a mirage produced by a rebel misreading. Instead, we would be obligated to treat it as a serious and distinct stage of Langland's career, analogous to the early Wordsworth's enthusiasm for the French Revolution, or the Irish nationalism of the early Yeats. The second possibility would hold that while Langland's political views did indeed remain the same throughout his career, they are most clearly expressed not in the C-text but the B-text, and that those aspects of the C revisions that seem to retreat from the radicalism of the B-text represent the fear of the external sanction rather than some internal conviction. This trajectory would assume a deeply disillusioned Langland similar to the one suggested by Susan Crane, hiding his sympathies for those who put themselves to the plough in ironic acknowledgments of the status quo. One can find an analogy in subsequent literary history for this possibility as well: the Milton of *Paradise Lost,* who acknowledges the defeat of his revolutionary ideals not by repudiating them but by repudiating the enduring immorality of the society they failed to transform.

Either of these models is as consistent with the textual evidence as the misreading hypothesis. But they both also allow the B-text a much fuller range of ideological specificity. In particular, either of them would enable us to take seriously the poem's radical strain and the philosophic depth it provided to the most important popular social movement of its time. Whether one ultimately decided Langland's radical nationalism was a stage in his career from which he later retreated, or a life-long commitment driven underground in the aftermath of the Rising, the ideological position itself would remain as the complex, nuanced, fully worked-out product of one of the period's most prominent thinkers. Recognizing it broadens our picture of the economy of political discourses in the period and enables us to view the rebels of 1381 more clearly as full participants in that economy. It gives us a fuller sense of the past, which means a fuller sense of the present. The radical promise that Langland and his rebel readers found in nationalist ideals constitutes a half-hidden provocation for the postcolonial critique of modern nationalism, the more so for being unfulfilled. Such provocations are among the most important of medieval culture's many legacies to modernity, particularly to modernity in its radical strain, for they remind modern radicalism of its own incompletion. To return once again to Benjamin, one of modernity's own most urgent prophets: "Like every generation that preceded us, we have been endowed with a *weak* Messianic power, a power to which the past has a claim. That claim cannot be settled cheaply" ("Theses," 254).

NOTES

This essay has greatly benefitted by the comments and suggestions of Christopher Baswell, Christine Chism, Rita Copeland, Susan Crane, John Ganim, Kathryn Lavezzo, James Simpson, Fiona Somerset, Paul Strohm, and Nicholas Watson.

1. In his eagerness to leave the religious past behind, Anderson ignores a fundamental incongruity between his project and Benjamin's. Benjamin is attempting to recuperate the power of religion for historical materialism, not escape it. In his fanciful opening he declares, "The puppet called 'historical materialism' is to win all the time. It can easily be a match for anyone if it enlists the services of theology, which today, as we know, is wizened and has to keep out of sight" ("Theses," 253).

2. Biddick, "Coming Out," offers a similar reading of Anderson and sees the same notion of temporality in the work of Edward Said.

3. Nicholas Watson reminds me that *Piers Plowman* is the first such poem with a known author. The very first English poem to attain a national audience is probably the *South English Legendary*.

4. For important recent exceptions, see Hudson, "*Piers Plowman*," Aers, "*Vox populi*," 432–39; and especially Galloway, "Making." The fullest and most authoritative exploration of the problem is Justice, *Writing*, 102–39, 231–51. Justice's conclusions support the standard view, though he is careful to cast the rebels' use of the poem as revision and critique, rather than simple misreading. I find this conclusion curious for it partially reinstates the barrier between the rebels and vernacular literacy that Justice is at great pains to remove everywhere else in this exemplary study. Justice argues that rebel approach to language is "documentary," instrumental, and "empirical," while Langland's interests are literary, penitential, and abstract (102–39). Langland was useful to the rebels because he showed them "how the concrete and empirical language of complaint might be rendered systematic and conceptual" (135–36). Justice treats the rebels as literate but not literary; apparently the ability to think systematically was something they otherwise lacked, including even John Ball, in spite of his clerical training. Their commitment to the empirical drives their divergence from Langland no less than their engagement with him. He offers them "resources of critique" that they use "first to criticize the poem" (127). He develops a digressive poetic

language that is "self-cancelling," advocating no other action than "penitential withdrawal," but the rebels take up "Langland's deliberately evasive locutions" and make them "definite and precise" (113–14, 120–22, 138). Justice points in particular to Carter's injunction that "peres þe plowman my broþur. duelle at home and dyȝt us corne," as a rejection both of the penitential and the poem's larger pilgrimmage toward truth: "The 'truth' Langland's pilgrims seek is something the rebels need not leave home to get, because it is something they already have" (122–24).

In point of fact, however, leaving home is precisely what the rebels have decided they need to do and Carter's main purpose is to spur them on. Moreover, in his eagerness to support this distinction between the documentary and the literary, Justice fails to note that John Ball's letter uses the figure of Piers in precisely the opposite way as Carter's: "biddeþ Peres plouȝman. go to his werk." Ball makes the rebellion synonymous with Piers's prophetic, penitential quest. If anything Justice's conviction that the rebel texts are "definite and precise" interprets their occasion rather than their rhetorical structures and assumes the very distinction between poetry and rebellion it purports to demonstrate. There is very little about these texts that is definite and precise, if they are treated purely as utterances. They are, as Walsingham observes, "full of enigmas" *(aenigmatibus plenam)*, and there is no reason not to give this observation the exegetical resonance that its use of the term *aenigma* seems to suggest. As I note below, like *Piers Plowman,* these texts are allegorical and prophetic. They are even penitential. Ball promises: "þe kynges sone of heuene schal paye for al." This formula means not only that the rebels are Christ's scourge, as Justice points out, but also surely that, because they are, Christ will forgive their sinful recourse to violence. We impute to these texts their instrumental, performative function because the chroniclers tell us what they were used for. I doubt that function is deducible from the language of the texts themselves. Indeed, their language is so lacking in apparent instrumentality, is so little tied to any particular tactic, that it is of no use whatsoever in settling the dispute among three chroniclers (Knighton, Walsingham, and the *Anonimalle* chronicler) concerning the exact moment of their production. In my view, it is the tension between their enigmatic, prophetic mode of address and their manifestly subversive function that constitutes their greatest challenge to modern historiography. For this tension reproduces within the rebel ideology itself the tension between prophesy and political subversion offered by the problem of the relation between the rebels and Langland's poem.

5. In his pivotal study, *England the Nation,* Thorlac Turville-Petre demonstrates beyond any doubt that a wide panoply of nationalist discourses were already available to English writers by the end of the thirteenth century. Noting that "Those who write on nationalism commonly argue that it is a modern phenomenon, that no such concept was possible in the Middle Ages, or that even if national feeling did exist, there were fundamental differences between medieval and modern perceptions of the nation," Turville-Petre contends "that it is the similarities between medieval and modern expressions of national identity that are fundamental, and the differences that are peripheral" (v). Nevertheless, accepting from Michael Ignatieff the distinction between "civic" and "ethnic" nationalism, he later concedes medieval nationalism was exclusively ethnic (that is, understood as "acquired by birth alone") (16–17). By contrast, the nationalism I identify in Lang-

land and the 1381 rebels seems predominantly civic, that is, based on a shared "'political creed.'" (Cf. Ignatieff, *Blood*, 3–4.)

6. As I mentioned in note 1, Benjamin is an important exception.

7. Cf. Clopper, "*Songes*," 167: "I do not think it can be argued that Piers, or, ultimately, Langland is a political 'conservative' in any simple sense; that is, someone who wishes to revert to a feudal system in the face of the challenges of the post-plague era."

8. See especially Hudson, *Premature Reformation*; Clopper, "*Songes*"; Kerby-Fulton, *Apocalypticism*; Justice, *Writing*; Scase, "*Piers Plowman*"; and some recent work by David Aers: *Community, Gender*, 20–72; and Aers and Lynn Staley, *Powers*, 43–76.

9. This trend began with Middleton, "'Kynde Name,'" and has taken definitive shape with the essays in Justice and Kerby-Fulton, *Written Work*. See also Justice and Kerby-Fulton, "Langlandian Reading Circles."

10. Curiously, most attempts to locate Langland in London do not suggest he had any interest in urban politics. For an important exception, see Simpson, "'After Craftes Conseil.'"

11. As Turville-Petre notes, in contrast to the border with Scotland, which, for at least one medieval mapmaker, was marked off by Hadrian's Wall, there was no clear marker for the English border with Wales (*England*, 2).

12. The line "By a wilde wildernesse and by a wodes side" is attested in thirteen witnesses. However Kane and Donaldson reconstruct the line as "And as I wente by a wode, walkyng myn one," apparently on semantic grounds.

13. See also Aers, *Chaucer, Langland*, 1–37, and *Community Gender*, 20–72; and Cole, "Trifunctionality." I should note that Clopper's own reading of this passage ("*Songes*," 153–55) is a good deal more cautious than mine. He reads Kind Wit and Clergy as synonymous, and takes *might of the commons* to refer back to the Knighthood, instead of the non-noble populace, as I do.

14. Ullmann, *Political Thought*, rather notoriously restricted this idea to the Germanic legacy, arguing somewhat inconsistently that it was driven underground by Christianity until allowed to re-emerge with Aquinas's rediscovery of Aristotle. For a brief discussion of the Ciceronian antecedents and additional bibliography, see Black, *Political Thought*, 28–29, 140–41, 204–05.

15. "Rex est a populi voluntate, sed, cum est rex, ut dominetur est naturale." John of Paris, *De potestate regia et papali*, xix. Cited and translated by Dunbabin, "Government," 515.

16. Genet argues that the *Fürstenspiegel* were particularly associated with Franciscans ("Ecclesiastics," 26). If so, this passage might be another example of Langland's particular fascination with the friars.

17. In an excellent paper entitled "Latinate Cacophony and the Vernacular Voice in *Piers Plowman*," Fiona Somerset takes the snippet offered by the commons to be "a vernacular voice in Latin," and notes that its most obvious significance is that it shows the commons speaking for themselves, "commenting on their own status relative to the king." My thanks to Professor Somerset for sharing a copy of this paper with me.

18. One of these is Walsingham. However, Galloway, "Making," convincingly argues that Walsingham's bias has been overstated.

19. See also Aers, "*Vox populi*," 432–37.

20. "...the said commons had among them a watchword in English, 'With whom do you hold?' and the answer was, 'With King Richard and with the true commons': and those who did not know how to respond, or who did not want to, were beheaded and put to death."

21. "...les communes leverount encontre lui et viendrent devaunt luy et susmistrent qil fuist traitour al roy et al roialme et qe malvyhsment et maliciousement les vodroit avoir defaitz par abbetement del faux enquest pris devaunt lui; pur quel enchesoun ils lui fesoient iurere sur le liver qe iames apres ne deveroit en tiels sessions sere, nestre iustice des enquerres; et lui fesoient notifier a eux toutz les nouns des iurrours, les quels toutz qils purroient prendre, decollerent et mistrent a la mort et lour measones treierent a la terre."

22. "Placuitque statim sermo vulgaribus Londoniarum, et ipsi in primis foedum reputantes, si quicquam Duci ante eos injuriae aut damni aliquid irrogaret, illico velut amentes cucurrerunt, et, ignibus in gyro conjectis, destructioni loci vacabant."

23. "Nam quis unquam credidisset, non solum rusticos, sed rusticorum abjectissimos, non plures, se singulos, audere thalamum Regis, vel matris eius, cum baculis subintrare vilissimis, et unumquemque de militibus deterrere minis, et quorundam nobilissimorum militum barbas suis incultissimis et sordidissimis manibus contrectare, demulcere; et verba modo familiaria serere de socialitate cum eisdem habenda de caetero, modo de fide servanda ipsis ribaldis, modo de juramento praestando, ut communiter cum eis regni quaererent proditores, cum ipsi manifeste proditionis notam devitare non possent, quippe qui vexilla et pennicellos erigentes, tali modo cum armata manu pro modulo suo, scilicet modo praetacto, incedere non timebant?" "Raising flags and pennants" refers to the Statute of Treason of 1352; it is one of the specific grounds named by that statute.

24. "Primerement, notre Sire le Roi dessuis dit desirant.... meement de faire & purvoier ore de bone Ordinance, pur mettre le Roi & son Roialme en paix & quiete sur le grant truboill & rumour q'estoient nadgaires moevez en certeins parties del dit Roialme, parmy la levee & insurrection de certeins menues Communes & autres, & sur lour horrible & dispitouse Maufait encontre Dieux, la Paix de la Terre, le Regalie, l'Estat, Dignitee, & la Coroune notre Seigneur le Roi; combien que mesme le Communes colurerent lours ditz Malfaitz en autre manere, en disantz, q'ils veulloient avoir nul Roi sinoun notre Seigneur le Roi Richard." (Trans. Dobson, *Peasants' Revolt*, 327).

25. "...il se parti de ses gens tous seuls, et dist: 'Demorés chi. Nuls ne me sieue.' lors vint il au devant de ces folles gens, qui s'ordonnoient pour vengier leur cappitainne, et leur dist: 'Signeur, que vous fault? Vous navés autre cappitainne que moi: je sui vostres rois; tenés vous en pais.'"

26. "Fertur revera cum superbia magna dixisse, pridie quam ista fierent, apposita manu suis labiis, quod ante quatriduum omnes leges Angliae de ore suo et labiis emanarent."

27. Keen remarks that with their "demand for heads of named traitors," the rebels' "attitude was not very different from that of the commons in the Good Parliament, who raised like them the cry of 'traitors about the king'" (*England*, 272).

28. "Pur qay ne voilliez aler en vostre pais?"

29. Harding ("Revolt") suggests Tyler refers to Edward I's Statute of Winchester, promulgated in 1285, a claim Justice makes one of the centerpieces of his view that rebel

ideology was localist and rural (*Writing*, 170–72). Harding argues that this Statute, which concerned local obligations to bear arms, came "to represent an ideal of communal self-policing" ("Revolt," 166) and that "Wat Tyler's demands for a return" to it "stand in a long tradition of debate between the king and the people of England on the proper administration of Justice" (174). Harding makes a case that is both ingenious and learned, and the specificity of legal learning it imputes to the rebels is extremely attractive. Nevertheless, it also leaves some crucial questions unanswered. First, in the evidence Harding cites the Statute of Winchester is always referred to specifically as a statute, not a law, and it is typically referred to not on its own, but together with the related Statutes of Northampton and Winchester (167). Even as shorthand for a broader ideal of communal self-policing, it seems a bit narrow to be the sole law of the land, or to fit Tyler's nearly apocalyptic ambitions. Second, the Statute ties its obligations specifically to the ownership of property. Even if Harding is right about the statute becoming shorthand for a communal ideal, he never explains how that ideal might have become attractive to those who did not own land. Finally, as Harding himself notes, the Statute assumes an opposition between the king on the one hand and an undifferentiated populace on the other. He never explains how Tyler might have specifically understood it as an ideal that put king and true commons on one side and all the landowners on the other.

30. "... le roy fist arrayer les comunes en deux raunges et fist crier devaunt eux qui vodroit confermer et graunter a eux destre free et touts lour vounes generalment et qils purroient aler par tute le roialme Dengleterre et prendre toutz les traitours et les amener a luy salvement et il ferroit execucione de eux com la ley demande."

31. As Crane puts it: "The same revisions that, in ideological terms, restrict the commons also betray, in the very act of revision, that ideal systems are constructed rather than fixed truths. While the direction of the revisions validates suppression, the text's mobility simultaneously asserts the temporal contingency of the revised model under which the plowman is as silent and without agency as the plow" ("Writing Lesson," 212).

REFERENCES

Aers, David. *Chaucer, Langland and the Creative Imagination*. London: Routledge, 1980.

———. *Community, Gender, and Individual Identity: English Writing 1360–1430*. London and New York: Routledge, 1988.

———. "*Vox populi* and the Literature of 1381." In *Cambridge History*, ed. Wallace, 432–53.

Aers, David, and Lynn Staley. *The Powers of the Holy: Religion, Politics, and Gender in Late Medieval English Culture*. University Park: Pennsylvania State University Press, 1996.

Anderson, Benedict. *Imagined Communities: Reflections on the Origin and Spread of Nationalism*. Rev. ed. London and New York: Verso, 1991.

The Anonimalle Chronicle, 1333–1381. Ed. V. H. Galbraith. Manchester: Manchester University Press; New York: Barnes & Noble, 1970.

Auerbach, Erich. *Mimesis: The Representation of Reality in Western Literature*. Trans. Willard R. Trask. Princeton: Princeton University Press, 1968.

Barron, Caroline. "William Langland: A London Poet." In *Chaucer's England*, ed. Hanawalt, 91–109.

Benjamin, Walter. "Theses on the Philosophy of History." In *Illuminations*, ed. with an
    introduction by Hannah Arendt, trans. Harry Zohn, 253–64. New York: Schocken
    Books, 1969.
Bhabha, Homi K. *The Location of Culture.* London and New York: Routledge, 1994.
Biddick, Kathleen. "Coming Out of Exile: Dante on the Orient Express." In *The Postcolonial
    Middle Ages*, ed. Jeffrey Jerome Cohen, 35–52. New York: St. Martin's Press, 2000.
Black, Antony. *Political Thought in Europe 1250–1450.* Cambridge: Cambridge University
    Press, 1992.
Burns, J. H., ed. *The Cambridge History of Medieval Political Thought, c. 350–c. 1450.* Cam-
    bridge: Cambridge University Press, 1988.
Chaucer, Geoffrey. *The Riverside Chaucer.* 3rd ed. Ed. Larry D. Benson et al. Boston:
    Houghton Mifflin, 1987.
Clopper, Lawrence M. *"Songes of Rechelesnesse": Langland and the Franciscans.* Ann Arbor:
    University of Michigan Press, 1997.
Cole, Andrew W. "Trifunctionality and the Tree of Charity: Literary and Social Practice in
    Piers Plowman." English Literary History 62 (1995): 1–27.
Coulton, G. G. *The Medieval Scene: An Informal Introduction to the Middle Ages.* Cambridge:
    Cambridge University Press, 1930.
Crane, Susan. "The Writing Lesson of 1381." In *Chaucer's England,* ed. Hanawalt, 201–21.
Crowley, Robert, ed. *The Vision of Pierce Plowman.* London, 1550.
Dante Alighieri. *Monarchy and Three Political Letters.* Trans. Donald Nicholl and Colin Hardie.
    New introduction by Walter F. Berens. New York and London: Garland Press, 1972.
    Orig. pub. London: Weidenfeld and Nicolson, 1954.
Dobson, R. B., ed. *The Peasants' Revolt of 1381.* 2nd ed. Houndmills, Basingstoke, and Lon-
    don: Macmillan, 1983.
Donaldson, E. Talbot. *"Piers Plowman": The C-Text and Its Poet.* New Haven: Yale University
    Press, 1949.
Dunbabin, Jean. "Government." In *Cambridge History of Medieval Political Thought,* ed.
    Burns, 477–519.
Eulogium historiarum sive temporis. Ed. Frank Scott Haydon. 3 vols. Rolls Series 9. London:
    Her Majesty's Stationery Office, 1863.
Foucault, Michel. *The History of Sexuality.* Vol. 1. *An Introduction.* Trans. Robert Hurley.
    New York: Vintage, 1980.
Froissart, Jean. *Chroniques de Jean Froissart.* Vol. 10 (1380–2). Ed. Gaston Raynaud. Paris:
    Société de l'histoire de France, 1897.
Fryde, E. B. *Peasants and Landlords in Later Medieval England.* Gloucestershire: Sutton,
    1996.
Galloway, Andrew. "Making History Legal: *Piers Plowman* and the Rebels of Fourteenth-
    Century England." In *William Langland's "Piers Plowman": A Book of Essays,* ed. Kath-
    leen M. Hewitt-Smith, 7–39. New York and London: Routledge, 2001.
Genet, Jean-Phillippe. "Ecclesiastics and Political Theory in Late Medieval England: The
    End of a Monopoly." In *The Church, Politics, and Patronage in the Fifteenth Century,* ed.
    Barrie Dobson, 23–44. Gloucester: Sutton; New York: St. Martin's Press, 1989.
Gewirth, Alan. *Marsilius of Padua—the Defender of the Peace.* London: Macmillan, 1961.

Given-Wilson, Chris. *The English Nobility in the Late Middle Ages.* London and New York: Routledge, 1996.

Hanawalt, Barbara, ed. *Chaucer's England: Literature in Historical Context.* Minneapolis: University of Minnesota Press, 1992.

Harding, Alan. *The Law Courts of Medieval England.* London: Allen and Unwin; New York: Barnes and Noble, 1973.

———. "The Revolt Against the Justices." In *The English Rising,* ed. Hilton and Aston, 165–93.

Higden, Ranulph. *Polychronicon, together with the English Translations of John Trevisa and of an Unknown Writer of the Fifteenth Century.* Ed. Churchill Babington and Joseph Lumby. 9 vols. Rolls Series 41. London: Her Majesty's Stationery Office, 1865–86.

Hilton, Rodney. *The Decline of Serfdom in Medieval England.* London, Melbourne: Macmillan; New York, St. Martin's Press, 1969.

———. *Bond Men Made Free: Medieval Peasant Movements and the English Rising of 1381.* London and New York: Methuen, 1973.

———. *Class Conflict and the Crisis of Feudalism.* Rev. ed. London and New York: Verso, 1990.

Hilton, Rodney, and T. H. Aston, eds. *The English Rising of 1381.* Cambridge: Cambridge University Press, 1984.

Homans, George Caspar. *English Villagers of the Thirteenth Century.* Cambridge: Harvard University Press, 1941.

Hudson, Anne. *The Premature Reformation: Wycliffite Texts and Lollard History.* Oxford: Clarendon, 1988.

———. "*Piers Plowman* and the Peasants' Revolt: A Problem Revisited." *Yearbook of Langland Studies* 8 (1995): 85–106.

Ignatieff, Michael. *Blood and Belonging: Journeys into the New Nationalism.* New York: Farrar, 1994.

Justice, Steven. *Writing and Rebellion: England in 1381.* Berkeley, Los Angeles, and London: University of California Press, 1994.

Justice, Steven, and Kathryn Kerby-Fulton. "Langlandian Reading Circles and the Civil Service in London and Dublin, 1380–1427." *New Medieval Literatures* 1 (1997): 59–83.

———, eds. *Written Work: Langland, Labor, and Authorship.* Philadelphia: University of Pennsylvania Press, 1997.

Keen, M. H. *England in the Later Middle Ages.* London and New York: Routledge, 1986.

Kerby-Fulton, Kathryn. "*Piers Plowman.*" In *Cambridge History,* ed. Wallace, 513–38.

———. *Reformist Apocalypticism and "Piers Plowman."* Cambridge and New York: Cambridge University Press, 1990.

Knighton, Henry. *Knighton's Chronicle 1337–96.* Ed. and trans. G. H. Martin. Oxford: Clarendon Press, 1995.

Langland, William. *Piers Plowman: The B Version.* Ed. George Kane and E. Talbot Donaldson. Berkeley: Athlone / University of California Press, 1975.

———. *Piers Plowman: The C Version.* Ed. George Russell and George Kane. Berkeley: Athlone / University of California Press, 1997.

Lewis, C.S. *The Allegory of Love: A Study in Medieval Tradition.* London: Oxford University Press, 1936.

Lyon, Bryce. *A Constitutional and Legal History of Medieval England.* New York, Evanston, and London: Harper, 1960.

Maddicott, J. R. "The County Community and the Making of Public Opinion in Fourteenth-Century England." *Transactions of the Royal Historical Society,* 5th ser., 28 (1978): 27–43.

Manly, J. M. "*Piers Plowman* and Its Sequence." In *The Cambridge History of English Literature.* Vol 2, *The End of the Middle Ages,* ed. A. W. Ward and A. R. Waller, 1–42. Cambridge: Cambridge University Press, 1908.

———. "The Authorship of *Piers Plowman.*" *Modern Philology* 7 (1909): 83–114.

Middleton, Anne. "Narration and the Invention of Experience: Episodic Form in *Piers Plowman.*" In *The Wisdom of Poetry: Essays in Early English Literature in Honor of Morton W. Bloomfield,* ed. Larry D. Benson and Siegfried Wenzel, 91–122. Kalamazoo: Medieval Institute Publications, 1982.

———. "Introduction: The Critical Heritage." In *A Companion to "Piers Plowman,"* ed. John A. Alford, 1–25. Berkeley, Los Angeles, and London: University of California Press, 1988.

———. "William Langland's 'Kynde Name': Authorial Signature and Social Identity in Late Fourteenth-Century England." In *Literary Practice and Social Change in Britain, 1380–1530,* ed. Lee Patterson, 15–82. Berkeley, Los Angeles, Oxford: University of California Press, 1990.

Nairn, Tom. *The Break-up of Britain.* London: New Left Books, 1977.

Pearsall, Derek. "Langland's London." In *Written Work,* ed. Justice and Kerby-Fulton, 185–207.

Robertson, D. W., Jr., and Bernard F. Huppé. *"Piers Plowman" and Scriptural Tradition.* Princeton: Princeton University Press, 1951.

Rotuli Parliamentorum; ut et Petitiones et Placita in Parliamento. Ed. J. Strachey. 7 vols. London: House of Lords, 1767–83.

Saul, Nigel. *Knights and Esquires: The Gloucestershire Gentry in the Fourteenth Century.* Oxford: Clarendon, 1981.

Scase, Wendy. *"Piers Plowman" and the New Anticlericalism.* London and New York: Cambridge University Press, 1989.

Simpson, James. *"Piers Plowman": An Introduction to the B-Text.* London and New York: Longman, 1990.

———. "'After Craftes Conseil clotheth yow and fede': Langland and London City Politics." In *England in the Fourteenth Century: Proceedings of the 1991 Harlaxton Symposium,* ed. Nicholas Rogers, 109–27. Stamford: Paul Watkins, 1993.

Skeat, W. W., ed., *The Vision of William Concerning "Piers Plowman" Dowel, Dobet, Dobest. . . . The Whitaker Text; or Text C.* EETS 54. London: Trübner, 1873.

Smith, Brian S. *A History of Malvern.* Worcester: Leicester University Press, 1964.

Southern, R. W. *Medieval Humanism.* Oxford: Blackwell, 1970.

Spivak, Gayatri Chakravorty. *A Critique of Postcolonial Reason: Toward a History of the Vanishing Present.* Cambridge and London: Harvard University Press, 1999.

Strohm, Paul. *Hochon's Arrow: The Social Imagination of Fourteenth-Century Texts.* With an appendix by A. J. Prescott. Princeton: Princeton University Press, 1992.

Trevelyan, George Macaulay. *England in the Age of Wycliffe*. 3rd ed. London and New York: Longmans, 1900. Reprint, New York: AMS, 1975.

Turville-Petre, Thorlac. *England the Nation: Language, Literature, and National Identity, 1290–1340*. Oxford: Clarendon, 1996.

Ullman, Walter. *Medieval Political Thought*. Harmondsworth: Penguin, 1975.

Wallace, David, ed. *The Cambridge History of Medieval English Literature*. Cambridge: Cambridge University Press, 1999.

Walsingham, Thomas. *Historia Anglicana*. Ed. Henry Thomas Riley. London: Her Majesty's Stationery Office, 1863–64.

Watson, Nicholas. "Visions of Inclusion: Universal Salvation and Vernacular Theology in Pre-Reformation England." *Journal of Medieval and Early Modern Studies* 27 (1997): 145–87.

Watt, J. A. "Spiritual and Temporal Powers." In *Cambridge History of Medieval Political Thought*, ed. Burns, 367–423.

Wright, Thomas, ed., *The Vision and Creed of Piers Ploughman*. 2nd ed. London, 1856.

Piers Plowman and the
National Noetic of Edward III

D. Vance Smith

> *'tis your thoughts that now must deck our*
> *kings . . .*
>
> —*Henry V*

> gnome *(judgment), again, certainly implies*
> *the ponderation or consideration* (nomesis)
> *of generation, for to ponder is the same as to*
> *consider; or, if you would rather,* noesis *is*
> neouesis *(the desire of the new); the word*
> neos *implies that the world is always in*
> *process of creation.*
>
> —Plato, *Cratylus*

I begin this essay by admitting my wariness about the ethics of thinking nationally, thinking of the nation as the ground for thinking, the mnemonic place filled with the disciplinary imagery of its sovereign community. I'm skeptical because of what must be obliviated in memorializing the nation—for that is what we do when we think of a nation, of the work of its dead that goes on in us, we who must continue to reanimate them[1]—not just the suppression of difference but the suppression of alternatives to the national noetic, the set of changing narratives and images that represent the nation as an always-already emerging, developing place while ensuring that it remains, in fact, in the condition most retrograde to our desire.[2] The idea of the nation is virtually a synonym for modernity, for the emergence of capital, for the Enlightenment, for the recovery of learning. The emergence of a nation is the obliviation of a heterogeneous past that has become recalcitrant, epiphenomenal, and irregular.[3] As Ernst Renan said, "forgetting is a crucial factor in the creation of a nation" ("What Is a Nation?" 11).[4] This forgetting is not just the obliteration of the events that lead up to the founding of a nation, but a shadow that falls over its history precisely when the nation seems most contingent, most in doubt, most determined to define its symbolic clarity, its national and notional unrepeatability. As I write this, it has become more evident than ever that we live in a community of nations for whom the state of emergency is not only not exceptional but the condition of law itself, a point Walter Benjamin made almost sixty years ago: "the 'state of emergency' in which we live is not the exception but the rule" ("Theses," 257).

Six hundred years before Benjamin wrote that, the confusion and expense of the Hundred Years War was the focus of an English national emergency, one that—because it involved the very logic of emergence, of the way in which representation works—appears in inchoate, lateral, and dispersed forms. Forms of social status, the ethical status of money, the admissibility of usury, are all part of a larger subterranean discourse that concerns, without quite calling it such, the formal structures of a political economy. But in the absence of what we would recognize as a discourse of political economy, the most suitable narrative form for such a subtle, complex, and oblique complex of practices is the meditative, agglutinative poem like *Winner and Waster* and, especially, *Piers Plowman*. The economic practices that *Piers Plowman* in particular describes, whether it accepts, condemns, or ambiguously appropriates them, are represented in terms that impinge on the national economy. The microcosmic practices of "regraterye," for instance, as Pearsall argues, are not criminalized in city and guild ordinances,[5] yet they are a part of a very evident concern on the part of Edward III with the fate of the national economy, and of a series of initiatives that he took in an attempt to manage the political economy of the nation.

Every condemnation of usury, brokering, and tortious exchange promulgated by London officials during Edward's reign was the result of a directive issued by him under the privy seal, that is, by his own authority.

In many ways, indeed, the economic imaginary of *Piers Plowman* is inseparable from the deep interest Edward took in managing the political economy of England. We will need not only to examine more closely Langland's own appropriations of money as a metaphor, but the intrinsically metaphorical properties of money itself, as they affect the economics of the national noetic. The question of who possesses money is important, but so is the question of how money works, or how it was imagined to work in the Middle Ages, for the poem's understanding of merchants is derived in some important ways from the medieval phenomenology of money.[6] In attempting to reconcile earthly and heavenly economies, and in attempting to imagine productive, positive roles for both money and merchants, the poem opts for neither of the solutions available to medieval writers on merchants: to condemn them or to integrate them in a coherent social scheme. They are placed in the margin of the pardon that Truth sends, neither wholly part of the body of the Pardon nor wholly separated from it. The writing of the poem itself is disturbed by some of the problems that characterize money: its instability, its tendency to be mistaken for the value it signifies, its inherently metaphorical nature—problems, we could say, that plague every form of communal imagination, if not as glaringly as in the metaphysics of coinage.[7]

Understanding the difference between this symbolic, communal capital and the narrower form of economic capital involves separating the differences between the kinds of value that a community consciously defines before the rest of the world, offering it in exchange for other things, for the conversation of communities, and the kinds of value that hide themselves as natural, that masquerade as inextricable beings from the world itself, the value that cannot simply be offered to others.[8] I want to examine this complex proposition as literally and as materially as possible, by looking at a group that is more than usually defined by the conveyance of a sign and is imagined in ways we cannot fully account for. It is a group whose very communality is defined by the translation of value between communities, but whose own intrinsic, communal value helped to define, or was pressed into service to shore up, the very idea of English *communitas* under Edward III—the merchants. Their *communitas* is made up of a substance that elicits, in its own right, extraordinary imaginary identifications, yet that is also the object of communal and international deliberation: money, both the repository of communal value and its disappearance, the substance that threatens to displace the very imaginary identifications that give rise to it in the first place. Money is a communal idea, but even more precisely, it represents the public face of a communal idea, the identity, the witness to an *ousia aphanës*, the invisible substance, that a community uses to present itself to the world and to encourage those who use the coin to accept that communal idea.[9] By placing merchants in the margin of a document describing the structure of English society, Langland traces and accommodates the crucially unstable mercantile subject in an attempt to pursue Edward's national *noesis* without falling prey to a national symbolics based on the atavistic model of the three estates. Like Edward, Langland is acutely responsive to the modes of thinking that money not only demands but creates—a phenomenology of exchange, a *noesis* of *numisma*. The poem's several references to itself as an incipient economy encourage us to think of exchange as more than a superfluous activity, more than the useless work of a "spille-time" whose enjoyment lies in mere spending, to paraphrase just one critique (Reason's). It is precisely the failure of traditional responses to superfluity to think economically, to imagine the use of surplus only as charitable giving or as unproductive expenditure, that encourages *Piers Plowman* to imagine its own activity, an activity that it candidly admits might participate in various forms of superfluity, in terms of the burgeoning economic practice of merchants. It might be more accurate to say that in comparison with other vernacular writing, Langland writes an account of mercantile activity that acknowledges its intractability without condemning it or rendering it ironic, not so much an account of the inevitability of exchange in human interaction, an account that would make it equivalent to the social bonds of "treuthe" in the feudal imaginary, but a *withdrawal* from explicit criticism of it, as much of a retraction of antimercantile tropes as his revisions in the C-text in the face of incipient anti-Lollard prosecution.[10]

In one of Ezra Pound's long, brilliant, and perverse tirades against usury in the Cantos, he argues that banking works by exploiting a latent tension in usury, a tension that had not yet been exploited by the nineteenth century:

> It "hath benefit of interest on all
> The moneys which it, the bank, creates out of nothing.
> Semi-private inducement. . . .

> . . . 'Very few people
> will understand this. Those who do will be occupied
> getting profits. The general public will probably not
> see it's against their interest.'"[11]

But is this tension between publicity and secrecy, or rather the exploita-
tion—and creation—of a secret by an instrument of the national economy a new twist on usury? Is it the emergence of a sophisticated modernity? In the Middle Ages the condemnation of usury is thorough and so
ubiquitous that our tendency, even as medievalists, has been to assume
that it's precisely the adherence to prohibitions against usury that keeps
the medieval economy, well, medieval, pre-economic, precapitalist.

    In his account of Langland's narration of the exigencies of street-
level trade in London, for example, the great Langland scholar Derek
Pearsall calls attention to the poem's various examples of the urban
pathologies of exchange, "regraterye," false weighing, "hokkerye," and
others, arguing that finance and trade in Langland's political economy
"cannot in themselves be legitimated" ("Langland's London," 193). It's
what merchants do that poses, in these terms, the largest threat to the
utopian fantasies of *Piers Plowman,* because of their tendency—almost
obligation—to practice usury. As Pearsall says, Langland does not "wish
to think of trade as anything more than a primitive form of barter or exchange" (194). As I will be arguing shortly, it is precisely these apparent
occlusions of an approving, positive account of the work of capital that
indicates the affinity of Langland's complex vision of exchange with the
statutes, ordinances, and writs issuing from Parliament, king, and may-
oral courts, which take for granted the force of capital and the essential
movement of money. While many of these citations are clearly unfavor-
able, many others are more difficult to dismiss as instantiations of a
generally illegitimate practice. Indeed all versions of the poem cite "chaffare" as a practice preferable even, perhaps, to the withdrawal from the
economic practiced by anchorites and hermits: "summe chesen chaffare—þei cheueth þe bettre" (C.Pro.33; B.Pro. 33; A.Pro.31). Langland
seems to be developing an economics out of the labor of the poem itself,
a change signaled by his announcement at the very beginning of the
C version, the third version, that what he sees in the dream is "Al þe
welthe of the world and þe wo bothe" (10). In other words, an economics
that is endemic to the poem, neither unavoidably usurious nor illicit,

and that imagines wealth, the possession of substance or capital, as the enjoyment that is the antonym of woe and that initiates the poem.[12]

We can hardly say that traditional mercantile practices, particularly as they are the subject of concern in the Edwardian social and economic initiatives, are unnoticed or that they cannot be imagined to have larger social consequences. In the strange political economy that emerges in the Pardon Passus, the crucial scene of the poem, where a pardon is sent from Truth to all the estates of fourteenth-century England, merchants are represented, in one of the most complex examples of Langlandian ambiguity, as both integral to it and outside it, quite literally (in the only use of the Middle English word in this sense) at the "margyne" of the pardon that Truth sends. And we might recall the work of secrecy in Pound's Canto on usury when we notice that the merchant's pardon is sent to them by Truth under "secret seal," an intimation that the role of merchants in the public economy already involves—or demands—some form of secrecy in the fourteenth century.

The poem's immensely sophisticated meditation on the nature and extent of mercantile transactions raises profound questions not only about the function of social margins, but also about the complex phenomenology of exchange, an activity that encroaches dangerously on the margins of writing itself. Even in the poem's own terms, the very example that Pearsall cites to support his argument that the poem articulates a primitive precapitalist economy, one that might go by the name of a barter or gift economy, is one that discloses both of these facets of the poem's mercantile imaginary. These simpler terms of exchange, Pearsall suggests, are the ones "under which Conscience had earlier exonerated merchants, declaring that 'marchandise is no mede,' since 'hit is as a permutacoun apertly [openly, publicly], on peneworth for another'" ("Langland's London," 194). Yet the conditions under which this is possible are far from simple. The infamous grammatical metaphor that follows this description of exchange, indeed, divulges in part a sophisticated and elaborate account of the political economy, concerning the relative nature of "meed," "mercede," "pay," "coest" and the effects of those who "inlyche . . . coueyte": "As relacoynes indirect reccheth thei neuere / Of the cours of case so thei cache suluer. / Be the peccunie ypayed, thow parties chyde, / He þat mede may lacche maketh lytel tale. / Nyme he a noumber of nobles or of shillynges, / How þat cliauntes acorde acounteth mede litel" (C 3.387–92). No less perplexing than the rest of this brilliant and multivalent metaphor, this passage has the double complexity of a meditation on the social effects of exchange, examining the work that money performs on its own in displacing what Marx refers to as one *Gemeinwesen* with another, a "community" with merely a "common essence" or "common substance." Langland's passage, indeed, uncannily anticipates Marx's observation of the effect of money in exchange, in which "relacoynes indirect" are precisely the product of money as a form of possession. Money, Marx argues, "does not at all presuppose an individual relation to its owner; possession of it is not the development of any particular essential aspect of his individuality, since this social relation exists at the same time as a sensuous, external object which can be mechanically seized, and lost in the same manner. Its relation to the individual thus appears as a purely accidental one."[13] Langland's analysis of the effects of exchange is thus remarkably akin to Marx's much later observation of the fetishistic, "indirect" nature of social relations in exchange, and suggests the potential of grammaticality as an instrument of economic analysis. And at the very least, Langland's citation of money itself in the heart of this complex metaphor indicates his appreciation of its intrinsic, not to mention extrinsic, complexity.

The question of who possesses money is important, but so is the question of how money works, or how it was imagined to work in the Middle Ages, for the poem's understanding of merchants is derived in some important ways from the medieval phenomenology of money. The gold noble that Edward III introduced may be the clearest example of the complex ideas that inhered in the coin, ideas that are a part of the very design and purpose of that coin in particular. It shows that Edward's national thought was anything but systematic and coherent, a nationalism of expediency and exigency. His determination to cross into foreign markets is declared in the obverse of the gold noble of 1344, which shows Edward crossing the sea in a ship.[14] Besides signifying his abstract territorial desires, it also clearly memorializes his stunning victory at Sluys, a victory that began England's long assertion of dominion over the waves, linking together England's military and economic conquest of its extimate neighbor France. To paraphrase Žižek, France was imagined as the thief of England's enjoyment, a point made insistently if inadvertently by Henry Knighton's stunning series of misrecognitions in his account of Edward's spectacular defeat of the French navy at Sluys in 1340. A reconaissance party reported that the French had "prestanciores naues, et grandiores, quales non prius uiderant," including, in their midst, one called the *Christopher* "pre sua excellencia" (*Chronicle*, 28). What Knighton doesn't say is that this ship was actually Edward's, captured two years before, a ship that becomes an important figure in Edward's attempt to retake the Continent with the bullion marked with the sign of this ship.

Edward's noble also evokes in several ways the notion that the basic sign of exchange—money—is transitive. Like all units of currency, these nobles functioned only by being circulated. The legend on their reverse summed up especially clearly that idea, but it also hinted at the errant and nomadic state of money in late-fourteenth-century England. The legend on the coin is a citation from Luke's account of Christ's escape from a hostile crowd outside his boyhood home of Nazareth by slipping through the crowd unnoticed—"IHC transiens per medivm illorvm ibat." It irresistibly recalls the ability of money to slip away unnoticed, a phenomenon that paradoxically is commented upon frequently in the Middle Ages. Money was invented for the purpose of exchange, argued Aquinas, following Aristotle, who had pointed out the usefulness of money in transporting wealth easily from one region to another: signifying its own disappearance, the "proper and principal use of money is its consumption or alienation in exchange."[15] It does not merely disappear once it is used: its disappearance is its very use, its ability to allow its owner to acquire the real commodities he or she desires. Money is not something that can be enjoyed for its own sake, or whose use is enjoyment (usufruct); it merely marks a passage, the transfer of substance from one point to another, the acquisition of the things that are really needed or desired. Money, as Aristotle says, is an "intermediate." Scholastics will examine what this means more fully, using, as Henry of Ghent does, terms borrowed from the medieval physics of motion and the grammatical principle of transitivity to describe money as a *medium* and not a *terminus*.[16] But money is not just transitive; it is also elusive. But more—or less—than that, the coin's citation of Luke summons up a host of complex and powerful associations. The motto was widely reputed to be used in alchemical transformation, as an incantation in the production of unusually pure gold, in a technology whose ultimate purpose was the recreation of purified, transformed, stable bodies.[17] And it is a motto concerned with embodiment in other ways. It was frequently written on amulets and bound to the body on strips of parchment, themselves the fragments of bodies.[18] But more directly it associates the king on its obverse with the king on its reverse: Edward with Christ, the earthly king portrayed, also, in a ship that could be none other than his own *Christopher,* the Christ-bearer, retaken from the French at Sluys. The Christological symbolics of English destiny, its national noetic, surfaces again in 1356, just after King John of France had been captured at Poitiers, in "multis...locis" on the Continent: "Ore est ly Pape deuenu Fraunceys, e Ihesu deuenu Englays, / Ore serra ueou qe fra plus, ly pape ou Ihesus" (Knighton, *Chronicle,* 150). The reference to the pope at Avignon is specific and pointed; the reference to the English Christ is both general and, as we have seen, specific, referring also, it seems, to Edward's coinage, in which he assumes the figure of Christ crossing the waters. And it echoes Edward's bodily advent in France, the tangible correlation of the passage symbolized by the coin, in which Edward himself, the king of the sea, embodies the motto that once referred to Christ, and in doing so becoming more English. Edward become Jesus: first the English king as the international, evanescent body of value, now the central body of the Middle Ages incarnated as an English national subject, conveyed into France unseen by the alchemy of English international money, and appearing as the image of England, the substantial body that the coin's *symbolon* could only hint at. Nothing sums up quite so well the changing alliances, the presence *in altero,* the cross-purposes, of national identifications. Edward's imperial ambitions at the start of the Hundred Years War enacted many such ironic reversals of communal representation, and the semiotic contradictions of a coin intended to signify England's arrival on the Continent, yet that simulated a foreign coin, a semiotics already present in those foreign markets, are nothing compared to the vast flow of foreign monetary capital that paid for Edward's attempt to make France part of the *communitas* of the English realm.[19] It is clear from Edward's many legislative initiatives that he was well aware of the deleterious effect of exchange on the *communitas* of the realm, and more particularly on its tendency to collapse and make permeable the stable social categories on which monarchical regulation depended.

The history of Edward III's gold nobles delineates the dependence of coinage on alienation, on achieving honor outside its own country, in some unintended, and quite literal, ways. In 1344 Edward issued a gold coinage in order to arrest the outward flow of English silver to foreign markets. It failed by August of that year precisely because it did not circulate widely enough in those foreign markets. The same design, however, appeared on subsequent issues of the noble, which eventually achieved wider circulation. It is a sign of Edward's desire to circulate his coinage in foreign markets, indeed, that he commissioned two Florentines, who became wardens of the English Mint, to design it specifically to appeal to the foreign markets.

But even without thinking in terms of political or national initiatives, the notion of what a pennyworth might be, of what modes of commensuration come into play in order to make one equivalent to another, is anything but straightforward. The strangeness of money, indeed, is a notion that Shakespeare builds deep into the structure of *Timon of Athens*, with its famous encomium to gold, the "visible god, / That solder'st close impossibilities."[20] *Piers Plowman*'s grammatical metaphor's attention to the social dimension reminds us that value was theorized in the thirteenth and fourteenth centuries not as a proportionate individual need, as it had been for Aristotle, but as a common determination, what Albertus Magnus called "opus civilis" or "opus in communitatis usus,"[21] precisely the kind of social determination of monetary function whose displacement Langland condemns later in the analogy. Not only did theories of exchange borrow from the highly elaborated technology of geometric calculation, but they also developed numerous ways of representing the worth that inhered in money, in what, exactly, a "pennyworth" included. The labor of the merchant could be represented in the adequation of value, the degree to which money represented the proportional exchange of goods, as that of transportation, risk, his accumulated good reputation, his expertise, the mental labor involved in bringing something to market.[22] Older provisions to the general principle that nothing could be "superadded" to the price demanded in exchange included such notions as *lucrum damnum* or *lucrum cessans*, which compensated the merchant for profit that might have otherwise been made.[23] A more widely accepted exception known as *damnum emergens* indemnified the merchant for any loss he might have suffered, a principle that Patience alludes to and rejects in his encomium on poverty, in which someone may "wynne" charity "thogh he chafare" as long as "he chargeth no loes" (C.16.148). More pointedly, the notion of a profit arising precisely out of loss is the very figure that Langland uses in C.5 to describe the writing of the poem, a profit that will cancel out and justify—and indeed be justified by—the successive losses of time that have thus far characterized the poem: "A bouhte suche a bargayn he was þe bet euere, / And set al his los at a leef at the laste ende" (C.5.96–97). The suitability of this analogy for the unfolding definition of a "life work" is only troubled further by Langland's apparent, but not unprecedented, conversion of something meant to be an exception, the profit that is justified by loss, into an accepted principle, the cancelling of loss by the emergence of profit. But almost everywhere one looks for extrinsic references to the "chaffare" that the writing of the poem is becoming, one finds disturbing evidence that Langland is deliberately pressing into metaphorical service aspects of "chaffare" that are the focus of considerable legislative attention, and that, as the treatment of money in the grammatical metaphor tells us, is bound up in the extrinsic world of the political economy, as well.

Coveitise is perhaps the most mercantile figure in *Piers Plowman* apart from the merchants themselves. In him, Langland confronts directly the detrimental practices of mercantile exchange, without necessarily suggesting that the logic of exchange is one of intractable depravity.

> Eschaunges and cheuesances with suche chaffare I dele
> And lene folke that lese wol a lyppe at euery noble
> And with Lumbardes lettres I ladde golde to Rome
> And toke it by taille here and tolde hem there lasse
> Lentestow euere lordes for loue of her mayntenaunce
> ʒe I haue lent lordes loued me neuere after
> And haue ymade many a knyʒte bothe mercere and drapere.
>   (B. 5.245–51)

Although, as we will see, Langland is clearly writing within a literary tradition that delights in antimercantile tropes, and although much of his own treatment of merchants is inflected by this tradition, his denunciation of exchange practices is not completely derivative or secondary. Coveitise's confession is an account both of the sophistication of late-fourteenth-century flows of capital and of the particular excesses and abuses that merchants committed. He cites such practices as bills of exchange ("Lumbardes lettres"), which were instruments allowing amounts to be transferred safely between countries, and which also allowed merchants to profit from differentials in exchange rates,[24] the complex economic implications of the burgeoning practice of maintenance, in which the accumulation of social capital—the bestowing of badges and livieries—compromised the real capital of members of the gentility, and the more complex reticences of the distraint for knighthood, whose effect we have already seen in the conflated social categories that appear in the writs for registrations of debt in staple towns.[25] Even more pointedly, this portion of Coveitise's confession incorporates the specific legislative initiative against usurers that was a part of the Edwardian social and economic interventions in the middle of the century.

In 1363 Edward issued a general writ, under the privy seal, against usurers, requesting the mayors and aldermen of the staple towns to pass an ordinance against usury and "male chevance."[26] A resourceful synthesis of economic, social, and spiritual reasons that usury is dangerous (it consumes the soul, honor, and goods of anyone who practices it, and destroys the "droit et leal marchandise" of the city), the ordinance is particularly lucid about the inherently deceptive nature of usury. It is a "faux et abhominable contract," dangerous because of its appropriation of legitimate practices of exchange, taking place under their very "couverture et colour." The figure the ordinance is apparently playing with at this point is that of the verbal integument or of the rhetorical color, since the language of exchange is precisely what is at stake. As a document required to be published throughout the city,[27] it concerns the means by which usurious contracts are represented in order to warn the general public against them. The threat of usury is substantial precisely because its terminology is identical to that of legitimate exchange: usurers call their practice "'eschange' ou 'chevisance,'" but, as the ordinance goes on to suggest, it might more properly be called 'meschaunce'" (*Liber Albus*, 368). The purported publicity of this ordinance may account for the currency of the terms that could be associated with usury. Most immediately, we might notice that Langland uses precisely the words "eschaunges and cheuesances" to describe Coveitise's usurious activity. But as the ordinance recognizes, one of the problems in recognizing and combating usury was its simulation of licit modes of exchange, particularly when usurious merchants are adept at appropriating such terms. The B-text's incomplete appropriation of the ordinance's condemnation of usury produces a more general condemnation of all acts of exchange, an indiscriminate indictment of all merchants. This, as the ordinance clearly establishes, is not the point of calling attention to "eschaunges and cheuesances," but to elicit a more acute understanding of the subtlety and complexity of exchange, to urge on consumers a more sophisticated understanding of the dangerous proximity of usury. In the C-text, indeed, Langland deletes the passage concerning exchange altogether, and has Coveitise cite the principal canonical argument against usury, that it is a theft of time: "what buryn of me borewede a bouhte the tyme" (C.6.247). Changes such as these support the poem's general elaboration in successive versions of a more sophisticated and subtle notion of exchange, one that is pointed towards the possibility that it might be intrinsically and ethically worthy despite its sociological dangers.

The casual, even delighted, anticipation of a massive "bargayn" in the C.5 passage, for instance, seems a purposive use of a term that is singled out in London ordinances to represent some of the most deleterious aspects of commerce. Responding to a royal writ ordering them to eradicate usury and "male chevance," the mayors and aldermen issued an ordinance that, like the original writ, condemned what it called such "bargaynes," proposing punishments ranging from forefeiture to exile.[28] Like these, the practices that the poem describes, whether it accepts, condemns, or ambiguously appropriates them, are represented in terms that impinge on the national economy. The microcosmic practices of "regraterye," for instance, as Pearsall argues, are not criminalized in city and guild ordinances, yet they are a part of a very evident concern on the part of Edward III with the fate of the national economy, and of a series of initiatives that he took in an attempt to manage the political economy of the nation. Every condemnation of usury, brokering, and tortious exchange promulgated by London officials during Edward's reign was the result of a directive issued by him under the privy seal, that is, by his own authority. In many ways, indeed, the economic imaginary of *Piers Plowman* is inseparable from the deep interest Edward took in managing the political economy of England.

Langland's apparently puzzling fabrication of a proto-estate of merchants in the famous Pardon Passus is less strange when we consider that Edward III had tried repeatedly to forge an estate of merchants throughout his reign as a means of circumventing the commons and appropriating the access to capital represented by merchants. The passage and subsequent revisions of the legislation descended from the Statute of Acton Burnell in 1285 elaborated a clearly defined national, and not merely urban, role for merchants, strengthened by the adoption of forms of the civil law that applied to both native and foreign merchants. This *Lex Mercatoria* was widely recognized throughout both England

and western Europe, and had a role even in the English chancery, which allowed a modified form of it to be used in the registration and collection of debts. But more than that, the history of its adoption and incorporation into the practice of commerce in fourteenth-century England suggests that its effects could hardly fail to be noticed by anyone who engaged in trade of any kind, or anyone living near a staple, market, or fair. An examination of the forms and practices of mercantile activity in the fourteenth century leads us to a sense of its massive effect on forms of registration and designation, its forging of systems of inscription that transcended manorial courts and localities, the increasing reliance of the government on the marketplace as a site of order, control, and the promulgation of legislation.[29]

Under Edward III, especially, the government came increasingly to rely on merchants themselves to fund increasingly expensive ventures, especially his French wars. At first Edward relied on foreign merchant houses like the Bardi and Peruzzi for infusions of capital, often in the form of outright loans, and the granting of monopolies to syndicates of powerful English merchants. As a means of circumventing the interests of magnates and the Commons as it was represented in Parliament, Edward tried several times, and in various forms, to convene an Estate of Merchants that would be able to provide capital to the Crown directly. But by the late 1340s the interests of the merchants closely allied with the maintenance of royal capital and the larger group of what one petition calls the "poor merchants" had become so incompatible that the final attempt to assemble an Estate of Merchants in 1349 involved no more than five of the seventy-six summoned in any useful way (Unwin, "Estate," 222). These lesser merchants, that is, those whose capital was not inextricably bound up in the economy of the royal household, were, as E. E. Rich says, "anxious to avoid Edward's attempt to deal with them as a political institution, and pleaded that duly enrolled Statutes, made in Parliament, were the only guarantee of good faith and permanence" (*Staple Court Books*, 26–27). The mid-century history of the legislative view of merchants is one that sees them eventually seeking refuge as a Commons entity, not as a separate body, in order to evade the extortions and demands that Edward attempted to place on them in his attempts to convene an Estate of Merchants.[30] What this may lead us to is an appreciation not of William Langland's open-mindedness in including in an attenuated way the body of merchants in the Pardon sent from Truth, but his echoing of various petitionary attempts to include merchants in the guarantees and freedoms extended to the deliberative body of the Commons. In the emergent fiscal and constitutional practice of and around the writing of the poem, merchants are thus not so much an incipient social body in their own right as they are a part of a fragmented body, as it turns out, in the process of being reintegrated. The pervasiveness and unsettled social place of the merchants in the legislation of the second half of the fourteenth century is inseparable from accounts of the status of money, but also of related attempts to forge social identities and signifying practices, in which the establishment of just price, a stable currency, and recognizable, legible bodies figures prominently. Hence, in the first version of the poem, Langland has the merchants thanking Will because he has "co[pie]de þus here clause" (A.8.44) in the Pardon, a document whose sociological ambit includes the very constituencies addressed by the social legislations of the 1350s to the early 1360s: the statute and ordinances of laborers (in which Langland has an undeniable interest), the statute of the staple of 1353, the sumptuary legislation of 1363—all of which included merchants and various modes of exchange, and all of which are motivated, above all, by a profound sense that the political economy is being wrecked by forms of excess.[31] Will's payment of "greet mede" by the merchants, a payment of woolen clothes, manages to cite all of these persistent concerns, concerns that remain as unresolved and troubling as does the place of "chaffare" as a whole in the poem.

Running through this set of legislative initiatives is a persistent concern with the quantity and quality of money, addressed with a desperation that suggests the framers of the statutes believed the imbalances of the political economy could be redressed by controlling the form and flow of money. As far back as 1335 an entire statute was devoted to the problem of counterfeit money, which was seen to cause "damage & oppression de nostre people," proposing a series of measures that England's "bone moneye soit multiplie": prohibitions against importing false money and counterfeit sterling, melting coins to make metal objects, taking money out of the realm without licence, the institution of specific sites for sanctioned exchange, and the creation of "searchers" to ensure that all of the statute's provisions are being enforced (*Statutes of the Realm*, 1:273–74). In 1343 the provision for searchers was reiterated, along with the general desire for the increase of "bone Monoie dargent," stressing that they were to pay particular attention to the export of silver money or in other forms, except in the case of "les grandez," whose domestic economy required silver vessels ("vessealx dargent pur servir lour hostelx": *Statutes of the Realm*, 1:299). The provisions that established the principle of free trade, removing most of the restrictions on trade that had favored monopolies, which was one of the first effects of the aligning of mercantile interests in general with the Commons, permitted the exchange of gold and silver without the making of profit as a means of keeping the circulation of coinage unrestricted (*Statutes of the Realm*, 1:322). And the important Ordinance of the Staples included measures designed to shore up the "commone cours" of English money by requiring foreign merchants to use sanctioned exchanges where they could exchange their money for "monoie de nostre coigne dor & dargent covenablement a la Value" (*Statutes of the Realm*, 1:338)

This persistent concern with the debasement and diminution of currency that weaves through these statutes of social legislation echoes the concern with money in *Piers Plowman*, which is overwhelmingly concerned, too, with its value and the integrity of its form and substance. The recurrent metaphor of false money not only runs through sections of the poem that take up the mid-century legislative concern with designating status, but that also concern the question of writing. In the C-text "lettred men" are compared to the false money that the statutes are anxious about, to coins like the "loscheborw," which London records warn against, and coins whose base metal is debased and alloyed:[32]

Me may now likene lettred men to a loscheborw oþer worse
And to a badde peny with a gode printe:
Of moche [m]one þe metal is nauhte
And ȝut is þe printe trewe and parfitliche ygraue. (C.17. 73–76).

This passage appears in a section of the poem whose relation to the equivalent section in the B version is both complex and revealing, because the C.5 passage in many ways supplants it. In the C-text this section of the poem is initiated by an encounter with the interlocutors who have "arated" Will in C.5, Reason and Conscience, and the gluttonous feast of the Doctor of Divinity, a "man lyk a frere" (30), whose insistence

on eating "mete of more cost" served by Scripture nicely satirizes both
the presumptuousness of higher learning and the putative avaricious-
ness of the fraternal orders. The next two passus are concerned with
both of these intertwined themes, in a virtuoso display of the spiritual
and social consequences of the economic practices it describes, and the
significance of designation, representation, and grammar, all conjured
up in the image of the striking of false money. The reiterated associations
of these two themes with various figures who task it is to construe authors
or to set forth narratives—and their unfolding in a part of the poem that
is also tied up with Langland's veiled self-designations—suggest that
this integral metaphor is, in some sense, the treasure that the poem has
sought to expound, articulate, spend reasonably, since its own beginning.
But these two passus are also riddled with a concern over the dangers
represented by possession.

The passus opens with a magnificent reference to the literal force of
the central Christian metaphor of redemption—Truth heard of the plow-
ing of the half-acre and "purchased" Piers a pardon—yet the merchants'
parlous state is discussed immediately after the relatively secure position of kings, knights, and bishops. The status of merchants in the passus is accordingly ambiguous: they are situated "in [th]e margyne" of the
bull (B.7.18), appended to the document, but part of neither its original
writing nor its discursive structure. Their legitimacy is, apparently, covert
or exceptional, the product of a particular dispensation rather than anything implicit in the act of exchange: "vnder his secret seel truþe sente
hem a lettre" (B.7.23), urging them to "bugge boldly what hem best likede"
and "saue þe wynnyng" in order to engage in public acts of charity. That
is, apparent and demonstrably public gratuitous acts are necessary to
redeem the procedures of exchange. But the exclusion made for merchants is assuredly not directed at the act of exchange itself, for, if anything, it urges merchants to pursue it even more persistently and pur-
posively, to continue not just to buy but to buy boldly "what hem likede,"
even despite the passage's observation that what makes exchange most
perilous to the merchant's soul is the very "couetyse of wynnynge." But
the remainder of Truth's letter urges that exchange be directed toward
the public good, toward the improvement of roads, bridges, hospitals,
and the plight of the poor and those in religious orders. This is a clearly
sociological vision of exchange, in which the individual effects, the en-

gaging in exchanges that "sownen into synne," are largely irrelevant to the public manifestations and regulation of exchange. This is, in other words, a phenomenology of exchange closely akin to Edward III's, in which a close analysis of the marketplace is not subsumed by moralizing conclusions about it, but in which the ethics of exchange is pressed into the service of, and indeed partly defined by, the demands of what the Ordinance of Labourers calls the public commodity (*Statutes of the Realm*, 1:309). The latitude of exchange was, indeed, defined by regal intervention, as a 1365 writ suggests.

Sent to the mayor and aldermen of London under the privy seal, it commands them to summon before them all anyone whom they suspect of engaging in "eschaunges" of any kind, and compel them to take an oath that they will make exchanges only with merchants who are "loial et conu," and that they will undertake to make no "emport ou paiement hors de nostre dite roialme."[33] Its concerns and language are clearly consistent with the aims and interests of Edward's mid-century economic initiatives, except that it shows both the degree to which Edward was prepared to intervene personally in matters of exchange and, more tacitly, the ethical complexity of Edward's ideological appropriation of exchange mechanisms in an age when the surveillance of exchange was virtually identical with the conviction that it was all usurious. The writ includes the notable provision that, while no merchants were to engage in these practices deleterious to the individual soul and the public commodity, exceptions to it could be made at the instance of the king himself, "par lettres desouz nostre Secre Seal" (*Liber Albus*, 372). The warrant to violate precisely the procedures that purportedly ensure the security of the realm's economy is itself surprising and somewhat paradoxical, since it is issued by the king's personal authority under the privy seal. In this light, the "lettre" that Truth sends "vnder his secrete seal" in *Piers Plowman* emerges as a more complex dispensation than even a scrupulous reading of the poem by itself would suggest. For what is being enacted for the merchants in the Pardon Passus is a subtle and intricate documentary indictment of exchange that permits the very things that it indicts,[34] the pursuit under a special warrant of a practice that its very exceptionality ensures will be remediative.[35] Thus deviant forms of exchange are tolerated if they can be converted to the public commodity, and covetous practices of exchange, driven by what the merchant "best likede," can be, if their "goed amende" the welfare of the public, the very conversion of the soul, its final habitation where, says Truth, "y mysulue dwelle."

Notes

1. As Marx famously said, "The tradition of all the generations of the dead weighs like a nightmare on the brain of the living" (*18th Brumaire*, 9).

2. I'm using the word *noesis* here because it suggests, as the epigraph shows, the work of contemplation, but, as Hegel and Husserl have used it, it also emphasizes the condition of coming to knowledge, not the acquisition of it. The phenomenological difference between coming to know *(noesis)* and the contents of knowledge *(noemata)* is a distinction worth preserving—indeed, one we must preserve—if we are to save ourselves from the overt disciplinarity of the national symbolic and the deadly politics of the national imaginary. A further, useful sense is the rhetorical figure of *noema*, in which the meaning only unfolds in the whole discourse, the opposite, as Putnam says, of synecdoche.

3. For brief—and not necessarily approving—discussions, see Anderson, *Imagined Communities*, 17–40; Gellner, "Coming"; and particularly Gourgouris, *Dream Nation*.

4. "If nation-states," as Anderson argued subsequently, "are widely conceded to be 'new' and 'historical,' the nations to which they give political expression always loom out of an immemorial past" (*Imagined Communities*, 19). On the disciplinarity of historical memory, see my "Irregular Histories."

5. "The practice of 'regraterye' was particularly associated with 'brokeres'....It hardly seems necessary to point out that these are not 'criminal' practices, nor are they necessarily against the public interest": Pearsall, "Langland's London," 205 n. 30.

6. Money becomes the sign of a deterritorialized subject, figuring its subjection to a nomadic imperative. As Michel Serres says, "[m]oney is the trace of the excluded [and] banished person" (*Parasite*, 149).

7. The similarity between money and language has been noticed since at least Aristotle; Langland uses the phrase "speche of suluer" (C.3.109). For useful discussions of the convergence of the linguistic and the monetary sign, see Shell, *Money, Language*; Goux, *Coiners*; Shoaf, *Dante, Chaucer*.

8. "Symbolic capital, a transformed and thereby *disguised* form of physical 'economic' capital, produces its proper effect inasmuch...as it conceals the fact that it originates in 'material' forms of capital which are also, in the last analysis, the source of its effects": Bourdieu, *Outline*, 183. And this movement is by definition irrational: it's the converse of the capacity for self-alienation, for exchange, that Lévi-Strauss described as the essential symptom of sanity. See *Elementary Structures; Savage Mind; Introduction*.

9. Marc Shell's brilliant discussion of the dialectics of appearance and disappearance in Greek economic thinking includes a useful reading of Plato's and Herodotus's story of the ring of Gyges in terms of the politics and communal fashioning of appearance, and argues that the ring *(symbolon)* thematizes the opposition of visible and invisible substance in the transfer of property (*Money, Language*, 11–62).

10. For useful appraisals of the influence of Lollardy, imagined and real, on Langland's writing of the C-text, see Cole, "Langland"; Gradon, "Langland"; Lawton, "Lollardy."

11. Canto 46. The quotation here is taken from Hollis, *Two Nations*, 251–52. The most useful discussion of Pound's "usury" cantos is in Rabaté (*Language, Sexuality*, 183–206).

12. Louise Bishop, "Law of Property," usefully sketches forms of possession in the poem that impinge on the civil definition of *possessio* and the polysemousness of the will, but is necessarily restricted to moments of conveyance or transfer.

13. Marx, *Grundrisse*. Earlier in the "Chapter on Money" Marx makes the same point in relation to the familial metaphor that runs through Langland's grammatical metaphor: "In the money relation, in the developed system of exchange . . . the ties of personal dependence, of distinctions, of blood, education, etc. are in fact exploded, ripped up (at least, personal ties all appear as *personal* relations); and individuals *seem* independent (this is an independence which is at bottom merely an illusion, and it is more correctly called indifference)" (*Grundrisse*, 163).

14. For discussions of the noble, see Sutherland, *English Coinage*, 72; Oman, *Coinage*, 169 ff.; Craig, *The Mint*, 62 ff.; Brooke, *English Coins*, 120.

15. Thomas Aquinas, *Summa Theologica* II-II, 78, 1, c. Cited in Langholm, *Economics*, 241. In a brief summary of forms of possession in his *questio* on usury, John Buridan makes a similar point: "proprius vsus pecunie consistatiri consumpcione pecunie & dispersione" (*Quaestiones*, Lib. I, q. 12, fol. xvii). See also his *Super decem libros ethicorum*, Lib. IV, q. 2, fol. lxxi: "custodia non est vsus pecunie." Elsewhere, he argues that the regulation of the flow of money is a matter of public policy, and that exchanging it freely hinders its proper end, the moving of goods from one place to another: "ordo nature pecunie & proprius finis est commutatio de bonorum aliorum: mo[neta] campsoria ars siue commutatio de pecunia dat pecuniam per pecunia & per consequens sit abusus" (*Quaestiones*, Lib. I, q. 11, fol. xv).

16. Henry of Ghent, *Quodlibet* VI, 22; cited in Langholm, *Economics*, 203. See also Coleman, "Jean de Ripa"; Covington, *Syntactic Theory*, 48–82.

17. For a brief discussion, see my "Body Doubles."

18. See Skemer, "Written Amulets."

19. Ephraim Russell estimated that the Bardi and Peruzzi banking families had loaned about £359,600, and the Florentine chronicler Villani estimated the debt at 1,365,000 florins, which "valeano un Reame." Quoted in Russell, "Societies," 129 and 131.

20. *Timon of Athens*, 4.3.379–80. Marx quotes the passage in his discussion of money in *Grundrisse* as an example of what he calls its function as the "equation of the incompatible" (163). The complexity of exchange leads Foucault to classify it with the general human sciences as one of the early modern modes of resemblance. The power and subtlety of his analysis derives in no small measure from his keen attention to the commensurability of exchange and grammar, and to the difficulty of the notion of commensurability or value itself: "in order that one thing can represent another in an exchange, they must both exist as bearers of value, and yet value exists only within the representation (actual or possible), that is, within the exchange or the exchangeability" (Foucault, *Order*, 190).

21. Albertus Magnus, *Alberti Magni super ethica*, ed. Kübel. Cited in Kaye, *Economy*, 76. By the thirteenth century, Kaye observes, the complexity of this sociological conception

of exchange had become sufficiently complex that the techniques of more elaborated disciplines such as geometry were borrowed to fit the question of worth into the scholastic apparatus of adequation, allowing for elaborate and subtle delimitations of the objective, social, calculation of appropriate worth in exchange: "As the geometric *figura* of exchange was de-subjectified, it came to represent the marketplace as a kind of mechanism of equalization, in which the cross-conjunction of common estimation and common need 'automatically' determined market prices" (76).

22. For a summary of all of these, see Kaye, *Economy*, 139–40.

23. See McLaughlin, "Teachings." The canonist Hostiensis described twelve exceptions to the general prohibition against this superaddition (that is, against usury), which he laid out in mnemonic form.

24. See Roover, "L' évolution."

25. That is, Coveitise's boast encompasses not just the general phenomenon of aristocratic indebtedness, but also the very real emergence of knights (or bachelors and esquires) who call themselves merchants. See the first chapter of my *Arts of Possession*.

26. See *Calendar of Letter Book G*, fol. 119. The later entries of the writ and ordinance are printed in *Liber Albus*, 367–71.

27. As the privy seal writ specifies. *Liber Albus*, 368.

28. *Calendar of Letter Book G*, fol. 119, 38 Edw. III. The writ and ordinance were later copied into the *Liber Albus* (142–46).

29. The clearest example of this is the practice of recognizance of debt, but the emergence of law merchant took other forms as equally motivated by a desire to delineate clearly and quickly the passage of debt and capital: bills for free passage (freedom from prise) for anyone carrying goods to and from a staple (*Statutes of the Realm*, 1:335); the installation of "Corecters" to oversee the legitimacy of contracts of exchange (*Statutes of the Realm*, 1:341); numerous attempts, as we will see, to stabilize and regulate coinage and exchange. For the argument that markets become the place where legislation is announced, see Masschaele, "Urban Trade." The history of relations between the king and various representative factions of merchants, which included at various times the richest two or three and at others a putatively comprehensive gathering, is too complicated to describe fully here, but excellent introductions can be found in Unwin, "Estate"; Bewes, *Romance*; Rich, *Staple Court Books*; Plucknett, *Legislation*, 136–61; Harriss, *Public Finance*, 420–65; Britnell, *Commericialisation*.

30. "In 1343 the petitions of the merchants represent a separate body of interests consulted before the rest of the Commons; and a treaty with that body, in which the greater and the lesser exporters were combined, was used as a means of extracting concessions from Parliament. In 1348 the petitions emanating from the merchants and representing a variety of different interests, are mingled with those of the Commons and the many petitions of the Commons express to a large extent the grievances of the merchants." Cf. Will's copying of the merchants' cause. Unwin, "Estate," 220.

31. In the Ordinance of Labourers the wages of artificers are addressed, but so is the selling of victual by "Butchers, Fishmongers, Regrators, Hostelers, Brewers, Bakers, and Pulters" (*Statutes of the Realm*, 1:308) "per precio rationabili," so that these sellers would have "moderatum lucrum, non excessivum." The Statute of Labourers empowers justices

to investigate the practices of "those that sell Victual by Retail" (*Statutes of the Realm*, 1:313); the sumptuary legislation included a prohibition of the practice called engrossment, by which merchants as a group ("appelle Fraternite & gilde de Marchaunt") would drive up the price of their goods by withholding them from the market, and regulations for the clothing that merchants were entitled to wear (*Statutes of the Realm*, 1:379 and 381). Both practices are framed as destructive to the realm as a whole, "au roi come as grant & commones"; "a tresgrant destruccion & empoverissement de tote la terre."

32. The *Liber Albus*, for instance, cites the "Breve pro Moneta vocata 'Lusseburghe,'" entered into Letter Book G (575). See *Calendar of Letter Book G*, fol. 149.

33. *Calendar of Letter Book G*, fols. 161–161v (1365). A similar writ was issued to sheriffs in 1364. *Calendar of Letter Book G*, fol. 146v. The 1365 writ is printed in *Liber Albus*, 371–73.

34. That is, its relation to the larger legislative initiatives that underwrite it is similar to the complex one traced by Anne Middleton in the C.5 passage, which emerges as an "incipient prosecution" under the labor statutes of 1388.

35. Giorgio Agamben describes the exception that founds the principle, like the performative declaration that cannot be performative because it is exemplary, as the arbitrary limit of the *nomos* itself. See, for example, *Homo Sacer*, 15–29; "Messiah and the Sovereign."

REFERENCES

Agamben, Giorgio. *Homo Sacer: Sovereign Power and the Base Life*. Trans. Daniel Heller-Pousen. Stanford: Stanford University Press, 1998.

———. "The Messiah and the Sovereign." In his *Potentialities: Collected Essays in Philosophy*, trans. Daniel Heller-Pousen, 160–74. Stanford: Stanford University Press, 1999.

Albertus Magnus. *Alberti Magni super ethica commentum et quaestiones*. In *Opera Omnia*, vol. 14, ed. Wilhelm Kübel. Aschendorff: Monasterii Westfalorum, 1968–72.

Anderson, Benedict. *Imagined Communities: Reflections on the Origin and Spread of Nationalism*. London and New York: Verso, 1983.

Benjamin, Walter. "Theses on the Philosophy of History." In *Illuminations*, trans. Harry Zohn, 253–64. New York: Schocken Books, 1969.

Bewes, Wyndham Anstis. *The Romance of the Law Merchant*. London: Sweet and Maxwell, 1923.

Bishop, Louise. "Will and the Law of Property in *Piers Plowman*." *Yearbook of Langland Studies* 10 (1996): 23–41.

Bourdieu, Pierre. *Outline of a Theory of Practice*. Trans. Richard Nice. Cambridge: Cambridge University Press, 1977.

Britnell, Richard H. *The Commercialisation of English Society, 1000–1500*. Manchester: Manchester University Press, 1996.

Brooke, G. C. *English Coins: From the Seventh Century to the Present Day*. London: Methuen, 1966.

Buridan, John. *Quaestiones super VIII libros politicorum Aristotelis*. Paris, 1513.

———. *Super decem libros ethicorum Aristotelis ad nicomachum*. Paris, 1513.

Calendar of Letter Books Preserved Among the Archives of the Corporation of the City of London: Letter Book G. Ed. Reginald R. Sharpe. London: Francis, 1905.

Cole, Andrew. "Langland, Wycliffism, and the Invention of Lollardy: The C-Text Response and Revision." Ph.D. diss., Duke University, 2000.

Coleman, Janet. "Jean de Ripa O.F.M. and the Oxford Calculators." *Mediaeval Studies* 37 (1975): 130–89.

Covington, Michael A. *Syntactic Theory in the High Middle Ages: Modistic Models of Sentence Structure.* Cambridge: Cambridge University Press, 1984.

Craig, John Herbert McCutcheon. *The Mint: A History of London Mint from A.D. 287 to 1948.* Cambridge: Cambridge University Press, 1953.

DeRoover, Raymond. *L'évolution de la lettre de change, xive–xviiie siècles.* Paris: Colin, 1953.

Foucault, Michel. *The Order of Things: An Archaeology of the Human Sciences.* New York: Random House, 1970.

Gellner, Ernest. "The Coming of Nationalism and Its Interpretation: The Myths of Nation and Class." In *Mapping the Nation,* ed. Gopal Balakrishnan, 98–145. London: Verso, 1996.

Gourgouris, Stathis. *Dream Nation: Enlightenment, Colonization, and the Institution of Modern Greece.* Stanford: Stanford University Press, 1996.

Goux, Jean-Joseph. *The Coiners of Language.* Trans. Jennifer Curtis Gage. Norman: University of Oklahoma Press, 1994.

Gradon, Pamela. "Langland and the Ideology of Dissent." *Proceedings of the British Academy* 66 (1980): 179–205.

Harriss, G. L. *King, Parliament, and Public Finance in Medieval England to 1369.* Oxford: Clarendon, 1975.

Hollis, Christopher. *The Two Nations: A Financial Study of English History.* London: Routledge, 1935.

Kaye, Joel. *Economy and Nature in the Fourteenth Century: Money, Market Exchange, and the Emergence of Scientific Thought.* Cambridge: Cambridge University Press, 1998.

Knighton, Henry. *Knighton's Chronicle 1337–96.* Ed. and trans. G. H. Martin. Oxford: Clarendon Press, 1995.

Langholm, Odd. *Economics in the Medieval Schools: Wealth, Exchange, Value, Money and Usury According to the Paris Theological Tradition 1200–1350.* Leiden: Brill, 1992.

Langland, William. *"Piers Plowman": The A Version.* Ed. George Kane. London: Athlone Press, 1960.

———. *"Piers Plowman": The B Version.* Ed. George Kane and E. Talbot Donaldson. London: Athlone Press, 1975.

———. *Piers Plowman by William Langland: An Edition of the C-Text.* Ed. Derek Pearsall. Berkeley: University of California Press, 1979.

Lawton, David. "Lollardy and the 'Piers Plowman' Tradition." *Modern Language Review* 76 (1981): 780–93.

Lévi-Strauss, Claude. *The Savage Mind.* Chicago: University of Chicago Press, 1966.

———. *The Elementary Structures of Kinship.* Trans. James Harle Bell, John Richard von Sturmer, and Rodney Needham. Boston: Beacon, 1969.

———. *Introduction to the Work of Marcel Mauss.* Trans. Barbara Freeman. London: Routledge, 1987.

Liber Albus. Ed. Henry Thomas Riley. London, 1859.

Marx, Karl. *Grundrisse: Foundations of the Critique of Political Economy.* Trans. Martin Nicolaus. New York: Vintage, 1973.

———. *The 18th Brumaire of Louis Bonaparte.* Beijing: Foreign Languages Press, 1978.

Masschaele, James. "Urban Trade in Medieval England: The Evidence of Foreign Guild Membership Lists." In *Thirteenth-Century England,* ed. P. R. Cross and S. D. Lloyd, 5:115–28. Woodbridge: Boydell, 1995.

McLaughlin, T. P. "The Teachings of the Canonists on Usury." *Mediaeval Studies* 1 (1939): 81–147.

Oman, Charles William Chadwick, *The Coinage of England.* Oxford: Clarendon, 1931.

Pearsall, Derek. "Langland's London." In *Written Work: Langland, Labor, and Authorship,* ed. Steven Justice and Kathryn Kerby-Fulton, 185–207. Philadelphia: University of Pennsylvania Press, 1997.

Plucknett, T. F. T. *Legislation of Edward I.* Oxford: Oxford University Press, 1949.

Rabaté, Jean-Michel. *Language, Sexuality and Ideology in Ezra Pound's Cantos.* Albany: State University of New York Press, 1986.

Renan, Ernst. "What is a Nation?" Trans. Martin Thom. In *Nation and Narration,* ed. Homi Bhabha, 8–22. New York: Routledge, 1990.

Rich, E. E. *The Staple Court Books of Bristol.* Bristol: Bristol Record Society, 1934.

Russell, Ephraim. "The Societies of the Bardi and Peruzzi and Their Dealings with Edward III, 1327–1345." In *Finance and Trade Under Edward III,* ed. Unwin, 93–135.

Serres, Michel. *The Parasite.* Trans. Lawrence R. Schehr. Baltimore: Johns Hopkins University Press, 1982.

Shell, Marc. *The Economy of Literature.* Baltimore: Johns Hopkins University Press, 1979.

———. *Money, Language, and Thought: Literary and Philosophical Economies From the Medieval to the Modern Era.* Berkeley: University of California Press, 1982.

Shoaf, R. A. *Dante, Chaucer, and the Currency of the Word: Money, Images, and Reference in Late Medieval Poetry.* Norman, OK: Pilgrim Books, 1983.

Skemer, Don. "Written Amulets and the Medieval Book." *Scrittura e Civiltà* 23 (1999): 253–305.

Smith, D. Vance. "Body Doubles." In *Becoming Male in the Middle Ages,* ed. Jeffrey Jerome Cohen and Bonnie Wheeler, 21–42. New York: Garland, 1997.

———. *Arts of Possession: The Middle English Household Imaginary.* Minneapolis: University of Minnesota Press, 2002.

Statutes of the Realm. London, 1810.

Sutherland, C. H. V. *English Coinage, 900–1700.* London: B.T. Batsford, 1973.

Unwin, George. "The Estate of Merchants, 1336–1365." In *Finance and Trade Under Edward III,* ed. Unwin, 179–255.

———. *Finance and Trade Under Edward III.* Manchester: Manchester University Press, 1918.

PART V

ENGLAND AND ITS NEIGHBORS

Translating "Communitas"

Lynn Staley

Translatio, the act of transferring authority, significance, of transplanting, grafting, of transposing, was a concept that for the literate meant that ideas, meanings, words, or things would be moved from one sphere to another.[1] The very act of removal was intended to convey the carefully interlocked sets of meanings that had obtained in the original sphere to the new sphere, thus investing the new medium with the power of the old. Or, to use France as the prime example of the arts of translation, if the authority of the empire was to be transferred from a pagan and classical world to the powers of an emerging Christian civilization, the symbols or rituals of Rome must also be relocated in the Christo-centric kingship of the early Frankish nation. Charlemagne or Pepin would thus graft Roman *imperium* onto themselves in a transfer of significance that located the majesty of Rome and the powers of Christ the conqueror in men whose power demanded an authoritative iconic status. The motto of the victorious Christ, "Christus vincit, Christus regnat, Christus imperat," which was used as a sort of charm, invested swords, belts, and coins with extraordinary powers (Kantorowicz, *Laudes regiae*). Everyday things, the "things" that were used to define community, became emblems linking the communities of France with that of Christian empire. If texts were the objects of *translatio,* they must be transplanted into the soil of the vernacular with the academic apparatus, the culture to which and out of which they speak somehow intact. That culture, the culture of the academy, is one of privilege and power; to relocate it in a vernacular sphere is to transfer wisdom, to "give" it to its patron, usually a prince.[2]

What is, in fact, moved from one place to another is privilege, the power, the set of meanings, the species that are thereby singled out and given new and protected life.

In part, the story of medieval institutions is a history of translations, from Rome to France or Germany or England, from the libraries of the Golden and Silver Ages to those of the monks of Benedict, from the highly stylized world of a Constantine to that of a Henry or a Louis, from the lecture halls of the late antique world or of the medieval university to the prince, the court, finally, to the laity. But it is also a history that underlines the ways in which *translatio* was so firmly linked to invention, to the recognition that the old could not be so easily grafted onto the new, that the very act would create a new entity, and that the continual acts of translation of kings, advisers, thinkers, and poets were also ways of coming to terms with inheritances that must necessarily change or become obdurate and useless. The concept of translation was thus directly relevant to the medieval understanding of the ideology of rule, and perhaps nowhere is this congruence so aptly, or so futilely, illustrated as in the cultural relationship between England and France during the reign of Richard II. The 1390s are a crucial period of English political consciousness, but only by turning to Richard's Continental inheritance does the urgency of the last decade of the century become understandable. Nigel Saul has recently and eloquently argued for the influence of Valois kingship upon Richard's views of himself and his role, but it is the carefully worked out sacramentalism of French regality, especially as it was expanded upon by Charles V, that I believe should be seen as providing Richard with the key to his own needs.

Richard, or those who surrounded him, came too late to the recognition that England did not, like its rival France, have an ideology of sacramental kingship that served also to define the political community. By the time Richard and/or his advisers sought to "invent" such a theory for England, the context for translation had changed, and the terms they attempted to appropriate could not define an ideal of English communal identity. Ironically, the events of the Merciless Parliament that established the need also made any attempt at wholesale translation impossible. Though the cultural presence of Philippe de Mézières in England, as well as works like the Wilton Diptych, suggest just how powerful an attraction sacral reality as a component of kingship had, the additional Wycliffite challenge to sacramental change had created an environment where the very subject of sacrality was contested. The tensions that this essay seeks to articulate are thus focused upon the making of a regal identity as a process that is inevitably bound up with the concept of community. In the end, I turn to Chaucer, whose deft handling of his royal rooster suggests that the icon that has been toppled cannot be put back together along the same lines. If it is the business of rulers to imagine identities for themselves and the communities they thereby constitute, they must create knowingly, out of the past, but in the language of the present.

By the last half of Edward III's reign England's need for an ideology of rule becomes, in hindsight at least, apparent, in part because the world that was emerging from the ongoing war between France and England seemed no longer completely accountable in the language of chivalry. In late December 1375 English and French diplomats had met in Bruges to negotiate a peace between the two nations. That conference, along with the military engagements or nonengagements between England and France during the last decade or so of Edward III's previously illustrious reign, which coincided with that of Charles V of France (1364–80), saw the waning of English prestige. Charles, though risking the scorn of his contemporaries for his strategy of delay, of military harassment, and of diplomacy, placed France in a far stronger position than she had been since the Hundred Years War began when Edward claimed the French throne as its rightful heir.[3] The terms of warfare began to change. In 1356 Edward, the Black Prince, had captured John II of France at the battle of Poitiers. Negotiations for his release broke down, and in 1360 a large English army invaded France. This campaign was less spectacular; John's son, the future Charles V, refused to give battle, adopting a policy of skirmish and harassment that wore down the English forces.[4] Exhausted by weather and hunger, the English no longer had the upper hand in negotiations. The situation did not change when Charles acceded to the throne in 1364. In her account of the reign of Charles V, Christine de Pizan reports that the Duke of Lancaster scorned Charles for an "attorney" and not a "sage prince." Upon hearing of the quip, Charles replied "Si nous sommes avocats, nous leur batirons tel plaid que le sentence les ennuiera" (Armitage-Smith, *John of Gaunt*, 66). His threat that he aimed at a sentence of exhaustion displayed both his understanding of the attack upon his chivalric reputation and his refusal to be baited in such crude terms. He had other and more substantial ends in mind that could not be gained by wasting time and energy in empty gestures of noblesse oblige.

His ends, praised by Christine for whom he was the exemplar of the sage prince, were to be gotten in negotiation; they were the fruits of wisdom, or of wise rule. Unlike Edward III, Charles V had inherited a coherent theory of sacral kingship. From at least the coronation *ordo* of 1250, the French court, in collaboration with the ecclesiastical centers of Rheims and St. Denis, began to evolve an ideology of the French monarchy that set it apart from all other species of rule (Le Goff, "Coronation Program," 55). With its careful delineation of myths of descent, as well as its employment of cultic symbols, the French court created a myth of sacral kingship that was increasingly documented and articulated during the fourteenth century, when the Valois' claim to legitimacy became the occasion for the Hundred Years War.[5] Charles V seems to have been particularly sensitive to the need to maintain and to enhance the status of the French monarch. In his now classic study of the myths of kingship, *The Royal Touch,* Marc Bloch argued for Charles V as a king who set out to strengthen the monarchy, particularly after the crisis of the battle of Poitiers, or to strengthen the monarchy's hold on the minds of its subjects (79). Though the French kings were not the only ones who claimed to have been granted the healing touch—English kings also touched for scrofula, and did so as late as Charles II—Bloch emphasizes the uniquely powerful aura that surrounded the French royal cult.

To a great degree he associates the unique status of the French Crown with the carefully constructed myths of descent that had been developed over the centuries by the monastery of St. Denis that, as Gabrielle M. Spiegel describes it, "became the official custodian and interpreter of royal history, virtually without parallel in the Middle Ages."[6] Though lacking the histories of Charlemagne, of Clovis, and of the dove's miraculous gift of the Holy Ampule containing the oil that was used to anoint the kings of France at their coronation, England did have Edward the Confessor. Henry III had perceived the need for a royal cult and had attempted to create in Westminster Abbey an embodiment of English royal identity. His efforts to use the figure of St. Edward as a model for English kingship did not outlive his own reign. That they were revived by Richard II, particularly after the death of Anne of Bohemia, says much about Richard's mature understanding of the uses of history, or about the sensitivity of his court to the language of power in the last decade of the century (Binski, *Westminster Abbey*, 6–7, 199). If Richard or his courtiers studied English history (which they did), they also studied the French use of history.[7]

Even by the thirteenth century, kingship was constructed differently in France. The law was linked more closely to the king himself, and, were "his peace" threatened, the king had more powers to encroach upon well-established institutions than did the king of England. But such a theocratically conceived kingship must also be maintained, and maintained by more than sheer might.[8] Charles V certainly inherited myths that endowed him with a sacral identity and a coronation *ordo* that centered power in him in ways that the English *ordo* did not allow, but he also emerged as a stunning model for the sovereign who might wish to create an officially sanctioned culture. Here, again, he demonstrated his sensitivity to the history of the French Crown's patronage of a humanism that was rooted in vernacular textuality.[9] Throughout the thirteenth century the French court had been engaged in the production of a variety of historical texts that centered power in the Crown, but it also sponsored books on good rule that anchored the ideas of sacral kingship to those of Aristotelian statecraft. Thus, Philip III had appointed Giles of Rome, former student of Thomas Aquinas, as the tutor to Philip IV, the Fair, for whom Giles wrote the *De regimine principium*. When Philip acceded to the throne in 1286, he asked that a vernacular translation be made (Molenar, *Livres du gouvernement*). The Valois kings were particularly involved with commissioning religious, political, historical, and literary texts. However, it is John II, the father of Charles V, who specifically initiated a program of artistic patronage for political ends.[10] John founded the royal library that was housed in the Louvre and commissioned Pierre Bersuire to translate Livy's *Ab Urbe Condita* and the Dominican Jean de Sy to translate the Bible into French. His four years' captivity in England did not alter his commitment to creating an official French culture, for he continued to acquire and commission texts (Sherman, *Imaging Aristotle*, p.4; Sinclair, *Melbourne Livy*, pp. 15–16).

But it is to Charles V that the real accolades for cultural production go; moreover, it is his interest in creating a *vernacular* political culture that seems especially significant for England during a period when English political thinkers must have been looking for some direction. In the late 1380s or early 1390s, what would the English have found in the court of Charles V? By that time, Charles was dead, but the political legacy he had founded had continued to provide France under Charles VI with stability. To put it bluntly, Charles V meddled magic with Aristotle, a feat of political alchemy that, even now, looks like a brilliant achievement. In royal manuscripts such as the *Grandes Chroniques* of France, the *Coronation Book of Charles V,* and in the *Traité du Sacre,* the first treatise on the French coronation ceremony, all either continued and shaped by Charles or commissioned by him, we can find evidence for a kingship whose power is sacramentally derived.

At a time when the Valois claim to the throne of France was under siege either literally or metaphorically by England, Charles was careful to link himself to the ritual practices of the past. The *Grandes Chroniques* had been begun under Louis IX and were produced from the Abbey of St. Denis from the 1270s through the early fourteenth century. They helped to shape the royal image by providing a coherent theory of French kingship as sacral. Charles V commissioned a continuation of the *Grandes Chroniques* that added to them accounts written at court about his father's reign, as well as his own. Thus, to the traditional history of the Merovingian, Carolingian, and Capetian kings was added the history of the Valois.[11] Charles, however, did not simply have the chronicle continued, he continued to tinker with the history. As A. D. Hedeman has demonstrated, he commissioned three distinct stages of execution, including both new material and miniatures that served to legitimize the Valois dynasty by linking it to the figure of Louis IX, king and saint.[12] What is thereby articulated is a "religion royale," carefully put together by a man whom John of Gaunt had scornfully referred to as only an "advocat."

Similarly, the *Coronation Book of Charles V* and the *Traite du Sacre,* both of which were passed to the Duke of Bedford, regent of France, at the death of Charles VI in 1423, play heavily upon the magical elements of French coronation ritual.[13] The *Coronation Book* is a splendid artifact of Charles's magnificence, sumptuously copied and illustrated. The illustrations themselves (there are thirty-eight of them) are designed to indicate the momentous nature of the event they record. Beginning at the point in the ceremony when the king arrives at the church door and is met by the bishop, they capture the sacramental meaning of coronation in the colors and type of clothing both Charles and his queen, Jeanne of Bourbon, are wearing during each stage of the ceremony. What is made visual here is the fact of investiture, that what happens when a king of

France is crowned is a form of re-dressing that has less to do with earthly power than it has to do with the miraculous action of the Holy Spirit upon a king anointed with the oil of Clovis. Even the powers vested in the churchmen who celebrate the ceremony are subtly secondary to the drama taking place between king and God. Thus, though the churchmen are agents for such divine magic, their robes, embroidered with the fleur-de-lis of France, proclaim them as ancillary to the king, in whom France is concentrated and constituted.

The *Traité* proclaims its magic more overtly.[14] The first treatise on the French coronation ceremony, it was composed by Jean Golein, a Carmelite and professor at the University of Paris, who was also confessor to Jeanne of Bourbon. Golein was known for his translations, most importantly for his French translation of Durandus's *Rational of Divine Offices,* to which he appended his treatise on the French coronation ceremony. The original manuscript was in the library of Charles V and bears his signature. Like the *Coronation Book,* it passed to the duke of Bedford, but was purchased in England in 1441 and is now back in France (Paris, Bibliothèque nationale de France, MS fr. 437). By commissioning Jean Golein to translate into French William Durandus's (ca. 1230–96) popular *Rational of Divine Offices,* which is a highly symbolic discussion of the Latin liturgy, and to insert a treatise on the French coronation ceremony into it, Charles V evinced his absolute comprehension of the very terms of the power he sought to unite and pass on.[15] Golein's opening sentence links the consecration of a French king, and Charles in particular, to the sacramental symbolism and efficacy discussed by Durandus. He begins with an account of the sacred oil, with which only the French kings were supposedly anointed. Whereas all kings were anointed, only the French were anointed with "sainte liqueur celestiele qui est en la sainte ampole la quele est a saint Remi de Reins conservee et gardee, comme celle qui fu du ciel aportee par la main des angelz pour oindre les nobles et dignes Roys de france . . ." (Jackson, "*Traité,*" 309). The French king therefore need recognize no temporal lord: he is subject to divine law and invested with his power (which is also his meaning) by a divine act of oblation. Golein assimilates the anointing to the baptism of Christ in a way that stresses sacramental change: "Aussi comme il plut a dieu le pere a dire a son filz en lonction du baptesme. *Hic est filius meus dilectus in quo michi complacui,* et le saint esperit descendi en forme de columbe qui loingni *oleo leticie pre participibus suis.* Et le filz en char humaine recut celle sainte consecration" (309–10). Anointed, then newly clothed in regalia whose meanings are "mystical," the king "est signifiance de mixtion Royal avec prestrie, de quoy il est escript *Vos estis genus electum regale sacerdocium*" (316). The king is thereby more than the royal defender of the Church; he himself has a priestly function.

Golein's treatise, which is as ornately symbolic as Durandus's, follows Durandus's program in explicating the meaning of each detail of the coronation ceremony. Since Durandus's *Rational* is devoted to the meaning of the sacraments, Golein is, by association, stressing the sacred character of the dramatic text he thereby explains. By its end, the king has been transformed by the *sacre,* or by Golein's discussion of it, into a figure for divine efficacy. But, as a sacerdotal figure, he is also the one through whom grace operates. He can make because he has been made. Short of proclaiming Charles divine, it is hard to see how much farther Golein could have gone in his effort to associate the French Crown with sacramental ordering, with the alignment of cause and effect. There are many statements of royal power, power that scholars have quite rightly suggested that Richard came to envy during the final years of his reign, when he tried to adapt Valois majesty to his own public image (Saul, *Richard II,* 349; Jones, *Royal Policy*). For example, Golein insists that the king of France recognizes no temporal lord, that he communicates directly with the holy. Golein then includes two prayers, one of the king to the Virgin Mary and one to Jesus Christ, that are not included in the official *ordo* of Charles V (Jackson, "*Traité,*" 311, n. 43). Not only does he allegorize each part of the ceremony, but he devotes a good deal of attention to the *regalia,* discussing the meaning of symbols of power, like the scepter and banner, and items of clothing that make up the newly clothed king. Golein brings his treatise to a close by reaffirming the priestly and therefore *male* nature of the French king ("Ne onques femme naprocha si pres de ordre prestral comme lonction Royal"), suggesting more or less baldly that a study of the French coronation ceremony demands someone adept in the terms of theology (323, 324). He claims, of course, more than political science; he claims a special wisdom underlies the royal mystique, or he claims divine magic of the type that inhabits sacramental change. As in the sacrament of the altar, the ministers of the Church are servants of a power they do not themselves possess. All lies in the king's touch.

This is heady stuff, and, along with Raoul de Presles and Nicolas Oresme, Golein formed part of a distinguished company of men whom Charles V entrusted with creating a national literature of rule in the vernacular. Charles added to his vernacular library of instructive texts (which can be seen as an index of his far-reaching political sensibility) by maintaining a corps of clerics who supplied translations into French of politically relevant works by John of Salisbury, Seneca, Vincent of Beauvais, Barthalemeus Anglicus, Petrarch, Aristotle, and St. Augustine.[16] Thus, in addition to devotional manuscripts, Scripture (both Latin and French), coronation *ordines,* historical chronicles, and works of mathematical and scientific instruction (as well as many geomancies), he displayed a pragmatic interest in texts that grounded political order in a firmly Aristotelian endorsement of natural ordering. The thirteenth-century writers, Giles of Rome and Brunetto Latini are of obvious importance here, for both were transmitters of Aristotelian political thought.[17] Both *Li Livres dou Tresor* and *De regimine principium* describe the body politic as a manifestation of the prince himself: the prince's ability to create a system of order for himself and his household is the central determinant of the well-ordered state. If Brunetto Latini seems more interested in explaining how to construct the image of lordship within what is a political arena and Giles of Rome more inclined to outline the underlying philosophy of good governance, both writers reflect the Aristotelian emphasis upon a natural order that the well-governed man or state must recognize or else risk personal and/or civil chaos. Giles of Rome begins with the techniques of self-government, covering the emotions, the passions, the virtues, and habits. In Book II he describes the family, a man's relations with wife and children, as well as the details of household management. Only in Book III does he move to the subject of civil government. What he articulates is a series of homologous and interdependent systems, in which a man's reasoned and loving care for his own nature and those of his wife and children cannot be separated from his ability to rule wisely an obedient people. This same method of organization gave Christine de Pizan the rhetorical structure for *Le Livre des fais et Bonnes Meurs du Sage Roy Charles V,* which she was commissioned to write after Charles's death.[18] She not only drew upon historical sources like the *Grandes Chroniques* in her presentation of French kingship and origins, but assimilated Charles to Aristotle's wise ruler, whose sagacity, justice, largess, chastity, familial devotion, sobriety, truth, and piety form the core of a nation whose chivalric glory magnifies the wisdom of its prince. Christine's portrait of Charles was as true to life as an icon can be, for Charles was indeed learned, temperate, deeply patriarchal, known for his interest in his own children and for his regard for his queen, and at all times conscious of the prestige and stability of the crown he inherited.

The control Charles exerted over the production of French cultural texts was minute. For example, as C. R. Sherman and A. D. Hedeman have demonstrated, Charles did not simply commission the rewriting of history; he or his court oversaw the miniatures of the king inserted into such manuscripts. They thereby presented a consistent and recognizable portrait type of the king that was used even in the initials that decorated royal charters.[19] This is the image of the wise ruler who presided over a kingdom organized according to the principles of a common good. Thus what Charles promulgated was far more than a reputation for *bibliophilia*. By insisting on the translation of key classical texts into French, he sponsored a deed "pour le profit et utilité de votre royaume" (Sherman, *Imaging Aristotle*, p. 7). This phrase, which appears in Raoul de Presles's preface to his translation of the *City of God*, is cast in language that, as Sherman notes, also appears in official documents recording payments to artists; in other words, it is official language. Thus, Charles has asked for the translation, which serves the good of "his" realm. The humanism for which Charles is praised is directly related to the state of France, or to the household of the king, that relational construct presided over by the beneficent and wise ruler.

Kingdoms, like households, were conceived of as corporate hierarchies; thus, instruction was necessary for all entrusted with responsibility. If young men were to grow into wise rulers (in the broadest sense of that term), they must be taught the elements of good rule. If young women were to become good wives, they must be taught how to understand their position within such a corporate body and how to maintain that body in as orderly a manner as possible. Here, the *Ethics*, the *Politics*, and the pseudo-Aristotelian *Economics* became the authoritative texts necessary for a political education. Oresme described the *Ethics* as teaching good morals and the *Politics* as teaching the art and science of government; the *Economics* taught the more mundane but equally necessary art of household management.[20] Oresme clearly saw all three Aristotelian texts as interdependent, for he links them at the beginning of the *Yconomique*, saying that the *Ethics* are about the mastery of the self, the *Economics* about managing a family group, and the *Politics* about establishing the science of managing groups or of governing cities (801). In the work itself, he presents the household as a kind of kingdom whose borders need be very carefully guarded. If externally contained, internally the household should be well organized, with a place for everything. Within the boundaries of this kingdom, the wife serves as the sub-regent, who exercises powers of dominion within it, but not over her husband's money. The success of the husband's care for the education and regulation of wife, servants, and children is manifest in the children themselves who, if carefully trained, will grow up to care for the parents in their old age. The emphasis throughout is upon the naturalness of the marriage bond and upon the rationality that is a key component of all human relationships. If this is a picture of a little kingdom, it is a kingdom in which the powers of the just husband (or prince) are unlimited because they are just.[21]

Furthermore, the *Yconomique* seems less focused upon the nobility than upon a household not defined so much by class than by methodology of rule, since the household may or may not have more than one servant. In other words, the *Yconomique* does not present itself as an exclusively aristocratic *ordo* that depends upon knightly culture, but as a discussion of a household as strictly monarchic as that of Charles's France. In fact, what Charles had, with a good deal of effort and intelligence, established in France was his own authority. When he came to the throne, he was not perceived as a figure of strength, but he not only managed to deal with both internal and external threats to his position but manufactured for himself an image that came to be identified with that of France itself. This text also sparked a vogue for books of household management during the fourteenth century, books that seem to have held a real interest for Charles V. He had had Pietro Crescenzi's *Duodecim libri ruralium commodarum* (1300) translated; the last quarter of the century saw four works, all in French, of the same type: Jean de Brie's *Le bon verger* (1375), Jean Bautilher's *La somme rurale* (1380), the anonymous books of the Knight of la Tour Landry (1371), and of the *Menagier de Paris* (1393).[22] The political relevance inherent in *Le Livre de Yconomique* is manifest in the opening statements whereby a household, which "unlike a state has only one figure of authority," is expressly compared to a monarchy, to a nonconstitutional government where power is not shared. The wife is not seen as a servant but as someone who requires rules delineating her role and the type of training and instructions required to create of her a sort of sub-regent whose dominion is derived from her husband's favor and will (Oresme, 786, 809–11).

As with other texts commissioned or encouraged by Charles V, the theory of government that underlies the discussion of marriage is designed to emphasize its corporate nature. Sherman notes that Oresme's glosses on the *Economics* emphasize the companionate nature of marriage, which she links to that between Charles V and his queen, Jeanne de Bourbon (*Imaging Aristotle,* 301). However, the picture of marriage that is fundamental to Charles's cultural program is itself a political construct.[23] Similarly, in the *De Moneta,* Oresme's treatise on coinage that he derived from Aristotle's *Politics,* Oresme seeks to articulate the corporate rationale validating all forms of commercial exchange accomplished through coinage bearing the stamp of the authority issuing it, but not belonging to that authority. Rather, the coin of the realm belongs to the realm, and the prince has no right to tamper with its standards. Such a prince would thereby exercise tyrannical powers over something belonging to the public.[24] If the face on the coin signifies the good of the realm, the face produced and placed into circulation by the court of Charles V was that of benign control.

More important yet, the quality of control exerted by Charles V was of a sophisticated variety that maintained itself by staging textual performances of dissent. For example, *Le Songe du Vergier,* the long dialogue between a Clerk and a Knight seeking to define the powers of the two arms of the state, was written at the request of the king and finished in a Latin version in 1376. The French text was in the hands of the king by 1378 (*Songe,* ed. Schnerb-Lièvre). Whether or not Oresme himself wrote the work as some think, its author was clearly familiar with Oresme's writings. It is addressed to the king, whom it praises for his power, wisdom, and peace, for the tranquility of his people, and for his humility. The *Songe* does not hesitate to address itself to issues of profound significance for the medieval conception of the political corporation. The Knight and the Clerk debate the relative powers of the monarch and the pope, the ways in which ecclesiastical corruption compromises ecclesiastical authority, the merits of sexual abstinence and marriage, ecclesiastical wealth, and the moral status of the mendicant orders; they end by debating the doctrine of the Immaculate Conception. The author gives the last word to the Church in the Clerk's affirmation of the doctrine and his praise of Mary, but the *Songe* nonetheless stands as a testimony to the powers of the state and of the French king, in particular. By creating a space for debate, by frequently putting into the Knight's mouth some of the more extreme positions (including a dispraise of chastity that sometimes can seem like an early Wycliffite attack on clerical abstinence), the author of the *Songe* subtly presents a picture of Charles V that declares his manifold power, his utterly pacific and intellectual nature that never stoops to tyrannical control. Thus, in the Epilogue, where the dream is passed on to the king for his discretion and understanding, Charles is imaged as the one who, in deciding the relative merits of the opposing arguments, effects a mutually beneficial peace between the powers of church and state. In other words, Charles looks to no higher power for adjudication. Both the more aggressive Knight and the Clerk defend the special status of the French Crown, the sanctity of which does not depend on a ceremony of the Church (else all kings would share in this status) (75–78). Implicitly, the powers of the Church are presented as secondary (or separate) to those of the king: the Church depends upon the king of France for its defense from those who, like the Knight, would seek to undermine its authority.[25] While the work presents itself as debate, it raises potentially inflammatory subjects only to muffle them in a stream of rhetoric that is finally deferred to the king for his judgment.

If we compare this work to the sorts of criticisms aimed at ecclesiastical authority by John Wyclif at about the same time, the nature of Charles's policy appears even more studied. By allowing an official forum for a vernacular exploration of the nature of civil power, he at once sanctions dissent and demystifies it. In the realm of the just prince, the body politic is allowed its voice. The dialogic murmur of the academy has a place within the magically sacral rule of the heir to Clovis. The issue finally is the king's face, the face patterned and produced and stamped on the coins that signify the people's business. In his *De Moneta*, Nicolas Oresme had discussed the literally bimetallic nature of coinage and the fact that the king must not alter the ratio unless the value of the metals is materially altered by a new source of supply. Charles V understood more than the art of money; he understood the principle of alloyed mixtures.

The one metal gave strength to the other—the magic of anointing, the rational arts of good rule; if the alloy held, the coin rang true.

What I have sketched is a recipe for statecraft that went far beyond in sophistication anything in the England of the 1370s or 1380s. Moreover, it is a recipe that Charles certainly inherited, understood, and reworked, but one that seems to have become attractive to English thinkers (or comprehensible to them) over a decade later. The conflict, and thus the relationship, between the two countries was complicated by the deaths of the Black Prince and of Edward III, by the accession of a child to the English throne in 1378, by the death of Charles V, by the English Rising of 1381, and by the developing crisis of regal authority (in which I include the tensions among court factions over the war with France) in England, and, finally, but not the least, by the controversies that were generated by and around the figure of John Wyclif. If Charles V had made a safe place for debate in his household, the English household looked more like the barely contained chaos of Chaucer's *Parliament of Fowles*.[26] Moreover, during the last years of his reign, Edward III was in no condition to think his way through to a policy on the royal image. It was a subject that concerned him in the early days of his authority and one that was clearly of interest to those surrounding him.[27] The manuscript made for presentation at the marriage of Philippa of Hainaut to Edward late in 1326 powerfully suggests an attempt to co-opt for him the model of the good ruler that the Valois kings were so eager to appropriate for themselves.[28] The compilation begins with Brunetto Latini's *Tresor*, which gave the ruler all he needed to know about the universe, about the vices and the virtues, and about the rhetoric of government, the romance *Le dit de Fauvain* by Raoul le Petit, a treatise by Julius Caesar (perhaps the Gallic Wars?), a copy of Giles of Rome's *De regimine*, the Statutes of England, a translation of the Pater Noster into French, and the coronation *ordo* of the kings of France.

However, by the time that Charles V was cementing his military strategy of negotiation and harassment and what Daniel Poiron has described as his centralization of culture (*Le Poète*, 616), Edward III was far removed from the business of governing, his oldest son, Edward the Black Prince, was incapable of exercising such authority, and John of Gaunt was set on the course of a career that never quite earned him the prize he wanted. Moreover, the complicated and many-pronged threat to authority that was already taking shape in England needed a sovereign of real insight and ability, one given to the sort of study that characterized France's "lawyer king." For example, the challenge to ecclesiastical authority posed by John Wyclif in the mid 1370s was sponsored by John of Gaunt, in part, in an effort to undo the work of the Good Parliament of 1376 (Holmes, *Good Parliament*). In the years between the Good Parliament and the Papal Schism of 1378, Wyclif broadcast his ideas with the tacit support of the duke of Lancaster. John of Gaunt wished to promote clerical taxation; John Wyclif, as Michael Wilks has described him, sought to reform the realm.[29] However, Wyclif was not sui generis. Giles of Rome had said that all human power was invalid without a foundation of supernatural grace; Richard Fitzralph had denied lordship to anyone in a state of mortal sin (Gwynn, *English Austin Friars*, chapter 4). Nor had Wyclif been silent during his years at Oxford. But with the Papal Schism, Wyclif's arguments about the foundations of authority acquired real force and consequently threatened the status quo in ways that were not acceptable to Gaunt. Nonetheless, Wyclif's perceived threat to authority grew out of a decade when English authority had already weakened itself. The shadow cast by Alice Perrers onto the English throne could only have seemed darker in comparison to the eminence of Jeanne of Bourbon, who embodied the ideal of the true wife and queen. The picture in *Piers Plowman* of Lady Meed captures the irresolutions of a world where *commercium* seemed no longer to bear the impress of the king's face.

But to what status quo was Wyclif a threat? To argue that the social order of the late Middle Ages, and particularly its construction by the Valois kings and especially by Charles V, was inextricably bound up with an intense and carefully worked out sacramentalism is not to deny a religious mystery in favor of a social one.[30] It is rather to suggest the ways in which what seem two spheres, theological and social or political, mutually respond to one another. The French understanding of kingship and its legacy in the Valois articulation of royal potency can be seen as a development of sacramental theology, just as the fervor that came to define the late medieval theological discussions of the sacraments can be seen as, in some measure, a response to the economic and political shifts of the period. Neither purely materialistic nor purely intellectual or devotional, the worlds of faith and politics continually alter one another because they are not distinct. Charles's cultural program, to which the emphasis upon sacramental kingship was integral, encouraged and/

or patronized studies of statecraft, of household management, of the education of the young, of the coinage of money, of the place of the
Church, and of the role of the sovereign. This cultural program was one
part of his response to the national or political situation he faced early in
his reign. But, the difficulties that presented themselves to Charles V
upon his succession to the French throne were very different from what
lay ahead for Richard II. Moreover, Charles was not only older and had
already assumed much responsibility while his father, the king, was in
captivity in England, but he had had a chance almost to fail early in his
public life. Richard came to the throne as a boy who had known nothing
of rule, much less of failure. Moreover, he came to an England that not
only contained the "normal" amount of anticlericalism associated with
papal taxes and charges of corruption and conflicted interest, but an
England where the increasing theological speculations of John Wyclif
gave an added edge to what might be otherwise simply excoriated as the
ethical and/or institutional lapses in the marriage between church and
state.

Until Wyclif began to challenge papal authority and the doctrine of
transubstantiation, he can be seen as belonging to the world of Oxford, a
world of vigorous academic argument that sometimes spilled over into
the public sphere when it was useful for it to do so. But after 1377 or
1378, when Wyclif was called to account by Gregory XI for his political
views and chose to question or to reject Rome's authority to censure
him, he began to take a path that would lead him finally out of Oxford.[31]
In 1379 he attacked the theology of the Eucharist, averring that the miracle of faith does not depend upon the words of a priest, that the words
make the occasion, not the miracle; the miracle takes place in the heart.
But what saved Wyclif from the severest penalties for so challenging the
spiritual authority of the Church to make and unmake was, as K. B.
McFarlane suggested, the very crisis of authority that obtained in England for the rest of Wyclif's life (*John Wycliffe*, 89). Edward III, who had
not truly reigned for almost a decade, had died in 1377, and a boy sat on the
English throne. In 1378 Gregory XI died, and Christendom was for thirty
years ruled, depending upon its political allegiances, by one of two popes.
Rome would not risk alienating England by persecuting an English the-
ologian, and Wyclif, though censured by the English ecclesiastical authorities, was nonetheless allowed to write and die in peace. Deprived of
Oxford, he was not deprived of his powers of rhetoric. The authority he

questioned, by its very weakness, made it possible for him to continue to question it.

The two issues—papal authority and the Real Presence in the Eucharist—are, of course, linked.[32] Wyclif did not deny the presence of Christ in the elements of the Mass. He denied that a priest could turn bread and wine into the actual body and blood of Christ, thus altering substance while the accidents of bread and wine remained. Wyclif, as he himself pointed out, was not alone in affirming the sacramental and spiritual (rather than the sacramental and actual) presence of Christ in the Eucharist, but, by the fourteenth century, such views were heterodox. For Wyclif, not only did the doctrine of transubstantiation seem idolatry of the carnal, but giving that magical power of change to a possibly corrupt human being, whose words were thought to alter the nature of matter, seemed to place the emphasis upon the wrong aspect of the Mass. Why should he worship false magic when there was more than enough true magic in Christ's presence in the hearts of the faithful? In May 1381, around the time he vacated Oxford for Lutterworth, he published his *Confession,* which contained his views on the Eucharist.[33] Here he reiterated his arguments against the doctrine of transubstantiation, backing them up with Scripture, as well as with authorities like Ignatius, Cyprian, Ambrose, Augustine, and Jerome. In the *Confession,* Wyclif raises an earlier set of authorities against those of the contemporary church, but, in effect, he raises the evidence of the human senses and the recesses of the human heart against the hierarchically conceived authority of the Roman curia and its priests. In so doing, Wyclif did more than raise the standard of nonconformity (to appropriate K. B. McFarlane's term); he began a process by which authority itself could be ignored or rejected. And he located that process in the heart. He insisted upon the faithful and predestined heart, but the heart itself, as anyone—Chaucer included—knows, is never still for long. Once Wyclif's views became theologically extreme, rather than politically useful, he lost the overt support of men like John of Gaunt.[34] They, like Charles V of France, would have understood all too well upon what base power lay.

Moreover, in England, Wyclif's questioning of ecclesiastical authority and sacramental magic came at a time of great social and political stress when civil authority was itself a subject of critical inquiry. The Rising in 1381, the political tensions of the 1380s, parliamentary dissatisfaction with the young Richard II, which culminated in the acts of the

Appellants near the end of the decade all helped to create a world with very different needs and a very different lexicon than the world overseen by Charles V. What England had was not so much a world whose verities were lost or eroding, but a world where the very identity of authority—and consequently of community—was not yet clearly defined. Nor did England have a king who could see his way to a solution for a potentially bad situation; it lacked the safe arena, the "theater," to use the Knight's term for Theseus's tournament space, for dissent. Instead, it had conflict, some of it in the streets of London, some of it in Parliament. Let us return to Wyclif's *Confession* in which he affirms the real presence in the host but not Christ's actual, essential presence. About midway through his argument, he stops to sum up the three ways in which "secta nostra" differs from the "sectae signorum" (Shirley, *Fasciculi*, 125). The word *secta*, of course, was a charged term, thrown about by many in an effort to categorize an opposing group as essentially marginal, wrongheaded, or subversive. Here, Wyclif uses it to characterize the established, prelatical Church, modifying it with the word *signorum*, meaning of signs, of symbols, of tokens, of images. In the context of the middle years of the fourteenth century, especially considering the efforts the French court had made to reinforce just such a belief in a sacramentally endowed view of lordship, Wyclif's stark dismissal of a whole universe of meaningful signs, of images that embodied, in some mysterious way, a divine essence, comes like a statement of negation. What you see is what you get: "our sect" adores the sacrament of the altar, but the outlines of the material universe are not affected by the act of consecration. Though he allows for mystery, it is a different mystery, one where the Aristotelian concept of good rule no longer is married to the magic, healing person of the king. What was played out later in the scene between Wat Tyler and the young King Richard at Mile End may not have been inspired by Wyclif, but perhaps the authorities were right to see the two challenges as part of the same challenge—what was threatened was sacrament itself.[35]

However, even more germane to the issue of sacramental kingship and community is the drama produced by the lords during the Merciless Parliament of 1387–88. The accounts we have of the Merciless Parliament are powerful testimonies to the Appellants' self-conscious use of Parliament as a theater of the realm. Their dramatic entrance, arm in arm, wearing golden coats, and the judicial order of the trials themselves, all carefully written into the official historic record of proceedings, evince just how thoroughly they understood the uses of political ritual. Thus, at the parliament's end, the lords, who had also masterminded the trials of Michael de la Pole, Nicholas Brembre, Simon Burley, Robert de Vere, and others, then "in full and cheerful submission" made the customary allegiances to their king.[36] After both king and lords had re-taken oaths binding them to one another in law, the king agreed to pardons for the perpetrators (thus preventing himself from avenging the harm done to him and his associates); after the epilogue of feudal homage was concluded, the parliament came to an end.

The immediate "audience" for this production was the king himself, who watched and participated in what undermined his own sovereignty. In order to maintain his throne, he had little choice. Where he quibbled— and this is leaving aside his ongoing pleas for his close associates, his assertions of their innocence of the charges brought against them—is over the issue of sacrality. Two incidents drawn from the written and frequently conflicting contemporary accounts of the Merciless Parliament capture an underlying conversation about sacrality that went on to become the defining concern of Richard's mature reign, which was also, I believe, a quest for a regal and communal identity.[37] What is especially intriguing about these two events and the various written accounts of them is their position in the semi-liminal space of the Merciless Parliament when all the participants inhabited positions and roles not necessarily connected to the roles and positions they had inhabited previously and would inhabit afterwards.[38] For Richard the opportunities were many— whether player, victim, or king, or all three, he could only succeed by determining an identity for himself. But, for the chronicle writers who recorded these events, that search for a royal identity—made either by Richard himself or by his advisers—was also bound up with the articulation of an emerging national identity, an identity that was challenged by what was billed as a Lollard threat to the order of the realm.

The first event that I would like to discuss, which Michael Wilks has noted, is the investigation, or discussion, of Lollardy that occupied four days of the Merciless Parliament, just after the trials of Sir Simon Burley, Sir John Beauchamp, Sir James Berners, and Sir John Salisbury. The Monk of Westminster says that a great deal of talk broke out in full Parliament about the Lollards, their preaching and their books that led people astray. Though some Lollards were summoned to appear before a tribunal headed by the pope's subcollector, the Lollards refused to answer the charges against them because they did not grant the members of the tribunal (some of whom were friars) authority over them (Hector and Harvey, *Westminster Chronicle*, 318–20). A few weeks later, when the Monk again recounts the King's concern for the life of Sir Simon Burley, the subject of these Lollards and their condemnation by the pope's tribunal is again noted. Directly thereafter the Monk describes Burley's execution (330–32). Henry Knighton also includes an account of Lollard errors immediately after his brief account of the events of the Merciless Parliament. His account of the Lollards is fuller than that of the Monk of Westminster's. According to Knighton, the Lollards were summoned to Parliament and reproached for their errors, which he then lists. Knighton's list is closely related to the *Twenty-Five Articles*, the confessional tract designed to answer objections to Lollardy raised by outsiders.[39] After he catalogues the false beliefs of the Lollards, he describes both the lords and the commons as beseeching the King to remedy a situation that threatened to swamp the ecclesiastical vessel ("navem"), the "ark" of the faith wanting governance and the realm itself ("regnum Anglie") at risk (Knighton, *Chronicle* 438–39). The king responded by not only ordering his bishops to do their duty, to chastise offenders, scrutinize books, and seek to unite the people in orthodox faith, but sent out letters patent to every county in the kingdom, ordering that books and beliefs be scrupulously examined. Just before Knighton includes the text of the letter, he remarks that this had little effect because "nondum hora correccionis aduenit" (438–39). Knighton's concern with the "hour of correction" (still some years in the future) deflects attention from the curious set piece of a Lollard trial inserted into an account of the Merciless Parliament. A play within a play, it purports to stage a semi-idyllic relationship between the king and his Parliament at a time when the king himself hung in the balance. Moreover, that semi-idyllic relationship between king and Parliament is figured as a workable hierarchical relationship, in sharp contrast to the force, and show of force, that drove the Merciless Parliament.

Let me turn to an earlier portion of Knighton's script, whose very drama and color capture the high theater of the events.[40] In his entry for 26 December 1387, Knighton describes the Appellants and their army, arms and armor shining, drawn up before the gates of London, receiving the keys to the city from its mayor. After encamping in the city, which quite naturally had no desire to risk their displeasure, the next day they

went to the Tower to meet with the king. They found Richard in a vineyard there, in a tent, ("sedentem in papilione apud Turrim in quadam
uinea, regaliter cum indumentis aureis strata") "royally arrayed with hang-
ings." The scene, or Knighton's description of it—the regally hung tent,
the vineyard, the king who appears to command the scene—makes a
point that the Monk of Westminster's account does not make. The Monk,
who correctly assigns this scene to 30 December, describes the Appellants
and five hundred armed men visiting the king. They find him in the
open, enthroned near the chapel, and do him reverence by prostrating
themselves three times before him. After this, they adjourn to the chapel
where they castigate the king for his bad faith and force him to submit
to the rule ("regimini dominorum") of the lords. Walsingham, too, emphasizes the force of the lords, their overpowering the king, who, according to Walsingham, was threatened with deposition. One chronicler in a
manuscript from Whalley Abbey, Lancashire, described by M. V. Clarke
in 1937, states that Richard was actually deposed for three days but was
reinstated because Thomas of Woodstock and Henry of Derby quarreled
about the succession.[41] In sharp contrast to these accounts of Richard's
ordeal, Knighton's biblical scene with its vineyard and tented king seems
to hold out the promise of a sort of renewal or harmony. The conversation he includes between king and lords is cast in the courtly speech of
host and guest, not of prisoner and guards.

Knighton's account of the Lollard investigation in the midst of the
Merciless Parliament similarly figures Richard's power as part of the organic unity of the realm. Thus, the lords petition the king for a remedy
for the incipient chaos of Lollardy, and the king listens and consents to
the wise counsel of the *whole* Parliament ("Rex uero sano consilio tocius
parliamenti") (Knighton, *Chronicle,* 438). Richard is then presented as
"ordering" ("iussit"), as the agent of the will of those who are acting for
the good of the realm, as having the power to span the realm with his letters patent and directives. Knighton inserts a copy of this letter into the
chronicle at this point. He follows it with a unique document, apparently
from parliamentary commons, asking Richard to assume his regality, to
redress the abuses prompted by the Appellants (442–50). Shortly thereafter, he presents his account of the Merciless Parliament. Knighton's
account of the events of 1387–88 seems designed to represent sacramental kingship even as the Appellants were transgressing the boundaries
between anointed king and lord. Moreover, the accounts by both the

Monk of Westminster and Knighton seem to suggest that the lords tried to displace their own violations of sanctuary (in that term's broadest sense) upon the Lollards, who can be accused of splitting the Church and thus the kingdom. Whether or not Wilks is right in thinking that the Lollards must have opposed the Appellants (and thus were members of the king's party, possibly in Parliament), this written account of the scene strongly suggests that what was at issue was sacramental power or authority.

The twenty-five errors of the Lollards that Knighton includes in his account of the Merciless Parliament relentlessly question the authority of the clergy to mediate between humankind and God. From the opening statement, which asserts that no pope since St. Sylvester has been a true pope, to subsequent denials of the powers of the clergy to grant indulgences, offer absolution for sin, or excommunicate sinners, the opinions quiz the status of ordained priests. Other "errors" include the call for priestly purity, apostolic poverty, and disengagement from secular offices and an assertion that the consecrated bread of the sacrament of the altar is a sign of a thing, not the thing itself ("signum rei, non ipsa res") (436). The remainder focus upon the self, upon the efficacy of solitary prayer, confession, and devotion, and upon the idolatry encouraged by devotion to the saints. The "agenda" is certainly a familiar one to anyone who has read Lollard treatises, but, within the context of the Merciless Parliament and the business it had set itself of dismantling Richard's network of friends and associates, it seems a peculiarly studied effort to offset any potentially negative thoughts about the official transgressions of the Appellants with a vivid account of the Lollard threat to order. The text of Lollard error that Knighton creates manifests that the Lollard challenge was to the fundamental idea of sacramental authority that underpinned the order of medieval ecclesiastical *and* social institutions. By implicitly locating spiritual authority in the self, they inevitably raised the specter of pluralism, of relativism.

What the Appellants were engaged in—the forceful correction of the king's misgovernance—was not unlike what the Lollards proposed to do in the ecclesiastical realm. The lords' infringement upon the king's person—canopied within a semi-idyllic vineyard —Richard certainly saw as a violation of his sanctity. The vineyard is, of course, a potent detail. Knighton probably embellished the scene between the king and the Appellants, for his account is certainly different from the Monk of Westminster's, who was closer to the action. However Knighton's version has a point, for he captured something of the encounter's importance for him, just as his attempt to turn it into a conversation rather than a show of force suggests his own reading of how kings and lords ought to behave. What he describes is a scene that resonates with the imagery of Old Testament kingship, just as Richard's positioning himself as enthroned in the open, rather than within the chapel, bespeaks his own awareness of the moment's dramatic needs and thus his understanding of the location of center stage. (The Monk of Westminster's account of the lords' prostration before Richard evinces a similarly dramatic impulse with its own message of political relationships, but it is less elaborately drawn than Knighton's.) By giving such primacy to the inquiry by the Merciless Parliament into Lollard error, an inquiry that is also recorded by the Monk of Westminster, Knighton points up the theme of authority, spiritual in this case, and links it firmly to a picture of a king who acts with the advice and will of Parliament. He has, in effect, made a picture whose truth is ideological rather than actual.

A similar urgency about sacrality underlies the Monk of Westminster's account of a second key event of the Merciless Parliament, the arrest of Robert Tresilian in late winter 1388. Tresilian, accused of being a false justice, had been one of the justices to whom Richard had turned in late summer 1387 when he needed an answer about the extent of royal power.[42] Though brought to trial, Tresilian had so far eluded his captors until parliamentary proceedings were already underway.

There are various accounts of his arrest. According to the Monk of Westminster, he was found in one of the sacrist's houses within the sanctuary of Westminster (Hector and Harvey, *Westminster Chronicle*, 310, n. 4). In order to take him, the lords had to ignore the bounds of sanctuary, something that had brought trouble to John of Gaunt in 1377, when he insulted the bishop of London in St. Paul's (Armitage-Smith, *John of Gaunt*, 151–53). This time there was no trouble from an angry mob. However, accounts of the incident suggest that contemporaries saw it as significant enough to warrant careful fashioning.[43] The Monk of Westminster, as he does for the entire Merciless Parliament, provides two versions of what happened. The first is taken from the Parliament Rolls. Officially, "Robert Tresilyan fuist pris hors de Westm' et amesne en plein parlement," thus outside Westminster. Later, the Monk offers his own version, which I have already mentioned. Froissart botches the order of the events and their parliamentary significance and presents the capture of Tresilian as high farce, the Chief Justice lurking in an inn as a tenant, who is then recognized and apprehended by a squire of the duke of Gloucester's. Favent presents an equally colorful version in which he foregrounds the crowd that apprehends Tresilian. Near the end of his Latin account of the arrest, Favent captures the popular voice in the cry, "We havet him. We havet him." Knighton describes Tresilian as hiding before his discovery, and Walsingham simply describes Tresilian as captured early. These accounts do not broach the issue of sanctuary, and the accounts of Froissart and Favent compose a sequence of events in which the crowd is the active force behind Tresilian's apprehension and arrest. Favent goes even farther and describes Tresilian as wearing russet, as a wolf in sheep's clothing. He then describes Richard's friends, whom the Appellants had accused of treason, as thorns, thistles, and tares, language that, of course, was also used to describe the followers of John Wyclif. But the Monk of Westminster flatly states that the justice "was in the sanctuary of Westminster." He describes the arrest as a violation of sacred space, wherein he was forcibly dragged in the fell hands of the above-named lords out of the sanctuary. The scene, then, is a dramatically different one, depending on who is describing it. The Monk of Westminster depicts the lords as the driving force. He describes the duke of Gloucester as taking a mace and arresting Tresilian himself, shielding the judge from an angry crowd. The Rolls of Parliament are more remote, and Favent describes what is a popular arrest by the city itself, going so far as to suggest that Tresilian and the others, disguised as servants of the king, were rather to be seen as thorns and tares in the field of the realm, thus as violators of a higher order.

What is at issue here is more than parliamentary ethics or procedure. As Tresilian, who was no innocent himself, argued, he had the privilege of sanctuary. It was an argument later made by King Richard, whose own sacred space had been violated by the position he was made to take in the proceedings. The subject of Westminster's privileges were, of course, of a good deal of interest to the Monk who wrote its chronicle, and he refers to the issue several times, giving the arguments a good deal of space (Hector and Harvey, *Westminster Chronicle,* 312, 324). The incident serves as an occasion for talking about what could not be discussed. Walsingham is most succinct. Just before the parliament, Richard had attempted to change his mind about meeting with Parliament. The

lords told him that if he did not do as he had agreed, they would renounce him. Later, Walsingham tersely describes Richard's role in the
sentence against his old tutor, Sir Simon Burley, making it clear that
the king had no choice: "Deinde exactum est juramentum a Rege, ad
standum regulationi procerum; et non solum a Rege, sed a cunctis regni
incolis, idem juramentum est expetitum" (*Historia,* 2:174–75). The privileges of Westminster may well have been transgressed, but what was at
stake here was the broader concept that also underlay that of sanctuary.

(There is an irony only history can produce in the fact that the Chan-
cellor of England, Thomas Arundel, pronounced a judgment against
those privileges, to which the king and his associates dissented. As archbishop of Canterbury under Henry IV, who at this point stood with the
Appellants, Arundel would threaten with treason all who violated England's sacred spaces. But for now, Richard defended the Church, Arundel, the secular realm, or secular pragmatism. On the other hand, though
the incident was covered over in the official record of Tresilian's arrest
and recreated in other terms by Favent, both the duke of Gloucester and
Sir John Cobham recognized the enormity of what they had done but
not wished entered in the official record and in May of 1388 presented
themselves to the abbot of Westminster for his correction.)

As many historians have pointed out, most recently Nigel Saul, it is
the search for an ideology of power that seems to have preoccupied
Richard during the last decade of his reign. But in the accounts of the
Merciless Parliament, we can find evidence for a submerged or displaced
conversation that helps us understand why the issue of Lollardy is en-
twined through the written history of the period. As scholars like Gordon
Kipling and Geoffrey Koziol have reminded us, political ritual constitutes
a language of conflict and ambiguity, a measure of perceptions, or a test
of strength. In Richard's early attempts to define himself as sacred
space—or in the chronicle writers' curiously elastic descriptions of scenes
that may or may not have occurred—we can find the beginnings of a
royal performance already understood as iconic at a time when the very
subject of signs, of sacramental reality, was a subject of contestation.
What seems to have been performed, or written as performed, was expi-
atory, in the sense that the lords knew the dangers of devaluing royal
power and, at the same time, displaced that devaluation onto another play,
the Lollard inquiry that would flame out in the early fifteenth century.

Here we find in the ritual performances of power and powerlessness a conversation about sacrality that would continue, at least until Henry shut it down by snuffing out the signifier.

To move forward to the mid-1390s is to move into a court where Richard's attempt to foster the ideology of a Valois-style kingship are well documented. However, it is the pronounced sacramental emphasis of that ideology that recalls the events of the 1380s and the incipient iconoclasm of both the Wycliffites and the Appellants.[44] In the work of Philippe de Mézières there is an explicitly worked-out program for international peace that depends upon an understanding of the role sacramental kingship might play. For all his wordiness and despite what can seem his overly conceited prose, Philippe de Mézières had a shrewd understanding of the demands of political rhetoric. His overarching concern with the political and spiritual fissures of Europe during the late fourteenth century, when the war between France and England was compounded by the Papal Schism, seeks a solution to actual problems in a language of concord. What he offers—an order of international chivalry devoted to the Passion and an endorsement of marriage as a figure for domestic and international harmony—is a sacramental "cure" for a world too steeped in actual conflict.[45]

Philippe de Mézières was a man of the world, who knew the East, the Mediterannean, and the political circles of both France and England. He was gripped by the need to reclaim the Holy Land for the Christian West and by the need to reunite the Christian West, which was split by the Hundred Years War and then by the Schism that bifurcated the body of Christ. He drew the first plan for the foundation of a new order of chivalry in 1367–68, in 1384 he wrote a second redaction, and the third in 1396.[46] For seven years, from 1373 to 1380, Philippe was closely bound to the court of Charles V. After Charles's death, he withdrew to the Paris convent of the Celestines, where he continued to work on redactions of his treatise on the Chivalry of the Passion. He not only wrote a long and very detailed Rule for his new Order of the Passion but also an abridged version, known as *La Sustance de la Chevalerie de la Passion de Jhesu Christ*, copies of which appear to have been privately owned. One of these, now Oxford, Bodleian Library, MS Ashmole 813, was once owned by the Arundel family. Possibly it was sent to Thomas Arundel, whose grandfather, the earl of Lancaster, was one of the early supporters of the order, or it may have been given to Richard's brother, the count of Huntington by Robert the Hermit who came to England from France to urge support for the order.[47]

Philippe de Mézières's treatise on chivalry argues for a sacramentally conceived institution, a community that will contain and transform disruptive passions. His new order of chivalry also has the advantage of uniting otherwise warring nations, of offering them a new form of dress, currency, and set of ideals that will bring together European knighthood under a single banner. The Rule is practical in the sense that it includes details for governing and running the order and does not require its members to renounce the world or their worldly married states, while presenting worldly knighthood as validated by the Passion of Christ. Though it has obvious connections to other military orders, Philippe de Mézières clearly saw it as addressing the issues of the late fourteenth century. Social harmony might thus be guaranteed by a sacramentally conceived international order of chivalry that reformulated the details of daily life as aspects of a religiously conceived body, a corporate whole. The six pictures representing the costumes of the order in MS Ashmole 813 designate each as a knight or a lady "de la religion"; the "commune" banner and arms are similarly designated as "de la religion."

For Philippe de Mézières the contemporary "moment" was one of war and schism and could only be mended through sacramental observance. Philippe played on an international stage, and, in the last fifteen years of the fourteenth century, he paid particular attention to the situation between France and England. From 1368, when he first expounded his ideal for the foundation of the Order of the Passion, until 1397, after the disaster of Nicopolis, he worked to bring together the warring factions of Europe in a new order of chivalry. He did this, not only in the various redactions of his treatise on the order that have already been mentioned, but by soliciting the help of key members of the European nobility and by finding in Robert the Hermit an emissary who could go back and forth between the French and English courts. In 1393, during the peace negotiations at Leulinghen, Robert the Hermit made an impression upon Charles VI, as well as upon the English delegates, including John of Gaunt. Thereafter, he became a messenger for the projected peace between the two countries.[48]

In May of 1395 Philippe de Mézières collected his ideas about that peace into a treatise, which he titled *A Letter to King Richard II*. The treatise, which is as heavily conceited and ornamented as anything he ever wrote, has as its project two interrelated goals: the establishment of a lasting peace between France and England, which, in turn, will heal the schism in Christendom itself, and the creation of the new Order of the Passion, which will make possible the retaking of the Holy Lands. The seal to be set upon the peace is marriage between the two royal houses. This marriage may result in the two objectives of healing and conquest. In the Introduction to the *Letter*, Philippe sketches in a sacramental world whereby kings are like precious stones, and peace between the kings will heal the Church. The journey overseas by these two kings will be sanctified by a new order of knighthood. Marriage will seal the peace between the kings, and the carbuncle (Richard) and the diamond (Charles) will be further sanctified by means of wine from the vineyards of Engadi. Fantastic as it sounds, the *Letter* nonetheless offered intelligent diplomatic advice to a world Philippe saw as wounded, as a victim of its own pervasive self-interest and courtly preoccupation. The body of Christ can therefore only be healed by sacramental remedies. By way of encouraging royal initiative, he describes the two kings as champions of Christ, eager to right the wrongs that have been done him. One of those initiatives, possible since the death of Queen Anne in 1394, is a negotiated marriage between Richard II and the young daughter of Charles VI. As for the "goods" of royal marriages, Philippe specifies they obtain the succession, make honorable alliances, achieve or preserve peace in kingdoms, and allow kings to live honestly and chastely according to the sacrament of marriage. Though he praises chastity, Philippe says that kings should marry. He then goes on to other subjects, including war, saying that the two kings should fear shedding royal blood, that when they make war on one another they risk becoming the "serfs" of their subjects. In other words, Philippe, like many a royal counselor before him, emphasizes the royal prerogative in order to underline the degree of responsibility a king must take for the health of his country, or, in this case, the world. What he advises is as hardheaded as the counsel of Chaucer's Prudence in the *Melibee:* recognize the situation for what it is, recognize your mutual responsibility for it and the likely venality of courtiers; choose peace, alliance, triumph. The marriage that will be the seal of responsible action looks forward to the immersion of the two royal stones in the precious wine from the Engedi vineyards, or, in the parlance of the theologians, all sacraments look forward to or prepare for that of the Eucharist. Philippe thus presents a world's problems and offers them up to rational action and sacramental remedy.

Philippe de Mézières's blend of political shrewdness and sacramental devotion is central to both his understanding of the international situation and his presentation of a solution. While his suggestions—diplomatic marriage and a transnational fighting force—were traditional responses to schism and fissure, his insistence that these proposals must be understood as more than diplomatic acts of speech provided (or was meant to provide) the participants in history with a perspective upon themselves that was more than political or ethical. Just as Charles V had meddled magic with Aristotle to arrive at a recipe for his own understanding of kingship, so Philippe urges his reader(s) to see ethical behavior in the light of its metaphysical significance. That Philippe had found the terms of a language that meant something to his intended audience is clear from the hints of his influence that we can detect. For example, Philippe de Mézières called Robert the Hermit, John de Blaisy, Louis de Giac, and Otto of Granson his "four evangelists"; between 1390 and 1395 they preached the "new Gospel of the Order of the Passion." They probably carried with them manuscripts of the *Sustance Abregie,* one of which is MS. Ashmole 813 (Coopland (1975), xxxiii-iv; Hamdy (1963), 5). The manuscript (MS Ashmole 813) was in the possession of the Arundel family until it became the property of Lord William Howard (1563–1640). Moreover, in *De la Chevallerie de la Passion de Jhesu Crist* (Paris, Bibliothèque de l'Arsenal MS 2251), which also contains the praises of the four men mentioned above, Philippe de Mézières left a list of key members of the international nobility who were supporters of his order.[49] The list testifies not only to the appeal Philippe's ideas had for men who were bound together by class and breeding if not by country, but to his own appraisal of the need to build a constituency within the courts of the kings he sought to persuade.

Moreover, the list, and particularly the English courtiers who appear on it, suggests a fascinating, if sometimes paradoxical, conversation among the privileged and powerful.[50] Otto of Granson, whom Chaucer praised as a poet/maker in the *Complaint of Venus,* was a knight of Savoy aligned with Richard II and in the entourage of John of Gaunt. The English knights were Edmund of Langley, the duke of York; his son, the earl of Rutland; Thomas Mowbray, the earl of Nottingham; Henry Percy, earl of Northumberland; John Gilbert, treasurer, bishop of St. David's; Mons. le Despenser (who may be either Henry, the bishop of Norwich, or Thomas); Mons. Hue le Despenser; Sir Louis Clifford, knight in the retinue of Joan of Kent, a Wycliffite, and a friend of Chaucer's; Thomas West (who may have been an associate of Chaucer's); William Heleman; John Harlestone (who may also have been known to Chaucer); William Fenistone; Raoul de Persy, brother to Hotspur and son of Henry Percy; Mons. Hervy filz Hue; Mons. Symon Felbrig; Mons. Richart Albery; Mons. Hervy Guine; Mons. Thomas Herpignen; Mons. de Rochefort; Mons. Robert Morley; Piteux, escuier; Richart Chelmesinch, escuier du king.

The arrangement of the list suggests a fierce attention to categories. The first group is that of the four, who are like the evangelists. Second, Philippe names the members of the French court, beginning with the duke of Bourbon and Jean Boucicaut, the marshall of France. He then names knights from Spain, from Gascony, from Navarre, and from Germany. After the German come the English names and one Scottish one. He then lists French knights who have offered to help the order, John, duke of Berry, and Louis, duke of Orleans, head this sequence. After this group, which also includes the name of Pope Benedict XIII, three other English knights are added, those of Thomas, duke of Gloucester, John of Gaunt, duke of Lancaster, and "Le conte de Nornthone/ frere du roy d'Engleterre."[51] Not only are the knights divided according to nationalities, but the groups themselves are ranked according to social status and power. However, this display of nation and rank is meant to serve the higher purpose of dissolving such distinctions by creating a new community with its own ranks, currency, and codes whose scope is international and whose ideals are those of the Passion. The categories evince Philippe's attention to the values of courtship, the overarching ideal his reading of the ways in which those values might be translated into the legal tender of another sort of nation. The Euro-centric world he envisioned was one whose stability could only rest on an absolute, the Passion of Christ, and be guaranteed by the Sacrament of the Altar, the feast that focused the devoted eyes of the Christian faithful. There is consequently no room in Philippe's vision for what cannot be assimilated to the Eucharist. He had no sympathy for Jews, none for pagans, and women figure only as wives, thus as hierarchically arranged in relation to the knights who are to be the prime movers of this new world. What he sought was a solution to a world he saw as broken, a solution that, for him, could only be effected from the top down and by a renewed attention to sacramental ordering. He did not appeal to peasants or merchants, but to princes and nobles. Whatever his appeal and influence in France, and even G. W. Coopland, whose work on Philippe de Mézières is unparalleled, admits we cannot finally know how figures like Philippe or Robert the Hermit actually were seen by their contemporaries, his "presence" in England testifies to the ongoing power of the court of Charles V.

Perhaps the most mysterious and arresting voice from Richard's court is the Wilton Diptych, which probably belongs in the juncture between Richard's attempts to rule as king in his own right and his disastrous assumptions of "Valois" majesty that become most apparent around 1397. It seems only natural to refer to it, as many have done, as an icon. It confers upon itself more than a simple artistic status.[52] Like the Westminster portrait of Richard (ca. 1395), the Wilton Diptych presents Richard as frozen in eternal youth at a point around 1395–96, when Richard had already had his tomb effigy made showing him in full maturity, bearded, the twenty-eight year old man and king who would lie beside Anne of Bohemia as one more sagacious figure of English rule in that great cathedral. If Richard in 1395, soon after the death of Queen Anne, had his tomb made, he also had both public and private images of himself made that deliberately recalled the boy who had first been consecrated as king.[53] Those who place the Wilton Diptych in the mid-1390s on the basis of heraldic and diplomatic evidence have strong arguments; we need also, however, to see the work as another piece of the conversation about the images of rule that went on during the latter part of Richard's reign.

The Richard of the Wilton Diptych kneels, the focal point for a web of images that validate a sacramentally conceived chivalric kingship. Directly behind him stands St. Edward the Confessor who holds a ring. The detail recalls the ring St. Edward gave to the pilgrim, a story that forms such an important part of his legend. But by 1395–96 the ring may also have been meant to present Richard as sacramentally bound, or married to his realm. William of Sudbury, at Richard's request, had provided a complicated series of metaphors that explicitly linked sacramental kingship to the institutions of both marriage and chivalry. Thus, by way of explaining the coronation regalia, William says that the ring serves as a sign of the marriage contract and a knight's arms as a sign of the honor of his office, so the regalia is a sign of office. He goes on to say that the clothes, which he traces to King Alfred, the first English king, have been consecrated by the pope.[54] In terms of the legend of St. Edward, the ring binds king and Church; in terms of the theory of sacramental kingship that Richard apparently wished to articulate, or to have articulated, the ring is a sign of the sacramental union between himself and the body politic. Directly across from St. Edward in the Wilton Diptych, the Blessed Virgin's thumb and forefinger encircle the Christ child's foot in exactly the same gesture used by St. Edward to hold the ring. Christ's physical body remains securely in the Virgin's hand, even as the haloed baby reaches out to bless (or greet) the young king whose open hands mirror those of the Child. The mortal body encircled and the token of encirclement mirror one another, while the sacramental king and the babe by whom sacrament proceeds gaze upon each other in attitudes of courtly welcome.

We, of course, or Richard himself, for whom the Wilton Diptych was probably intended, gaze upon these icons of power. What Michael Camille has described as a "democratization of the gaze" that a king's image ought to effect locates all viewers in relation to the kneeling king (*Gothic Idol*, 282–83). The Wilton Diptych comes to us as an artifact of late-fourteenth-century English culture, but both it and the Westminster portrait of Richard II were commissioned. They are images that were intended for certain uses. They offer the king an image of magnificence, of cultic rule, of sacramental transformation. They do not suggest that the magic that transforms men to kings or men to knights, that binds king and people, or invisible hosts to the material world, is in any serious way contractual, that it depends upon worthiness for its reality, that it can be subjected to the sorts of questions about authority Wyclif persistently asked or Chaucer's pilgrims ask in their advance upon Canterbury.

To turn to Chaucer and ask that he sum up a conversation about the definition of regal authority is to ask the master of indirection for an answer he can only give obliquely. However, his own development as a writer gives evidence that he came to understand that the world in which he lived and out of which he wrote could no longer be thought about in the terms of sweepingly diagnostic allegory. For one thing, it was no longer simply a world composed around the court, nor was his language controlled by the aesthetics of courtly forms. Chaucer's interrogations in

Troilus of individual actions and public events that suggest the relationship between self-understanding and an understanding of history and an acknowledgment of one's place in it also emerges in later Canterbury works, such as *The Nun's Priest's Tale,* which I have argued elsewhere is, in part, a sort of comic echo of *Troilus.*[55] Through Chauntecleer, who learns the lesson of agency and so escapes history's net, returning his "community" to a greater degree of safety, Chaucer touches on some of the political dangers that must have been apparent to him and others in the court of the 1390s. Though the rooster at the end of the tale wins our regard because of his wits, the rooster at the beginning is as brilliantly detailed as any figure in the Wilton Diptych:

> His coomb was redder than the fyn coral,
> And batailled as it were a castel wal;
> His byle was blak, and as the jeet it shoon;
> Lyk asure were his legges and his toon;
> His nayles whitter than the lylye flour,
> And lyk the burned gold was his colour. (VII.2859–64)

With red comb, black shiny beak, azure legs and toes, white nails, and burned gold color, Chauntecleer is the very image of a royal rooster. He sits high up, on a perch in the hall, surrounded by his wives, who are his sisters and paramours. A number of critics have commented upon the heraldic, formal, and courtly qualities of Chaucer's description of Chauntecleer, thereby steering our understanding of it away from strict realism and towards its striking visual appeal.[56] What we see is not a rooster, but the icon of a rooster, and at a time when Richard began to adapt some of the Valois mannerisms of regality to his public appearances in his own hall.[57] The gender comedy of the tale and the exquisite rendering of the beast fable work to shield us from the portrait of iconic kingship on its perch. However, Chauntecleer's fascination with his own image of magnificence almost brings his realm into utter ruin, into the type of chaos reminiscent of the Rising of 1381:

> So hydous was the noyse—a, benedicitee!—
> Certes, he Jakke Straw and his meynee
> Ne made nevere shoutes half so shrille
> Whan that they wolden any Flemyng kille. (VII.3393–96)

In "remembering" the Rising and the violence against resident aliens in London's streets, Chaucer does not stop to decry civic chaos but, instead, suggests it is a consequence of a failure of true authority. Chauntecleer's studied posturing and his willingness to listen to flattery threaten more than his own life and unleash the disorder submerged within any attempt at communal ordering. In performing power, Chauntecleer has lost control, something he is clever enough—even when in mortal danger—to tempt the fox into emulating: "Sire, if that I were as ye, / Yet sholde I seyn, as wys God helpe me, / 'Turneth agayne, ye proude cherles alle!...'" (VII.3407–09). Troilus's failures, like the regal rooster's, may be private, but Chaucer uses them to detail the utter inadequacy of a chivalric world that can neither know itself nor comprehend the terms by which it purports to speak. Chaucer's farewell to his book at the end of the poem writes paid at once to tragedy and to the very institutions that are fundamental to its form. To be in Troy is to be without escape from Troy, its history, its mannerisms; to see it is to leave it, as the narrator does. That he returned in works like the tale of Chauntecleer is not to say he returned but that he chose to see what type of ending might bring release in comedy.[58]

If Chaucer's fable looks back to his own work, it also looks out upon a world—captured in *The Canterbury Tales*—whose contingencies cannot allow a simple borrowing of signs from another culture and time. Tellingly, Chauntecleer traces out a comic trajectory in which the formalized iconic authority of a barnyard fowl is replaced by empirical shrewdness. The community presumably reconstituted around the newly savvy Chauntecleer is implicitly less vulnerable because its "governor" has escaped the fates of his parents so eloquently recalled by the flattering fox. French majesty—whether in feathers or cloth of gold—is not easily translated into the flock's common tongue. Although Chaucer does not detail the arguments of John Wyclif or analyze the actions of the Appellants, he presents a world in *The Canterbury Tales* where the hierarchical mysteries of class, gender, and religion are the subjects under constant review by a wide variety of debunkers. Whatever his own views, the talk on the road to Canterbury runs strongly against the need for magic.

In giving Chaucer the last word, I position him in the ambiguously defined space he appropriated for himself, suggesting that we can catch echoes within his works of conversations held on much higher levels of power than those he frequented. But I also suggest that Chaucer made himself into a poet whose rare quality could only have emerged from a world in search of stabilizing images of rule. The search, moreover, was a real search, in the sense that the English court, particularly after Richard's declaration of his majority in 1389, soon after his humiliation at the hands of the Appellants, actively sought to produce a royal image as magically endowed as that of the French kings. Richard's interest in the Valois monarchy is well known. What is less understood is the nature of the conflict about the language of sovereignty. What was the king to be? There were many who thought they could answer the question, and Chaucer had the quickness in moments like *The Nun's Priest's Tale* to record a conversation about the use (or appropriation) of images that was also and inevitably a debate about the nature of the English community. He did more than record: he suggests that if acts of translation are attempts to appropriate the terms of empire, translators might think again. Empires dissolve and become acts of translation, or, put another way, translation succeeds only by dissolving the past into a contingent present.

NOTES

I would like to thank Derek Brewer, Ardis Butterfield, and Thomas F. X. Noble for giving me the opportunity to read portions of this essay at sessions of the International Congress on Medieval Studies, Kalamazoo, in 1997, the New Chaucer Society in 1998, and the International Congress on Medieval Studies, Kalamazoo, in 1999.

1. Any discussion of translation as a cultural practice must be indebted to Copeland, *Rhetoric*.

2. See Copeland's discussion of Jean de Meun's preface to his translation of Boethius. Copeland, *Rhetoric*, 135.

3. For discussions of Charles V in relation to English policy, see Armitage-Smith, *John of Gaunt*; Goodman, *John of Gaunt*; Ormrod, *Reign*.

4. I am using Goodman, *John of Gaunt*, 35–37, here, partly because he recounts the campaign in terms of personalities. The Black Prince and John of Gaunt were playing by an older set of rules, whereas Charles had created a type of nonbattle that eschewed the glamour of pitched battle. But I am oversimplifying the situation in France, where there was a great deal of suffering. The war was, after all, fought in France, and the people of France paid the toll for the war in high taxes, in destroyed crops, in damaged towns. That Charles V could hold to his policy says much about his own understanding of the terms of sovereignty. For careful analyses of the situation in France, see Hanneman, *Olivier de Clisson*, chapters 4–6; Palmer, *England, France,* Introduction and chapter 1; Wright, *Knights and Peasants*.

5. See Beaune, *Birth*; Spiegel, *Chronicle Tradition*, "Moral Imagination," and *Romancing*, Introduction, for important accounts of the ways in which texts were used to create a history of legitimization.

6. Spiegel's is the classic study. See Spiegel, *Chronicle Tradition*. Bloch's analysis of the power of the French cult in relation to the relative weakness of the English is borne out by Binski, *Westminster Abbey*, 6.

7. For a discussion of French influence upon English royal ceremony, see Saul, *Richard II*, 342–49, 465.

8. For studies that discuss the legal histories of England and France in the late Middle Ages, see *Cambridge History*, ed. Burns, especially the essays by Canning ("Law, Sovereignty") and Dunbabin ("Government"); Ullman, *Principles*. The above remarks are indebted to Ullman, chapter 4.

9. For a discussion of the French and English coronation *ordos*, see Ullman, *Principles*, 201–06. On the English coronation, see Richardson, "Coronation"; Schramm, *History*. For important discussions of the ways in which textuality became ancillary to French kingship, see Sherman, *Imaging Aristotle*; Spiegel, *Chronicle Tradition*.

10. The phrase belongs to Sherman, whose *Imaging Aristotle* articulates this aspect of French court culture in the fourteenth century. The phrase appears on p. 4, but I am deeply endebted to Sherman, not only for the citations that follow, but for insights into the French court that enabled me to think creatively about the English court under Richard.

11. I am drawing here upon Hedeman, *Royal Image*, 95. For the texts, see Delachenal, *Chronique*; Viard, *Grandes Chroniques*.

12. See Hedeman, *Royal Image*, 109. But I cannot do justice here to the intricacy of the argument, which sheds real light on the contruction of a textual culture.

13. The *Coronation Book* is still in England, in the holdings of the British Library (Cotton MS Tiberius B VIII). The illustrations, which form a distinct section, have been removed and bound separately. The volume has been edited; see Dewick, ed., *Coronation Book*.

14. For a complete edition of the *Traité*, see Jackson, "*Triate*." For a rich account of its author, Jean Golein, see Jackson's Introduction.

15. See Jackson, "*Traité*," Introduction, for the manuscript history.

16. On Charles's library, see Delisle, *Recherches*. On the translators, see vol. 1, chapter 9. See also Sherman, *Imaging Aristotle*, Bibliography.

17. See Molenar, *Livres dou gouvernement*, and Brunetto Latini's *Book of the Treasure*. The *Liber Albus* (ed. Riley), compiled in London in 1419, contains extracts from Brunetto Latini's *Treasure* in French as guides for London's mayors.

18. For a discussion of Christine's debt to Giles of Rome, see I, *Livres des Fais*, I:xxx–xxxvi.

19. Sherman, *Portraits*, 34–35, 64, 79; Hedeman, "Copies"; Hedeman, *Royal Image*. This oversight also included the queen's image; see Sherman, "The Queen."

20. Babbit, *Oresme's "Livre"*; Oresme, *Yconomique*. Sherman, *Imaging Aristotle*, argues that Oresme planned the program of illustrations for his translations and did so with an eye to instruction.

21. On Giles of Rome and the powers of the prince, see Dunbabin, "Government."

22. Oresme, *Yconomique*, 786. Though Menut, the editor, insists that these volumes are not strictly "indebted" to Aristotle's *Economics*, they share the same broad (and inevitably political) interest in teaching the arts of stewardship and management. However Sherman, *Imaging Aristotle*, argues for an organic textual development; see chapter 24.

23. See Fradenburg, *City*, for a discussion of marriage as a political metaphor.

24. See Johnson, *The "De Moneta."* See also Spufford, *Money*, 295–301.

25. These are ideas directly linked to Oresme's championship of Gallicanism. Thus, the king of France was described as independent of the papacy in temporal matters and the General Council as superior to the pope. The clergy and the king needed to cooperate in order to preserve the liberties of the French church, but the French king was consistently affirmed as having a unique status in regard to the Church. See Babbit, *Oresme's "Livre,"* chapter 6. Babbit links the *Songe* to Oresme; see p. 137.

26. I have written on this period and on this poem. See Aers and Staley, *Powers*, 188–213. See Aers, "The *Parliament*," for an account of the poem as deliberately irresolute. I do not mean to imply that France was without conflict. For a far more nuanced discussion of the situation in France, see Palmer, *England, France*, who provides a close look at the ways in which those who guided Charles VI, particularly Philip the Bold, coped with the decade after the death of Charles V.

27. Ormrod, *Reign*, describes Edward III as one of the "most image-conscious" kings of the later Middle Ages (45). For an analysis of Edward's reign, see his study.

28. I am drawing here upon the description of the manuscript (Paris, Bibliothèque nationale de France, MS fr. 571) to be found in Michael, "Manuscript." For recent political readings of the manuscript's preparation and contents, see Butterfield, "French Culture"; Wathey, "Marriage."

29. Wilks, "*Reformatio Regni.*" See also Wyclif, *Tractatus de Civili Dominio*.

30. For recent work on the complex relationship between sacramental theology and late medieval institutions, see Beckwith, "*Sacrum Signum*"; Rubin, *Corpus Christi*.

31. See Leff, "John Wyclif"; McFarlane, *John Wycliffe*, 79–88.

32. On this, see Gwynn, *English Austin Friars*, 257. For a cogent discussion of Wyclif's views on the sacrament, see Keen, "Wyclif," 1–16. Keen sees Wyclif's attack on the Real Presence as growing out of his work on the *De Veritate Sacre Scripture*.

33. For the *Confession*, see Shirley, *Fasciculi*, 115–32. The *Confession* was answered point-by-point by Thomas Winterton; see 181–238. See also Wyclif's *De Eucharistia*.

34. The degree of Gaunt's involvement with Wyclif is a matter of debate, as is the degree to which the government supported Wyclif during this period. For the argument, see McFarlane, *John Wycliffe*, chapter 3; Holmes, *Good Parliament*; Hudson, *Premature Reformation*, 60–73; Rex, *Lollards*, chapter 2. Though Wyclif challenged only ecclesiastical authority, his argument about dominion left open the door to challenging secular authority, as some followers seemed to do. See Hudson, *Premature Reformation*, 359–67.

35. Paul Strohm (*Empty Throne*, 139–41) discusses the Lollards' views on the Eucharist as threatening to the entire Lancastrian project.

36. The language here is the Monk of Westminster's ("cum omni subjeccione ac grato animo"). See Hector and Harvey, *Westminster Chronicle*, 342–43.

37. On identity making during this period, see also Staley, "Gower."

38. Much has been written on the Merciless Parliament. See especially, Goodman, *Loyal Conspiracy*; Saul, *Richard II*, chapters 8, 9. For a discussion of the Parliament in relation to Chaucer, see my chapter, "Chaucer and the Postures of Sanctity," in Aers and Staley, *Powers*, esp. 217–33.

39. See Knighton, *Chronicle*, 432–39. For the *Twenty-Five Articles*, Arnold, *English Works*, 3:455–96. For discussion, see Hudson, *Premature Reformation*, 210–11.

40. For the following account, see Knighton, *Chronicle*, 424–27. See Martin's Introduction for a discussion of Knighton's handling of his sources. For the Monk of Westminster's account, see Hector and Harvey, *Westminster Chronicle*, 226–27.

41. Clarke, *Fourteenth Century Studies*, 91. See also Saul, *Richard II*, 189.

42. See Saul, *Richard II*, 173–75; Chrimes, "Questions."

43. For the Monk of Westminster's own account, see Hector and Harvey, *Westminster Chronicle*, 310–13; for the account from the Parliament Rolls, which he also includes, see 282–83. For Favent, see McKisack, "Narracio." For Froissart, see *Chroniques*, 5:25–28.

44. Near the end of his reign Richard had supposedly found the oil given to Thomas á Beckett and asked to be sealed with it. Richard would have known that the kings of France were sealed with the oil of Clovis. Though Richard was denied, Henry IV made sure he was properly signed at his coronation. See Saul, *Richard II*, 423–24.

45. For editions of his works with good introductions, see *Le Songe*, ed. Coopland and *"Letter,"* ed. and trans. Coopland; *La Sustance*, ed. Hamdy; Williamson, *Le Livre*. See also Molinier, "Description."

46. See *La Sustance*, ed. Hamdy for a discussion of the manuscript history of these various redactions.

47. The attribution to the count of Huntington is made by the Bodleian annotator on the reference cards for the manuscript.

48. I am indebted to Coopland here; see his Introduction to *"Letter,"* esp. xxiii–iv.

49. See the dissertation by Brown, "De la Chevallerie," for an annotated edition of this manuscript, which includes the list. For Philippe's "four evangelists," see Palmer, *England, France*, 188.

50. I am here referring to Brown's transcription of the list on pp. 260–67 of her dissertation. In the cases of the Despenser, Thomas West, Harlestone, and Percy, I am using her annotations. See Brown for other suggestions about the identity of men on the list. When it is not clear to whom the designation refers, I leave it as it appears in the original.

51. None of Richard's half brothers carried this title; see Brown, "De la Chevallerie," 267 for suggestions.

52. Though some scholars wish to date the Diptych early in Richard's reign, I find the strongest arguments those that locate it in the 1390s. Literature on the Wilton Diptych is vast. Two recent volumes contain some of the most interesting recent work on the piece and its relationship to Ricardian ideology. Both books have ample bibliographies and give full reviews about the arguments about dating that are integral to the Diptych's meaning. See *Making*, ed. Gordon; *Regal Image*, ed. Gordon, Monnas, and Elam.

53. I here refer to the likely function of the Wilton Diptych, which is portable and probably intended for Richard's own devotional use.

54. Richard of Cirencester, *Speculum Historiale*, 2:26–39. For Edward the Confessor, see Book IV. See also Richardson, "Coronation," who notes that the ring is indeed part of regalia; see pp. 136–37 for the oblation Richard made at his coronation.

55. All quotations from Chaucer's works are taken from *The Riverside Chaucer*. On *Troilus* and Chaucer's handling of history, see Patterson, *Chaucer,* chapter 2; Wetherbee, *Chaucer;* Fleming, *Classical Imitation*. For my earlier essay on *The Nun's Priest's Tale*, see Staley, "'To Make.'"

56. See Davies, *Lyrics,* 334; Salter, "Medieval Poetry," 19. For other comments about this passage, see *Nun's Priest's Tale*, ed. Pearsall, 150–51.

57. See Saul, *Richard II,* 340–58, for an analysis of the mannerisms of Richard's court.

58. For an argument that Chaucer invented tragedy as we know it, and for speculations about Chaucer's definition of comedy and comic form, see Kelly, *Chaucerian Tragedy,* chapter 3. In my essay on *The Nun's Priest's Tale,* I suggest that the tale offers a pattern for comic form in Chaunticleer's literal (rather than metaphoric) movements.

REFERENCES

Aers, David. "The *Parliament of Fowls:* Authority, the Knower and the Known." *Chaucer Review,* 16 (1981): 1–17.

Aers, David, and Lynn Staley. *The Powers of the Holy: Religion, Politics, and Gender in Late Medieval English Culture*. University Park: Pennsylvania State University Press, 1996.

Armitage-Smith, Sydney. *John of Gaunt*. New York: Charles Scribner's Sons, 1905.

Arnold, T. *Select English Works of John Wyclif*. 3 vols. Oxford: Clarendon Press, 1869–71.

Babbit, Susan M. *Oresme's "Livre de Politiques" and the France of Charles V*. Transactions of the American Philosophical Society, 75.1. Philadelphia: American Philosophical Society, 1985.

Bak, János M., ed. *Coronations: Medieval and Early Modern Monarchic Ritual*. Berkeley: University of California Press, 1990.

Beaune, Colette. *The Birth of an Ideology: Myths and Symbols of Nation in Late-Medieval France*. Trans. Susan Ross Huston. Berkeley: University of California Press, 1991.

Beckwith, Sarah. "*Sacrum Signum:* Sacramentality and Dissent in York's Theater of Corpus Christi." In *Criticism and Dissent in the Middle Ages,* ed. Rita Copeland, 264–88. Cambridge: Cambridge University Press, 1996.

Binski, Paul. *Westminster Abbey and the Plantagenets: Kingship and the Representation of Power, 1200–1400*. New Haven: Yale University Press, 1995.

Bloch, Marc. *The Royal Touch: Sacred Monarchy and Scrofula in England and France*. Trans. J. E. Anderson. London: Routledge and Kegan Paul, 1973.

Brown, Muriel Anderson. "*De la Chevallerie de la Passion de Jhesu Crist: An Annotated Edition* (Bibliothèque de L'Arsenal Ms. 2251)." Ph.D. dissertation, University of Nebraska, 1971.

Burns, J. H. ed., *The Cambridge History of Medieval Political Thought*. Cambridge: Cambridge University Press, 1988.

Butterfield, Ardis. "French Culture and the Ricardian Court." In *Essays on Ricardian Literature in Honour of J. A. Burrow*, ed. A. J. Minnis, Charlotte Morse, and Thorlac Turville-Petre, 82–120. Oxford: Clarendon Press, 1997.

Camille, Michael. *The Gothic Idol. Ideology and Image-Making in Medieval Art.* Cambridge: Cambridge University Press, 1989.

Canning, J. "Law, Sovereignty and Corporation Theory, 1300–1450." In *Cambridge History of Medieval Political Thought*, ed. Burns, 341–66.

Chaucer, Geoffrey. *The Nun's Priest's Tale.* Ed. Derek Pearsall. Vol. 2, part 9 of *A Variorum Edition of the Works of Geoffrey Chaucer.* Norman: University of Oklahoma Press, 1984.

———. *The Riverside Chaucer*, ed. Larry D. Benson. Boston: Houghton Mifflin Company, 1987.

Chrimes, S. B. "Richard II's Questions to the Judges, 1387." *Law Quarterly Review* 72 (1956): 365–89.

Christine de Pizan, *Le Livre des Fais et Bonne Meurs du Sage Roy Charles V.* Ed. S. Solente. 2 vols. Paris: Librairie Ancienne Honaré Champion, 1936.

Clarke, M. V. *Fourteenth Century Studies.* Ed. L. S. Sutherland and M. McKisack. Oxford: Clarendon Press, 1937.

Copeland, Rita. *Rhetoric, Hermeneutics, and Translation in the Middle Ages: Academic Traditions and Vernacular Texts.* Cambridge: Cambridge University Press, 1991.

Davies, R. T., ed. *Medieval English Lyrics: A Critical Anthology.* London: Faber and Faber, 1963.

Delachenal, R., ed. *Chronique des Regnes de Jean II et de Charles V.* 4 vols. Paris: Société de L'Histoire de France, 1916.

Delisle, L. *Recherches sur la Librairie de Charles V.* 2 vols. Paris: Champion, 1907.

Dewick, E. S., ed. *The Coronation Book of Charles V of France (Cottonian MS Tiberius B.VIII).* Henry Bradshaw Society, 16. London, 1899.

Dunbabin, Jean. "Government." In *Cambridge History of Medieval Political Thought*, ed. Burns, 477–519.

Fleming, John V. *Classical Imitation and Interpretation in Chaucer's Troilus.* Lincoln: University of Nebraska Press, 1990.

Fradenburg, Louise Olga. *City, Marriage, Tournament: Arts of Rule in Late Medieval Scotland.* Madison: University of Wisconsin Press, 1991.

Froissart, Jean. *Chroniques.* Trans. John Bouchier, Lord Berners. 6 vols. New York: AMS Press, 1967.

Goodman, Anthony. *The Loyal Conspiracy: The Lords Appellant under Richard II.* Coral Gables, FL: University of Miami Press, 1971.

———. *John of Gaunt: The Exercise of Princely Power in Fourteenth-Century Europe.* New York: St. Martin's Press, 1992.

Gordon, Dillian, ed. *Making and Meaning: The Wilton Diptych.* London: The National Gallery, 1993.

Gordon, Dillian, Lisa Monnas, and Caroline Elam, eds. *The Regal Image of Richard II and the Wilton Diptych.* London: Harvey Miller Publishers, 1997.

Gwynn, A. *The English Austin Friars in the Time of Wyclif.* London: Oxford University Press, 1940.

Hamdy, A. H., ed. *La Sustance de la Chevalerie de la Passion de Jhesu Crist. Bulletin of the Faculty of Arts.* Alexandria University, Egypt, 18 (1963): 45–55; 1–104.

Hanneman, John Bell. *Olivier de Clisson and Political Society in France under Charles V and Charles VI.* Philadelphia: University of Pennsylvania Press, 1966.

Hector, L. C. and Barbara F. Harvey, eds. and trans. *The Westminster Chronicle, 1381–1394.* Oxford: Clarendon Press, 1982.

Hedeman, Anne. "Copies in Context: The Coronation of Charles V in His *Grandes Chroniques de France.*" In Bak, *Coronations,* 72–87.

———. *The Royal Image: Illustrations of the Grandes Chroniques de France, 1274–1422.* Berkeley: University of California Press, 1991.

Holmes, George. *The Good Parliament.* Oxford: Clarendon Press, 1975.

Hudson, Anne. *The Premature Reformation: Wycliffite Texts and Lollard History.* Oxford: Clarendon Press, 1988.

Jackson, R. A. "The *Traité du Sacre* of Jean Golein." *Proceedings of the American Philosophical Society* 113 (1969): 305–24.

Johnson, Charles, trans. *The "De Moneta" of Nicholas Oresme and English Mint Documents.* London: Thomas Nelson and Sons Ltd., 1956.

Jones, R. H. *The Royal Policy of Richard II: Absolutism in the Later Middle Ages.* New York: Barnes and Noble, 1968.

Kantorowicz, E. H. *Laudes regiae. A Study in Liturgical Acclamations.* University of California Publications in History 33. Berkeley: University of California Press, 1946.

Keen, Maurice. "Wyclif, the Bible, and Transubstantiation." In *Wyclif in His Times,* ed. Anthony Kenny, 1–16. Oxford: Clarendon Press, 1986.

Kelly, Henry Ansgar. *Chaucerian Tragedy.* Woodbridge: Boydell and Brewer, 1997.

Kipling, Gordon. *Enter the King: Theatre, Liturgy and Ritual in the Medieval Civic Triumph.* Oxford: Clarendon Press, 1998.

Knighton, Henry. *Knighton's Chronicle, 1337–1396.* Ed. and trans. G. H. Martin. Oxford: Clarendon Press, 1995.

Koziol, Geoffrey. *Begging Pardon and Favor: Ritual and Political Order in Early Medieval France.* Ithaca: Cornell University Press, 1993.

Latini, Brunetto. *The Book of the Treasure.* Trans. Paul Barrette and Spurgeon Baldwin. New York: Garland Publishing, 1993.

Leff, Gordon. "John Wyclif: The Path to Dissent." *Proceedings of the British Academy* 52 (1960): 143–80.

Le Goff, Jacques. "A Coronotion Program for the Age of Saint Louis: The Ordo of 1250." In Bak, *Coronations,* 46–57.

McFarlane, K. B. *John Wycliffe and the Beginnings of English Nonconformity.* New York: The Macmillan Company, 1953.

McKisack, May. "Narracio de Modo et Forma Mirabilis Parliamenti apud Westmonasterium." *Camden Miscellany,* 3rd series, 37 (1926): 1–24.

Michael, M. A. "A Manuscript Wedding Gift from Philippa of Hainault to Edward III." *Burlington Magazine* 20 (1985): 582–89.

Molenar, Samuel P., ed. *Li livres dou gouvernement des rois: A XIIIth Century French Version* of *Egidio Colonna's Treatise, "De regimine principium."* New York: Columbia University Press and MacMillan, 1899; reprint New York: AMS Press, 1966.

Molinier, A. "Description de deux manuscrits contenant la 'Règle de la Militia Passionis Jhesu Christi de Philippe de Mézières.'" *Archives de l'Orient Latin* (1881): 335–64.

Oresme, Nicole. *Le Livre de Yconomique d'Aristote.* Ed. and trans. Albert D. Menut. Transactions of the American Philosophical Society, n.s., 47.5. Philadelphia: American Philosophical Society, 1957.

Ormrod, W. M. *The Reign of Edward III: Crown and Political Society in England, 1327–1377.* New Haven: Yale University Press, 1990.

Palmer, J. J. N. *England, France and Christendom.* Chapel Hill: University of North Carolina Press, 1972.

Patterson, Lee. *Chaucer and the Subject of History.* Madison: University of Wisconsin Press, 1991.

Philippe de Mézières. Le Songe du Vieil Pelerin. Ed. G. W. Coopland. 2 vols. Cambridge: Cambridge University Press, 1969.

Philippe de Mézières "Letter to King Richard." Ed. and trans. G. W. Coopland. Liverpool: Liverpool University Press, 1975.

Poiron, Daniel. *Le Poète et le Prince.* Paris: Presses Universitaires de France, 1965.

Richard of Cirencester. *Speculum Historiale.* Ed. John E. B. Mayor. 2 vols. London, 1869. Reprint Wiesbaden: Kraus Reprint, 1970.

Richardson, H. G. "The Coronation in Medieval England: The Evolution of the Office and Oath." *Traditio* 16 (1960): 111–203.

Riley, H. T., ed. *Munimenta Gildhallae Londoniensis: Liber Albus, Liber Custumarum et Liber Horn.* London: Longman, Brown, Green, Longmans, and Roberts, 1859.

Rubin, Miri. *Corpus Christi: The Eucharist in Late Medieval Culture.* Cambridge: Cambridge University Press, 1991.

Salter, Elizabeth. "Medieval Poetry and the Visual Arts." *Essays and Studies* 22 (1969): 16–32.

Saul, Nigel. *Richard II.* New Haven: Yale University Press, 1997.

Schramm, Percy Ernst. *A History of the English Coronation.* Trans. L. G. W. Legg. Oxford: Clarendon Press, 1937.

Sherman, Claire Richter. *The Portraits of Charles V of France, 1338–1380,* Monographs on Archaelogy and the Fine Arts 20. New York: New York University Press, 1969.

———. "The Queen in Charles V's *Coronation Book:* Jeanne de Bourbon and the *Ordo ad Reginam Benediendem." Viator: Medieval and Renaissance Studies* 8 (1977): 255–98.

———. *Imaging Aristotle: Verbal and Visual Representations in Fourteenth-Century France.* Berkeley: University of California Press, 1995.

Shirley, W. W., ed. *Fasciculi Zizaniorum Magistri Johannis Wyclif cum Tritico, ascribed to Thomas Netter of Walden.* London: Longman, Brown, Green, Longmans, and Roberts, 1858.

Sinclair, Keith V. *The Melbourne Livy: A Study of Bersuire's Translatio Based on the Manuscript in the Collection of the National Gallery of Victoria.* Melbourne: Melbourne University Press, 1961.

Le Songe du Vergier. Ed. Marion Schnerb-Lièvie. 2 vols. Paris: Centre National de la Recherche Scientifique, 1982.

Spiegel, Gabrielle M. *The Chronicle Tradition of St. Denis: A Survey.* Medieval Classics: Texts and Studies 10. Brookline, MA and Leyden: Classical Folia Editions, 1978.

———. "Moral Imagination and the Rise of the Bureaucratic State: Images of Government in the *Chroniques des Rois de France,* Chantilly MS 869." *Journal of Medieval and Renaissance Studies* 18 (1988): 157–73.

———. *Romancing the Past: The Rise of Vernacular Prose Historiography in Thirteenth-Century France.* Berkeley: University of California Press, 1993.

Spufford, Peter. *Money and Its Use in Medieval Europe.* Cambridge: Cambridge University Press, 1988.

Staley, Lynn. "'To Make in Som Comedy': Chauntecleer, Son of Troy." *Chaucer Review* 19 (1985): 226–44.

———. "Gower, Richard II, Henry of Derby and the Business of Making Culture." *Speculum* 75 (2000): 68–96.

Strohm, Paul. *England's Empty Throne: Usurpation and the Language of Legitimation, 1399–1422.* New Haven: Yale University Press, 1998.

Ullman, W. *Principles of Government and Politics in the Middle Ages.* New York: Barnes and Noble, 1961.

Viard, Jules, ed. *Les Grandes Chroniques de France.* 5 vols. Paris: Société de L'Histoire de France, 1920.

Walsingham, Thomas. *Historia Anglicana.* Ed. H. T. Riley. 2 vols. London: Longman, Green, Longman, Roberts, and Green, 1863–64.

Wathey, Andrew. "The Marriage of Edward III and the Transmission of French Motets to England." *Journal of the American Musicological Society* 45 (1992): 1–29.

Wetherbee, Winthrop. *Chaucer and the Poets: An Essay on Troilus and Criseyde.* Ithaca: Cornell University Press, 1984.

Wilks, Michael. "*Reformatio Regni:* Wyclif and Hus as Leaders of Religious Protest Movements." *Studies in Church History* 9 (1972): 109–30.

———. "Thomas Arundel, the Appellant Archbishop." In *Life and Thought in the Northern Church, c.1100–c.1700: Essays in Honour of Claire Cross,* ed. Diana Wood, *Studies in Church History,* subsidia 12, 57–86. Woodbridge: Boydell, 1999.

Williamson, Joan B., ed. *Philippe de Mézières: Le Livre de la Vertu du Sacrement de Mariage.* Washington: Catholic University of America Press, 1993.

Wright, Nicholas. *Knights and Peasants: The Hundred Years War in the French Countryside.* Woodbridge: Boydell Press, 1998.

Wyclif, John. *Tractatus de Civili Dominio.* Ed. Reginald Lane Poole. 4 vols. London: Trübner, 1885; reprint, New York: Johnson Reprint Co., 1966 (Introduction to vol. 4 by Johann Loserth).

———. *De Eucharistia.* Ed. Johann Loserth. London: The Wyclif Society, 1895.

The Captivity of
Henry Chrystede:
Froissart's *Chroniques*,
Ireland, and Fourteenth-
Century Nationalism

Claire Sponsler

Near the end of Book IV of his *Chroniques*, Jean Froissart describes an encounter in Richard II's chambers with an Anglo-Irish knight named Henry Chrystede, "ung escuier d'Angleterre" about fifty years of age, whom Froissart meets on his return visit to England in 1395. Noting with approval that Chrystede is "moult homme de bien et de prudence grandement pourveu" (*Oeuvres,* 15:167–68) and is fluent in French, Froissart is pleased when Chrystede recognizes that Froissart is "ung historien" (15:168) (as he has heard from Sir Richard Stury) and engages him in conversation, promising a story he can use in his chronicle. The tale Chrystede is eager to tell concerns Richard II's recent expedition to Ireland, a military undertaking in which Chrystede played an important role thanks in no small part to his own personal history.[1] According to the story he relates to Froissart, Chrystede was raised in Ireland, where he became a member of the household of Thomas, earl of Ormond, whose family had long been among the most powerful of the Anglo-Irish colonists. In the late 1350s, when Ormond is sent to the border to fight the

Gaelic Irish, he takes Chrystede along. Out riding one day, the colonists are ambushed by the Gaelic Irish; Chrystede is captured by a man named Brin Costerec, who takes his victim to a fortified house surrounded by woods, stockades, and stagnant waters. There Chrystede is held captive for seven years, marries one of Costerec's daughters, and has two daughters of his own.

Up to this point, it might seem that Chrystede is narrating a tale of happy assimilation, in which whatever anguish accompanied his capture has been forgotten as he goes native, embracing the indigenous customs of his captors even to the extent of intermarriage with them. But Chrystede's captivity story continues on to a different, more complicated ending, one that removes him from the hands of his Gaelic captors and returns him to his "homeland" of England. This rescue operation comes about when some years later Brin Costerec is himself captured in battle by the English, who learn from him that Chrystede is still alive. As a condition of his ransom, Costerec will be freed only if Chrystede is repatriated to England with his wife and daughters. Having grown fond of his son-in-law, however, Costerec is unwilling to go along with this plan. But the English remain adamant, and although Costerec manages to strike a bargain in which one of Chrystede's daughters is allowed to remain in Ireland, Chrystede's wife and younger daughter are forced to leave and take up residence near Bristol.[2] Both of his daughters subsequently marry and have children, Chrystede tells Froissart. The one in Ireland gives birth to three sons and two daughters; the one in England, to four sons and two daughters, thus neatly splitting Chrystede's extended family between Ireland and England. Even after being repatriated, Chrystede's own connection to Ireland apparently remains strong if we can take as evidence the fact that despite now living in England he continues to speak Gaelic with his wife and to teach it to his grandchildren as best he can.

The final twist in Chrystede's story, which takes him back once again to Ireland, comes in 1394–95 when Richard, needing assistance in his efforts to gain the submission of the Gaelic, puts Chrystede in charge of "civilizing" the four Irish kings he has conquered. Presumably because he recognizes the importance of behavior and manners in shaping or at least displaying identities, Richard orders Chrystede to teach the Irish kings English customs and "proper" ways of dressing, eating, and comporting themselves. Chrystede appears to have carried out his task capably, even though he cannot completely erase the Irishness of the kings whose foreign appearance attracts the attention of the Englishmen who watch as the kings are knighted by Richard II in the cathedral church of Dublin in 1395.

Froissart's recounting of Chrystede's personal history opens a window onto the complexities of Anglo-Irish relations and nationalist sentiments at the end of the fourteenth century, as Chrystede is forced to live within the shifting borders of English, Gaelic Irish, and Anglo-Irish communities. At the same time, Froissart's decision to retell Chrystede's story within his grand history of French and English affairs during the fourteenth century comments on Froissart's own tangled identity and his muddled national allegiances. Chrystede describes what happens to one individual caught up in the on-going English colonization of Ireland, while Froissart's retelling of that story takes place in the late stages of the decolonization of England from French rule. This interplay between colonization and decolonization, between Anglo-Irish and Anglo-French tensions, raises a number of important questions. Why does Froissart choose to recount Chrystede's story at such length and in Chrystede's own words, given that his chronicle, like his own life, in important ways elides rather than intensifies differences between the French and the English? What significance does Chrystede's account hold for Froissart within the context of his historiographic project, particularly in light of Froissart's own snarled national affiliations? What comment does Chrystede's story make on Richard II's downfall, which was precipitated in part by rumors that in the wake of his "quarrel with London" he planned to abandon England and rule from Ireland? What is the appeal of this captivity story for the chronicler and his anticipated audience of francophone gentlemen in England and on the Continent?

To think of it from Chrystede's side, what effect has his captivity had on his own identity? Where do his allegiances lie—with the English, the Irish, or in between? Given the hard-line position taken by the English in the Statutes of Kilkenny (1366), which attempted to arrest the "degeneracy" of the Anglo-Irish by ordering them to forsake all Irish sports and entertainments and to use English surnames, to speak the English language, and to follow English customs, what are we to make of Chrystede's allegiance to his Irishness and his obviously successful use of that Irishness in service to the English Empire? The English demand that Chrystede be repatriated, even, apparently, against his wishes, suggests

a determination to protect "Englishness" that was consistent with repeated schemes for anglicizing the Irish. Yet Chrystede's mongrel identity—not entirely one thing or another—flies in the face of this and other
efforts undertaken throughout the fourteenth century to draw sharper
distinctions between the Irish and the English.[3]

While there are a number of circumstances that help make sense of
Froissart's decision to include Chrystede's narrative in his chronicle, circumstances I shall return to shortly, it seems clear that one reason Froissart accords this captivity story such a privileged position at the end of
his chronicle is because the story fascinates him. It fascinates him, I
would argue, because it crystallizes within one man the confusions of
ethnic identity and national affiliation that shaped English life in the late
fourteenth century, confusions that spoke to Froissart's own cultural pre-
dicament, as well as to that of countless others among his readership. In
the remainder of this essay, I examine Chrystede's captivity story as
recounted in the *Chroniques,* with an eye to what this story can tell us
about nationalism at the end of the fourteenth century. In Froissart's
narrative of Chrystede's personal history, we can see some of the private
and public consequences of a growing sense of nationalism, particularly
in terms of England's relations with its borderlands during a fractious
half century of intertwined colonization and decolonization. Whereas in
the thirteenth century, England's quarrels with France had been a concern only of the king and magnates, after the middle of the fourteenth
century, thanks to Edward III's victories of 1346–54 and to his domestic
propaganda, English involvement with France became an *English* undertaking, as Robin Frame has pointed out (*Ireland and Britain,* 181). At the
same time, as Frame also notes, English expansion "ceased within the
archipelago" (181) and state-sponsored English settlement, with the exception of those in Normandy and Maine in the early fifteenth century,
halted. Chrystede's story calls attention to itself as a narrative about what
happens to individuals caught within these altered national contours.

ENGLAND AND IRELAND, 1100–1400

In one sense, there is nothing unique about Chrystede, since the personal history of many Anglo-Irish colonists in the fourteenth century
would be likely to provide us with ample evidence of similar identity

confusion, given the history of English colonization in Ireland, a history whose early moments set the stage for later, more hardened attitudes toward ethnic and national difference. Following the first settlement of Ireland in the tenth and eleventh centuries—a period in the history of the Irish Sea province that one historian has likened to the North American Wild West, with speculators and settlers rushing in to grab land in the hope of quick riches—England gradually attempted to impose increasing control and order, grounded, at least initially, in a sense that the Irish provinces were a jewel in the crown of royal holdings.[4] For most of the late twelfth and thirteenth centuries, the Lordship of Ireland was shaped by royal power and the concerns of the London metropolis, both of which encouraged the making of clear distinctions between settlers and native Irish as a means of exerting control over both groups and thus furthering greater access to Irish lands by the colonists. In 1171, Henry II began consolidating relations with the Anglo-Norman barons and knights occupying the south and east of Ireland and accepted submissions from the Irish kings. These efforts culminated in the agreement of 1175 known as the treaty of Windsor, which Henry made with Rory O'Connor, king of Connacht and current high king of Ireland. The treaty distinguished between the lands of Henry and his men in the south and east and those of the Irish in the west and north. The plan was that Rory would act as Henry's agent in the north and west, collecting tribute and hostages, but the treaty quickly collapsed.

In 1185, the young King John was sent to take charge of the potential kingdom assigned to him, accompanied by various men who secured property in Ireland. As the actions of John's companions attest, Angevin desire for expansion in Ireland was fueled by the fact that Ireland provided possibilities for advancement for men of the court at a time when the availability of landed patronage in England had shrunk.[5] Although in the thirteenth century the Lordship became more crowded, Irish land continued to be redistributed, including through the marriage market, and English kings continued to regard Ireland as a place where their supporters could be enriched. During this stage of colonization, the close ties of the Anglo-Norman settlers to the king and metropolis makes it hard to distinguish a distinct Anglo-Irish baronage or a colonial identity among the settlers. In fact, the picture in thirteenth-century Ireland is less of a nation and colony than of an extended Angevin court with its interlocking networks and territories. Under Angevin rule throughout the 1200s, the native Irish kings of the north and west maintained a position in the Lordship, however separate and limited, and might even be asked for advice or included in policy decisions made by the Crown.[6]

By the fourteenth century, however, the colonists' political connections with England had changed, as had relations with the Gaelic Irish and, consequently, the identity of the settlers as well. The direct link that once existed between the Crown and native Irish leaders had faded as baronial power increased and the wealth of the Irish kings dwindled. This decline in the status of the native Irish is signaled by the fact that in the rare instances in which English royal records in the fourteenth century use phrases such as *rex hibernicorum* or *reguli hibernici* it is with the sense that they are not real kings. As the government expanded in Ireland, a much firmer line than had earlier existed was drawn between the English employed in it and the excluded Irish. Irishmen might have careers as captains in royal and magnate service, such as Aedh O'Toole of the Dublin mountains did in the 1350s, but unless they had been granted English law, they were excluded from public office and from central government. The gap between those inside and those outside the Lordship increased, with divisions by and large following ethnic lines and adopting a language of English solidarity. Anti-Gaelic sentiments were widespread, both in Ireland and in England. Reform-minded native bishops were hostile to Irish customs and attempted to stamp them out. Even the appearance of Irishness could be an impediment as the Gaelic themselves noticed. In 1333, for example, when Dermot O'Dwyer, a Gaelic lord from the southwest, was granted the king's peace and English law, he had "the hair of his *cúlán* cut in order to hold English law."[7] Frame points out that the shrinkage and weakening of Irish kingship formed part of a broader pattern of increasing imperial pretensions on the part of the English Crown and also intensified divisions between the Gaelic Irish and the English ("England and Ireland," 24).

As divisions hardened during the fourteenth century, the identity of the settler elite in Ireland became increasingly problematic, both for those who claimed it and for the metropolis.[8] By Edward III's time, when the English government played a more interventionist role in Ireland than at any time since King John,[9] many settlers had been in Ireland for a century and had effectively become Irish, adopting native customs, language,

and culture. This widespread assimilation is what the Statutes of
Kilkenny, passed in 1366, by a parliament presided over by Edward III's
son Lionel, duke of Clarence and earl of Ulster, addressed. The preamble
to the Statutes states:

> Whereas at the conquest of the land of Ireland and for a
> long time afterwards the English of that land used the English
> tongue, manner of riding and dress, and were governed and
> ruled . . . by English law . . . now many English of that land, for-
> saking the English speech, outward appearance, manner of rid-
> ing, laws and customs, live and conduct themselves according
> to the customs, appearance and tongue of the Irish enemies, and
> have also entered into many marriages and alliances between
> themselves and those Irish enemies; through which that land,
> its liege people, the English tongue, the allegiance owed to our
> lord the king, and the English laws there are subordinated and
> diminished, and the Irish enemies are exalted and raised up,
> contrary to right. (*Statutes and Ordinances*, 430–31)

The Statutes go on to forbid the English to marry, foster, or ally with the
Gaelic Irish or to use Brehon or March law.[10] The Gaelic Irish living
among the English were ordered to adopt English speech and surnames,
and the speaking of Irish was prohibited to the English and the Irish
among them. As Frame notes, the Statutes of Kilkenny represent not
only Lionel's sentiments but also the attitudes of those who assented to
them, that is, "the communities of the settled heartlands of eastern and
southern Ireland, whose knights and burgesses attended the parliament"
("'Les Engleys,'" 132) as well as magnates and higher clergy. Although
they represent the best-known example of attitudes toward the settlers
in Ireland, the Statutes are not unique but in fact echo documents drawn
up six years earlier by the second earl of Ormond—the same Ormond
served by Henry Chrystede—whose land and career lay mostly in Ireland.

The policing of identity voiced by the Statutes of Kilkenny is linked
to the colonists' increasingly loud proclamations of their Englishness,
despite—or perhaps as a consequence of—their growing assimilation
with the native Irish. Although there continued to be a dense network of
personal, institutional, and cultural contacts linking settlers and the

metropolis, sometime during the early fourteenth century there seems to have developed a clearer political entity of English Ireland, a political community that identified itself with the Lordship rather than with the metropolis or the court. This community of the "Anglo-Irish," or "the English of Ireland," was made up of those whose identity was defined in contrast with the native Irish, but whose "Englishness" was a vexed issue. The complexity of the terms "English" and "Irish" in this period make it difficult to know precisely what was meant by the various users of those terms, whose use, it must be said, often had specific political goals. But it is evident that distinctions were frequently made between "the English born in England" and "the English born in Ireland" in terms that seem to suggest a nascent colonial nationalism.

Frame persuasively argues that the public identity of the English in Ireland in the fourteenth century was a construct that sought to explain to themselves and others who they were and from where they had come ("England and Ireland," 26–27). This public identity was to a certain extent inaccurate, since the twelfth-century settlers probably spoke French, Welsh, and Flemish in addition to English, representing the heterogeneous groups who initially occupied Ireland.[11] Although the settlers were polyglot and multiethnic in origin, they were, Frame stresses, "the people of the king of England and some ingredients of an English political-legal identity were present in the Lordship from the start" ("'Les Engleys,'" 133). This political-legal identity bound the disparate settlers together and set them off from the native Irish. The stronger lines that had been drawn by the common law in mid-thirteenth-century England between free and unfree had similarly created a greater distinction between newcomer and native in Ireland, and the development of courts, offices, rights, and duties—governmental and juridical features spawned by the common law—increasingly encouraged the idea of a common English identity. Although as early as 1171 Giraldus Cambrensis reports Maurice fitz Gerald as saying, "we are English to the Irish and Irish to the English," it was not until the 1300s that descendants of colonists who had gone to Ireland in the late twelfth and early thirteenth centuries were commonly calling themselves "the English of Ireland" or "the English born in Ireland" if they were describing themselves to Englishmen in an English context, and referring to themselves as "the English" when in Ireland.[12] The need to profess a common Englishness was

underscored in ordinances drawn up by Edward III in 1357 that assert
that "both the English born in Ireland and those born in England and
dwelling in Ireland are true English" despite sometimes being in conflict (*Statutes of the Realm*, 1:363), a position reiterated by the annalist
who describes how when Lionel arrived in 1361 with his troops, he
united the people *(totum populum)* of England and of Ireland against the
Gaelic Irish (taking the English of England and Ireland as one).[13]

While the Lordship was a region whose customs were English and
whose elites were attached to England by ties of patronage, service, marriage, and landholding, it was also a place understood as distinct from
England. By the mid-fourteenth century the Anglo-Irish possessed, in
Frame's words, "a sense of history linked with a sense of place; a distinctive variant of English law and custom; facsimiles of English royal institutions, including Parliament; and a clutch of preoccupations (from dealings with an omnipresent native population to relations with a far-away
ruler) that amounted to a unique political agenda" ("'Les Engleys,'" 147).
Between the reigns of John and Edward III we pass, then, from an era in
which the Englishness of the settlers was being gradually defined to one
in which it was vociferously asserted and defended, even as it became
recognizably an Irish Englishness. By the time of Richard's reign, there
were two "English" political communities—one in England and one in
Ireland—that shared a common law, English regnal institutions, and preoccupations (with military service, taxation, enforcement of law). Anglo-
Ireland was overseas, but not completely foreign.

All of the parties involved—English in England, English in Ireland,
and Gaelic Irish—shared, however, a sense of the Gaelic Irish as being
distinctly different and in possession of an identity that marked them
off from others.[14] There is evidence that what we might call the language of racism was employed for political purposes at official levels by
both sides in medieval Ireland—with racial adjectives being used to distinguish between Gaelic and English Irish. Indeed, there was a continuous insistence that the Lordship was occupied by two distinct races.
Although the early settlers had been Welsh, Flemish, and French as well
as English, throughout the thirteenth century the English community
imposed its culture on the non-Gaelic and gradually developed a sense
of its own identity, not least in a feeling of superiority to the Gaelic Irish.
By the time Chrystede was born, the English in Ireland tended to think
of themselves as in some way English, to identify with Ireland as their

patria, and to regard the Gaelic Irish as wild, uncivilized, and their natural enemies.[15]

FROISSART'S RETELLING OF
CHRYSTEDE'S STORY

Born in the 1340s, if Froissart's guess as to his age is accurate, Henry
Chrystede entered the world in the midst of these changing relations between the English and the Irish. The impression we get from Froissart's
account is that Chrystede was well aware of the significance of his history for English and Irish relations and, moreover, that he was eager to
have his private life become a part of the public record. The desire to
enter into written history appears in fact to be what motivated Chrystede
to first approach Froissart at Leeds castle on the same Sunday on which
Froissart presented his "book of love" to Richard. In his conversation with
Froissart, Chrystede himself situates his personal history within the
broader frame of public events, within, that is, Richard II's expedition
to Ireland. Froissart, too, seems to have been interested in Chrystede's
life chiefly for the way it intersected with a major historical episode—
Richard's conquest of Ireland—and for the light it shed on Richard, at
whose birth Froissart had been present and whom he had come to England to see. For both the subject himself and his chronicler, then, Chrystede's private life appears to have been noteworthy primarily for what it
could say about broader public issues. This linking of the personal with
the public is a persistent feature of the *Chroniques*, particularly in Book
IV, and is a topic to which I shall return later.

A striking feature of Chrystede's personal history as retold by Froissart is Chrystede's ability to move seamlessly from objectifying stereotypes about the Irish to close identification with them. The opening para-
graphs of Chrystede's reminiscences echo in a surprisingly consistent
manner European myths about the wild and uncivilized Irish. Chrystede
begins his account by confiding that in order to understand Richard's
achievement, Froissart needs to understand that Ireland is one of the
most difficult countries to subdue, since it is a strange, wild place of tall
forests, large bodies of water, bogs, and uninhabitable regions ("car il est
fourmé estrangement et sauvagement de haultes forests et grosses yaues,
de crolières et de lieux inhabitables") (*Oeuvres*, 15:169). The Gaelic Irish,

he continues, hide in the forests where they live in holes dug under trees or in bushes and thickets, "comme bestes sauvages" (15:169). The Irish, moreover, are fierce and unnatural warriors, springing up suddenly from the ground to seize men from their horses and cut their throats. They slit open the bellies of their captives to remove their hearts, which some—who know their ways—say they eat "par grant délit" (15:170). In sum, they show no respect for proper manners or for gentlemen, since they have nothing to do with courteous behavior ("gentillesse") but live according to their traditional rough customs ("rudesse") (15:170).

With its exoticized picture of an untamed landscape populated by horrifying savages, Chrystede's description of Ireland is on most points consistent with late medieval English and French impressions of that country.[16] Popularly viewed as a foreign land to the west, a kind of wilderness within Europe, Ireland was analogous in its strangeness to the equally exoticized East lying in the opposite direction. Its proximity to Europe, rather than familiarizing Ireland, had the effect of making that country all the stranger. John Trevisa's 1387 translation of Ranulph Higden's *Polychronicon* (1352), to cite just one example, describes Ireland by noting that in the "uttermeste endes" of the world are often found "newe meruailles and wonders" and that is why the island of Ireland contains "meny grisliche meruayles and wondres" (1:361). For Trevisa, despite Ireland's nearness to England, Ireland seems like a place at the uttermost ends of the earth and hence not surprisingly is filled with marvels and wonders.

Although we might well puzzle over Chrystede's reasons for echoing the stereotypical view of Ireland, when such a view, as his account makes clear, is at odds with his own experience (a riddle I shall return to later), it is easier to understand why Froissart might have embraced this exoticized perception of Ireland, given that he had no first-hand knowledge of the country, but instead ample access to popular impressions of Ireland as well as motives for parroting them.

Froissart never traveled in Ireland, yet his sojourns in England could hardly have left him unaware of the country to England's west. Having journeyed to Scotland in 1365 and to the area of the lower Severn in 1366, while "clerc de la chambre" to Queen Philippa, Froissart had gained some knowledge of England's borders. More importantly in terms of his awareness of Ireland, Froissart was in England at crucial moments of the English occupation of Ireland: during Lionel's missions to Ireland in 1361 and 1366, and again in 1395 just as Richard II returned from his Irish expedition. All of this suggests that despite the absence of first-hand experience of Ireland, Froissart's understanding of that land might have been shaped by English attitudes toward it.

While Ireland could hardly be described as an obsession of Froissart's, he nonetheless includes descriptions of the country in several of his works. In addition to the two passages about Ireland in Book IV of the *Chroniques,* which lend a touch of the exotic to Froissart's return to England, Froissart also wrote about Ireland in his romance *Meliador,* drawing on myths of Ireland as a land of marvels populated by savages, myths that had been established as early as Giraldus Cambrensis's *Topographia Hibernica* of 1189.[17] The treatment of Ireland in *Meliador* is instructive. In this romance, written between 1365 and 1383 and set in England and Ireland, Froissart divides the British Isles into four kingdoms: Arthur's kingdom of Britain; Scotland; Ireland; and the kingdom of "Norgalles." Like Scotland, Ireland is decribed as a country of moors. Only one real place-name is given, that of Dublin. Indeed, the whole description of the country is vague, nebulous, and imbued with a general sense of its estrangement from civilized norms. In *Meliador,* however, Ireland is unexpectedly imagined as being separated from England only by a river two leagues wide (called the "Clarense," in apparent reference to Edward III's son Lionel, the duke of Clarence, who was also earl of Ulster and became Lieutenant of Ireland in 1361), rather than by fifty miles of sea. In other words, in Froissart's romance, Ireland is imagined as closer to England than it actually is, but it is depicted in stereotypical ways as strange and—as the text's inarticulateness about its attributes suggests—literally indescribable.[18]

A similar sense of close-to-hand alterity is stressed in a second account of Ireland that Froissart relates in the *Chroniques* only a few pages before Chrystede is introduced. The first new acquaintance Froissart makes on his return to England is an English knight named Guillaume de Lisle who happens to be lodging in the same hostel as Froissart in Ospringe. Seeing that Froissart is a foreigner and from France—Froissart adds in an aside that the English think that everyone who speaks French is French (*Oeuvres,* 15:144)—Guillaume de Lisle befriends Froissart (who in another aside observes that the gentlemen of England are courteous and easy to become acquainted with). Guillaume advises Froissart that the best way to meet Richard II is to ride to Leeds, where King

Richard is staying. The two men then set off together.[19] As they ride along,
Froissart asks Guillaume if he had been on the Irish expedition with
Richard. When Guillaume admits that he had been, Froissart immedi-
ately asks if he visited the place called "le trou Saint-Patris," St. Patrick's
Purgatory in Loch Derg in Ulster, a place thought to be a portal to hell.[20]

Guillaume, as it turns out, has indeed ventured to this well-known
tourist attraction and, when Froissart asks if the stories he has heard
about it are true and presses him to describe the "merveilles" and the
"nouvelles" (15:145) he saw and heard there, Guillaume relates the following mysterious event. At St. Patrick's Purgatory, Guillaume and another knight had entered the gate of the cavern and gone down three or
four steps when they were overcome by sleepiness, dropped to the ground,
and slept the whole night through. While asleep, they had strange dreams
and imaginings, many more than they would have in their own beds at
home, but when they woke in the morning they could not remember
any of their dreams and considered the whole experience to have been a
delusion, a "fantosme" (15:146), as Guillaume puts it. Although Froissart
would like to pursue the subject and to learn more about the voyage to
Ireland, they are interrupted when other knights ride up to speak with
Guillaume.

Guillaume's story constitutes the first anecdote about Ireland in the
Chroniques, an anecdote that despite its brevity both sets up Chrystede's
narrative and reveals a good deal about Froissart's attitudes toward Ireland. One of the things that Froissart's exchange with Guillaume shows
is that as a chronicler Froissart is interested in testing the validity of
hearsay and the possibility of the existence of marvelous phenonema.[21]
This concern with veracity is demonstrated when Froissart repeatedly
asks Guillaume if what popular rumor says about Saint Patrick's Purgatory is true. Interestingly, the answer is ambiguous. On the one hand,
Guillaume's account of his inexplicable sleepiness and the dreams that
follow suggest something supernatural at work. On the other hand, Guillaume himself seems unimpressed by what happened to him, considering it all to have been a fantasy. Guillaume's dismissal of his experience
as all a delusion is allowed to stand unchallenged by Froissart, who lets
the topic drop despite his earlier eagerness to hear about "merveilles."

Whether Froissart includes this episode in order to feed a public
taste for exoticism and marvels or to satisfy his own curiosity, within the
structure of the Chroniques it works to set the stage for Chrystede's story,

which—when it begins not many pages later—conjures up the same wild and savage Ireland found in Guillaume's account. Chrystede's description in fact presents an evolved echo of what Guillaume has told Froissart—one in which "merveilles" and "fantosmes" are replaced by desolate and rugged landscapes—yet his version is not, for all that, much different from Guillaume's. Chrystede continues to rely on myths about Ireland and his perspective seems influenced by the xenophobia that the many years of the Anglo-French wars and royal propaganda had spawned among the English.

What is remarkable is that Froissart and Chrystede reassert these myths of Ireland and voice this xenophobia even as both are contradicted in the person of Chrystede himself. This disjunction becomes clear as Chrystede continues his account. For after describing the homeland and habits of the wild Irish, Chrystede next relates that he is by birth Anglo-Irish and has been brought up in Ireland in the household of Thomas, earl of Ormond, a wealthy Anglo-Irish baron and a man with strong ties to the English court who also had roots in Ireland. Ormond was a fluent speaker of Gaelic and resided in Leinster, and was just the sort of assimilated Anglo-Irish the Statutes of Kilkenny might have had in mind. Given these circumstances of birth and upbringing, which immersed him in a Gaelicized English culture, it is startling when Chrystede resorts to xenophobic discourses, as Froissart quotes him doing. We might be tempted to imagine Froissart himself fabricating these stories and attributing them to Chrystede, and that is certainly a possibility. But it is more likely that Chrystede himself, despite the contradictions involved, repeats to Froissart what both men know to be an outsider's stereotypical perception of the "wild Irish." If the latter possibility is in fact what happened, then these xenophobic discourses stand as signs that Chrystede has distanced himself from Gaelic culture, at least enough to be able to mimic widely held external views of the Gaelic Irish.

Just as Chrystede's upbringing is at odds with xenophobic myths about the Gaelic Irish, so too is his treatment by them. Once captured, Chrystede is spared the barbaric rituals of mutilation and cannibalism he has just described to Froissart as the inevitable practice of the Irish toward their captives. Instead, and against all of the stereotypes of the savage Irish, Chrystede is treated kindly and is taken in by his captor, Brin Costerec—who lives in a fortified house, which is later described in assimilationist fashion as a "manoir" (15:173) near the town of Herpelepin—

and embraced as part of his family.[22] Far from suffering in his subsequent captivity, Chrystede thrives, perhaps in considerable comfort if
the term "manoir" with its connotations of landed wealth is any indication. The gentrified satisfactions of matrimony and progeny also accrue
to Chrystede, with marriage and children adding to his happiness and
prosperity. Although Chrystede is silent about his own feelings for his
Irish captor-relatives, he relates that his father-in-law comes to feel so
much affection for him that he can hardly bear it when, seven years
later during the campaigns of Arthur McMorrough, king of Leinster,
against Lionel, when Costerec is captured by the English during a battle,
he is forced by them to give up his captive son-in-law as the only way of
ransoming his own life. Despite Chrystede's silence on the matter of his
own feelings toward his father-in-law, it is hard not to imagine a reciprocal level of emotional attachment from his side as well.

Oblique evidence of what Chrystede's real attitude toward his captor
might have been can be found in a consideration of his socioeconomic
standing during his captivity. Chrystede's position within Costerec's
household looks remarkably similar to but even better than what he had
enjoyed in Ormond's employ. In Ormond's household, Chrystede's status was that of a subordinate, while in Costerec's household he becomes
heir apparent. Similarly, Costerec's affection for Chrystede echoes but
exceeds that of Ormond, whom Chrystede earlier describes as having
taken a special liking to him—apparently in large part because the young
Chrystede was a fine horseman. Despite attempts in the narrative to
establish a clearcut difference between Gaelic and English Irish and to
demonize the Gaelic Irish, Chrystede's experiences suggest that the line
between the two ethnic groups is blurred and that for a nonlanded man
seeking to improve his lot in life, there might be ample opportunities
among the Gaelic Irish for social and economic advance—opportunities
greater than those offered within English or Anglo-Irish society.

The change in representational registers that occurs part way through
Froissart's recounting of Chrystede's story—the transition from echoing of popular myths about Irish barbarism to voicing implicit sympathy
for and even admiration of them—might well be an expression of the
captive's inevitable dilemma, which often forces a refiguring of experience and attitudes during captivity as allegiances to the homeland grow
dim under the passage of time and the need to forge relations with the
capturing group. The representational change in Chrystede's story might

also point to class-based differences in perception of the Gaelic Irish, with nonelites less likely to endorse xenophobic discourses whose aim in part was to maintain hierarchies favoring the English landed classes.

Whatever its origins, Chrystede's sympathetic identification with his captors proves short-lived. When he is exchanged for his captured father-in-law and repatriated to Bristol along with his wife and younger daughter, Chrystede adopts an outsider's perspective that requires him to reject identification with the Gaelic Irish and makes it possible for him to anatomize their customs in a detached and objectifying way. Sometime between this moment of repatriation to England in the 1370s and his encounter with Froissart in 1395, Chrystede adopts a new subject position, one at least superficially consistent with English views of the Irish even if it cannot entirely shake off Chrystede's earlier feelings of alliance with his Irish captors.

CHRYSTEDE AS GO-BETWEEN

Chrystede's refashioned attitudes are put to the test when he is appointed by Richard II in 1395 to instruct the four Irish kings in the ways of the English—a job he gets by virtue of his fluent Gaelic, one mark of his Irishness that he has not put aside. In Richard's service, Chrystede becomes a go-between who uses the lingering traces of his Irish identity to "civilize" the four kings whom Richard had forced into submission. In taking on this job, Chrystede converts the experiences of his youth among the Gaelic and English Irish into empire-building assets, effectively identifying with the English against the Irish. As a go-between, Chrystede becomes a conduit for the flow of power from the dominant culture—in this particular situation, English culture—onto the subordinate one. Importantly, what Chrystede agrees to do for Richard is not to bring the Gaelic kings to submission—Richard has already accomplished that himself—but to educate them in the ways of the English, that is, to reshape their appearance and manners so as to help them pass for English and thus presumably bring them more effectively under the sway of England. Chrystede's task is one of remolding, as he is charged with instructing the Gaelic kings in the external apparatus of assimilation with the norms of the would-be dominant culture. What Richard sought, as Chrystede's assignment makes clear, is not just political but cultural control over

the Irish; and Chrystede agreed—with what degree of willingness or re-
luctance we do not know—to assist him.

In the eyes of the Anglo-English barons, Richard's expedition to Ireland in the mid-1390s was long overdue. In 1386 Richard had made his
close friend, Robert de Vere, duke of Ireland, and in that same year de
Vere, along with retinues of the earl of Ormond and Sir Roger Drury,
planned to go to Ireland. But there was danger of invasion from France
and feeling was running high against the king's favorites. The parliament of 1386 not surprisingly reversed de Vere's plans and the king left
Westminster for ten months starting in February of 1387, during which
time he toured the midlands and the north country. Richard's attempt to
recover power at the end of the year failed and de Vere fled overseas;
many of the king's friends were executed in the Merciless Parliament of
February 1388. By 1394, however, a truce had been made with France
and there was nominal peace with Scotland. Richard's wife Anne of
Bohemia died on 7 June 1394; almost immediately afterwards, Richard
made preparations for an expedition to Ireland, ordering all men born
in Ireland to return there in preparation for his arrival. When Richard
sailed at the end of September, he took along the largest army ever sent
to Ireland during the Middle Ages, a total of perhaps eight thousand to
ten thousand men.[23]

Richard arrived in Ireland on 2 October 1394, with his army and
five great peers, armed with a policy of conquest and conciliation.[24] His
goal was peaceful submission of the Gaelic Irish and their withdrawal
from lands usurped from Anglo-Irish magnates. At Dublin castle, in
February of 1395, after a series of military successes, Richard worked out
a plan to pardon the rebel English who had allied themselves with the
native movement; he was equally prepared to admit the Gaelic Irish to
full legal status. Although he had little success with the Anglo-Irish,
Richard achieved remarkable submissions from the native chiefs.[25] This
was the task for which Chrystede was enlisted, being assigned the four
Irish kings who submitted to Richard, Ó Néill (Ulster), Mac Murchadha
(Leinster), Ó Conchobhair (Connacht), and Ó Briain (Thomond).[26] Frame
argues that one of Richard's problems when Irish leaders came to submit to him was a lack of familiar conventions for the type of lordship
over ethnic rulers that had come so naturally two centuries earlier when
the Irish kings submitted to Henry II ("England and Ireland," 25). Richard
tried to solve the problem by redefining the position of the Irish in En-

glish terms, going so far as to re-educate them culturally, as Chrystede's account shows.[27] Chrystede pointedly remarks that it was Richard's express desire that the Irish kings conform to the English pattern in behavior, bearing, and dress ("de manière et contenance et de habis," Froissart, *Oeuvres,* 15:174), since he wished to dub them knights.

To that end, Chrystede is instructed to live with the four kings in a house in Dublin, provided by Richard, and to educate them. At first, Chrystede merely watches the kings, regarding them as they conduct themselves according to their customary manner, a manner that Chrystede presumably once shared but toward which he now pretends revulsion. Chrystede's attitude toward the four kings is consistent with what might be expected from an Englishman and belies the fact that he lived, apparently quite happily, among the Gaelic Irish for over seven years. He finds them rude and uncouth—"très-rudes et de moult gros engien" (15:174)—and complains of the great difficulty he encounters in moderating their behavior. After a few days of observation, Chrystede steps in to change their appearance and behavior. He teaches them English table manners, introduces them to English dress, especially breeches, and trains them in English horsemanship, including the use of a saddle. He briefly wades into deeper waters, inquiring about their religious beliefs, but is rebuffed. For the most part, however, Chrystede describes the kings as remarkably compliant, once they understand that they must abandon their previous practices for English usages since that is what Richard demands. Chrystede's account of the compliance of the four kings is consistent with the historical record, which suggests that some Gaelic Irish in the fourteenth century became anglicized, despite the many who held fast to their own culture.[28]

After Chrystede had completed his task, the four kings were knighted in the cathedral church in Dublin, wearing rich robes as befit their rank.[29] Familiar feudal forms accompanied the oath-taking ceremonies, in which the submitter removed his cap, girdle, and weapons, knelt, and put his hands between the king's. The oath was taken in Irish then translated into English and was followed by ceremonial kissing of the Gospels.[30] Despite Chrystede's civilizing work, the English and others stared at the four kings, Chrystede states, since they were clearly foreign and different in appearance from the English and other nationalities ("car ils estoient trop estranges et hors de la contenance de celux d'Angleterre et d'autres nations," 15:178) and because, Chrystede adds, people are naturally curious to see novel things ("nature s'encline à voulentiers veoir toutes nouvelles choses," 15:178). Chrystede's work as a go-between, then, is only partially successful, since despite his efforts at helping the Gaelic kings assimilate, they remain recognizably alien—"trop estranges"—and even non-European, in the eyes of the English, thus demonstrating the limits of cultural assimilation and the resilience of visible or imagined signs of ethnic or racial difference.

Chrystede's confrontation with essential and ineradicable differences between the Gaelic Irish and the English, despite vigorous efforts to elide those differences, meshes with what seems to have been historical reality. On the one hand, Richard was willing to go to great lengths in order to create the impression that the Gaelic Irish were his subjects and hence in some way similar to all his other subjects. Dorothy Johnston notes that it was normal for the Anglo-Irish chancery, in mentioning local hostilities, to refer to *Hibernicos inimicos* who were often aided by *Anglicos rebelles,* but that Richard and the English chancery in the 1390s consistently described disturbers of the peace simply as *rebelles* contrasting them with *fideles ligeos* of the king. This choice of label, Johnston argues, represents an attempt to unite the Irish under sovereignty of the king and to suggest that the rebels could be pardoned if they submitted ("Richard II," 3). Richard's letter to archbishop Colton of Armagh, thanking the archbishop for his help in dealing with Ó Néill and other rebels, expresses these sentiments, explaining that "we wish . . . to ordain and establish such governance throughout our land of Ireland that our faithful lieges will be pleased and our rebels punished for their faults."[31] On the other hand, in spite of Richard's attempts at consolidation under his sovereignty, he continued to acknowledge racial differences between the Gaelic Irish and the English. Although contemporary English narrative sources sometimes in ignorance called a man *Hibernicus* simply because he came from Ireland,[32] Johnston observes that such carelessness was unusual in official writings—in Ireland the chancery carefully distinguished by race even the allied participants in local disturbances, no matter how indistinguishable they might have looked to an outsider (3–4). Richard II's recognition of this is shown in his invariable inclusion of a racial adjective when a man of English blood of any rank submitted to him.[33] Richard himself, then, would not in all likelihood have been surprised that the innate otherness of the four Gaelic kings could not be erased by Chrystede's assimilation attempts.

The persistence of these signs of racial identity raises questions about how thoroughly Chrystede was able to refashion himself. Despite the apparent ease with which he adopted an English attitude toward the Irish kings, there are discordant moments in his account, moments of slippage that undercut Chrystede's supposed rejection of his Gaelic past. The first slip occurs when, in the course of his education of the kings, Chrystede asks them about his father-in-law; Brin Costerec, he discovers, is still alive but very old. This detail, despite the fact that Chrystede mentions it in an off-hand and unemphatic way, suggests that Chrystede has kept alive stronger attachments to his Gaelic captor than he has allowed us to see, attachments that to some extent unsettle his easy attitude of allegiance to an English perspective. Another slip comes in connection with the fundamental reason for Chrystede's job—that he is still fluent in Gaelic. Chrystede informs Froissart that not only do he and his wife still speak Gaelic at home but they are also teaching it to their grandchildren as much as possible (*Oeuvres*, 15:173–74). What are we to make of this renegade linguistic behavior, which flies in the face of attempts to anglicize the Irish while preventing the gaelicization of the English? Isn't Chrystede, by continuing to speak Gaelic and even teach it to his offspring, preserving an important link with his Gaelic past and exhibiting nostalgia for what he has lost? Yet another moment of slippage comes when, while instructing the four Irish kings, Chrystede at one point quizzes them on the rituals of knighting common among them (15:176). What is odd about this line of questioning is that Chrystede tells us that he knows all about these rituals and so doesn't really need to ask. We are presented, then, with the image of a man who is deliberately suppressing insider knowledge in order to play the role of the outside reformer. But clearly he has not forgotten that earlier knowledge, despite recognizing that it has to be ignored. Taken together, these slippages suggest that Chrystede is less settled in his new identity than he might like Froissart—and perhaps even himself—to believe.

Mongrel Identities

Chrystede's conflicted identity intersects in key ways with Froissart's own rather uncertain subject position, which is perhaps one reason Chrystede's story resonates as strongly with Froissart as it apparently does.

Like Chrystede, Froissart has been resident—although under more willing circumstances—in a foreign land. Unlike Chrystede, who has for the
most part quietly lived with the consequences of his crosscultural experiences, Froissart has dedicated his writing career in large part to exploring
the nature of the relations between the two lands he has inhabited. The
four books of the *Chroniques* take as their subject the entangled histories
of France and England in the fourteenth century and because of Froissart's tendency to view history through the lives of individuals, issues of
national identity inevitably come to the forefront in his account.

The end of Book IV of the *Chroniques* is preoccupied with the affairs
of England, but these affairs have a distinctly personal cast and explicitly
involve Froissart himself. Particularly in the section in which Froissart
describes his encounter with Chrystede, issues of Froissart's own private
history are never far from the surface of the public events he recounts.
Composed between 1390 and 1404, and surviving in only one version,
Book IV covers the years from 1389 to 1399; unlike the earlier books of
the *Chroniques* it was thus written nearly contemporaneously with the
events it describes and at a time when Froissart was in his fifties. Book
IV starts during the reign of Charles VI with the entry into Paris of Isabel
of Bavaria and ends with the death of Richard II, chronicling in between
the entangled affairs of France and England during the last decade of
the fourteenth century. At midpoint in that decade, Froissart makes the
momentous decision to return to the country he has not seen for some
twenty-seven years. He seizes the opportunity for travel provided by a
four-year truce, which has created a lull in the Anglo-French hostilities,
and sets out. Froissart cites "plusieurs raisons" for making the voyage:
nostalgic memories of his youth spent at the court of Edward III and the
"honneur, largesse et courtoisie" (15:140) with which he had been treated
there, as well as the historian's wish to confirm the accuracy of his accounts by seeking confirmation from sources at the English court ("pour
justifier les histoires et les matières dont je avoie tant escript de euls")
(15:141). Finally, he is also motivated by a desire to present a handsome
copy of his writings on love and morality to Richard II, whom he has not
seen since the day many years before when the newly born king-to-be
was baptized in the cathedral at Bordeaux.[34]

Excitement and anticipation spur Froissart on, he tells us, making
his travel preparations easy, but his enthusiasm is dimmed when he
reaches Dover and discovers to his surprise that the city's hostels are

filled with strangers ("nouveau poeuple") who do not know him and
whom he does not recognize (15:142). After this sobering reminder of the
vicissitudes of time, Froissart moves on to Canterbury, where he visits
the shrine of St. Thomas and waits for King Richard, whom he has
learned is coming to Canterbury on pilgrimage after his campaign in
Ireland. Once again, Froissart remarks on his loneliness and estrangement from the scene around him, commenting that "tout me sembla
nouvel, ne je y congnoissoie âme, car le temps estoit moult changié en
Angleterre" (15:143). It is in this context of loneliness and the shock of
change that Froissart falls in with Chrystede and hears a story that could
scarcely fail to speak to his own sense of displacement.

A characteristic feature of Froissart's historiographic technique is
his heavy reliance on informers and his frequent inscription of their accounts—often verbatim—into his narrative. As a historian, Froissart not
surprisingly depends on having people tell him about important events,
battles, and occurrences. But rather than quietly stealing their information and presenting it in his own voice, Froissart incorporates them into
his narrative, constructing his informers as characters who become every
bit as interesting as the men whose exploits they recount; indeed, his informants often become the heroes of their own tales, as happens in the
case of Chrystede. Froissart needs his informers, but they also need
him; they exist in history because Froissart recounts their tales. And
they know this—seeking him out, as Chrystede does, in order to find a
place in his book.[35]

As Stephen Nichols notes, the use of verbatim accounts by informers
is an obvious reason for the appeal of Froissart's chronicle, capturing as
it does the liveliness of actual speech and filtering impersonal historical
events through the conduit of individual persons ("Discourse," 281). In
the case of Chrystede, the use of verbatim reports also strengthens the
bonds between the chronicler and his narrators. Nichols identifies four
types of discourse in the *Chroniques:* short, direct quotations, which are
often used for heightening the drama of a particular moment; longer direct quotations spoken by one person about one topic, which allow a view
of history filtered through a person; collective discourse, which achieves
a chorus-like effect of public opinion; and dialogue, which encourages
concentration on speakers and personalities. In the section dealing with
Chrystede, Froissart employs a combination of dialogue and long, direct
quotation. The dialogue, all of which takes place between Froissart and

Chrystede, comes at the beginning and again at the end of the section, and to a large extent functions as an establishing shot does in cinema: it provides a legible context within which readers can locate Chrystede's story. In this framing dialogue, Froissart plays the role of eager audience, leading Chrystede on and, once Chrystede has concluded, affirming the importance of his story. Interestingly, when Chrystede ends his account by telling Froissart that he wishes that the chronicler could have been present at the knighting ceremony in Dublin cathedral since he would have agreed that it was a novelty to see the four Irish kings, Froissart concurs, adding that in fact he would have been there had it not been for the death of Queen Anne, which made him postpone his journey. This close identification between historian and informant, between the one who would have been there if he could have been (doesn't that describe all historians?) and the one who was, seems worth noting in the context of the emphasis on belonging and place that informs this section of the *Chroniques*.

The chronicler's own history had provided him with ample reminders of the tenuousness of national and political affiliations. For much of his adult life, Froissart had a peripatetic existence, with spilt allegiances. Born into the merchant middle classes of Valenciennes, he came to England in the 1360s, perhaps in search of a patron. His first histori-cal work, presented to Queen Philippa, who like Froissart came from Hainault, is now missing but may have been a verse chronicle.[36] While resident at the English court, he visited Scotland in 1365 and also jour-neyed to the west country in the company of Edward Despenser, a journey later described in the Rome version of his *Chroniques*. He was present at Bordeaux in 1367 when Richard II was born and in 1368 went to Italy with Lionel of Clarence. After Philippa's death, on his return from Italy, he went back to the Netherlands, not to return to England until the 1390s. His later patrons were the English sympathizer Robert of Namur, count of Flanders, for whom Froissart began writing his prose *Chroniques* at the end of the 1360s, and subsequently Wenceslaus of Bohemia and Guy de Chatillon, count of Blois, both of whom were French sympathiz-ers. As this brief biography suggests, Froissart was accustomed to mov-ing between cultures and nations; as the *Chroniques* demonstrate, he had a professional interest in what happens when they collide.[37]

Froissart's personal and professional life, then, helps explain his fascination with Chrystede's captivity story, a fascination that is underscored by the very nature of the captivity narrative as a genre. Captivity comprises a distinct category of cultural encounter, a subgenre that Urs Bitterli has called the "direct encounter," in which the traveler encounters the Other without the accoutrements of power—without the theological certitude or military might that usually safeguard and wall off the traveler from the dangers of the foreign. Captives, alone and powerless, offer the possibility of the self's integration with the Other in a way rarely experienced by voluntary travelers. Unlike other travelers, captives typically learn the language, live and work alongside their captors, and often intermarry or in other ways participate in the foreign culture's social interactions. In short, captives often have the chance to "go native" and blend with the alien culture, even if not always by choice. The stories produced by captivity—the literature of direct encounter—would seem to provide a unique perspective on the meeting of cultures, a perspective that replaces the distance common to most travel accounts with the intimacy and familiarity of an insider's view.

Although they promise an insider's perspective, captivity narratives usually serve the interests of the social groups for which they are written rather than the societies about which they write. More often than not, captivity stories become yet another part of the processes through which social groups legitimize their power and define themselves through systems of inclusion and exclusion. Captivity narratives can thus be seen as part of a group's ongoing efforts at appropriation (who is one of "us") and exclusion (who is one of "them"). In Froissart's hands, Chrystede's direct encounter with Irish culture quite explicitly addresses these themes of inclusion and exclusion so crucial to the building of national self-consciousness.[38] But as the ensuing narrative shows, deciding just who is "us" and who "them" proves difficult for Chrystede and indeed for Froissart as well. When Froissart and Chrystede turn to stereotypes about the "wild Irish" we can see them searching for a way to use dominant cultural attitudes to strengthen the line between "us" and "them." That the recourse to stereotypes ultimately fails suggests not just that Chrystede's experience cannot be so readily categorized, but also that "us-them" categories are themselves ill-defined for Chrystede and Froissart. In most of the other captivity episodes found in the *Chroniques*, Froissart comfortably relies on assumptions about capture and ransom as part of the code of civilized warfare guiding the wealthy classes, a code shared by French and English elites and honed through the many battles of the

Hundred Years War. In most of these episodes, captivity and ransom raise no troubling issues of political or national identity whatsoever. Only when such codes break down, usually under pressure from nonelites who do not subscribe to them, do we glimpse anything like the concerns that become so prominent in Chrystede's story, in which the captive offers a relational form of identity shaped out of a melding of subject positions and social contexts, which oscillates between identification with the Other and revulsion at it.

As Stephen Greenblatt has noted, the native seized "as a token and then displayed, sketched, painted, described, and embalmed is quite literally captured by and for European representation" (*Marvelous Possessions*, 119). Greenblatt argues that witnessing is crucial to European dreams of possession of the New World, a witnessing "understood as a form of significant and representative seeing," since to see is to know the truth even about things that might seem unbelievable (122). The premium placed on witnessing gives rise to persistent claims in early travel writing about personal experience and the authority of the eyewitness.[39] The captive takes these tropes a step further, while also complicating the authenticating function of the eyewitness, since the captive is not just an observer but also a participant, however reluctantly, in the alien culture being described. Going beyond even close observation, the captive becomes an object of exchange, an agent of communication, a model of assimilation, and a marker of difference—all conflated into one in the body of the captive, which itself comes to represent an interplay between self and other, familiar and foreign cultures.

In the case of Chrystede, however, the power dynamic of captivity in early modern European encounters with the New World is reversed—it is not the invading culture that seizes captives, but the invaded one. Chrystede's situation resembles that found in the many captivity stories of colonial America, in which British colonists are captured by Native Americans; it also foreshadows the assimilation stories that feature as anecdotes in a number of early modern travel accounts.[40] Like many of these stories, Chrystede's captivity starkly confronts the invader culture with the unpleasant truth that perhaps not everyone agrees that it is superior and perhaps not everyone, given the choice, would prefer to live under it. By actually enjoying his captivity and flourishing during it, Chrystede troublingly raises the specter of cultural discontent in ways that threaten to undermine English assumptions of superiority and preference.

An important question about Chrystede and his captivity story is how much it might have resonated not just with Froissart but with Froissart's aristocratic and gentle English and French readers, readers who in the 1390s remained more linked than separated by blood, language, and customs, in spite of the rifts created by the Hundred Years War.[41] Chrystede's story comments on their plight in an age of growing nationalist sentiment and, despite a lull in the armed conflict between France and England, a growing division between the two countries, as Froissart himself is forced to realize when he returns to England after his long absence. It is possible to see Chrystede's seemingly successful negotiation of the complexities of transnational allegiances as offering a desirable—even if in most cases impossible to imitate—model for resolving increasingly pressing problems of identity construction within the late medieval nation. At the same time, however, Chrystede's inability to resolve completely his identity conflicts stands as a troubling reminder of the personal consequences of a hardening of national boundaries for those who straddle them.

Froissart saw his chronicle as a moral treatise that would recount the great marvels and feats of arms ("les grans merveilles et li biau fait d'armes") of the Anglo-French wars for his imagined audience of young gentlemen or bachelor knights ("jones bacelers," *Oeuvres,* 2:8) eager for social and economic advance ("tout jone gentil homme, qui se voellent avancier," 2:8). His intent, in his own words, was to pack his book full of examples that would be of help and encouragement to these readers in their endeavors ("matère et exemples de yaus encoragier en bien faisant," 12:3). That Chrystede's story spoke to at least some of Froissart's readers—specifically, those who commissioned or produced manuscripts of his chronicles—is suggested by the fact that Richard's Irish expedition and Froissart's encounter with Chrystede are scenes chosen for illustration in a number of manuscripts of the *Chroniques.* Laurence Hanf-Lancner and Marie-Laetitia Le Guay comment that in the nine illuminated manuscripts of the twenty extant copies of Book IV, the images fall into two broad categories—symbolic and dramatic. The symbolic ones have a celebrative function and usually accompany ceremonial moments of chivalry or royalty: entries, coronations, funerals, tournaments; the dramatic scenes underscore events that seized the contemporary imagination ("L'illustra-tion," 102–03). The latter category obviously includes Froissart's accounts of Ireland, which might similarly be taken as fascinating contemporary readers.

Froissart's acute sense of the utility of what he writes about, specifi-cally what would interest and assist his readers in their quests for social self-definition and strategic advance, also makes him recognize the political benefits of Chrystede's story, especially in other contexts of col-onization. This comes across most clearly when Froissart concludes his interview with Chrystede by asking him how the Irish kings were brought to submission, since when he returns home to Hainault, he will be asked why the duke Aubert de Baviere is unable to do the same with the Frisians (15:179). As this query suggests, Froissart sees Chrystede's ac-count as useful to the elite of his own country of Hainault, whose prob-lems with the Frisians resemble those of the English with the Irish. Clearly Froissart sees a pointed connection between the English troubles with Ireland and other hot spots on the borders of the European nations.

The story of Chrystede's Irish captivity, as Froissart himself seems to have recognized, can be seen as part of what Robert Bartlett has called "the Europeanization of Europe" (*Making*, 269), those processes of cul-tural homogenization that increasingly elided regional or local differ-ences in the later medieval period. Evidence suggests that the Anglo-Irish colonists were caught up in this Europeanization. For example, the collection of poems in London, British Library, MS Harley 913, produced in a Franciscan house in Ireland, shows what a well-educated Anglo-Irishman might have been reading in a religious community; tellingly, its contents represent international tastes, with Latin, French, and English literature dominating.[42] What made the Gaelic Irish seem so strange and caused them to capture the imaginations of northern Europeans was that they resisted these moves toward Europeanization and continued to stand outside the homogenized cultural norm.

As much as the Anglo-Irish colonists of the late fourteenth century might have been swept up in a general homogenization of culture, they could not entirely shake off their own distinctiveness, even if that dis-tinctiveness was never so strongly marked as was the otherness of the Gaelic Irish. As J. A. Watt argues, medieval Ireland fits the modern defi-nition of a colony: it was a country to which Anglo-Normans and English-men emigrated and settled, appropriating the lands of the indigenous population, displacing the native ruling classes, building a new society in the image of the one they left behind, and retaining a dependency on the home government ("Approaches," 313). For these colonists, questions of national and racial identity were especially vexed, since they did not fall neatly into any one group. The Gaelic Irish Remonstrance of 1317, the plea sent to Pope John XXII by Domnall Ó Néill asking for the right to uphold the birthright of national freedom from the English, voices this sense of cultural indeterminacy when it describes the English Irish as calling themselves a middle nation, a nation apart.[43] Debates about the "degeneracy" of the Anglo-Irish in the fourteenth century seem to attest to this "middle nation" status since the word "degeneracy" in this context refers to those in the process of losing the characteristic traits of their nation: like Chrystede, they were quite literally *de genere,* out of their genus or proper, that is, English, national place (Watt, "Approaches," 310).

Richard II attempted a second expedition to Ireland at the century's end, an expedition that—had it not been cut short by the maneuvers of the man who would depose Richard and become Henry IV—might have written a different ending for England's relations with Ireland and perhaps for the history of English nationalism as well. In March 1396, Richard sealed a twenty-eight-year truce with France, seconded by his marriage to the French king's daughter. But this French alliance aroused suspicions and uneasiness added to by Richard's grandiose dreams of being elected king of the Romans (he also projected an Italian expedition). Richard went again to Ireland in June 1399, several months after John of Gaunt's death in February of the same year. Rumors spread that he was planning to settle permanently in Ireland, exploiting England's wealth from the west.[44] Once in Ireland, Richard launched an attack against MacMurrough, who claimed to be the rightful king of Ireland, but never succeeded in engaging the Irish leader in battle. Marching south from Dublin to burn MacMurrough out of the woods, Richard received word that Henry had landed in Yorkshire to claim his inheritance. On July 27, Richard sailed home, by mid-August he was Henry's prisoner, and by September 30, Henry had made himself king. Ireland was left in disorder and confusion. Faced with the more pressing need to establish his position in England and to deal with threats of France and Scotland, Henry largely ignored Ireland and its colonists.[45] It is tantalizing to imagine how—had Richard succeeded in his Irish endeavors and established his court there—the relation between national center and margins might have been reversed, and how the mongrel identities of the middle nation might have became the norm. Instead, Henry and the Lancastrians began a decades-long propaganda campaign designed to stress the distinctive identity of the English—their language and their culture—in order to legitimize Lancastrian rule and strengthen support for taxation to support the wars against France. The result of the propaganda efforts would be to increase the English sense of Englishness and to demarcate them from the people on England's borders and across the Channel.

Froissart would, of course, have known about the outcome of Richard's Irish efforts and about Richard's own demise, and this knowledge might have colored his account of Chrystede's Irish captivity. Froissart would not have known about the final resolution to the Anglo-French conflicts of the Hundred Years War, but he would certainly have recognized, as his return journey to England made so palpably real to him, that the old bonds between England and France, strongest at elite levels of society, had by the late 1390s been severed. In this context, Chrystede's personal history might well have spoken to Froissart's own mixed national and ethnic allegiances. From a broader perspective, Chrystede's indeterminate identity, neither entirely Gaelic, English Irish, or English, stands as a sign of larger social and political changes. Lacking a way to assemble his various identities into one synthetic whole, Chrystede is forced to choose among them according to his changing circumstances. For modern readers, Chrystede thus offers a glimpse into shifting patterns of national affiliation in the late fourteenth century, patterns that had not yet assumed their later, harder contours. What, then, is perhaps most poignant about Chrystede's story is that it represents the loss of what might have been had history taken a different tack—away from the hardening of lines of national and political identities that would characterize England and Europe's entry into the modern world.

Notes

1. For a discussion of Richard II's Irish campaigns and their relationship to his own troubled rule, see Curtis, *Richard II*, esp. 26–54 and McKisack, *Fourteenth Century*, 490–93.

2. From Anglo-Saxon times on, Bristol was an important port linking England with Ireland and the main commercial center in the Irish Sea region, hence Chrystede's repatriation would presumably not entirely have severed his ties with Ireland.

3. See, for example, the case of Robert Sygn, who was brought from Ireland to England by William of Windsor when he was fourteen and lived for forty years in Yorkshire, but as late as 1415 was still pleading in court for permission to remain; cited in Cosgrove, "England and Ireland," 527.

4. A concise survey of economic changes in the Irish Sea province can be found in Hudson, "Changing Economy"; the discussion of the Crown's attitude is on 55–57. The royal interest in Ireland is attested by the fact that from the time of King John the title "lord of Ireland" took precedence over French titles used by earlier English kings and the *dominium Hiberniae* was to be found on royal seals, headings of royal documents, and coins used by the king's subjects; see Frame, "England and Ireland," 15.

5. The extensive recourse to Irish property for purposes of royal patronage in the late thirteenth century is documented in Lally, "Secular Patronage." For a general discussion of the Angevin Empire, see Ramsay, *Angevin Empire*, and Flanagan, *Irish Society*.

6. Frame, "England and Ireland," 20–21, sketches the dynamics of Angevin rule in Ireland.

7. *Statutes and Ordinances*, 210–11; cited in Frame, "'Les Engleys,'" 142.

8. Stringer's discussion ("Nobility and Identity") of Anglo-Irish identity in relation to one baronial line, the de Vecsy family, offers a useful point of comparison with Chrystede.

9. Lionel's expedition marks the start of large-scale military intervention in Ireland, intervention that was chiefly financed by the English Exchequer under the control of William of Windsor from 1369 to 1372 and 1374 to 1376; see Otway-Ruthven, *History*, 277–308.

10. A cogent discussion of the Statutes of Kilkenny can be found in Otway-Ruthven, *History*, 291–94, who points out that very little of what is mentioned in the Statutes is new, but that they represent a codification of existing attitudes (291).

11. For an analysis of the polyglot nature of the twelfth-century settlers, see Bliss and Long, "Literature."

12. See Giraldus Cambrensis, *Expugnatio Hibernica*, 80–81.

13. Cited in Frame, "'Les Engleys,'" 142.

14. For an excellent discussion of the issue of racial identity in Ireland, see Lydon, "Nation and Race"; my discussion in this paragraph draws extensively on Lydon's essay.

15. See the *Annals* of the English Franciscan John Clyn (d. 1349), who wrote at Kilkenny. Clyn shows cross-national alliances but also affixes national labels to the English and Irish, awarding the English favorable epithets. Also see Henry II's words describing the Gaelic Irish as uncivilized and undisciplined, steeped in vice, and given to mutual slaughter and barbaric marriage customs; cited in Richter, "First Century." Attitudes toward the Irish as uncivilized and undisciplined had long been encouraged by the Irish reforming clergy and expressed by Canterbury and Rome; see Watt, *The Church*. Cosgrove, "England and Ireland," 527–28, notes a number of fourteenth-century English references to the "wild Irish." For depictions of the wild Irish in English satire, see Snyder, "Wild Irish."

16. Ireland captured the attention of another Frenchman besides Froissart. Jean Creton accompanied Richard II on his second Irish expedition and wrote a metrical account of the events leading up to Richard's deposition starting with his time in Ireland; see Creton's "Histoire du roy d'Angleterre Richard." A survey of English attitudes towards

Ireland can be found in Rambo, *Colonial Ireland*; see 119–23 for a concise summary of stereotypes about the "wild Irish" and about Ireland as combined wasteland and otherworld.

17. See the discussion of *Meliador* by Boivin, "L'Irlande."

18. Diverres, "Geography," usefully describes the imagined geography of England employed by Froissart in *Meliador*.

19. A miniature on fol. 27 in the lavishly illustrated version of the *Chroniques* found in London, British Library, MS Harley 4380 shows Froissart riding with Guillaume de Lisle, Jehan de Grailly, and three other men; the miniature is reproduced in Coulton, *Chronicler*, 63. Inaccurately, Harley 4380 also depicts Froissart riding with Chrystede and two other men, fol. 34b (cf. Coulton, *Chronicler*, 64).

20. Another and nearly contemporary account can be found in the travel narrative of Raymond, viscount of Perelhos and of Roda in Roussillon, who in the winter of 1397 made a pilgrimage from his native Pyrenees to St. Patrick's Purgatory. Raymond was taken under the protection of the Irish chieftain Ó Néill and spent Christmas with him. Raymond's account (in Provençal) offers a valuable description of Gaelic Irish manners and customs; see Jeanroy and Vignaux, *Voyage*, and Mahaffy, "Two Early Tours." For a discussion of the legends of St. Patrick's Purgatory, see Wright, *St. Patrick's Purgatory*.

21. On the use of the marvelous in the *Chroniques*, see Zink, "Froissart."

22. It seems that Chrystede's father-in-law lived in a crannog or lake dwelling; see Watt, "Approaches," 333.

23. Good overviews of Richard's Irish campaigns can be found in Lydon, "Expeditions," and Otway-Ruthven, *History*, 326–27.

24. Richard landed at Waterford on 2 October 1394 with some six thousand troops. His two expeditions were the natural climax to the fourteenth century armed intervention, as has been argued by Lydon, *Lordship*, 239–40.

25. In this letter, Richard descibes the population of Ireland as divided into the "wild Irish our enemies," "Irish rebels," and "obedient English." Curtis, *Richard II*, 35, interprets "Irish rebels" as degenerate English, but Otway-Ruthven, *History*, 333–34, more convincingly argues that they were Gaelic Irish who never submitted to English authority. The chief difference between the Irish position toward Edward II in 1317 and Richard II in 1395 was that the Edward Bruce invasion had given the Gaelic Irish hope of an overthrow of English lordship, whereas Irish nationalism melted in the face of the overwhelming military force Richard brought with him. Watt concludes that in Ireland "nationalism was stirring, but coexistence and accomodation were often the stronger force in practical life" ("Approaches," 351).

26. By the 1390s the Leinster Irish represented the greatest threat to the Lordship. MacMurrough's hegemony, which included many Anglo-Irish, meant he could effectively hold the government ransom; see Johnston, "Richard II," 14. But despite MacMurrough's claim to be *Rex Lagenie*, he wished to legitimize his position within the Anglo-Norman Lordship, explaining one reason why he might have decided to submit to Richard. Anglo-Irish institutions could enhance a Gaelic chief's power just as Gaelic ones did for great Anglo-Irish lords.

27. Richard's efforts had little lasting result as contemporaries were aware; cf. Adam Usk, who noted: "sed modicum ibi profecit quia, licet Hiberniences sibi ad uotum placere

tunc se fingentes, statim post eius recessum rebellare noscuntur"; translated by Chris Given-Wilson as "he accomplished little there, however, for although the Irish pretended to submit to his will, as soon as he had departed news arrived that they had rebelled" (*Chronicle*, 18–19).

28. See also Raymond of Perelhos's story of how Ó Néill wanted to hear about the customs of the kings of France, Castile, and Aragon, but still felt Irish ways were the best and most perfect in the world ("els teno lors costumas melhors e plus perfieytas del mon"); cited in Mahaffy, "Two Early Tours."

29. Records describe how the Irish came before Richard and took oaths of allegiance in Irish, which were then translated into English. The Gaelic Irish submitters often came ritually bound with cords around their necks; removed their girdles, caps, daggers, and mantles; and knelt. The English Irish did the same but took their oaths in English. See Curtis, *Richard II*, 57–118, for the Latin text that includes details of the accompanying rituals of submission. Johnston, "Richard II," 2, n. 6, notes that while Froissart's account of the knighing of the four Irish chiefs is inaccurate on details of place and date, there is evidence that on different occasions Ó Néill, Ó Briain, and Ó Conchobhair were indeed knighted (see the PRO, KR Mem. Roll 22 R.II, E 159/175, Michaelmas term). Gillespie comments that Jean Creton, the French squire who accompanied Richard to Ireland in 1399, says he was unable to remember the names of all those whom the king knighted on this occasion ("Richard II's Knights," 146).

30. Johnston describes the ceremony in detail ("Richard II," 7).

31. The letter is printed in *Anglo-Norman Letters*, no. 7; qtd. in Johnston, "Richard II," 3–4.

32. See Walsingham, *Ypodigma Neustria*, 366–67.

33. Curtis makes this argument (*Richard II*, 79, 91).

34. For a detailed discussion of Froissart's return to England, see Medeiros, "Voyage."

35. For Froissart's use of informants, see Calin, "Narrative Technique."

36. The standard biography of Froissart remains that of Shears, *Froissart*; see also Lettenhove's introduction in Froissart, *Oeuvres*, vol. 1.

37. For a discussion of Froissart's relations with Edward, see Barber, "Jean Froissart," 37. On Froissart's origins, see Vale, *Edward III*, 42.

38. It is perhaps worth noting that an earlier Irish captivity story shows no interest in questions of national allegiance. A tenth-century Irishman named Moriuht, along with his wife, was captured in a slave raid. After various adventures, Moriuht escaped from servitude and went in search of his wife, which led him to Rouen. Both were given sanctuary and remained there; see Ormont, "Satire," 193–210.

39. Campbell describes how beginning with the accounts of Marco Polo and William of Rubruck European travel accounts increasingly come to rely on the tropes of eyewitness recording of actual experiences (*Witness*, 87–121).

40. The scholarship on captivity stories in colonial America is large; for representative studies suggesting the range of the research, see Pearce, "Significances," Sekora, "Red, White, and Black," and Strong, *Captive Selves*. See also the assimilation stories recounted in the sixteenth century by Bernal Diaz, *Conquest*, 60–65, or in the thirteenth century by Jean de Joinville, *Life*, 262.

41. For a discussion of Froissart's audience, see Ainsworth, *Jean Froissart*, 73–74.

42. The poems are discussed in Lydon, "Middle Nation" 14–15 and in Turville-Petre, *England*, 155–75.

43. Lydon, "Middle Nation," 1–26, provides a comprehensive discussion of this "middle" status. Of the remonstrance, Watt says: "It seems difficult to find any word more accurate than 'nationalism' to describe the principles and emotions that find expression in the remonstrance" ("Gaelic Polity," 350).

44. One of the London chronicles, written around 1435, cites documents on Richard's deposition, which complain of Richard's trip to Ireland that when he went he "toke away alle the Jewelles, and lete hem be bore with him with oute the assent off the States off the Rewme; wherthurh the Rewme was gretly hyndred and empoueryd"; see London, British Library, Cotton MS Julius B II fol. 32v, printed in *Chronicles of London*, 34. See also Creton, "Histoire du roy."

45. See Otway-Ruthven, *History*, 309–38, for a summary of Henry IV's problems with Ireland.

REFERENCES

Ainsworth, Peter F. *Jean Froissart and the Fabric of History: Truth, Myth, and Fiction in the Chroniques*. Oxford: Clarendon Press, 1990.

Anglo-Norman Letters and Petitions from All Souls MS. 182. Ed. M. D. Legge. Oxford: Clarendon Press, 1941.

The Annals of Ireland by Friar John Clyn and Thady Dowling. Ed. R. Butler. Dublin: Irish Archaeological Society, 1849.

Barber, Richard. "Jean Froissart and Edward the Black Prince." In *Froissart: Historian*, ed. J. J. N. Palmer, 25–35. Woodbridge: Boydell Press, 1981.

Bartlett, Robert. *The Making of Europe: Conquest, Colonization and Cultural Change, 950–1350*. Harmondsworth: Penguin, 1993.

Bernal Diaz del Castillo. *The Conquest of New Spain*. Trans. J. M. Cohen. London: Penguin, 1963.

Bitterli, Urs. *Cultures in Conflict: Encounters Between European and Non-European Cultures, 1492–1800*. Trans. Ritchie Robertson. Stanford: Stanford University Press, 1989.

Bliss, A., and J. Long. "Literature in Norman French and English." In *New History of Ireland*, ed. Cosgrove, 708–15.

Boivin, Jeanne-Marie. "L'Irlande et les Irlandais dans l'oeuvre de Froissart: métamorphoses d'un mythe." In *Et c'est la fin pour quoy sommes ensemble: hommage à Jean Dufournet*, ed. Jean-Claude Aubailly et al., 3 vols, 1:227–41. Paris: Editions Champion, 1993.

Calin, William. "Narrative Technique in Fourteenth-Centruy France: Froissart and His Chroniques." In *Studies in Honor of Hans-Erich Keller*, ed. Rupert T. Pickens, 227–36. Kalamazoo: Medieval Institute Publications, 1993.

Campbell, Mary B. *The Witness and the Other World: Exotic European Travel Writing, 400–1600*. Ithaca: Cornell University Press, 1988.

Chronicles of London. Ed. Charles L. Kingsford. Oxford: Clarendon Press, 1905.

Cosgrove, Art. "England and Ireland, 1399–1449." In *New History of Ireland*, ed. Cosgrove, 525–32.

———, ed. *A New History of Ireland*. Vol. 2, *Medieval Ireland, 1169–1534*. Oxford: Clarendon Press, 1987.

Coulton, G. G. *The Chronicler of European Chivalry*. London: The Studio, 1930.

Creton, Jean. "Histoire du roy d'Angleterre Richard." Ed. and trans. John Webb. *Archaeologia* 20 (1824): 1–123.

Curtis, Edmund. *Richard II in Ireland and the Submissions of the Irish Chiefs*. Oxford: Clarendon Press, 1927.

Diverres, A. H. "The Geography of Britain in Froissart's *Meliador*." In *Medieval Miscellany Presented to Eugène Vinaver*, ed. Frederick Whitehead, A. H. Diverres, and F. E. Sutcliffe, 97–112. Manchester: Manchester University Press, 1965.

Flanagan. Marie Therese. *Irish Society, Anglo-Norman Settlers, Angevin Kingship: Interactions in Ireland in the Late Twelfth Century*. Oxford: Clarendon Press, 1989.

Frame, Robin. "England and Ireland, 1171–1399." In *England and Her Neighbors, 1066–1453: Essays in Honour of Pierre Chaplais*, ed. M. Jones and M. Vale, 139–55. London: Hambledon Press, 1989. Reprinted in his *Ireland and Britain*, 15–30.

———. "'Les Engleys nées en Irlande': The English Political Identity in Medieval Ireland." *Transactions of the Royal Historical Society*, 6th series 3 (1993): 83–103. Reprinted in *Ireland and Britain*, 131–50.

———. *Ireland and Britain, 1170–1450*. London: Hambledon Press, 1998.

Froissart, Jean. *Oeuvres*. Ed. Kervyn Lettenhove. 15 vols. Brussels: Victor DeVaux, 1867.

Gillespie, James L. "Richard II's Knights: Chivalry and Patronage." *Journal of Medieval History* 13 (1987): 143–59.

Giraldus Cambrensis. *Historia et Topographia Hibernica*. Ed. J. S. Brewer. Vol. 5 of *Giraldi Cambrensis Opera*. London, 1861–91.

———. *Expugnatio Hibernica: The Conquest of Ireland*. Ed. and trans. A. B. Scott and F. X. Martin. Dublin: Royal Irish Academy, 1978.

Greenblatt, Stephen. *Marvelous Possessions: The Wonder of the New World*. Chicago: University of Chicago Press, 1991.

Hanf-Lancner, Laurence, and Marie-Laetitia Le Guay. "L'illustration du livre IV des *Chroniques* de Froissart: Les rapports entre texte et image." *Le Moyen Age* 96 (1990): 93–112.

Higden, Ranulph. *Polychronicon, together with the English Translations of John Trevisa and of an Unknown Writer of the Fifteenth Century*. Ed. Churchill Babington and Joseph Lumby. 9 vols. Rolls Series 41. London: Her Majesty's Stationery Office, 1865–86.

Hudson, Benjamin T. "The Changing Economy of the Irish Sea Province: A.D. 900–1300." In *Britain and Ireland*, ed. Smith, 39–66.

Jean de Joinville. *The Life of Saint Louis*. In *Chronicles of the Crusades*, trans. M. R. B. Shaw, 161–353. London: Penguin, 1963.

Jeanroy, Alfred, and Alphonse Vignaux. *Voyage au purgatoire de St Patrice*. Toulouse: E. Privat, 1903.

Johnston, Dorothy. "Richard II and the Submissions of Gaelic Ireland." *Irish Historical Studies* 22 (1980): 1–20.

Lally, J. E. "Secular Patronage at the Court of Henry II." *Bulletin of the Institute of Historical Research* 49 (1976): 159–84.

Lydon, James F. "Richard II's Expeditions to Ireland." *Journal of the Royal Society of Antiquairies of Ireland* 93 (1963): 135–49.

———. *The Lordship of Ireland in the Middle Ages.* Toronto: University of Toronto Press, 1972.

———. "The Middle Nation." In *The English in Medieval Ireland,* ed. James Lydon, 1–26. Dublin: Royal Irish Academy, 1984.

———. "Nation and Race in Medieval Ireland." In *Concepts of National Identity in the Middle Ages,* ed. Simon Forde, Lesley Johnson, and Alan V. Murray, 103–29 Leeds: University of Leeds Press, 1995.

Mahaffy, J. P. "Two Early Tours in Ireland." *Hermathena* 18, no. 40 (1914): 3–9.

McKisack, May. *The Fourteenth Century, 1307–1399.* Oxford: Clarendon Press, 1959.

Medeiros, Marie-Thérèse de. "Voyage et lieux de mémoire: Le retour de Froissart en Angleterre." *Le Moyen Age* 98 (1992): 419–28.

Nichols, Stephen G., Jr. "Discourse in Froissart's *Chroniques.*" *Speculum* 39 (1964): 279–87.

Ormont, H. "Satire de Garnier de Rouen contre le poète Moriuht." *Annuaire bulletin de la Société de l'histoire de France* 31 (1894): 193–210.

Otway-Ruthven, Annette J. *A History of Medieval Ireland.* New York: St. Martin's, 1968.

Pearce, Roy Harvey. "The Significances of the Captivity Narratives." *American Literature* 19 (1947): 1–20.

Rambo, Elizabeth L. *Colonial Ireland in Medieval English Literature.* Cranbury, NJ: Associated University Press, 1994.

Ramsay, James H. *The Angevin Empire; or, The Three Reigns of Henry II, Richard I, and John (A.D. 1154–1216).* New York: Macmillan, 1903; reprint, New York: AMS, 1978.

Richter, M. "The First Century of Anglo-Irish Relations." *History* 59 (1974): 195–210.

Sekora, John. "Red, White, and Black: Indian Captivities, Colonial Printers, and the Early African-American Narrative." In *A Mixed Race: Ethnicity in Early America,* ed. Frank Suffleton, 92–104. Oxford: Oxford University Press, 1993.

Shears, Frederick S. *Froissart: Chronicler and Poet.* London: Routledge, 1930.

Smith, Brendan, ed. *Britain and Ireland 900–1300: Insular Responses to Medieval European Change.* Cambridge: Cambridge University Press, 1999.

Snyder, E. D. "The Wild Irish: A Study of Some English Satires Against the Irish, Scots, and Welsh." *Modern Philology* 17 (1919–20): 687–725.

Statutes and Ordinances and Acts of the Parliament of Ireland, King John to Henry V. Ed. H. F. Berry. Dublin, 1907.

The Statutes of the Realm: Printed by Command of His Majesty King George the Third. London: Eyre and Strahan, 1810–28. Reprinted London: Dawsons, 1963.

Stringer, Keith J. "Nobility and Identity in Medieval Britain and Ireland: The de Vecsy Family, c. 1120–1314." In *Britain and Ireland,* ed. Smith, 199–239.

Strong, Pauline Turner. *Captive Selves, Captivating Others: The Politics and Poetics of Colonial American Captivity Narratives.* Boulder: Westview Press, 1999.

Turville-Petre, Thorlac. *England the Nation: Language, Literature, and National Identity, 1290–1340.* Oxford: Clarendon Press, 1996.

Usk, Adam. *The Chronicle of Adam Usk, 1377–1421.* Ed. and trans. Chris Given-Wilson. Oxford: Clarendon Press, 1997.

Vale, Juliet. *Edward III and Chivalry: Chivalric Society and Its Context, 1270–1350.* Woodbridge: Boydell Press, 1982.

Walsingham, Thomas. *Ypodigma Neustria a Thome Walsingham.* Ed. Henry T. Riley. London: Longman, 1876.

Watt, J. A. *The Church and the Two Nations in Medieval Ireland.* New York: Cambridge University Press, 1970.

———. "Approaches to the History of Fourteenth-Century Ireland." In *New History of Ireland,* ed. Cosgrove, 303–13.

———. "Gaelic Polity and Cultural Identity." In *New History of Ireland,* ed. Cosgrove, 314–51.

Wright, Thomas. *St. Patrick's Purgatory: An Essay on the Legends of Purgatory, Hell, and Paradise Current during the Middle Ages.* London: John Russell Smith, 1904.

Zink, Michael. "Froissart et la nuit de chasseur." *Poétique* 11 (1980): 60–77.

AFTERWORD

THE BRUTUS PROLOGUE TO
SIR GAWAIN AND THE
GREEN KNIGHT

THORLAC TURVILLE-PETRE

In writing *England the Nation* I was concerned (I now think overconcerned) to demonstrate that the concept of national identity was available to writers in the fourteenth century. This seemed to me—as I suspect it does to everyone who knows anything about the Middle Ages—undeniable, though frequently denied by modernists who work on nationalism, who assert that it was a phenomenon that arose in the nineteenth century, or the late eighteenth, or the mid-sixteenth. More recently Adrian Hastings in *The Construction of Nationhood* has taken a broader look at the development of nationalism, locating the earliest expressions of English national identity in Bede's *Ecclesiastical History* and tracing the factors that influenced its unsteady growth and reformulations throughout the Middle Ages and later.

The focus of *England the Nation* was the half-century up to 1340, and I did not emphasize sufficiently that many of the factors that lay behind passionate expressions of nationalism were quite specific to this period. Historians talk about the "crisis" of these years, referring to the continual conflict with Scotland, the threats from France, the baronial discontents of Edward I's last years, the disastrous and humiliating reign of Edward II with its military defeats and civil war as well as famine and plague, and the uncertain start of Edward III's reign under the shadow of Mortimer and Isabella. In times of fear and discontent, nationalism is able to provide reassurance to a society anxious about its identity and cohesion. The concept of nationalism waits in the wings ready to be called forward, to assume whatever shape serves the moment, representing what the audience wants to see even as they know that many elements of the performance are fraudulent. Nationalism always deals in half-truths, distorting and suppressing, and it is evident that many of the writers of the early fourteenth century were aware of this as they struggled to construct a coherent concept of nationhood from irreconcilable materials. For example, the theme of the Norman Yoke that Robert Manning and Robert of Gloucester espoused depended upon a racial divide that had no basis in reality, and these authors, who were both reasonably good historians, were surely deliberately misrepresenting the situation in the interests of strengthening their image of an English identity that excluded the Normans.

It would be wishful thinking to suppose that such specious constructions have little staying power. It was not because it was disreputable that the theme of English nationalism was less attractive in the later fourteenth century. A more powerful reason was that it better served the interests of sophisticated Ricardian writers to turn their backs on the fashions of their parents and grandparents and instead to emphasize their attachment to European culture. Derek Pearsall is surely right in his perception in "Chaucer and Englishness" that "of national feeling or a sense of national identity...I find little or nothing in Chaucer" (90). It is a significant absence. It indicates that the battle for English that preoccupied writers early in the century had been won, in the sense that court poets such as Chaucer could be confident that English writings would not be despised as the products of a humbler culture. There was no need for authors to repeat that they were writing in English "for the loue of Inglis lede," even if Gower in *Confessio Amantis* implies surprising unease at this date in writing "A bok for Engelondes sake" (1.23); his curious observation "that fewe men endite / In oure englissh" (1.22) is perhaps motivated by a supercilious contempt for humbler scribblers. The fact was that English could now take its place as one of the established vernacular languages of literature. As Elizabeth Salter says of Chaucer: "His use of English is the triumph of internationalism" (*English and International*, 244).

As contributors to the present collection of essays demonstrate so clearly, writers became much more interested in looking at other ways of analyzing society and fashioned other kinds of community and identity. Some of these, such as the self-definition by the Lollards as a collective group, were prompted by urgent considerations specific to the moment that are explored by Jill C. Havens in this volume. Andrew Galloway shows that sober historians such as Higden offered sophisticated Ricardians a corrective to constructions of national identity that rely on foundation myths such as Brutus the Trojan and heroes of dubious authenticity such as Arthur.

The story of the founding of Britain in the *Anglo-Norman Brut* from the beginning of the fourteenth century and *Sir Gawain and the Green Knight* from the end provides a neat illustration of the different approaches and purposes of the Ricardians from their predecessors. Geoffrey of Monmouth's account of Brutus is the text that underpinned nationalist polemics of the early fourteenth century, and so it was constantly retold, adapted, and cited as justification for the construction of the nation. It was always recounted at length in the chronicles of England, since it gave Britain an ancestry as distinguished as the Roman Empire. Like Virgil's Aeneas, Geoffrey's Brutus, great-grandson of Aeneas, proves his valour through a period of wandering and exile. Over several pages the chronicler who assembled the *Anglo-Norman Brut* retells Geoffrey's account of how Brutus, having killed his father in a hunting accident, was expelled from Italy, and coming across another group of Trojans enslaved in Greece, released them and married the king's daughter. Sailing on, we are told, Brutus came to an island where there was a temple of Diana, who directed him to the island of Albion as his destiny and that of his descendants. Further battles, conquests, and liberations of oppressed peoples took place before Brutus finally landed at Totnes and began the foundation of New Troy.

Brutus's descendant Arthur becomes an emblem of Englishness, both to chroniclers and to their rulers. It might be thought that the fact that he was a Briton would have been an even more damaging objection than the fact that he never existed, but both objections were commonly swept aside in the interests of scoring political points. There is a striking example of this in the *Anglo-Norman Brut* where the chronicler heaps scorn on Roger Mortimer for his Arthurian pretensions: "he helde a rounde table in Walys to alle men þat þider wolde come, and countrefetede þe maner and doyng of Kyng Arthurez table; but openly he failed, ffor þe noble Kny3t Arthure was þe most worþi lord of renoun þat was in al þe worlde in his tymc" (262.7–11). Robert Manning took Arthur as his model for "Englishemen," and it was Edward I's failure to follow Arthur's example that demonstrated for Manning the mistakes of the last years of his reign, as I have argued elsewhere (Turville-Petre, *England*, 84, 101–03). In "Reading for England," Felicity Riddy also explores this theme and shows how "Arthurian texts in a sense created a nation" (331). The concept of Englishness was constructed upon a misappropriation of a falsehood, but it became a crucial element in the self-fashioning of a national identity.

To introduce his story, the author of *Sir Gawain and the Green Knight* adopted the Brutus prologue so familiar from the earlier chronicles, and at the end of the poem he refers to two distinct types of source: "þe best boke of romaunce" (2521) that supplied the story and the "Brutus bokez" (2523) that provided the frame. As line 2523 states, one function of the Brutus story is precisely to "bear witness" to the veracity of the romance, and that, of course, is a no less fraudulent use of pseudo-history than the *Anglo-Norman Brut* had made of it. Yet there is a rather more significant function of the prologue that signals the poem as a Ricardian work as much as Chaucer's poems, similarly designed to locate itself within a European context, and this marks *Gawain* off sharply from those earlier chronicles that had relied upon the same material to proclaim their Englishness.

The treatment of the episode in *Gawain* has of course none of the detail of the chronicles; the poet could safely assume the details would have been well known to his audience, and yet it should be noted that, for all its familiarity, the story has changed. The focus is not upon Brutus wandering as an exile from country to country, conquering, negotiating, liberating, searching for his divinely ordained homeland. Instead, the Trojan descendants of Aeneas are dispersed throughout Europe. Their tale consists not of battles, but instead of establishing, settling, building, and naming; the verbs are "biges" (9), "neuenes" (10), "bigynnes" (11), "lyftes vp" (12), and "settez" (14). It is fitting that the epithet used of Brutus, "Felix" (13), was that applied to founders of cities (Silverstein, "*Sir Gawain*," 196–202), for that is what is being emphasized here. Apart from Brutus, Aeneas's "highe kynde" as listed in *Gawain* are not figures from Geoffrey's story: Romulus and his founding of Rome is briefly

mentioned much later in Geoffrey's account; Ticius might reflect
Wace's Turnus, ruler of Tuscany, or be a corruption of the Tirius of commentaries on Virgil; and Langaberde is the ancestor of the Lombards according to Nennius (194–96). These are the Trojans, we read, who are
the founders of Europe, called "þe west iles" (*Sir Gawain*, 7). The utter
destruction described in the first two lines is balanced by the account of
reconstruction in the following lines 5–15. Any conflict and damage that
the European settlements involved is underplayed, as the Trojans become
"patrounes" (6). The word is often translated "overlords," but this is misleading if it excludes the modern sense of "patron." The entry for *patron*
in *OED* explains that the Latin *patronus* "had the senses of protector and
defender of his clients (viz. of individuals, of cities, or provinces)," and
that the technical Latin sense of the word is relevant here is reinforced by
its alliteration with the equally Latin and technical "prouinces." *MED*'s
citations for *patroun* support the senses "protector, benefactor, patron of
a church, patron saint," but *MED* perhaps misleads slightly by splitting
the word into two separate entries dependent on sense, listing under
patron(e citations in the sense of "model of behaviour" and other meanings that have been taken over by our modern form *pattern*. For the
Gawain-poet the civilizing Trojans were patrons to their contemporaries
and patterns to his fourteenth-century readers.

Yet the poet's word "depreced" in the same line seems to strike a
conflicting note, since it apparently has to do with pressing down and
hence subjugating. The word is used twice elsewhere in the poem in different senses, once at that crucial moment when the lady almost succeeds in bringing Gawain to the point, as she "depresed hym so þikke"
(1770), pushed him so hard. In the other instance Gawain asks the lady
to "deprece your prysoun" (1219), which editors gloss as a separate word,
cited only here by *MED*, meaning "release" (from French *de(s)presser*,
"free from pressure," rather than *depresser*). Editors are obliged to choose
and therefore to make over-precise, but users of language do not distinguish words sharply in this way. Most speakers of English are surprised
to discover that lexicographers distinguish two adjectives "light"; the two
ranges of meaning might well alert them to the existence of separate
words, but they are not so perceived, and therefore ambiguity, accidental
or deliberate, is always a possibility. So, too, with "depreced" in line 6.
It seems to me that the word is deliberately ambiguous here: did the
Trojans, in becoming patrons of European provinces, win domination

by conflict or free peoples from their enslavement? In fact they did both in Geoffrey of Monmouth's account, with Brutus releasing the Trojan exiles in Greece from "thraldom and bondage," and shortly afterwards destroying the land of Gascony (*Anglo-Norman Brut*, 6.20, 8.18). Arthur Lindley has urged us not "to restrict the play of meanings in the text" of *Gawain* and to be more receptive to the ambiguities of the vocabulary of the poem ("Pinning Gawain Down," 26–42), and ambiguity is undeniably a feature of this opening stanza. Who are these Trojans? Noble or treacherous; oppressors or liberators; bringers of bliss or of blunder?

Where the earlier chroniclers had used the Brutus story to assert the uniqueness of England, the *Gawain*-poet adopts it in order to stress the very opposite. Through the noble Trojan ancestry that the English share with other Europeans, English culture claims an international heritage. Geographically, it has to be admitted, Britain is something of an outpost, "fer ouer þe French flod" (13), but its people were civilized by the same distinguished race, "hyghe kynde," as other provinces in Europe. As a result of this, Brutus and his descendants Arthur and Gawain can represent a court culture that is international, not one that is specifically English, a culture that they share with the French across the water. When Bertilac is showing off his good manners to Gawain, the poet calls them "Frenkysch fare" (1116), a metaphor no doubt, but one that still carries within it the sense that manners are part of a shared culture, so that Bertilac in his Cheshire palace would be equally at home in the courts of France. The poet's only use of the word "English" is itself significant, since he reports that the "Englych" call the pentangle "þe endles knot" (629). These supposed English may call it so in their ignorance (even if there is no other record of them doing so); the poet, by four times calling it the "pentaungel," aligns himself with educated people who have at their fingertips the correct technical expressions: "þe pure pentaungel wyth þe peple called / with lore" (664–65). For Manning "English" was associated with an aggressive patriotism; for the *Gawain*-poet it becomes a mark of a cultural chauvinism, the very opposite of the international values that Gawain signifies with his pentangle and that should become the pattern for modern Englishmen. The poet's contemporary Jean Froissart is the most striking example of this internationalism fostered by his constant travels to aristocratic patrons across Europe, recounting the experiences that united his English and French exemplars of chivalry and praising chivalric conduct even-handedly wherever he finds it (see

Claire Sponsler's essay in this volume). In a similar spirit the *Gawain*-poet was interested in analyzing the virtues of those knightly values that overrode the conflicts between European nations.

Chaucer sets his poem on the road to Canterbury to which his pilgrims head "from every shires ende / Of Engelond" (*Canterbury Tales*, I.15–16); Gawain travels north through Logres across the Dee and into the Wirral. Neither poet could have written as he did without a strong consciousness of English identity, of the nation's history, geography, and language, but for neither of them was national identity a topic that they were concerned to dignify with their attention. They were more interested in claiming a place for themselves in the world of European culture.

REFERENCES

Anglo-Norman Brut (Middle English translation): *The Brut, or the Chronicles of England*. Part I. Ed. Friedrich W. D. Brie, EETS o. s. 131. London: Oxford University Press, 1906.

Chaucer, Geoffrey. *The Riverside Chaucer*. Ed. Larry D. Benson et al. Boston: Houghton Mifflin, 1987.

Gower, John. *Confessio Amantis*. In *The Complete Works of John Gower*, ed. G. C. Macaulay, vols 2–3. Oxford: Clarendon Press, 1901.

Hastings, Adrian. *The Construction of Nationhood: Ethnicity, Religion and Nationalism*. Cambridge: Cambridge University Press, 1997.

Lindley, Arthur. "Pinning Gawain Down: The Misediting of *Sir Gawain and the Green Knight*." *Journal of English and Germanic Philology* 96 (1997): 26–42.

Middle English Dictionary. Ed. Hans Kurath et al. Ann Arbor: University of Michigan Press, 1952–2001.

Pearsall, Derek. "Chaucer and Englishness." *Proceedings of the British Academy* 101 (1999): 77–99.

Riddy, Felicity. "Reading for England: Arthurian Literature and National Consciousness." *Bibliographical Bulletin of the International Arthurian Society* 43 (1991): 314–32.

Salter, Elizabeth. *English and International: Studies in the Literature, Art and Patronage of Medieval England*. Cambridge: Cambridge University Press, 1988.

Silverstein, Theodore. "*Sir Gawain*, Dear Brutus, and Britain's Fortunate Founding: A Study in Comedy and Convention." *Modern Philology* 62 (1965): 189–206.

Sir Gawain and the Green Knight. ed. J. R. R. Tolkien and E. V. Gordon. Revised by Norman Davis. Oxford: Clarendon Press, 1967.

Turville-Petre, Thorlac. *England the Nation: Language, Literature, and National Identity, 1290–1340*. Oxford: Clarendon Press, 1996.

Contributors

Kathleen Davis is assistant professor of English at Princeton University. Her essays have addressed issues of gender and translation, particularly as they relate to medieval national discourse. She is the author of *Deconstruction and Translation,* and is currently working on the book project *Unbirthing the Nation: The Middle Ages and Postcolonial Time.*

L. O. Aranye Fradenburg is professor of English, women's studies, and comparative literature at the University of California, Santa Barbara. She is the author of *Sacrifice Your Love: Psychoanalysis, Historicism, Chaucer* (Minnesota, 2002) and *City, Marriage, Tournament: Arts of Rule in Late Medieval Scotland.*

Andrew Galloway is associate professor of English and medieval studies at Cornell University. Currently editor of *The Yearbook of Langland Studies* and section editor (1350–1500) of the online Literature Compass, he has most recently written on Chaucer's negotiations with "authority" and Gower's and the chroniclers' views of the "Merciless Parliament." He is collaborating on an annotation of *Piers Plowman* and, with Russell Peck, an edition of Gower's *Confessio Amantis,* and he is preparing a volume on Middle English literature for Blackwell's History of English Literature series.

Jill C. Havens is an instructor of English at Texas Christian University. She is founder of the Lollard Society and coeditor of *Lollards and Their Influence in Late Medieval England.*

Peggy A. Knapp is professor of English at Carnegie Mellon University and author of *Chaucer and the Social Contest* and *Time Bound Words: Semantic and Social Economies from Chaucer's England to Shakespeare's.* She founded and for many years edited *Assays: Critical Approaches to Medieval and*

Renaissance Texts. She has also written on medieval, early modern, and contemporary poetry, drama, narrative, and film.

Kathy Lavezzo teaches English at the University of Iowa. She is completing a book, *Angels on the Edge of the World: Literature, Geography, and English Identity in the Middle Ages.*

Larry Scanlon is associate professor of English at Rutgers, The State University of New Jersey. He is editor of *Studies in the Age of Chaucer* and is currently finishing a book on sexual regulation, medieval writing, and postmodern theory.

D. Vance Smith is associate professor of English and Jonathan Dickinson Bicentennial Preceptor at Princeton University. His books include *The Book of the Incipit: Beginnings in the Fourteenth Century* (Minnesota, 2001) and *Arts of Possession: The Middle English Household Imaginary* (Minnesota, 2003).

Claire Sponsler teaches English at the University of Iowa. She is author of *Drama and Resistance: Bodies, Goods, and Theatricality in Late Medieval England* (Minnesota, 1997) and coeditor of *East of West: Cross-cultural Performance and the Staging of Difference.*

Lynn Staley is Harrington and Shirley Drake Professor in the Humanities at Colgate University. She is the author of *The Powers of the Holy: Religion, Politics, and Gender in Late Medieval English Literature* (with David Aers); *Margery Kempe's Dissenting Fictions; The Shepheardes Calender: An Introduction;* and *The Voice of the Gawain-Poet.* She has edited and translated *The Book of Margery Kempe* and is now completing the book *Chaucer, Richard II, and the Languages of Power in Late Fourteenth-Century England.*

Thorlac Turville-Petre is professor of medieval English literature and head of the School of English Studies at the University of Nottingham. His publications include *The Alliterative Revival; The Wars of Alexander; Alliterative Poetry in the Later Middle Ages: An Anthology; A Book of Middle English* (with J. A. Burrow); and *England the Nation: Language, Literature, and National Consciousness, 1290–1340.*

MEDIEVAL CULTURES

Index